ENCYCLOPEDIA OF
WORLD
FOOTBALL

ENCYCLOPEDIA OF
WORLD
FOOTBALL

Tim Hill

Bath New York Singapore Hong Kong Cologne Delhi Melbourne

This edition published by Parragon in 2009

Parragon
Queen Street House
4 Queen Street
Bath BA1 1HE, UK

Text © Parragon Books Ltd 2004
Photographs © GettyImages

Produced by Atlantic Publishing

A catalogue record for this book is available
from the British Library.

ISBN 978-1-4075-6680-1

Printed in China

Contents

Introduction

In many ways football today bears little resemblance to the game which was born in a London tavern in 1863. The rules, kit and pitches were all very different back then. Professionalism was still twenty years away, and by today's standards participation was minuscule. But the spirit of those eleven clubs which became founder members of the Football Association – those that wanted to focus on a kicking game and let the ball-carrying rugby people go their own way – remains to this day. Fans, now as then, carry the pleasure of victory and pain of defeat around with them; results and performances are, by turns, precious jewels and onerous burdens. No other sport permeates so many people's lives to such an extent.

If England was the cradle of football, the game quickly spread through missionary zeal. In the postwar era the pupils have all too often outshone the masters, with the glorious exception of 1966. Whether South American, Spanish, Italian, German, Dutch – or English – football is the best is open to question. Many of the great players, teams and coaches from these countries, and others, are profiled in these pages. Their achievements can be recounted but there are as many different judgments as there are fans. From the same facts spring myriad opinions.

Compiling lists of footballing greats is a game all fans love to play. It is an art rather than a science. Statistics, important as they are and much as we love to pore over them, can only reveal so much. To make virtually any selection is to run the risk of generating more heat than light. Would you have Schmeichel or Banks in your dream team? Moore or Baresi sweeping? Duncan Edwards or Patrick Vieira driving the midfield? Ryan Giggs or Jimmy Johnstone flying down the wing? Van Basten or Ruud van Nistelrooy leading the line? Or maybe none of the above. And who gets the vote as the greatest of them all? Di Stefano, Cruyff, Maradona, Pele, Zidane?

Just because a question is imponderable doesn't make it any the less fascinating. Have Arsene Wenger's achievements eclipsed those of Herbert Chapman? Has Sir Alex Ferguson taken over from Sir Matt Busby as United's greatest ever manager? How would the Ajax side of the 1970s have fared against the AC Milan team of the early 1990s? Did France's World Cup-winning team of 1998 assume the mantle as the greatest ever, and if so did they take it from the Brazilian side of 1970?

Football is a game of shifting sands with few certainties or definitive answers. We enjoy its glorious subjectivity. It is for this very reason that many fans are wary about the introduction of technology. We like referees to make decisions – even flawed ones – because we like debates about the game to continue long after the whistle has blown. Football is about human passion, not clinical efficiency. *The Encyclopedia of World Football* is packed with profiles, information and statistics about the beautiful game, but not judgments. It will settle many arguments, and no doubt provoke many more.

Legends *of* Football

Tony Adams

Florian Albert

Born: 15 September 1941
Clubs: Ferencvaros
National Team: Hungary

Florian Albert arrived on the scene just as the great Hungary side of the 1950s was breaking up. He became the star of the 1960s team and a legend at Ferencvaros, where he spent his entire 18-year playing career. Technically excellent, Albert was both a maker and taker of chances. He made his debut for Hungary at 17 in a 3–2 win over Sweden in Budapest. He was joint-top scorer at the 1962 World Cup, when Hungary reached the quarter-finals. But his finest performances probably came four years later. Hungary again went out at the quarter-final stage, but Albert turned in a scintillating performance in a 3–1 victory over reigning champions Brazil at the group stage. He was named European Footballer of the Year in 1967, the only Hungarian to receive that award.

Tony Adams

Born: 10 October 1966
Clubs: Arsenal
National Team: England

Tony Adams was the linchpin in Arsenal's mean defence for well over a decade. He made his debut for the Gunners as a 17-year-old and his international debut in a 4-2 win over Spain in February 1987. On the last day of the 1988-89 season he helped Arsenal to a dramatic victory at Anfield, giving the Gunners their first title since 1971. In 1990-91 Adams picked up his second championship medal, Arsenal conceding just 18 league goals during the season. Adams missed part of that campaign, having been imprisoned for a drink-driving offence. In 1992-93 he won both the FA Cup and League Cup, Arsenal beating Sheffield Wednesday on both occasions. There was success in Europe too, with a Cup Winners' Cup victory over Parma in 1994. The crowning moment as far as the domestic game was concerned came in 1998, when Arsenal won the Double, emulating the achievement of the famous 1971 side. An outstanding captain as well as a superb defender, Adams won 64 caps in a 13-year international career. He cut his managerial teeth with Wycombe Wanderers, but lasted just four months in his first top-level job, at Portsmouth, after taking over at Fratton Park in October 2008.

Carlos Alberto

Born: 17 July 1944
Clubs: Fluminese, Santos, Botafoga, New York Cosmos
National Team: Brazil

Carlos Alberto was the captain of Brazil's World Cup-winning side of 1970, considered by many to be the greatest team of all time. An outstanding full-back, he was ever ready to spring forward and join the attack. This facet of his game was best illustrated in the 1970 final itself, when he exploded forward to latch onto Pele's sublime pass and thunder home Brazil's fourth goal against Italy. Carlos Alberto also enjoyed success at club level, winning the South American Championship with both Fluminese and Santos. By the time the 1974 World Cup came round, the great Brazil side of four years earlier had largely been broken up. Carlos Alberto spent the latter part of his career in North American playing for New York Cosmos alongside the likes of Beckenbauer and Pele. Carlos Alberto's coaching career includes spells in charge of the Oman and Azerbaijan national sides.

Ivor Allchurch

Born: 16 October 1919
Clubs: Swansea City, Newcastle United, Cardiff City, Swansea City
National Team: Wales

Ivor Allchurch was a stylish inside-forward who began and ended his career at Swansea. He spent 12 years at the Vetch Field with spells at Cardiff and Newcastle United in between. He made his debut for Swansea in 1949–50 and his 166 league goals remains a record for the Welsh club. His time at Newcastle was spent during a not particularly successful period for the club and unfortunately Allchurch played out his entire career for mediocre teams.

At international level, Allchurch enjoyed greater success. Along with John Charles, he was the star of the Welsh side that reached the quarter-finals of the 1958 World Cup, losing narrowly to Brazil. Allchurch's spectacular goal in the game against Hungary had placed them in that fortunate position and was one of 23 goals that he scored for his country. He won 68 caps for Wales and played his last international match in 1966. Ivor Allchurch died in 1997.

Ivor Allchurch

Jose Altafini

Born: 24 July 1938
Clubs: Palmeiras, São Paulo, AC Milan, Napoli, Juventus, Chiasso
National Team: Brazil, Italy

Only a handful of players have appeared in a World Cup for two different countries, Ferenc Puskas being the most famous of them. Jose Altafini is another member of that club. He played in the 1958 tournament for Brazil as a 19-year-old, though he didn't feature in the final. His direct, powerhouse performances at centre-forward persuaded AC Milan to bring him to Italy just after Brazil's victory. Altafini proved to be a goalscoring machine for Milan. His performances contributed towards the development of the ultra-defensive 'catenaccio' system, which was aimed at stifling the league's free-scoring marksmen. Altafini played for Italy in the 1962 World Cup but the team was eliminated at the group stage. A year later he set a competition record by scoring 14 goals as AC Milan won their first ever European Cup. Altafini's tally included two in the final against Benfica at Wembley.

Osvaldo Ardiles

Born: 3 August 1952
Clubs: Huracan, Tottenham Hotspur, Paris St-Germain, Tottenham Hotspur, Blackburn Rovers, Queens Park Rangers, Swindon
National Team: Argentina

Argentina celebrated victory in the 1978 World Cup partly thanks to their star midfielder Ossie Ardiles. Just two weeks after receiving his World Cup medal he had been snapped up by Spurs manager Keith Burkinshaw. At Tottenham Hotspur, he formed a deadly midfield alliance with Glenn Hoddle; the diminutive Ardiles had stylish ball control and thrived in the English game.

Spurs had only just been promoted back into the First division in Ardiles' first season at the club and they finished respectably in a mid-table position. In 1981, the club beat Manchester City to win the FA Cup and Ardiles collected the first of two medals he would win with Spurs. The following year, Ardiles helped his team win the FA Cup semi-final game against Leicester, but war had broken out between England and Argentina the day before and Ardiles opted to leave the club for France until the end of the conflict. He missed their subsequent victory in the final, but was back at Spurs the following year and played in the 1984 UEFA Cup final which Spurs won.

Gordon Banks

Roberto Baggio

Roberto Baggio

Born: 18 February 1967
Clubs: Vicenza, Fiorentina, Juventus, AC Milan, Bologna, Inter Milan, Brescia
National Team: Italy

Even at the age of 35 Roberto Baggio had a lot of supporters among Italian fans when it came to picking the World Cup squad for 2002. Giovanni Trapattoni decided against including him, bringing down the curtain on a marvellous international career. Baggio was outstanding at Italia '90, his performances persuading Juventus to part with a world-record £8 million. Fiorentina fans were inconsolable at the loss of the 'Divine Ponytail', as Baggio was dubbed. He helped the Turin club to win the UEFA Cup in 1993 and promptly picked up both the European and World Footballer of the Year awards. He was in brilliant form as Italy made it all the way to the final at USA '94, only to miss the vital penalty which handed victory to Brazil. He helped Juve to win the Serie A title in 1995, moving on to AC Milan the same year. Baggio expunged the memory of USA '94 by converting two spot-kicks at France '98, though Italy did go out on penalties again for the third tournament in succession. He wound down his career with Brescia, retiring in 2004.

Gordon Banks

Born: 30 December 1937
Clubs: Chesterfield, Leicester City, Stoke City, Fort Lauderdale Strikers
National Team: England

Gordon Banks, often considered to be England's greatest goalkeeper, began his career at Chesterfield in 1955, earning just £2 per match. His move to Leicester City in 1959 brought him greater recognition, despite being on the losing side of the FA Cup final in 1961. He picked up another loser's medal two years later.

In 1963, Banks made his debut for England and he remained in the team for almost a decade. He was a member of the glorious 1966 side, but perhaps his greatest moment came during the following World Cup tournament. Ten minutes into their game against Brazil at Guadalajara, Mexico, the world's greatest player, Pele, headed a thundering ball towards the inside far post. Banks managed to scoop it up over the bar, producing what many believed to be the finest save of all time. England were through to the quarter-finals, but without Banks, who had to withdraw due to illness. The defending champions went out to West Germany. Of 73 matches with Banks in goal, England lost only 9 and he kept 35 clean sheets.

Banks joined Stoke City in 1967, picking up his first club medal when they beat Chelsea in the League Cup final of 1971–72. The 34-year-old Banks signed a long-term contract with Stoke, but his career was sadly cut short when he lost an eye in a car accident in 1972.

Franco Baresi

Franco Baresi

Born: 8 May 1960
Clubs: AC Milan
National Team: Italy

Along with Paolo Maldini and Alessandro Costacurta, Franco Baresi formed the superb defensive platform on which AC Milan built their success in the late 1980s and early 1990s. Baresi was not the quickest defender, but his ability to read the game was almost uncanny. He made defending against the world's top strikers look easy with his superb positional play and impeccable timing. He was also quick to surge upfield and link up with the attack. Baresi spent his 20-year playing career at AC Milan, the club he joined as a 17-year-old. In that time he won six domestic championships and the European Cup twice, in 1989 and 1990. He missed out on a hat-trick of victories in Europe's premier cup competition when he was suspended for the 1994 final, in which Milan beat Barcelona 4–0. Baresi made his debut for Italy in 1982, and was a member of the squad which won that year's World Cup. Twelve years and 81 caps later, he bowed out of international football in the World Cup final against Brazil in the USA. He was Italy's star player, despite having recently undergone a cartilage operation, but did miss with his spot-kick in the penalty shoot-out. Milan retired the No. 6 shirt after his retirement in 1996.

Jim Baxter

Jim Baxter

Born: 29 September 1939
Clubs: Raith Rovers, Glasgow Rangers, Sunderland, Nottingham Forest
National Team: Scotland

'Slim' Jim Baxter's flame flickered all too briefly, but at his peak in the 1960s he played with the kind of flair and style that captivated all Scottish fans. He had mesmerizing skills and was also a consummate showman. Baxter signed for Rangers from Raith Rovers in 1960 and transformed the Glasgow side from a workmanlike unit into a team with great attacking flair. He helped Rangers win the championship in his first season and played a key role in helping them become the first British club to contest a major final. Rangers went down to Fiorentina in the inaugural European Cup Winners' Cup final but Baxter's reputation was considerably enhanced. Rangers won two more league titles and three Scottish cups during Baxter's five-year spell at the club. He headed south and had spells at Sunderland and Nottingham Forest, but he didn't quite produce the same magic on a regular basis. In 1969 he returned to Rangers, where he spent one final season before retiring. Capped 34 times, Baxter never graced a World Cup with his skills. But in October 1963 he was selected for a World XI which took on England at Wembley. England won 2–1 that day, but it was a different matter four years later, in April 1967. Playing for Scotland this time, Baxter was outstanding in a 3–2 win over England, their first defeat since winning the World Cup the previous year. Baxter died of pancreatic cancer in 2001.

Cliff Bastin

Born: 14 March 1912
Clubs: Exeter City, Arsenal
National Team: England

Along with Alex James, Cliff Bastin was the star of the Arsenal side which dominated English football in the 1930s. A flying left-winger, Bastin went to Highbury in 1929, signed from Exeter City by talent-spotter supreme Herbert Chapman. He was just 16 when he first came to Chapman's attention, and the nickname 'Boy' Bastin stuck, despite the fact that he stayed with the club for the rest of his career. Bastin won the championship five times and the FA Cup twice. The first of those victories came when he was just 18, a record which stood until the 1950s. He was capped 21 times for England, scoring 12 goals. Bastin's 178 goals for Arsenal stood until 1997–98 when Ian Wright set a new Highbury record. He died in 1991.

Franz Beckenbauer

Born: 11 September 1945
Clubs: Bayern Munich, New York Cosmos, Hamburg
National Team: West Germany

Franz Beckenbauer is the only man to have won the World Cup both as a player and as a manager. Captain of West Germany when they won the World Cup in 1974, beating the favourites Holland, and manager when they won in 1990, his list of honours is unique. Known as 'Emperor Franz' or 'The Kaiser', Beckenbauer's commanding style of play in either a midfield position or as an attacking sweeper made him legendary.

Beckenbauer rose to prominence in the 1966 World Cup, having made his international debut during the qualifying campaign. He finished on the losing side in that tournament but by 1971 he had been made West Germany's captain. He led them to victory in the European Championships in 1972 and then achieved the double by lifting the world cup two years later.

Beckenbauer made his debut for the then unfashionable Bayern Munich in 1964. By 1966 they had become Germany's premier side, winning the Bundesliga title and domestic cup four times each between 1966 and 1974. Under Beckenbauer's leadership the team went on to dominate Europe, with a hat-trick of Champions Cup wins between 1974 and 1976. He won the European Footballer of the Year award twice, in 1972 and 1976, and then retired from international football in 1977, having won a record 104 caps.

In 1977, Beckenbauer accepted a £2.7million contract to play for New York Cosmos in the NASL. He briefly returned to Germany to play, but finally retired in 1983. That same year he became the replacement manager for Germany's national side. He took the team to the finals of the 1986 World Cup in Mexico, where they were beaten by Argentina 3–2. In Italy in 1990, Beckenbauer's team took their revenge, beating the Argentinians to win the trophy. He then retired as manager and returned to Bayern as club president.

Dennis Bergkamp

Born: 10 May 1969
Clubs: Ajax, Inter Milan, Arsenal
National Team Holland

Sublime skill, marvellous touch, incredible vision and a sizeable haul of memorable goals: such are the hallmarks of Dennis Bergkamp's footballing career. Named after Denis Law, Bergkamp was a teenage prodigy at Ajax in the late 1980s. He won both the European Cup Winners' Cup and the UEFA Cup with the Dutch club before moving on to Inter Milan in 1993. His two-year spell in Serie A was a frustrating one, though he did pick up another UEFA Cup winners' medal when Inter beat Austria Salzburg in the 1994 final. He moved to Arsenal in June 1995 for £7.5 million, then a record for the Highbury club. The Premiership proved to be the ideal stage for Bergkamp's skills. In 1997–98 he helped Arsenal to achieve the Double, although injury forced him to miss the FA cup final victory over Newcastle. His outstanding performances earned him both the PFA and Football Writers' Player of the Year awards, and he was voted

Franz Beckenbauer

third in FIFA's World Footballer of the Year poll. He scored the goal of the tournament in the quarter-final of France '98, a last-minute win against Argentina, though Holland went out against Brazil in the semis. Bergkamp scored 36 goals in 79 appearances for Holland, though that figure would undoubtedly have been higher had he not been hampered by his much-publicized fear of flying. He retired at the end of the 2005–06 season, signing off with a trademark curler against WBA at Highbury, Gunners fans dubbing the occasion 'Dennis Bergkamp Day' in honour of one of their greatest ever players.

George Best

Born: 22 May 1946
Clubs: Manchester United, Stockport County, Fulham, Los Angeles Aztecs, Motherwell, Hibernian, Bournemouth, Brisbane Lions
National Team: Northern Ireland

As a young man George Best had a wealth of natural talent, speed, strength, balance and poise, creativity and incredible ball control. Yet by his late twenties his career as a top-level footballer was all but over. The pressure of celebrity and a disastrous tendency to self-destruct were to end his career prematurely.

Born in Belfast in 1946, Best joined Manchester United when he was just 15. Such was Best's natural ability that when he decided to return to Belfast due to homesickness, Matt Busby travelled across the Irish Sea to persuade him to return. Busby recognized Best's raw talent and coaching staff were told not to try to teach him anything; he reasoned that such skill was best left alone. It was said of Best that he could have played in any outfield position – and outperformed the man who usually played there, and Busby claimed he had never seen another player so capable of beating an opponent.

Best made his playing debut for United in 1963 and just seven months later he made his first appearance for Northern Ireland. Although he won 37 caps, he never really had the chance to make an impact on the world stage. It was, however, his appearance in the European Cup of 1965–66 that brought the full glare of the media spotlight onto Best. He stunned Benfica by scoring twice in the first 10 minutes of the game. United won 5–1, beating the Portuguese giants at the Stadium of Light. Dubbed 'El Beatle', the good-looking and charming Irishman was an instant star.

In 1968, United became the first English team to win the European Cup, beating Benfica again, this time at Wembley. Best picked up the European and English Footballer of the Year titles and looked set to reap more honours, but success was beginning to take its toll. During the early 1970s relations with teammates and with new boss Tommy Docherty were becoming strained and Best's lifestyle was beginning to affect his health. When he walked out of Old Trafford in 1972, two days before his twenty-sixth birthday, his best playing days were behind him.

The following decade saw Best move between a succession of clubs in both Britain and America. In 1980 he began a first course of treatment for alcoholism, retiring from the game in 1983. Best continued to be in demand as a football pundit, but his health did not improve and he underwent a liver transplant in 2002. He died on 25 November 2005, aged 59.

George Best

Laurent Blanc

Born: 19 November 1965
Clubs: Montpellier, Napoli, Nimes, Saint-Etienne, Auxerre, Barcelona, Marseille, Inter Milan, Manchester United
National Team: France

The 1998 World Cup will long be remembered for France's stunning victory on home soil — and the trademark kiss that central defender Laurent Blanc planted on the forehead of goalkeeper Fabien Barthez before each game. The ritual was missing for the final, however. Blanc missed France's greatest day after being unjustly red carded for an alleged foul on Slaven Bilic in the semis. Even so, Blanc had contributed hugely towards his country's World Cup victory, in attack as well as defence. It was he who hit the golden goal winner against Paraguay in the second round. In 2000 France emulated West Germany's achievements of the 1970s by adding the European Championship to the World Cup. This time Blanc played in the final, a 2–1 victory over Italy. It was to be his 97th and final cap. By the summer of 2001, Blanc was approaching 36 and seemed to be winding down his playing career at Inter Milan. But long-time admirer Alex Ferguson brought the Frenchman to Old Trafford as a replacement for Jaap Stam, and also persuaded him to stay on for the 2002–03 season. Having made his debut for Montpellier back in 1983, Blanc thus completed 20 years in top-class football.

Laurent Blanc

Danny Blanchflower

Danny Blanchflower

Born: 10 February 1926
Clubs: Glentoran, Barnsley, Aston Villa, Tottenham Hotspur
National Team: Northern Ireland

Danny Blanchflower retired from professional football in 1964, having spent ten years at Tottenham Hotspur. Born in Belfast, he had begun his career at Glentoran and Barnsley, and in 1951 he moved to Aston Villa for £15,000. Just three years later he joined Spurs for £30,000.

During the 1960s, Blanchflower became a legendary member of the north London team. In the 1960–61 season, Spurs won the coveted Double and Blanchflower was the first captain of the century to lift both trophies in one season. That same year he received a second Footballer of the Year award, being only the second player to achieve that honour twice.

The following season, Blanchflower led his team to FA Cup victory over Burnley and followed that with an historic win over Atletico Madrid in the European Cup Winners' Cup final. Spurs became the first British side to win a European trophy.

Blanchflower also enjoyed an illustrious international career, playing 56 times for Northern Ireland. In 1957 he had captained the side to their first ever defeat of England at Wembley and in 1958 led them to the quarter-finals of the World Cup. Danny Blanchflower died in 1993, aged 67.

Zbigniew Boniek

played in both the 1982 and 1986 World Cups. Blokhin led Ukraine to the World Cup finals in 2006, the country's first appearance in a major tournament.

Steve Bloomer

Born: 20 January 1874
Clubs: Derby County, Middlesbrough
National Team: England

Steve Bloomer was the most prolific marksman of his day. An inside-forward with a deadly accurate shot, Bloomer began his career as an 18-year-old with Derby in 1892. He ended his career at the age of 40 in 1914 at the same club, although he did have a four-year spell at Middlesbrough along the way. These 22 years yielded a remarkable 352 league goals in 598 appearances. It was not until the 1936–37 season that Dixie Dean set a new mark, and only a handful of players have outscored him since. Bloomer's record 28 goals in just 23 games for England stood even longer, until the 1950s. The FA presented him with a portrait of himself when he won his 21st cap, which was a record at the time. After hanging up his boots, Bloomer took up a coaching job in Germany and was interned for the duration of the First World War.

Oleg Blokhin

Born: 5 November 1952
Clubs: Dynamo Kiev, Vorwärts Steyr
National Team: Soviet Union

In 1975 Oleg Blokhin became only the second player from the Soviet Union to win the European Footballer of the Year award, following in the footsteps of Lev Yashin. Franz Beckenbauer and Johan Cruyff were the outstanding players in European football so it was no mean achievement for the Dynamo Kiev player. The award came on the back of Kiev's 3–0 victory over Ferencvaros in that year's European Cup Winners' Cup final. The lightning-quick striker was outstanding throughout and made a huge contribution towards helping Kiev become the first Soviet side to lift a major European trophy. Blokhin hit one of the goals in that year's final, then repeated the feat eleven years later when Dynamo beat Atletico Madrid by the same score in the final of the same competition. Blokhin became the first Soviet player to pass the hundred-cap mark, hitting 39 goals. He

Zbigniew Boniek

Born: 3 March 1956
Clubs: Zawisza Bydgoszcz, Widzew Lodz, Juventus, AS Roma
National Team: Poland

The Poland side of the mid-1970s might have been the greatest the country has ever produced, but the star individual came from the next generation. Zbigniew Boniek won his first cap in 1976 and played in the World Cup two years later, where Poland went out in the second round. At Spain '82 Boniek was the outstanding player in a side which won through to a semi-final clash with Italy. Unfortunately, Boniek was suspended for that match and the eventual tournament winners prevailed 2–0. Boniek left Widzew Lodz for Juventus in the same year. Playing in a star-studded side including Michel Platini, Boniek scored the winner in Juve's 2–1 win over Porto in the 1984 European Cup Winners' Cup. The following year he picked up a European Cup winners' medal when Juventus beat Liverpool in a final that was overshadowed by the tragic events at the Heysel Stadium.

Alen Boksic

Born: 31 January 1970
Clubs: Hadjuk Split, Cannes, Marseille, Lazio, Juventus, Lazio, Middlesbrough
National Team: Yugoslavia, Croatia

Alen Boksic was a teenage prodigy, coming through the youth ranks at Hadjuk Split to make his first team debut at the age of 17 in 1987. He joined Marseille four years later, signing off for Hadjuk with the goal that beat Red Star Belgrade in Yugoslavia's domestic Cup final. He won the league and cup with the French club, but the crowning achievement came with a victory over AC Milan in the 1993 European Champions League final. He was the French league's top scorer that season with 23 goals. Beset by a bribery scandal, Marseille was forced to sell its star player. Lazio beat Juventus to his signature, but three years later Boksic did have a season at the Turin club. He then returned to Lazio, and in 1998 he helped the club reach the Italian Cup and UEFA Cup finals. The team won the former but went down 3–0 to Inter in the first UEFA Cup final to be decided over a single leg. Boksic was in the veteran class when he joined Middlesbrough but he graced the Premiership with his skills when he was fit and in form. Boksic was a member of an outstanding Croatia side in the 1990s, but injury forced him to miss France '98 when the country finished third in its debut appearance at a World Cup. He announced his retirement from international football in 2003.

Liam Brady

Born: 13 February 1956
Clubs: Arsenal, Juventus, Sampdoria, Inter Milan, Ascoli, West Ham United
National Team: Republic of Ireland

The sweetest of left feet and an elegant, languid style were the hallmarks of Liam Brady's cultured midfield play. The creative force in the Arsenal side for much of the 1970s, Brady played in a period of relative famine for the Gunners. The team was regularly languishing in mid-table, although there was a celebrated hat-trick of FA Cup final appearances. It was Brady who engineered their sole victory, over Manchester United in 1979. His superb burst in the dying seconds set up the winning goal scored by Alan Sunderland. Brady moved to Juventus the following year, and helped the Turin side to successive Serie A titles. He also played for Sampdoria, Inter Milan and Ascoli before returning to England, ending his career at West Ham. Brady played 72 times for the Republic of Ireland between 1975 and 1990.

His international career was coming to an end just as Ireland were enjoying their most successful spell ever under Jack Charlton.

Paul Breitner

Born: 5 September 1951
Clubs: Bayern Munich, Real Madrid, Eintracht Braunschweig
National Team: West Germany

When West Germany reached the 1982 World Cup final, Paul Breitner was the only survivor from the side which had won the tournament on home soil eight years earlier. Breitner scored in both games. His penalty cancelled out Cruyff's spot-kick in 1974, with Gerd Müller grabbing the winner. At Spain '82 Breitner hit a late consolation goal as West Germany went down 3–1 to Italy. Equally effective as a rampaging left-back or cultured midfielder, Breitner played in the mighty Bayern Munich team of the mid-1970s. Having also played in the Germany side that was crowned champions of Europe in 1972, Breitner was a member of the elite group of players to have simultaneously held winners' medals in the World Cup, European Championship and European Cup.

Liam Brady

Billy Bremner

Billy Bremner

Born: 9 December 1942
Clubs: Leeds United, Hull City, Doncaster Rovers
National Team: Scotland

Billy Bremner is fondly remembered by Leeds fans as a key player in Don Revie's great side of the late 1960s and early 1970s. His Leeds career spanned 16 years as they rose from Division 2 to compete in the 1975 European Cup final against Bayern Munich. He joined the club in 1959 and soon formed a playing partnership with Johnny Giles in which Bremner's superb passing and surging forward runs perfectly complemented Giles' artistry.

In 1968–69 and 1973–74, Bremner led his side to two League Championships and FA Cup victory over Arsenal in 1972. However, he was also to collect a number of runners-up medals: Leeds finished second in the league on five occasions during Bremner's era, and were beaten FA Cup finalists three times. The defeat by Bayern Munich prompted the end of his playing career at Leeds and he moved first to Hull City, then to Doncaster. In 1985 he returned to Elland Road as manager where he remained until 1988.

Bremner was capped 54 times for Scotland, one short of Denis Law's then record. He led the Scots to the 1974 World Cup, where they were unbeaten and unlucky to be eliminated on goal difference.

Bremner was one of the first players to be sent off at Wembley when he and Kevin Keegan resorted to fighting during the 1974–75 Charity Shield. Further controversy came when he received a lifetime ban from the Scottish FA following a charge of misconduct. Billy Bremner died in 1997.

Emilio Butragueno

Born: 22 July 1963
Clubs: Real Madrid, Celaya
National Team: Spain

Initially thought not good enough by Real Madrid, Emilio Butragueno proved his critics wrong to become one of the most feared strikers in world football in the 1980s. He was dubbed 'The Vulture' for his predatory instincts in the box.

His goals helped Real win the Primera Liga five times in succession between 1986 and 90. There were also back-to-back UEFA Cup victories in 1985 and 1986. He scored on his international debut, a World Cup qualifying match against Wales in 1984. He went on to score a record 26 goals in 69 appearances for Spain over the next eight years. His finest moment came in the 1986 World Cup, when he hit four goals as Spain thrashed a fine Denmark side 5–1 in the second round. Spain went out to Belgium on penalties in the quarter-final, with Butragueno having the consolation of finishing as joint-second top marksman, behind Gary Lineker.

Trevor Brooking

Born: 2 October 1948
Clubs: West Ham
National Team: England

Trevor Brooking's cultured midfield play was nurtured at the celebrated West Ham academy in the 1960s under Ron Greenwood. He spent his entire career at Upton Park, during which time he was the Hammers' key playmaker. Loyalty meant that an illustrious career yielded few honours. West Ham did win the FA Cup twice in Brooking's time, the first an expected victory over Fulham in 1975. The second, five years later, was more of a surprise. Arsenal went to Wembley as holders and strong favourites to retain the trophy, but a rare Brooking header was the difference between the teams on the day. Spain '82 finally gave Brooking the opportunity to show his skills on the World Cup stage, eight years after he had made his England debut. Injury prevented him from making an appearance until the crucial second-round match against Spain. Despite the fact that he was not fully fit, his old club boss Ron Greenwood threw him on as a late substitute to see if he could add to his tally of five international goals. He couldn't help the team to manufacture the goal they needed to progress in the tournament. It was 33-year-old Brooking's 47th and final cap. He was knighted in 2004.

Trevor Brooking

Cafu

Born: 19 June 1970
Clubs: Nacional Sao Paulo, Real Zaragoza, Palmeiras, Roma, AC Milan
National Team: Brazil

Brazil's most capped player, Cafu was already the only man to have played in three World Cup finals. He came on as an early substitute at USA '94 and four years later, he was an automatic choice in the side which ran out of steam so dramatically in the final against France. By the time Japan and Korea 2002 came round, he was in the veteran class, yet he was still regarded as the best in the business in his position as Brazil again lifted the trophy. When he captained Brazil to the quarter-finals at Germany 2006, Cafu joined a select group of players to have participated in four World Cups. These were fine achieve-ments for a player who was virtually dismissed when he was a teenager. He was playing in midfield for Nacional and wasn't thought to have the flair and creativity that such a position demands. He moved to Sao Paulo in 1989 and there, under the tutelage of Tele Santana, he was converted into an attacking right-back. After five successful years at Sao Paulo, culminating in his winning the South American Footballer of the Year award in 1994, Cafu headed for Europe. After a brief spell at Real Zaragoza, he returned home. He joined Roma in 1997 and played a major role in helping the club win its first *scudetto* for a decade in 2001. In 2003 he joined AC Milan, winning another Serie A title in his first season. He announced his retirement at the end of the 2007–08 season.

Eric Cantona

Born: 24 May 1966
Clubs: Auxerre, Martigues, Marseille, Bordeaux, Montpellier, Nimes, Leeds United, Manchester United
National Team: France

Eric Cantona became one of the first overseas players to carve a name for themselves in English football. When the rules on importing players from abroad were relaxed, a huge number of foreign footballers arrived in England and Cantona came to Leeds halfway through the 1991–92 season. His former club Marseille had just become French Champions and Cantona carried success with him, enabling the Yorkshire club to win their first championship title since the 1970s. In 1992, Howard

Eric Cantona

Wilkinson sold the 26-year-old to Manchester United, just as they were to begin their domination of the league.

With United, Cantona won four Championship medals, including the Double twice. In 1996, he was named Footballer of the Year as a result of his inspiring performances during that season, including his last-minute goal against Liverpool in the FA Cup final. Cantona had led United during that final, becoming the first foreign player to captain an FA Cup-winning team.

With his trademark upturned collar, Cantona was captivating to watch, performing complex skills with apparent ease. Unfortunately his career was soured by disciplinary problems. In January 1995, the fiery Frenchman was banned for eight months for aiming a kung-fu kick at a fan following a sending-off. He was renowned for arguing with players and managers alike, and were it not for his difficult relationship with the French FA he would probably have earned more than 43 international caps. Although his disciplinary record had improved by 1996, the Old Trafford hero decided to retire from the game at the end of the 1996–97 season, aged just 30.

Jan Ceulemans

Born: 28 February 1957
Clubs: Lierse, Club Brugge
National Team: Belgium

Jan Ceulemans was Belgium's star striker in the 1980s. He scored 26 goals in a record 96 international appearances, dropping back into a midfield role in the latter part of his career. Belgium's finest achievement in Ceulemans' time was a semi-final berth at the 1986 World Cup, where the team went down 2–0 to eventual winners Argentina. He was still there at Italia '90, when Belgium's hopes were dashed by a wonder strike from England's David Platt in the second round. Ceulemans would surely have garnered major club honours had he not chosen to remain in Belgium for his entire career. A proposed glamour move to AC Milan in 1981 fell through, apparently at his mother's behest!

Stephane Chapuisat

Stephane Chapuisat

Born: 28 June 1969
Clubs: Malley, Lausanne Sports, Bayer Uerdingen, Borussia Dortmund, Grasshoppers Zurich, BSC Young Boys
National Team: Switzerland

Along with Stephane Henchoz, striker Stephane Chapuisat has been Switzerland's top footballing export of the modern era. He left his native country for Germany in 1991, joining Bayer Uerdingen. He moved to Borussia Dortmund the following year and was instrumental in that team's revival after a long period of underachievement. Dortmund won the Bundesliga title in 1995 and 1996, the club's first championships since the 1960s. The crowning glory came with a European Champions Cup triumph in 1997. Chapuisat helped Dortmund get past Manchester United in the semis, then pull off an unexpected 3–1 victory over Juventus in the final. He scored an extra-time winner against arch-rivals Bayern Munich in the quarter-final of the same competition the following year, but Dortmund's progress was halted by Real Madrid in the semis.

Lured away from Swansea, where he had been apprenticed, Charles began his career as a central defender at Leeds United. In the 1953–54 season, Charles was switched to a centre forward role and the following season he put away 42 league goals a record to this day, and an achievement which brought him to the attention of the Italian giants. In 1957 he joined Juventus for a record £67,000 and he made an immediate impact. During his first season, he scored 28 goals in 34 games and soon became Serie A's top marksman. With the help of Charles, Juventus won the league title three times and the cup twice. By the time he left Italy in 1962, he had hit 93 goals in 155 games.

At the age of 18 years and 71 days, Charles was the youngest player to turn out for Wales. Although he missed his country's greatest moment in international football, reaching the quarter-finals of the 1958 World Cup, he had been a key figure in helping them to get there. Charles had been injured during the tough play-off match against Hungary, targeted by defenders wary of his goal-scoring ability. After a spell back at Leeds, Charles wound down his career with Roma and Cardiff City. He died in February 2004.

John Charles

John Charles

Born: 27 December 1931
Clubs: Leeds United, Juventus, AS Roma, Cardiff City
National Team: Wales

'The Gentle Giant' was an appropriate nickname for one of football's great gentleman players. Charles was 6 ft 2 in tall and 15 stone, strong and powerful, but he never used his physique in an aggressive manner; in a 16-year career he was never booked and never sent off. One of the first British players to enjoy success on the Continent, the Welshman spent 5 years at Juventus and is still fondly remembered by Italian fans.

Bobby Charlton

Born: 11 October 1937
Clubs: Manchester United
National Team: England

Football was in Bobby Charlton's blood. His uncle was Jackie Milburn, a legend on Tyneside in the 1950s, while his elder brother Jack also joined the professional ranks. In a career that spanned two decades, Charlton won just about every honour in the game, both at club and international level. He signed for Manchester United in 1955, as part of Matt Busby's plan to poach the best young talent in the country. On his debut against Charlton Athletic in 1956 he scored twice and, along with the rest of the 'Busby Babes', he looked set to dominate top-flight football.

The infamous Munich air crash in February 1958 practically wiped out that United side. Eight of the 'Babes' were killed in the disaster, but Charlton survived to become a key member of the new team that Busby would build. Just weeks after the tragedy, Charlton made his debut for England, earning the first of his 106 caps.

Early in his career, Charlton appeared as a winger or inside-forward, but he soon developed into a deep-lying centre-forward. He could pass with pinpoint accuracy and would burst forward to unleash shots with either foot. En route to victory in the 1966 World Cup, both Mexico and

Portugal were on the receiving end of his firepower. That same year, Charlton received the European Player of the Year award, in recognition of his performances during the tournament.

In 1968, Charlton captained Manchester United to their victory in the European Cup final, beating Benfica by 4 goals to 1. It was an emotional triumph for Charlton, Busby and the whole team, coming ten years after the deaths of so many teammates during a European campaign.

Charlton's final game for England came in 1970, in the quarter-final of the World Cup in Mexico. England were 2–1 ahead against West Germany at half-time, and Alf Ramsey's decision to substitute Charlton in the second half was believed by many to be a contributing factor in the subsequent defeat. In 106 appearances for his country, Charlton scored 49 goals, a record that remains unbeaten. His final league appearance, and final game for Manchester United, was in 1973. It was his 606th league game. In all that time, Charlton received only one booking, for time wasting – when his side were losing. Bobby Charlton was knighted in 1994.

Jose Luis Chilavert

Born: 27 July 1965
Clubs: Cerro Portero, San Lorenzo, Velez Sarsfield, Real Zaragoza, Strasbourg, Penarol
National Team: Paraguay

One of the game's great characters as well as a fine goalkeeper, Jose Luis Chilavert has been a dominant figure in Paraguay's success in recent years. The team's portly talisman was outstanding at France '98, and it took a late golden goal from Laurent Blanc in the second round to put Paraguay out of the tournament. Chilavert was there again at Japan and Korea 2002. He was approaching his 37th birthday, yet was still confidently predicting that he would get on the scoresheet with a penalty or one of his trademark free-kicks. This was no idle boast, as Chilavert had notched more than 50 goals from dead-ball kicks, which he practised tirelessly on the training ground. The team played poorly against Germany in the second round and went out to a late Oliver Neuville goal. Chilavert has played most of his club football in South America, his performances for Velez Sarsfield of Buenos Aires earning him the South American Footballer of the Year award in 1996. He had a spell at Real Zaragoza, and signed for French club Strasbourg at the age of 35. He was sacked in 2002 over contract irregularities and returned to Velez Sarsfield before retiring in 2004.

Bobby Charlton

Mario Coluna

Born: 6 August 1935
Clubs: Deportivo Lourenco Marques, Benfica, Lyon
National Team: Portugal

Along with Eusebio, Mario Coluna was Mozambique's greatest footballing export in the 1950s. At a time when many Portuguese clubs were trawling the colonies for talent, it was Benfica who stole a march on their rivals by signing the teenage centre-forward in 1954. Coluna spent the next 16 years at the club, with coach Bela Guttman converting him into a deeper-lying midfield role. He was hugely influential as Benfica took over from Real Madrid as the most successful club side in Europe in the 1960s. There were five European Cup final appearances in eight years, with Coluna getting on the scoresheet in the two victorious campaigns, against Barcelona in 1961 and Real Madrid the following year. Capped 73 times, Coluna captained Portugal in their 1966 World Cup campaign. Only a great save from Banks denied him from hitting a late equaliser in the team's semi-final clash with England. Even so, he ended his international career with 57 goals, a superb strike rate.

Alessandro Costacurta

Born: 24 April 1966
Clubs: Monza, AC Milan
National Team: Italy

AC Milan's penalty shoot-out victory over Juventus in the 2003 Champions League final brought 37-year-old Alessandro Costacurta his fourth winners' medal in that competition. Costacurta had been a stalwart in Milan's defence for 18 seasons, spending his entire career at the club apart from a one-year stint at Monza in 1986–87. Along with Paolo Maldini, Costacurta was a fixture in the side during a period of great success. Milan won the Serie A championship on six occasions during Costacurta's time at the club, although it was only in 2003, a few days after the victory over Juve at Old Trafford, that he added an Italian Cup winners' medal to his haul. Despite his successes at club level, Costacurta had to wait until 1991 to receive the first of his 59 caps. In the semi-final victory over Bulgaria at the 1994 World

Cup he picked up a second yellow card which kept him out of the final against Brazil. He was also suspended for the European Cup final win over Barcelona in the same year. Despite those disappointments, 'Billy' Costacurta has enjoyed one of the most successful careers of the modern era. He joined Milan's coaching staff after signing off as a player at the end of the 2006–07 season.

Alessandro Costacurta

Johan Cruyff

Born: 25 April 1947
Clubs: Ajax, Barcelona, Los Angeles Aztecs, Washington Diplomats, Levante, Ajax, Feyenoord
National Team: Holland

Johan Cruyff was the heart of a Holland side that gave the world 'Total Football'. Cruyff's name became synonymous with a style of play where any player could do anything on the field. The centre-forward could confuse his markers to devastating effect and the famous 'Cruyff turn' astounded fans and defenders alike when he first used it in a match. Beautifully balanced, nimble and agile, he roamed all over the pitch with the ball at his feet.

Cruyff's mother, who worked at Ajax as a cleaner, persuaded the coaching staff to take a look at her young son when he was just twelve. Cruyff joined their youth team and eventually made his first team debut for Ajax in 1965, aged 17. He scored in that first game. Between 1966 and 1973 Ajax won the domestic title six times and the cup on five occasions. They also won the European Cup three times in a row from 1971, dominating European football during the first half of the seventies. The part Cruyff played in this success was duly recognized and he was named European Footballer of the Year in 1971, 1973 and 1974, becoming the first player to win the prestigious award on three occasions.

In 1973, Cruyff joined Barcelona for a world record £922,000. The manager of the struggling Catalan club Rinus Michels was an ex-Ajax coach and he knew that Cruyff was the player to turn things around. In his first season Barcelona took the Spanish championship, ending a 14-year drought; among their victories was a 5–0 humiliation of arch-rivals Real away in Madrid.

Although Cruyff was to reap medals at club-level he never won a major trophy with Holland. The stunning Dutch side looked set to win the 1974 World Cup, meeting hosts West Germany in the final. He won a penalty for Holland in the first minute of the

game, but the Germans recovered and won the game 2–1. It was to be Cruyff's only appearance in a World Cup tournament. Much to the disappointment of the Dutch fans, he prematurely retired before the 1978 finals in Argentina.

Cruyff left Spain to play in the USA and he returned to Europe in 1981, enjoying a twilight spell at Ajax, winning two domestic titles. He then made a shock defection to Feyenoord where he picked up another championship medal. Cruyff went on successfully to manage the clubs where he had had his greatest playing days, Ajax and Barcelona.

Johan Cruyff

Teofilio Cubillas

Born: 8 March 1949
Clubs: Alianza, Basel, FC Porto, Alianza, Fort Lauderdale Strikers
National Team: Peru

Teofilio Cubillas was the star player in the Peru side of the 1970s and widely regarded as the finest the country has ever produced. The 21-year-old inside-forward hit five goals in Peru's run to the quarter-finals at the 1970 World Cup, making him the tournament's third top scorer behind Müller and Jairzinho. He repeated the feat eight years later in Argentina, where Peru topped a group including Holland and Scotland before going out in the second round. Only Mario Kempes, with six goals, found the net more often. He was less successful at club level, spells at Basel and Porto not proving to be too fruitful. But his 38 goals in 88 appearances for Peru established him as a legend in the country.

Kenny Dalglish

Born: 4 March 1951
Clubs: Celtic, Liverpool
National Team: Scotland

Kenny Dalglish was the most feared striker north of the border when Bob Paisley brought him to Liverpool from Celtic. Dalglish had begun his career at Parkhead aged just 16 and scored over 100 goals for Celtic in the ten years he spent there. Dalglish's move to Anfield in 1977 eased the loss of Kevin Keegan who had moved to Hamburg a month earlier. Over the next 13 years, Dalglish became a legend on the Kop. In his first season at Liverpool he scored 30 goals and looked set to repeat his Scottish record. In November 1983 his 100th goal for Liverpool hit the back of the net and Dalglish became the first double centurion – chalking up 100 goals on each side of the border. As a player, Dalglish won five Championship medals and three European Cups. When he became player-manager in 1985–86,

Kenny Dalglish

Liverpool won the Double. The player widely considered to be the greatest ever to wear the famous red shirt also won a record 102 caps for Scotland. He scored 30 goals at international level, equalling Denis Law's record.

Dixie Dean

Born: 22 January 1907
Clubs: Tranmere Rovers, Everton, Notts County, Sligo Rangers
National Team: England

Dean had started his career at Tranmere Rovers, and finished at Sligo Rangers, but Everton was his greatest love and he was certainly one of Everton's greatest players. William 'Dixie' Dean still holds the record for the most number of goals scored in one season, 60 in total, scored in 1927–28. During that record-breaking season Everton had scored 102 times in order to win the Championship. Fittingly, Dean broke the previous record of 59 goals, held by Middlesbrough's George Camsell, with a hat-trick at the last game of the season.

He had joined Everton in 1925, when they were languishing at mid-table, although his career was nearly over before it began when, in 1926, he was involved in a near-fatal motorcycle accident. Dean's prolific goal scoring was instrumental in changing Everton's fortunes. They won the league again in 1931–32, having been promoted from the Second Division and during that season, Dean had scored 44 times. He captained his team to victory in the 1933 FA Cup final, beating Manchester City 3–0. In 502 appearances in competitive football, Dean scored an amazing 473 goals, including 37 hat-tricks for Everton alone. Dean made 16 appearances for England, scoring 18 times.

He died in 1980, aged 73, just minutes after the whistle was blown at an Everton–Liverpool derby.

Dixie Dean

Marcel Desailly

Born: 7 September 1968
Clubs: Nantes, Marseille, AC Milan, Chelsea, Al Gharafa, Quatar Sports Club
National Team France

Marcel Desailly has been one of the world's premier players for more than a decade, equally accomplished in midfield or central defence. A product of the youth system at Nantes in the late-1980s, Desailly joined Marseilles, and with them he won the European Champions League in 1993. A year later he picked up another winners' medal, this time with AC

Milan, making him a member of a very exclusive club. He won the Serie A title twice in his four years at Milan, in 1994 and 1996. He was a key member of France's World Cup-winning team in 1998, though the 3–0 victory over Brazil ended on a slightly sour personal note as he became only the third player in the tournament's history to be red carded in the final. Desailly joined Chelsea shortly afterwards. He helped the club to FA Cup victory in 2000 and in the same year added a European Championship winners' medal as France beat Italy in the final. Desailly was still at the heart of France's defence as they suffered a shock exit at the group stage of the 2002 World Cup. In October of that year he won his 100th cap as France thrashed Slovenia 5–0 in a European Championship qualifier. Desailly retired after Japan and Korea 2002, having made a then-record 116 appearances for his country.

Didier Deschamps

Born: 15 October 1968
Clubs: Nantes, Marseille, Bordeaux, Marseille, Juventus, Chelsea, Valencia
National Team: France

Didier Deschamps was once famously referred to as a mere 'water carrier' by Eric Cantona. But there was more to France's World Cup-winning captain than mere fetching and carrying and midfield donkey work. He was not known for spraying 60-yard passes or mazy runs, his strength being receiving and giving the ball simply, not squandering possession, and linking the play superbly. Deschamps won the European Cup with two different clubs. He was in the Marseille side which overcame mighty AC Milan in 1993, then picked up another winners' medal three years later with Juventus, whom he joined in 1994. He also won the domestic championship in both France and Italy. But the crowning moment came at France '98, when Deschamps became the first French player to lift the World Cup. He retired in 2000, having notched up 103 caps for France. Deschamps coached the Monaco side which reached the 2003–04 Champions League final. In 2006 he returned to Juventus as coach in the wake of the match-fixing scandal which saw the club relegated to Serie B. He resigned in 2007, after steering the Turin club back to Italy's top division.

Didier Deschamps

Kazmierz Deyna

Born: 23 October 1947
Clubs: Wlokniarz Starogard Gdanski, LKS Lodz, Legia Warsaw, Manchester City, San Diego Sockers
National Team: Poland

England fans were distraught when Poland went to the 1974 World Cup in Germany at their team's expense. It was no fluke, however, as Poland played some very entertaining football in the tournament, finishing third. The tall, stylish Kazmierz Deyna was the midfield maestro of the team. His wonderful vision and superb passing were instrumental in strikers Lato and Szarmach becoming the tournament's top marksmen, with 12 goals between them. Two years earlier, at the same venue, Deyna had hit nine goals as Poland took the Olympic title, beating Hungary in the final. Deyna never quite managed to reproduce his best form when he sampled English football with Manchester City. He ended his career in the USA, where he died in a car accident in 1989.

Didi

Born: 8 October 1928
Clubs: FC Rio Branco, FC Lencoes, Madureiro, Fluminense, Botafogo, Real Madrid, Valencia, Botafogo
National Team: Brazil

Waldyr Pereira spent six hours a day practising his ball skills when he was growing up in Rio de Janeiro. That effort paid dividends in the 1950s, when he established himself as one of the finest midfield generals the game had ever seen. By then he was known as Didi — the Cobra. A pass master who could drop the ball on a sixpence, Didi was also deadly from free kicks. He scored a stunning 30-yarder in Brazil's 5–2 win over France in the 1958 World Cup semi-final. He picked up a winners' medal that year and was still there four years later, when he was nearly 34. Didi then joined the elite group of players to become a double World Cup winner. He played for several clubs in Brazil before being lured to Spain. However, during his spells with Valencia and Real Madrid he failed to find his best form. At the 1970 World Cup he coached an exciting Peru side which went down in the quarter-final — to Brazil.

Didi

Dunga

Dunga

Born: 31 October 1963
Clubs: Internacional, Corinthians, Santos, Vasco da Gama, Pisa, Fiorentina, Pescara, Stuttgart, Julilo Iwata
National Team: Brazil

As a hard-running, tough-tackling midfield anchorman, Dunga was not a player in the classic Brazilian mould. Many criticized his uncompromising style and questioned his appointment as Brazil's captain for the 1994 World Cup in the USA. But it was Dunga who had the last laugh, for although it was generally agreed that the 1982 side was more talented, it was the class of '94 that took the top honours, beating Italy on penalties. Dunga also led Brazil to the final four years later, but even his excellent captaincy and tactical astuteness couldn't compensate for Brazil's underperformance against France on that day. Dunga will be better remembered for his leadership and organisational skills than his artistry, but in 1994 he joined the ranks of those who have held the World Cup aloft. He won 90 caps, scoring seven goals. After the 2006 World Cup, Dunga was appointed coach to the Brazil side.

Duncan Edwards

Duncan Edwards

Born: 1 October 1936
Clubs: Manchester United
National Team: England

The 1958 Munich air crash robbed football of a possible legend with the death of Duncan Edwards. The star player of Matt Busby's 'Busby Babes', Edwards had debuted for Manchester United in 1953, aged only 16, and while he was with them he won two Championship medals, in 1956 and 1957. Although his position was at half-back, Edwards made his presence felt all over the pitch with a natural all-round ability and athleticism. He made 125 appearances for United and notched up 21 goals.

He was just 18 years and 183 days old when he became the youngest player to be capped for England, a record that remained unbroken until the debut of Michael Owen in 1998. Had he lived he would almost certainly have featured in the 1966 England squad. At his death, aged only 21, Edwards had already achieved 18 caps, scoring five goals.

Stefan Effenberg

Born: 2 August 1968
Clubs: Borussia Moenchengladbach, Bayern Munich, Fiorentina, Wolfsburg
National Team: Germany

When Bayern Munich brought rising star Michael Ballack from Bayer Leverkusen in 2002 he was seen as the man to replace Stefan Effenberg whose influence on the side had been enormous. The tall, blond midfielder was both elegant and effective. Bayern won a hat-trick of championships between 1999 and 2001, and Effenberg was in the side which

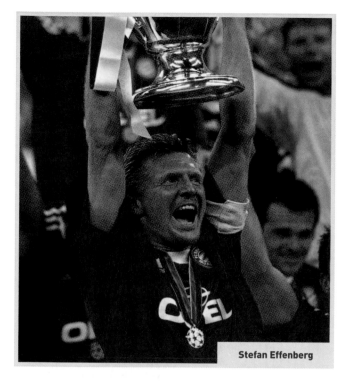

Stefan Effenberg

came within seconds of winning the 1999 European Cup, denied by Manchester United's two injury-time goals. Effenberg's reputation for being difficult was reflected in his international career. He was sent home from the 1994 World Cup after gesturing to fans following Germany's narrow win over South Korea at the group stage. Without him Berti Vogts' team crashed to Bulgaria in the last eight. Such behaviour meant that Effenberg won just 35 caps in nine years. After a spell in Serie A with Fiorentina, he returned to the Bundesliga with Wolfsburg before ending his career in Qatar.

Eusebio

Born: 25 January 1942
Clubs: Sporting Lourenco Marques, Benfica, Boston Minutemen, Toronto Metros, Las Vegas Quicksilver
National Team: Portugal

Eusebio da Silva Ferriera was born in 1942 and raised in Mozambique. Largely considered to be the greatest African-born footballer of all time, 'The Black Panther' or 'The Black Pearl' as he was known, Eusebio spent the majority of his career with Benfica. He arrived in Portugal in 1961, the subject of a fierce battle between Sporting Lisbon and Benfica. Virtually kidnapped by Benfica, he quickly became established as one of the top scorers in history. During a 15-year career in Portugal he put away 317 goals in 291 league appearances. Eusebio was the top scorer for the Portuguese League club every year from 1964 to 1973, leading Benfica to ten league championships and five cup victories. In 1968 and 1973, he was Europe's top scorer and his 46 goals in European competition is second only to the 49 of Real Madrid's Alfredo di Stefano. He was also Portugal's top marksman on seven occasions.

In his first season, Eusebio scored twice in Benfica's incredible comeback against Real Madrid in the European Cup final. Real's veteran star, Puskas, had scored a hat-trick and the match was tied at 3–3 when the rising star finished the game with two second-half goals to trounce the legendary Spanish side 5–3.

He made his international debut for Portugal in 1961. During the 1966 World Cup his tally of nine goals won him the golden boot of the tournament, although he was to leave the pitch in tears at the end of the semi-finals when Portugal were dismissed by England.

Eusebio left Benfica in 1974 and travelled to the USA where he played for a succession of clubs before retiring in 1977.

Eusebio

Giacinto Facchetti

Born: 18 July 1942
Clubs: Trevigliese, Inter Milan
National Team: Italy

Giacinto Facchetti was one of the world's top defenders for two decades. He rose to the top in the 1960s, when Italian football was revolutionizing the art of defending with the 'catenaccio' or 'bolted gate' system. Originally a striker, Facchetti converted to a full-back after joining Inter Milan in 1960. Under renowned coach Helenio Herrera, Facchetti was ruthlessly efficient in the man-to-man marking system that was employed, but was also quick to get forward and link up with the attack. Inter won the Serie A title three times in four years in the early 1960s, and lifted back-to-back European Cups in 1964 and 1965. Facchetti was first capped in 1963 and played for Italy 94 times over the next 14 years. He captained the side that lost 4–1 to Brazil in the 1970 World Cup final, and also played four years later when Italy surprisingly crashed out at the group stage. Facchetti died in 2006, two years after being elected Inter's president. The club retired the famous No. 3 shirt in his honour.

Tom Finney

Tom Finney

Born: 5 April 1922
Clubs: Preston North End
National Team: England

Tom Finney spent the whole of his career at Preston North End and after 24 seasons at the club, his goal total of 187 set a club record as yet unbroken. The 'Preston Plumber' was a talented and versatile footballer, operating on either wing or playing as a central striker. Preston was Finney's home town club, and his loyalty to them cost him the opportunity of collecting medals and honours, however his brilliance did not go unnoticed. In 1954 and 1957 he was named Footballer of the Year, and teammate Bill Shankly once said of him that he would be great in any era 'even if he'd been wearing an overcoat'.

Finney was a contemporary of Stanley Matthews and played alongside him for England between 1946 and 1958. He scored 30 goals in 76 appearances, setting a new record, which has since only been beaten by Bobby Charlton, Gary Lineker, Jimmy Greaves and Michael Owen.

Tom Finney retired from the game in 1960, eventually becoming club president for Preston. He was knighted in 1998.

Just Fontaine

Born: 18 August 1933
Clubs: AC Marrakesh, US Marocaine Casablanca, Nice, Reims
National Team: France

Just Fontaine's place in football's pantheon was secured with the amazing 13 goals he scored in the 1958 World Cup, a record which still stands. His haul came from just six games, one fewer than the maximum at present, as France took third place in the tournament. Moroccan-born Fontaine joined Nice in 1953, when he was 20. He moved to Reims three years later to replace Raymond Kopa, who had gone to Real Madrid. By the time Sweden '58 came round Fontaine was a fringe player in the international side. Injury to his Reims teammate Rene Bliard gave him his opening and the rest is history. Many of his goals came courtesy of brilliant assists by Kopa and the pair were in devastating form in the third place play-off against West Germany, in which Fontaine hit four goals in a 6–3 victory.

Hughie Gallacher

Hughie Gallacher

Born: 2 February 1903
Clubs: Queen of the South, Airdrieonians, Newcastle United
National Team: Scotland

Hughie Gallacher stood barely 5 ft 6 in tall, yet he is rated as one of the best centre-forwards of all time. He played for Queen of the South and Airdrie before heading south to join Newcastle for £5,500 in 1926. He quickly established himself as an idol on Tyneside after firing Newcastle to the championship in 1926–27, his first full season with the club. He hit 36 goals in 38 games during the campaign, which remains a club record. Gallacher was a complete striker and amazingly powerful in the air considering his lack of inches. He was capped 23 times for Scotland, scoring 22 goals. Gallacher's private life was more turbulent. He ended his days in straitened circumstances and commited suicide in 1957.

Garrincha

Born: 28 October 1933
Clubs: Pau Grande, Botafogo, Corinthians, Flamengo, Bangu, Portuguesa
Santista, Olaria, Atletico Junior Barranquilla, Red Star Paris
National Team: Brazil

Garrincha

Garrincha overcame incredible odds to become one of the
most dangerous wingers in the game in the 1950s and 1960s.
He contracted polio as a child, leaving him with a right leg so
badly twisted that doctors feared he might never walk again.
But the player whose nickname means 'Little Bird' became a
double World Cup-winner with Brazil, starring in the side
which won in Sweden in 1958 and retained the trophy in
Chile four years later. His blistering runs set up two goals for
Vava in the 5–2 victory over Sweden. He was the star of the
show in Chile after Pele limped out of the tournament
through injury. He ran England ragged in the quarter-final,
scoring two goals in a 3–1 victory. The second was a
memorable strike, a dipping, swerving 25-yarder. He hit two
more in the semis against Chile before being sent off. There
had been severe provocation, however, and the authorities
allowed him to play in the final, where Brazil beat
Czechoslovakia 3–1. He played in the 1966 tournament,
tasting international defeat for the first time at the age of 32.
The man who was Jairzinho's boyhood hero fell on hard
times after retiring from the game and alcohol abuse
contributed to his premature death in 1983.

Paul Gascoigne

Born: 27 May 1967
Clubs: Newcastle United, Tottenham Hotspur, Lazio, Rangers, Middlesbrough,
Everton, Burnley, Gansu Tianmu, Boston United
National Team: England

A Geordie by birth, Paul Gascoigne made an immediate
impact when he joined Newcastle United in 1985 aged 17.
Just three seasons later, Terry Venables paid a record
£2million to take him to Tottenham Hotspur.

He shot to fame at Italia '90, for both his inspirational
influence on a team that went to the semi-final, and for his
tears following being booked. Often considered the most
talented player of his generation, Gascoigne was a brilliant
footballer but his exuberance and occasional recklessness
were to cost him, both on and off the field. A rash tackle in
the 1991 FA Cup final against Nottingham Forest's Gary
Charles resulted in damage to his own cruciate ligament,
keeping him on the bench for the rest of the season. Injury
was to plague Gascoigne for much of his career. He spent

three years at Lazio, who had paid £5.5 million for him, but
his lack of fitness meant that his time there was difficult. In
1995 he returned to Britain, where a more positive stint at
Rangers earned him Scotland's Footballer of the Year award in
1995–96. At Euro '96, Gascoigne shone again, scoring a
memorable goal against Scotland under the tutelage of his
former Spurs boss, Terry Venables. However, Gascoigne would
never play for his country again. Beset by problems, he joined
Middlesbrough in 1998, then went on to Everton for a brief
spell. There were a few appearances at Burnley and a sojourn
to China. In 2004 he enjoyed a brief stint as player-coach at
Boston United and a year later was sacked after just six weeks
in charge of Conference North side Kettering Town.

Francisco Gento

Born: 22 October 1933
Clubs: Santander, Real Madrid
National Team: Spain

It is difficult to imagine anyone surpassing the European Cup
record set by Francisco Gento between 1956 and 1966. A
fast, tricky left-winger, Gento appeared in eight finals in that
11-year period, finishing on the winning side six times. He
hit the winner in the 3–2 victory over AC Milan in 1958 and
also got on the scoresheet against Fiorentina in the previous
year's final. Gento began his career at Santander but after
joining Real in 1953 he embarked on a glittering 17-year
career which also included twelve domestic championships.
He was capped 43 times for Spain, scoring five goals. He
played in the 1962 and 1966 World Cup finals, but Spain was
eliminated at the group stage in both tournaments.

Paul Gascoigne

Johnny Giles

Born: 6 January 1940
Clubs: Manchester United, Leeds United, West Bromwich Albion, Vancouver Whitecaps, Shamrock Rovers
National Team: Republic of Ireland

Johnny Giles joined Leeds from Manchester United in 1963 for the bargain price of £35,000. Leeds had been languishing in the Second Division, and during the next twelve years, Giles was instrumental in helping Don Revie's side develop into a force to rival Liverpool and Manchester United. A skilled and creative midfield player, Giles formed a dream partnership with Billy Bremner and by the end of his first season at the club, Leeds had won promotion to the First Division. Leeds would not finish lower than fourth for the next ten years and won the Championship twice during that time. Giles had already played for an FA Cup winning side when Manchester United had beaten Leicester in 1963, and collected a second winners' medal in 1972 with Leeds.

Despite two wins in the Fairs Cup, Giles missed out on a European Cup victory as Leeds lost to Bayern Munich in 1975. Following that defeat he left Leeds for West Bromwich Albion, ending his career at Shamrock Rovers. A Republic of Ireland international for nearly two decades, Giles won his 59th and final cap in 1979.

David Ginola

Born: 25 January 1967
Clubs: Toulon, Racing Paris, Brest, Paris St-Germain, Newcastle United, Tottenham Hotspur, Aston Villa, Everton
National Team: France

Flamboyant, stylish and a consummate entertainer, David Ginola was a player who lit up the game with individual flair and artistry. With superb balance and close control, Ginola's surging runs down the touchline were reminiscent of the golden age of wing play. He came to prominence at Paris St-Germain in the early 1990s, winning the Footballer of the Year award in 1992–93. The team finished runners-up to Marseille, and although that club was later stripped of the title for match-fixing, PSG were not awarded it by default. Premiership fans got a chance to see Ginola in action when Kevin Keegan signed him for Newcastle in 1995. He showed some of his best form on Tyneside before moving on to Spurs. Spells at Aston Villa and Everton in the twilight of his career were less successful as he lost a yard of pace and came to be seen as a luxury player. Ginola won just 17 caps for France, a poor return for a player of his skills. His reputation

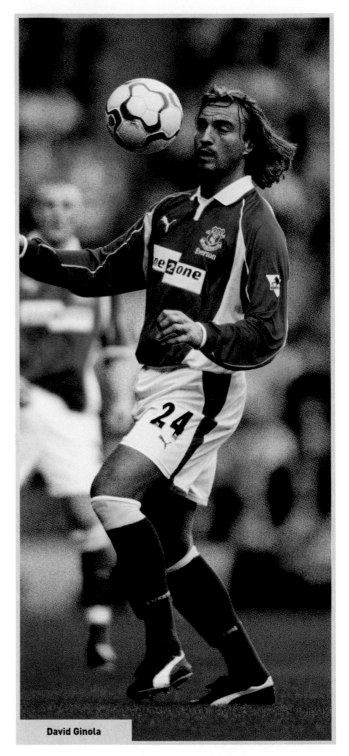

David Ginola

was tarnished by a crucial mistake which contributed to defeat by Bulgaria in a qualifier for the 1994 World Cup. It cost France a place in the finals and brought a swift end to Gerard Houllier's tenure as national team coach. Even when Ginola was in his prime in the mid-1990s, Houllier's successor Aime Jacquet regularly overlooked him.

Alain Giresse

Born: 1 January 1964
Clubs: Bordeaux, Marseille
National Team: France

Alain Giresse was a key member in one of the most stylish midfields of the modern era. Along with Michel Platini and Jean Tigana, Giresse played in France's superb side of the early 1980s. He scored a brilliant goal to put his country 3–1 up against West Germany in the semi-final of the 1982 World Cup. In a game that was marred by goalkeeper Harald Schumacher's brutal challenge on Patrick Battiston, West Germany came back to equalize and won the game on penalties. Two years later, Giresse picked up a winners' medal as France won the European Championship on home soil. He was nearly 33 years old when France took on Uruguay in the inaugural Intercontinental Cup match in August 1985. France won 2–0, with Giresse outshining the great Platini on that occasion. He played in the side that reached the semis once again at the 1986 World Cup in Mexico. Giresse played most of his club football at Bordeaux, with whom he won two domestic championships. He joined Marseille in 1986, having just scored the winner in the French Cup final against them for Bordeaux.

Jimmy Greaves

Jimmy Greaves

Born: 20 February 1940
Clubs: Chelsea, AC Milan, Tottenham Hotspur, West Ham United
National Team: England

Jimmy Greaves may have been replaced by Geoff Hurst during the latter stages of the 1966 World Cup finals, but he was an outstanding goal scorer. Slight and lithe, he was lightning-fast both physically and mentally, with a killer instinct in front of goal. During a nine year run at Spurs, Greaves scored an incredible 220 goals, 37 of which were put away in the 1962–63 season, club records which remain to this day. The Spurs boss, Bill Nicholson, had purchased Greaves from AC Milan, who he had joined in 1961. He came with a price tag of £99,999, deliberately kept short of £100,000.

Despite a public battle with alcoholism, Greaves scored a total of 357 goals during his career in the First Division.

He debuted for England in 1959, scoring the only goal in a 4–1 defeat by Peru. As an international player, his 44 goals for England were an impressive achievement, all the more so because they came in only 57 appearances. The only England players to have accumulated more goals are Bobby Charlton and Gary Lineker, with 106 and 80 caps respectively. Greaves retired from the game in 1971, going on to enjoy a career in the media.

Ruud Gullit

Born: 1 September 1962
Clubs: Haarlem, Feyenoord, PSV Eindhoven, AC Milan, Sampdoria, AC Milan, Sampdoria, Chelsea
National Team: Holland

Tall and powerful but with wonderful balance and touch, Ruud Gullit was a complete footballer who took over Johan Cruyff's mantle in the late 1980s. Gullit was comfortable in any position, an excellent finisher, superb midfield general and an elegant sweeper. Surinam-born Gullit began his career with Haarlem, then spent three years at Feyenoord before PSV Eindhoven prised him away in 1985. His goals spearheaded PSV's championship-winning campaign of 1987. Arrigo Sacchi paid a world-record £6 million that year to take Gullit, the World and European Footballer of the Year, to AC Milan, part of a Dutch triumvirate including Marco Van Basten and Frank Rijkaard. Milan became the dominant side in Europe, winning the European Cup in successive years. The 4–0 demolition of Steaua Bucharest in 1989 was a stunning performance, with a half-fit Gullit scoring twice. He left the field to a standing ovation after an hour, the game already over. A year earlier Gullit had gone one better than Cruyff by lifting a major trophy with Holland. He scored the first goal in the side's victory over the USSR in the 1988 European Championship final. He played in the team which lost to eventual winners West Germany in the 1990 World Cup but quit during the 1994 campaign after a spat with coach Dick Advocaat. Gullit joined Chelsea in June 1995, taking over as player-manager the following year when Glenn Hoddle was appointed England coach. He led the team to FA Cup victory in 1997 but was sacked in the spring of the following year. He had a brief managerial spell at Newcastle United, and in 2005 resigned after less than a year in charge at Feyenoord. In 2007 he took over the managerial reins at LA Galaxy but lasted less than a year with the MLS side.

Ruud Gullit

Gheorghe Hagi

Born: 5 February 1965
Clubs: FC Constanta, Sportul Studentesc, Steaua Bucharest, Real Madrid, Brescia, Barcelona, Galatasaray
National Team: Romania

Gheorghe Hagi's amazing ball skills have graced the football pitches of several countries over the past two decades, and also made him the linchpin of the Romania side for most of that time. Dubbed 'The Maradona of the Carpathians', Hagi made his international debut as an 18-year-old in 1984, while playing for Sportul Studentesc. Two years later he joined the country's premier side, Steaua Bucharest, although this was more akin to a requisition than a transfer. He won a string of domestic honours with Steaua, and the team also made it through to the 1989 European Cup final, where they were roundly beaten by AC Milan. Hagi starred in the 1990 and 1994 World Cups and was still there at France '98, where Romania beat England on the way to the second round. Hagi joined Real Madrid after Italia '90 and also had spells at Brescia and Barcelona. He became Galatasaray's biggest ever signing in 1996, and four years later he helped the Turkish club to a famous UEFA Cup triumph over Arsenal.

Gheorghe Hagi

Alan Hansen

Born: 13 June 1955
Clubs: Partick Thistle, Liverpool
National Team: Scotland

Alan Hansen was one of the most cultured and classy central defenders of the modern era. He won 17 major honours, a medal tally that few have surpassed. After joining Liverpool from Partick Thistle for just £100,000 in 1977, Hansen enjoyed thirteen years of unparalleled success at Anfield. He won eight league championships, and picked up two FA Cup and four League Cup winners' medals. There were three glorious European Cup successes, and he also appeared in the 1985 final, when Liverpool's defeat by Juventus was overshadowed by the death of 39 fans at the Heysel Stadium. Hansen's 26 caps for Scotland included the 1982 World Cup, when the team went out at the group stage on goal difference. He was surprisingly omitted from the squad for the 1986 tournament. Since retiring from the game, Hansen has carved out a successful career as a media pundit.

Alan Hansen

Johnny Haynes

Born: 17 October 1934
Clubs: Fulham, Durban City
National Team: England

With the abolition of maximum wages, Johnny Haynes became the first £100-a-week footballer, and although he could have reaped greater rewards elsewhere, he remained loyal to Fulham. Haynes was at Craven Cottage from 1952 to 1969, when the team was either in the Second Division or in the lower reaches of the First. Despite playing for an unfashionable club, Haynes established himself in the England side in the mid-1950s. He made 56 appearances for his country, the last 22 as captain, including during England's 1962 World Cup campaign. As an inside-forward, he was noted for his skilful passing, and alongside Bobby Robson he was at the heart of a run of six consecutive wins in 1960–1. A regular goalscorer, Haynes secured 18 goals for England.

A serious car accident in 1962 ended an international career which included two World Cups, but he continued to appear for Fulham for a further seven years. A free-transfer enabled Haynes to emigrate to South Africa, as player-manager of Durban City. He died in 2005.

Nandor Hidegkuti

Born: 3 March 1922
Clubs: Herminamezo, MTK Budapest
National Team: Hungary

Nandor Hidegkuti was a key player in the 'Magic Magyars' side which lit up international football in the 1950s. Nominally a centre-forward, Hidegkuti played in a withdrawn role. His immaculately-timed forward runs proved almost impossible to counter and yielded plenty of goals. Harry Johnston, England's centre-half when Hungary came to Wembley in 1953, was plainly bemused by Hidegkuti, who hit a hat-trick in a brilliant 6–3 victory. He was in the Magyars' side which marched all the way to the 1954 World Cup final, where West Germany pulled off a shock 3–2 victory. Hidegkuti won 68 caps in all, scoring 39 goals. Unlike his teammates Puskas and Kocsis, Hidegkuti spent his entire career in Hungary, with MTK Budapest, effectively denying himself a chance of major club honours, although he won the Cup Winners' Cup as a coach with Fiorentina in 1961. He died in 2002.

Glenn Hoddle

Glenn Hoddle

Born: 27 October 1957
Clubs: Tottenham Hotspur, Monaco, Swindon Town, Chelsea
National Team: England

Glenn Hoddle was one of the classiest midfielders in British football in the late 1970s and 1980s. His artistry on the ball rivalled the best that Europe or South America had to offer, and his skills were revered at White Hart Lane, where he spent twelve years. Spurs won two FA Cups and the 1984 UEFA Cup in Hoddle's time at the club. Although he won 53 caps, successive international managers tended to regard him as a luxury and he was never fully sure of his place. His gifts found their natural outlet when he joined Monaco in 1987. Hoddle spent four years in France before returning to Britain as player-manager, first with Swindon, then at Chelsea. He took over from Terry Venables as England coach after Euro '96 and led the team to the World Cup in France in '98. He was appointed Southampton manager in 2000 but the call came soon from White Hart Lane. Hoddle was sacked early in the 2003–04 season, taking over the reins at Wolves a year later. He left Molyneux after failing to gain promotion in the 2005–06 season.

Geoff Hurst

Geoff Hurst

Born: 8 December 1941
Clubs: West Ham United, Stoke City, West Bromwich Albion, Seattle Sounders, Cork Celtic
National Team: England

At the age of 24, Geoff Hurst earned his place in footballing annals by becoming the only man to score a hat-trick in a World Cup final. The West Ham striker entered the 1966 tournament with only five caps to his name, having scored just one goal. His first appearance was at the quarter-final stage, replacing Jimmy Greaves in the match against Argentina, and Hurst scored the only goal of the game. Greaves had lost his place in the team from that moment.

Hurst appeared for West Ham over 400 times between 1959 and 1972, and managed to acquire an FA Cup winners' medal in 1964 and a European Cup Winners' Cup medal the following year. He left the Hammers for Stoke City then West Bromwich Albion where he finished his top-flight career. Knighted in 1998 for his contribution to sport, Hurst was also a first class cricketer, batting for Essex in 1962.

David Jack

Born: 3 April 1899
Clubs: Bolton Wanderers, Arsenal
National Team: England

David Jack was 29 years old when Herbert Chapman targeted him as the man to replace Charlie Buchan after the latter retired at the end of the 1927–28 season. Jack had already had a glittering career at Bolton, with whom he won two FA Cup winners medals. An inside-forward with terrific ball skills and a keen eye for goal, Jack scored the first ever goal in a Wembley showpiece, the famous 'White Horse Final' in which Bolton beat West Ham 2–0.

Chapman caused a stir when he paid £10,890 to bring Jack to Highbury, doubling the previous transfer record. It proved an astute move, however, as Jack was a key figure in the all-conquering Arsenal side of the 1930s. He picked up three Championship medals and also made it a hat-trick of Cup successes when Arsenal beat Huddersfield in the 1930 final. He died in 1958.

Alex James

Jairzinho

Born: 25 December 1944
Clubs: Botafogo, Marseille, Cruzeiro, Portuguesa
National Team: Brazil

The natural successor to the outstanding Brazilian winger Garrincha, Jairzinho had lightning pace, mesmerizing skills and could score goals as well as create them. He was playing professional football with Botafogo by the time he was 15. First capped in 1963, he made the squad for Brazil's unhappy 1966 World Cup campaign. But it was in Mexico four years later that he had his finest hour. Jairzinho scored in each of Brazil's six games en route to winning the tournament, a World Cup record. A brace against Czechoslovakia at the group stage put him on seven goals in all, yet he only finished as second top scorer, three behind West Germany's Gerd Müller. Jairzinho had a brief spell in Europe, joining Marseille in 1971, but was soon back in his native Brazil with Cruzeiro. He scored the goal which beat River Plate in the 1976 Copa Libertadores final.

Jairzinho

Alex James

Born: 14 September 1901
Clubs: Raith Rovers, Preston North End, Arsenal
National Team: Scotland

Alex James was the outstanding player of Herbert Chapman's mighty Arsenal side of the 1930s. Probably the most complete player of his generation, James was equally adept in the scheming role or as a finisher. Chapman paid Preston £8,750 for his services in 1929. It proved to be money well spent. Over the next eight years James was the orchestrater-in-chief in a phenomenally successful spell which included four Championships and two FA Cup victories. James was a wayward star, however, and that contributed to the fact that he won a meagre eight caps for Scotland. One of those came in March 1928, when Scotland took on England at Wembley. James was outstanding, scoring twice in a 5–1 victory and cementing his place in the annals as one of the famous 'Wembley Wizards'. He died in 1953.

Pat Jennings

Pat Jennings

Born: 12 June 1945
Clubs: Newry Town, Watford, Tottenham Hotspur, Arsenal
National Team: Northern Ireland

It is a tribute to the esteem in which Pat Jennings was held that although he spent the majority of his career with arch-rivals Spurs and Arsenal, it created no friction or animosity. Softly spoken, genial and a model professional, Jennings played at the top level for more than 20 years. He joined Spurs in 1964, after spending a season at Watford. In 1977 he moved to Highbury, where his famous bucket-like hands continued to make outstanding saves for another eight years. He won the FA Cup with both clubs, and picked up a UEFA Cup winners' medal in 1972, when Spurs beat Wolves in the final. His record 119 caps for Northern Ireland included two World Cups. He retired on his 41st birthday, following his country's 3–0 defeat by Brazil in the 1986 tournament. Despite being a world-class 'keeper for more than two decades, Jennings is, ironically, probably best remembered for the goal he scored against Manchester United in the 1967 Charity Shield. A huge punt upfield sailed over Alex Stepney's head on the first bounce. The game ended in a 3–3 draw.

Jimmy Johnstone

Born: 30 September 1944
Clubs: Celtic, San Jose, Sheffield United, Dundee, Shelbourne
National Team: Scotland

The pocket-sized, flame-haired Jimmy Johnstone was a magician on the wing for the great Celtic side of the 1960s and early 1970s. He gave Inter Milan's Burgnich a torrid time in the 1967 European Cup final, having been in scintillating form throughout the competition. Three years later, when Celtic reached the final again, Feyenoord targeted Johnstone as the player they had to stop. He had been on top form against Leeds United in the semis, but in the final the Dutch side shackled him successfully and ran out 2–1 winners. In his 14 years at Celtic, Johnstone picked up nine domestic championship medals between 1966 and 1974. His 10-year international career yielded just 23 caps as Johnstone also had a reputation for wayward behaviour and inconsistency. He died in March 2006.

Jimmy Johnstone

Roy Keane

Born: 10 August 1971
Clubs: Cobh Ramblers, Nottingham Forest, Manchester United, Celtic
National Team: Republic of Ireland

Of all the superstars that have made Manchester United the dominant force in English football in the past decade, Sir Alex Ferguson points to Roy Keane as the most influential. He took over as the driving force in midfield from Bryan Robson, which was regarded as a tough act to follow. But since moving to Old Trafford from Nottingham Forest in 1993, when he was 21, Keane has developed into one of the most complete midfielders in world football. Fierce competitiveness, tireless running, great technical ability and superb leadership skills; such are the hallmarks of the man who has led United in their unprecedented run of success in recent years. Credit must also go to Brian Clough, who spotted Keane's potential when he was turning out for Cobh Ramblers in the Irish League. Clough paid just £10,000 to take the Irishman to the City Ground in what must rank as one of the bargains of all time.

In the five seasons between 1996 and 2001, United conceded the Premiership title just once, to Arsenal in 1997–98. Many highlighted the fact that Keane missed most of that campaign through injury as a crucial factor. Keane excelled at USA '94, where the Republic of Ireland did well before being knocked out by Holland. The team missed out at France '98, and Keane was regarded as a key figure as far as their chances at Japan and Korea 2002 were concerned. The infamous bust-up between Keane and manager Mick McCarthy meant that Keane was back home before a ball was kicked. 2002–03 saw Keane at his best: driving United on towards yet another title when it looked certain to go to Highbury for the second successive season. In 2003–04 United finished out of the top two for only the second time in a decade. Some of the junior players came in for criticism from Keane, who had set the standard for consistency and desire. He was openly critical of some of his teammates before parting company with United in November 2005. He joined Glasgow Celtic, helping the club he supported as a boy to wrest the crown from Rangers but was forced to announce his retirement because of injury in June 2006.

Keane became Sunderland manager in August 2006, and he steered the Black Cats back to the Premiership at the first attempt. He kept them up in his first season but quit in December 2008, joining Ipswich in April 2009.

Roy Keane

Kevin Keegan

Born: 14 February 1951
Clubs: Scunthorpe United, Liverpool, Hamburg, Southampton, Newcastle United
National Team: England

Kevin Keegan's career is testament to what hard work, commitment and self-belief can do. Not the most naturally gifted of footballers, Keegan was ultimately an impressive goalscorer and a valuable teammate, always looking to create opportunities for others.

Keegan began his career at Scunthorpe United, having been told he was too small to have any real success in the game. He was brought to Liverpool by Bill Shankly in 1971 and very quickly made himself a vital part of the team proving his detractors wrong. He scored in his debut for the club and netted 22 goals the following season, helping Liverpool to win both the championship and the UEFA Cup.

Keegan scored twice in Liverpool's 3–0 victory over Newcastle in the 1974 FA Cup final and two years later he received the Footballer of the Year award as they yet again took the league title and the UEFA trophy.

Keegan handed over his famous number 7 shirt, when he left Liverpool for Hamburg in 1977. The German club paid £500,000 for Keegan and during his time there he won the European Footballer of the Year award twice, in 1978 and 1979, the only British player to have done so. On his return to Britain, Keegan played for both Southampton and then Newcastle, the team where he

Kevin Keegan

ended his career. He returned to the Magpies in 1992, as manager, and swiftly led them from the bottom of the league to the top. His surprise move to Fulham was cause for celebration for the London club, who also benefited from his inspirational managerial skills.

Keegan had enjoyed an England career which lasted for ten years. He won 63 caps, 31 of which were as captain. His international playing career ended soon after the 1982 World Cup tournament, when Keegan was disappointed to be dropped by Bobby Robson from the European Championship qualifiers. In 1999, Keegan made an initially popular return to the England team as manager, following the controversial departure of Glenn Hoddle. Keegan did succeed in getting England through to the Euro 2000 qualifiers, but after a series of disappointing games he bowed out from the England job. Keegan re-established Manchester City as a Premiership club before stepping down in the 2004–05 season. In 2008, after two years out of the game, he made a surprise return to St James's Park, where he was hailed as the returning hero by the Toon Army, but Keegan's second spell on Tyneside lasted just eight months.

Mario Kempes

Mario Kempes

Born: 15 July 1954
Clubs: Instituto Cordoba, Rosario Central, Valencia, River Plate, Hercules, First Vienna, SV Austria Salzburg
National Team: Argentina

Mario Kempes scored six of the 15 goals which brought Argentina their first World Cup victory, on home soil in 1978. He was not only the tournament's top scorer but was voted the outstanding player too. His haul included a brace in the final, and for good measure he also set up Bertoni for the goal which sealed the team's 3–1 victory over Holland. Kempes was the only member of the team who was playing club football outside Argentina. He joined Valencia in 1976, having made his mark in the World Cup two years earlier. He was twice the Primera Liga's top scorer, although Valencia couldn't break the stranglehold of the two Madrid clubs during his five years there. The highlight came in 1980, when Valencia beat Arsenal in the European Cup Winners' Cup final. In the first major European final to be decided on penalties, Kempes missed his spot-kick but his blushes were spared when Brady and Rix also failed in their attempts. Kempes played for Argentina at Spain '82 but failed to make much of an impression as the team limped out in the second round.

Jurgen Klinsmann

Born: 30 July 1964
Clubs: Stuttgart Kickers, Stuttgart, Inter Milan, Monaco, Tottenham Hotspur, Bayern Munich, Sampdoria
National Team: Germany

Jurgen Klinsmann played in the Italian, French and English leagues, as well as his native Germany, establishing himself as one of the world's most lethal strikers in the 1980s and 1990s. His prolific scoring for Stuttgart prompted Inter Milan to take him to Italy in 1989. He helped Inter to win the 1991 UEFA Cup before moving on to Monaco the following year. By then he also had a World Cup winners' medal, having scored three goals in Germany's victorious campaign at Italia '90. It was seen as one of the coups of the year when Spurs unveiled Klinsmann as their new signing in 1994. He answered the fans who criticized him for going to ground too readily with some blistering performances. He hit 29 goals in his debut season and picked up the 1995 Footballer of the Year award. He returned to Germany and Bayern Munich in 1995, following some acrimonious wrangling with the north London club. He scored a record 15 goals as he fired Bayern to UEFA Cup victory in 1996. In the same year he captained the Germany side which triumphed in the European Championship. He wound down his career with Sampdoria and a second spell at Spurs, and grabbed another three World Cup goals at France '98. Forty-seven goals in 108 international appearances puts Klinsmann second behind Gerd Müller in the list of all-time German strikers. Appointed Germany coach in 2004, Klinsmann led the side to the semi-finals of the 2006 World Cup, where it lost to Italy in an extra-time thriller. He stood down after the tournament. Midway through the 2007–08 season he was named as Ottmar Hitzfeld's successor as Bayern Munich coach but left the club towards the end of the 2008–09 season.

Jurgen Klinsmann

Sandor Kocsis

Born: 23 September 1929
Clubs: Ferencvaros, Honved, Young Fellows, Barcelona
National Team: Hungary

Sandor Kocsis formed a devastating twin strike-force with Ferenc Puskas in the brilliant Hungary side of the 1950s. The two also played for Honved, at the time regarded as the best club side in the world. After winning the 1952 Olympic title, Hungary were favourites to lift the World Cup two years later. West Germany upset the form book in the final, though Kocsis had the consolation of ending the tournament as top scorer with 11 goals. He moved to Barcelona after the 1956 Revolution and won the Inter-Cities Fairs Cup with the Spanish club in 1960, beating Birmingham City in the final. The following year, Kocsis scored in the European Cup final against Benfica, but Barcelona went down 3–2. Nicknamed 'Golden Head' for his prodigious aerial ability, Kocsis scored a phenomenal 75 goals in his 68 appearances for Hungary.   He died in 1979, aged 49.

Ronald Koeman

Ronald Koeman

Born: 21 March 1963
Clubs: FC Groningen, Ajax, PSV Eindhoven, Barcelona, Feyenoord
National Team: Holland

Ronald Koeman emerged as one of the world's top sweepers in the 1980s. As well as being a formidable defender, Koeman was a great attacking weapon for both club and country. His long-range passing was superb and his shooting from distance, either from open play or dead-ball situations, was legendary. Koeman was a key player in the PSV Eindhoven side which dominated Dutch football in the late 1980s. PSV's Championship win in 1986 was the first of four in a row. 1988 saw Koeman add European Cup and European Championship winners' medals to his tally. In the former Koeman was on target in the shoot-out victory over Benfica. His form brought him the Dutch Player of the Year award in 1987 and 1988. He moved to Barcelona in 1989, and in 1990–91 the club began a four-year run as La Liga champions. Koeman also picked up a second European Cup winners' medal in this time. His 30-yard free kick in extra-time beat Sampdoria at Wembley. Koeman was also on target against England in the qualifiers for USA '94, helping Holland to reach the finals at the expense of Graham Taylor's side. His 78th and final cap came in that tournament. Koeman took over as manager of Ajax during the 2000–01 season, leading the club immediately to the domestic Double. Koeman quit during the 2004–05 season following a poor run of results After a season at Benfica he took over at PSV, replacing Guus Hiddink. In 2006–07 he notched his seventh Eredivisie title as a player and manager, but was soon on his travels again, taking over at Valencia. He led the Spanish club to domestic cup victory but indifferent league form led to his dismissal at the end of the season.

Raymond Kopa

Born: 13 October 1931
Clubs: Angers, Reims, Real Madrid, Reims
National Team: France

In the inaugural European Cup final in 1956 Raymond Kopa found himself on the receiving end of the great Real Madrid side. Kopa was the star player for Reims, but couldn't prevent the French club from going down 4–3 to di Stefano and Co. Kopa joined Real just after that game and went on to win a hat-trick of European Cup winners' medals as the club's dominance continued in the late 1950s. Kopa, the son of a Polish miner, was equally effective as a centre-forward or wide player. He hit 18 goals in his 45 appearances for France but was also responsible for countless assists. At the 1958 World Cup Just Fontaine's record 13-goal haul was in large measure down to Kopa's creativity. His performances in Sweden, together with the part he played in yet another triumphant European Cup campaign, won Kopa the European Footballer of the Year award. He remained the only Frenchman to be honoured thus until Michel Platini.

Hans Krankl

Born: 14 February 1953
Clubs: Rapid Vienna, Vienna AC, Barcelona, First Vienna, Barcelona, Rapid Vienna, Wiener Sportclub
National Team: Austria

A prolific centre-forward, Krankl began his career at Rapid Vienna. He was his country's top scorer on four occasions, and once hit seven goals in a league match. In 1977–78 he hit 41 goals, earning him the Golden Boot as Europe's top marksman. A year later Krankl was a Barcelona player. He was on target against Anderlecht and Beveren as Barca made it to the Cup Winners' Cup final. He also got what proved to be the winner

in the final itself, a thrilling 4–3 victory over Fortuna Dusseldorf. He sustained serious injuries in a car crash and returned to Rapid when he had recovered. In 1982 he helped fire Rapid to their first championship for 24 years, and in 1985 he scored in a European Cup Winners' Cup final for the second time. This time, however, he finished on the losing side, Everton running out 3–1 winners. Krankl was capped 69 times for Austria, scoring 34 goals. He played in both the 1978 and 1982 World Cups, helping the country reach the second round on each occasion. He began his management career with Rapid and went on to manage the national side but was sacked after he failed to get the team to the 2006 World Cup.

Hans Krankl (left)

Ruud Krol

Born: 24 March 1949
Clubs: Ajax, Vancouver Whitecaps, Napoli, Cannes
National Team: Holland

Ruud Krol was a key member of Rinus Michels' Ajax side which gave the world Total Football in the late 1960s and won a hat-trick of European Cups in the early 1970s. Krol could play at full-back or in central defence, although his ball-playing skills enabled him to be equally effective anywhere on the field. Krol made his debut in the national team at 20 and remained a fixture in the side for the next 14 years. His 83 caps would remain a Dutch record until Aron Winter and Frank de Boer overhauled it. He played every match at the 1974 World Cup, where Holland lost to West Germany in the final. Four years later, with Cruyff unavailable, Krol captained the side to a second final. It was another runners-up medal as hosts Argentina won the match 3–1. After a season with Vancouver Whitecaps, Krol had four years at Napoli before winding down his career with French club Cannes.

Grzegorz Lato

Born: 8 April 1950
Clubs: Stal Mielec, KSC Lokeren, Atlanta de Mexico, Toronto
National Team: Poland

Poland was an unheralded side when it reached the 1974 World Cup at England's expense. By the end of the tournament the team had made the world sit up and take notice, and none caught the eye more than Grzegorz Lato, whose seven goals made him the tournament's top scorer and helped the Poles to a third-place finish. Lato was there in 1978 too, when Poland made it to the second phase. In his third World Cup appearance, Spain '82, Poland again finished third. In all Lato played 20 World Cup matches, scoring a highly creditable ten goals. By the time he bowed out of international football in 1984, he had won over 100 caps, a Polish record. His 42 goals put him second only to Wiodzmierz Lubanski in the all-time list. Lato spent most of his club career with Stal Mielec, with whom he won the Polish championship in 1973 and 1976. In 1980 he moved to Belgian side KSC Lokeren, before ending his career in Mexico and Canada.

Marius Lacatus

Marius Lacatus

Born: 5 April 1964
Clubs: Steaua Bucharest, Fiorentina, Ovieda
National Team: Romania

Along with Gheorghe Hagi, Marius Lacatus is Romania's greatest player of the modern era. A pacy, tricky forward, Lacatus joined Steaua Bucharest in 1985. The club not only dominated the domestic championship in the second half of the decade but Lacatus also helped to make history as Steaua became the first Eastern European side to lift the Champions Cup. The 1986 final with Barcelona ended goalless and Steaua won the shoot-out. Lacatus impressed at Italia '90, where Romania went out on penalties to the Republic of Ireland in the second round. He had a spell with Fiorentina and Spanish side Ovieda before returning home to the club where he made his name. He was left out of the squad for USA '94 but was soon back in the team. Euro '96 was a disappointment, Romania losing all three of their group games. Lacatus was a veteran of 34 at France '98, where he helped Romania reach the last 16. He ended his career with 84 caps, scoring 13 goals.

Brian Laudrup

Born: 22 February 1969
Clubs: Brondby, Bayer Uerdingen, Bayern Munich, Fiorentina, AC Milan, Glasgow Rangers, Chelsea, FC Copenhagen, Ajax
National Team: Denmark

Brian Laudrup had a hard act to follow when he began his career at Brondby in the late 1980s. His father had been a Danish international, while brother Michael, five years his senior, had starred in the 1986 World Cup. He was voted Denmark's Player of the Year in 1989, the year he helped Brondby to win the country's domestic cup competition. On the international stage he was a member of the side which got into the 1992 European Championships by the back door – after Yugoslavia was banned from taking part – and then proceeded to win the tournament. His eye-catching performances during the competition attracted a lot of interest from clubs in some of Europe's stronger leagues. He had a spell in Germany before moving on to Serie A with Fiorentina, and then AC Milan. The big squads in Italy meant inevitable periods on the sidelines and it was only after his surprise move to Rangers that he recaptured his best form. His marvellous skills helped Rangers to win three Championships, and he also picked up the country's Player of the Year award. In 1998 he headed south for a brief spell at Chelsea. In the same year he helped Denmark reach the quarter-finals of the World Cup, where the team suffered a narrow 3–2 defeat against Brazil.

Brian Laudrup

Michael Laudrup

Born: 15 June 1964
Clubs: Brondby, Juventus, Lazio, Barcelona, Real Madrid, Vissel Kobe, Ajax
National Team: Denmark

Michael Laudrup was the elder of the two famous footballing brothers by five years. After starring for Brondby in the early 1980s this gifted playmaker joined Juventus, although for two seasons he was loaned out to Lazio. In his first season back at Juventus, 1985–86, he picked up a Serie A winners' medal. In 1989 he moved to Barcelona, whom he helped to win four successive La Liga titles. He also won the European Cup in his time at the Nou Camp, Barca beating Sampdoria in 1992. Another Spanish title came with Real Madrid in 1994–95, and after a spell in Japan he enjoyed a fine swansong season with Ajax. There was yet another championship medal with the Amsterdam club, making a total of seven in three different countries. Laudrup enjoyed a sparkling international career too. Denmark lit up the early stages of the 1986 World Cup, beating West Germany and putting six goals past Uruguay at the group stage before crashing to Spain in the second round. The Danes failed to reach the next two World Cups, and 34-year-old Laudrup bowed out of the game after another fine showing at France '98, where the team reached the last eight. He missed Denmark's greatest achievement in this period, victory in the 1992 European Championship, after a disagreement with coach Moller Nielsen. After a spell in charge of former club Brondby, Laudrup took over as coach of La Liga side Getafe CF in 2007. He resigned after one season in charge, taking over at Spartak Moscow in 2008.

Denis Law

Born: 22 February 1940
Clubs: Huddersfield Town, Manchester City, Torino, Manchester United,
National Team: Scotland

When Denis Law scored the backheeled goal for Manchester City that sent Manchester United down to the Second Division in 1974, it came as no surprise that there was no characteristic one-armed salute in celebration. Law had spent eleven years at United, making 399 appearances and scoring 236 goals for the side he passionately loved. During the 1960s, Denis Law had been 'The King' of the Stretford End; playing alongside George Best and Bobby Charlton, he had been a crucial part of one of the many great sides to play at Old Trafford. Law had helped United win the FA Cup in 1963, scoring one and making two of the 3–1 win over Leicester City. The following year he picked up the European Footballer of the Year award. Manchester United won the championship twice during Law's time with them, although their European Cup victory of 1968 had been achieved without him, due to injury.

His career had started at Huddersfield Town in 1957 and when he made his first move to Manchester City it was for a then record £55,000. The following season, £100,000 took him to Torino, another record fee, which was topped in 1962 when United paid £115,000 to bring him back to Britain. His return to Manchester City in 1973 was precipitated by deteriorating relations with manager Tommy Docherty and the transfer was free. That famous goal for City marked the end of Law's career.

Born in Aberdeen, Law made his international debut for Scotland aged only 18, the youngest to do so since 1899. In 55 appearances, his total of 30 goals has been equalled only by Kenny Dalglish.

Denis Law

Tommy Lawton

Born: 6 October 1919
Clubs: Burnley, Everton, Chelsea, Notts County, Brentford, Arsenal
National Team: England

Tommy Lawton was the teenage sensation who became the most highly regarded centre-forward in postwar England. In 1937, Lawton left his first club, Burnley, for Everton, who paid the princely sum of £6,500. His 35 goals in 1938–39 ensured championship success for Everton, who had finished only 14th the season before. When World War Two broke out, Lawton was the league's top scorer. War robbed Lawton of his prime playing years, and at the end of hostilities he played one season for Chelsea, scoring 26 goals in 34 matches before joining Third Division Notts County. In 166 appearances for the Nottingham club, Lawton scored 103 goals. He then moved to Second Division Brentford, as player-manager, in 1952. His career appeared to be drawing to a close, but Lawton made a surprise move to Arsenal, playing out his career in impressively good form. Despite playing in the lower division, Lawton was selected for the national side, scoring 22 goals in 23 games. He died in 1996.

Billy Liddell

Born: 10 January 1921
Clubs: Liverpool
National Team: Scotland

Liverpool became the first postwar champions in 1946–47 and their star player was Billy Liddell. Son of a Scottish coalminer, Liddell was recommended to Liverpool by Matt Busby when aged only 16, signing for the Reds in 1938, aged 18. He scored a hat-trick against Manchester City in only his second game. His career was interrupted by the war and robbed him of what would undoubtedly have been some of his best years. His prime position was as left-winger, although his versatility on the field meant that he played in every position except goal during his career.

Despite their success in the 1946–47 season, Liverpool were not a top side in the 22 years that Liddell spent at the club and from 1954 to 1960 Liddell carried the club during their wilderness years in the Second Division. He played 495 games for the club, scoring a then-record 216 goals. He won 28 caps for Scotland and featured in eight wartime internationals. Liddell also played in the Great Britain side that beat a Rest of Europe XI 6-1 at Hampden Park in 1947. In 1960, during the early days of Bill Shankly's reign, Liddell played his last game for Liverpool, and he died in July 2001. It is a testament to the esteem in which he was held that in his heyday the club was nicknamed 'Liddellpool'.

Billy Liddell

Gary Lineker

Born: 30 November 1960
Clubs: Leicester City, Everton, Barcelona, Tottenham Hotspur, Nagoya Grampus Eight
National Team: England

When Gary Lineker began his career at Leicester City in 1978, he didn't immediately stand out as a striker. However, by 1983 he had scored 26 in a season which saw his team promoted to the First Division. He joined Everton two years later and in his only season at the club, accumulated 30 league goals and the joint honours of the Professional Footballers' Association and Football Writers' Player of the Year awards. Lineker spent three years at Barcelona under Terry Venables, contributing to their Cup Winners' Cup victory in 1989. That same year he returned to England to join Venables at Spurs, where he picked up an FA Cup winners' medal in 1991.

It is for his career as an international goalscorer that Lineker is most celebrated. He netted 48 goals in 80 appearances, just one short of Bobby Charlton's record. Six of those goals came during the 1986 World Cup in Mexico, making Lineker the top marksman in the competition. At Italia '90 he scored four times for England, one crucial late equalizer keeping the side in the semi-final against West Germany, which was eventually lost on penalties. In 1992, he played his final game for his country against Sweden, his substitution in the final half-hour being a frustrating end to his international career. Lineker's playing career finished following two seasons at Grampus Eight in the Japanese League, and he has since enjoyed a highly successful career in the media.

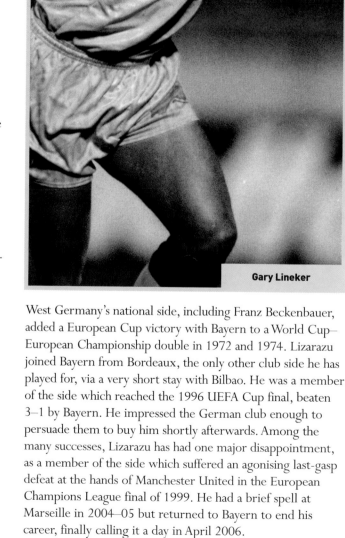

Gary Lineker

Bixente Lizarazu

Born: 9 December 1969
Clubs: Bordeaux, Atletico Bilbao, Bayern Munich, Marseille
National Team: France

Despite the disappointment of being in the French side which crashed out of the 2002 World Cup, Bixente Lizarazu still has a medal haul which most players can only dream about. He was France's stalwart left-sided defender in the team which completed a marvellous double by winning the World Cup on home soil in 1998, then added the European Championship two years later. Lizarazu then went one better, adding a European Champions League winners medal to his tally. That victory, for Bayern Munich in the 2001 final, gave Lizarazu a Treble not seen since the mid-1970s. Several members of

West Germany's national side, including Franz Beckenbauer, added a European Cup victory with Bayern to a World Cup–European Championship double in 1972 and 1974. Lizarazu joined Bayern from Bordeaux, the only other club side he has played for, via a very short stay with Bilbao. He was a member of the side which reached the 1996 UEFA Cup final, beaten 3–1 by Bayern. He impressed the German club enough to persuade them to buy him shortly afterwards. Among the many successes, Lizarazu has had one major disappointment, as a member of the side which suffered an agonising last-gasp defeat at the hands of Manchester United in the European Champions League final of 1999. He had a brief spell at Marseille in 2004–05 but returned to Bayern to end his career, finally calling it a day in April 2006.

Nat Lofthouse

Born: 27 August 1925
Clubs: Bolton Wanderers
National Team: England

Between 1946 and 1960, Nat Lofthouse played for Bolton Wanderers as their most successful ever marksman. During 14 years he scored 255 goals. The only other team shirt Lofthouse wore was for his country, making 33 appearances for England and chalking up an impressive 30 goals, placing him at joint fourth on the list of England scorers.

Idolised by Bolton fans, Lofthouse scored in every round of the 1953 FA Cup, and despite their subsequent defeat at the hands of Blackpool and Stanley Matthews, Lofthouse picked up the Footballer of the Year award. Five years later he captained Bolton to FA Cup victory, scoring two goals against a Manchester United side that had been decimated by the Munich air disaster.

It is for his brave contribution to England's victory against Austria in the 1951–52 season that Lofthouse is perhaps best remembered. Playing away to the best team in Europe at that time, he hit a first-half goal to put England in the lead. He then scored an impressive second-half winner, racing half the length of the pitch and being knocked unconscious by the keeper in the process. With that feat he earned himself the nickname 'Lion of Vienna'.

Nat Lofthouse

Sepp Maier

Born: 28 February 1944
Clubs: TSV Haar, Bayern Munich
National Team: West Germany

Along with Beckenbauer, Müller and Breitner, Sepp Maier was a member of an elite group of players who were simultaneously European Champions, World Champions and European Cup holders. Twenty-two-year-old Maier was a fringe player at the 1966 World Cup. However, he was soon established as West Germany's No. 1 'keeper and over the next 13 years he won 95 caps, putting him in Germany's top 10 in the all-time list. The national team was thought to be at its peak in 1972 when West Germany beat the Soviet Union in the final of the European Championship. It was still good enough to lift the World Cup on home soil two years later. Maier spent 19 years at Bayern Munich, racking up almost 500 Bundesliga appearances. Bayern's achievements included a hat-trick of European Cup victories in the mid-1970s, including a win over Leeds United in the 1975 final. Maier's incredible consistency earned him Germany's Player of the Year award in 1975, 1977 and 1978. The only major disappointment in a sparkling career came in 1976, when Maier for once had to settle for a runners-up medal in the European Championship.

Sepp Maier

Paolo Maldini

Born: 26 June 1968
Clubs: AC Milan
National Team: Italy

When Paolo Maldini led Italy to the 2002 World Cup finals, he confirmed that it would bring down the curtain on his international career. The tournament ended unhappily, denying Maldini the chance of lifting the one trophy that had eluded him at his fourth and final attempt. The greatest left-back of the modern era, Maldini made his Serie A debut as a 16-year-old for AC Milan, his one and only club. The Rosonneri were about to embark on a period of European domination, including three Champions Cup victories in six years. The last of those, 1993–94, saw Maldini receive the coveted World Player of the Year award, the first defender to be so honoured. Maldini passed Dino Zoff's record 112 caps for Italy in October 2000, twelve years after making his debut in the famous blue shirt. He played in the 1994 World Cup final, when Italy lost to Brazil on penalties. That will remain the closest he came to winning the greatest prize in international football. But seven years after leaving the international stage with a record 126 caps, he continues to anchor Milan's defence. In 2004 he won a seventh Serie A title, and three years later picked up his fifth European Cup winners' medal when Milan beat Liverpool in the final.

Paolo Maldini

Diego Maradona

Diego Maradona

Born: 30 October 1960
Clubs: Argentinos Juniors, Boca Juniors, Barcelona, Napoli, Seville, Newell's Old Boys, Boca Juniors
National Team: Argentina

For some, Diego Maradona was the world's greatest footballer throughout the 1980s. He was certainly one of the most controversial players of his generation, inspiring either adulation or anger wherever he went.

His career began in the working-class suburbs of Buenos Aires, where he and his friends formed a football team that was in turn signed up as a whole by Argentinos Juniors. In 1976, the 15-year-old made his league debut and the following year he was playing in an Argentina shirt. Cesar Menotti decided not to include Maradona in the 1978 World Cup, but he was still purchased by Boca Juniors for £1 million, who then sold him to Barcelona for £3 million.

Maradona's World Cup debut came in 1982, but it was not a happy introduction to the tournament. Succumbing to the pressures of international football, he made a bad lunge at Brazil's Batista and was red carded. In 1986, Maradona led Argentina to win the World Cup again, and during the tournament he scored one of the best World Cup goals ever seen and also one of the most controversial. His infamous 'Hand of God' goal against England in the quarter-final is perhaps the best remembered, but the other goal in that match, when he outwitted five defenders and Peter Shilton, was certainly the more impressive, demonstrating Maradona's amazing speed and agility. That same year, Maradona won the World Footballer of the Year trophy.

In 1984, he was bought by Napoli for an incredible £5 million. He repaid the investment in ticket sales and silverware. In seven seasons at the club he helped them to

win the *scudetto* twice, the Italian Cup and UEFA Cup. However, his career began to freefall in the early 1990s. In 1991, Maradona was handed a 15-month ban after testing positive for cocaine in a random drug test. His body ravaged by drug addiction, Maradona finally retired from the game in 1997, playing his final game for Boca Juniors. By then he had had a couple of undistinguished spells in club management, but his legendary status as a player was enough to secure him the job of Argentina coach in 2008.

Lothar Matthaus

Born: 21 March 1961
Clubs: Borussia Moenchengladbach, Bayern Munich, Inter Milan, Bayern Munich, New York Metro Stars
National Team: Germany

It is a testimony to the esteem that Lothar Matthaus was held in that he was still regarded good enough for Germany's national side at France '98, when he was 37 years old. The quarter-final defeat by Croatia was Matthaus's 25th World Cup match in what was his fifth appearance in the finals, a world record for an outfield player. Matthaus began his career at Borussia Moenchengladbach but it was with Bayern Munich – where he had two spells – and Inter Milan that he enjoyed his glory years at club level. He won the Championship and the UEFA Cup with both Inter and Bayern. The crowning moment of his career came at Italia '90 when he captained Germany to World Cup victory. His inspirational performances in midfield earned him the Player of the Tournament award, and he was also voted European and World Footballer of the Year. In the latter part of his career he followed in the footsteps of Franz Beckenbauer by dropping back into the role of sweeper, where he also turned

Lothar Matthaus

in many magnificent performances. He retired after Euro 2000, where he played his 150th and final game.

Stanley Matthews

Born: 1 February 1915
Clubs: Stoke City, Blackpool, Stoke City
National Team: England

When Sir Stanley Matthews died in February 2000, over 100,000 mourners attended his funeral. He had retired from the game 35 years earlier, yet such were his achievements that he had been held-high esteem for over six decades.

Matthews' playing career began in 1931 when he was 17, playing for his local team, Stoke City. During 17 years at the club, he established himself as the best outside-right in world football, earning himself the tag 'Wizard of the Dribble'. In 1947 Matthews joined Blackpool. Having lost two FA Cup finals in 1948 and 1951, when Blackpool got to Wembley again in 1953, all neutrals hoped he would finally get a winners medal. Things looked bleak when opponents Bolton went 3–1 ahead, but 38-year-old Matthews inspired a terrific comeback and Blackpool finished the game 4–3 winners. The match went down in footballing annals as 'the Matthews final'.

Matthews made his international debut in September 1934, scoring in a 4–0 defeat of Wales. Matthews was capped 84 times in an England career that lasted for 20 years and included appearances in the 1950 and 1954 World Cups. However, when England suffered a humiliating 1–0 defeat at the hands of the USA in the 1950 tournament, Matthews was not on the field. The selectors had decided to alternate Matthews and Tom Finney on the right wing and it was Finney who played that day in Brazil.

Matthews was 46 when he left Blackpool in October 1961, but incredibly he chose to return to Stoke rather than retire. After four more years of play he retired on 6 February 1965, five days after his 50th birthday. He had just been knighted in the New Year's Honours and went out in style, with a 3–1 win over Fulham. Twice voted Footballer of the Year, in 1948 and 1963, he was also named European Footballer of the Year in 1956, his final year as an international player and the first award of its kind.

Matthews set a number of records that still remain unbroken. He is the oldest player ever to appear in English football's top flight. At 42, he is the oldest England player. When he scored his final goal for England in 1956 against Northern Ireland he was 41 years and 248 days, making him the oldest player to score for England. Records can of course be broken, but Matthews' achievements and popularity will undoubtedly endure for many years to come.

Stanley Matthews

Sandro Mazzola

Born: 8 November 1942
Clubs: Inter Milan
National Team: Italy

Sandro Mazzola enjoyed a glittering career for Inter Milan and Italy in the 1960s and early 1970s. When he joined Inter in 1960, the club was languishing in the shadows of its Milan neighbours and Juventus, who had shared the past four Serie A championships. By 1963 the title went to Inter for the first time in nearly a decade, with Mazzola hitting 10 goals in 23 games. Mazzola won three more Championship medals over the next nine years. He also appeared in four European Cup finals, finishing on the winning side twice. He scored from the spot early in the 1967 final against Celtic but had to be content with a losers' medal that day. Mazzola was capped 70 times for Italy, scoring 22 goals. He played in the European Championship-winning side in 1968, and in the team which went down to Brazil in the World Cup final two years later.

Jimmy McGrory

Born: 26 April 1904
Clubs: Celtic
National Team: Scotland

Celtic legend Jimmy McGrory broke a host of goalscoring records and remains the only striker in the history of British football to average more than a goal a game. His 410 goals in 408 matches eclipsed even the likes of Dixie Dean, his great contemporary south of the border in the 1920s and 1930s. He broke the Scottish Division One record when he fired 49 goals in 1926–27, despite missing the last five games through injury. Seven years later he went one better, hitting the magic 50 mark, which remains a record for the Glasgow club. A marvellous poacher with a particular penchant for spectacular diving headers, McGrory scored a record eight goals in Celtic's 9–0 win over Dunfermline in January 1928. Amazingly, McGrory wasn't an automatic choice for Scotland as his playing career overlapped that of the great Hughie Gallacher. He died in 1982.

Sandro Mazzola

Dave Mackay

Born: 14 November 1934
Clubs: Hearts, Tottenham Hotspur, Derby County, Swindon Town
National Team: Scotland

Known as the 'Miracle Man' for surviving two broken legs, Dave Mackay was a wing-half for Spurs during their glory years in the early 1960s. In 1959, Mackay was purchased from Heart of Midlothian for £30,000. He had already won every major honour in Scottish football and was an established Scotland international.

At Spurs, Mackay enjoyed even greater success. They achieved the Double in 1960–61 and retained the FA Cup the following year. He missed the final of the European Cup Winners' Cup in 1963, when Spurs beat Atletico Madrid 5–1, but bounced back from injury to captain Spurs to a third FA Cup triumph in 1967.

In 1968, he moved to Derby County for just £5,000, a bargain for manager Brian Clough. He inspired the team on to their Second Division Championship in 1968–69, earning himself the Footballer of the Year title, an honour he shared with Tony Book. Mackay finished his career at Swindon Town, retiring in 1971.

Giuseppe Meazza

Born: 23 August 1910
Clubs: Inter Milan, AC Milan, Juventus, Varese, Atalanta
National Team: Italy

Giuseppe Meazza was not only a spectacular centre-forward but was regarded as one of the most complete players of his era. He played in both of Italy's World Cup-winning campaigns of 1934 and 1938, one of only two players to do so. Meazza was a teenage prodigy, making his debut for Inter Milan at 17 and winning the first of his 53 caps two years later. His 33 goals for Italy puts him second behind Luigi Riva in the all-time list. He hit two on his debut, against Switzerland in a 4–2 win in 1930. He headed the goal which won a brutal quarter-final replay against Spain in the 1934 World Cup. The following season he scored both of Italy's goals in their 3–2 defeat against England in the infamous 'Battle of Highbury'. Meazza captained his country to a 4–2 win over Hungary in the 1938 World Cup final. The crunch match was actually the semi-final against Brazil, and it was Meazza's spot-kick which proved decisive as Italy won the game 2–1.

Dave Mackay

Billy Meredith

Born: 30 July 1874
Clubs: Manchester City, Manchester United
National Team: Wales

Billy Meredith, 'the Welsh Wizard', is widely regarded as the game's first superstar. Meredith came from Welsh mining stock, and he himself was working underground by the age of 12. His parents were eventually persuaded to allow him to pursue a career in football and Meredith joined Manchester City in 1894. He quickly established himself as a skilful, free-scoring winger, and became known for the fact that he never took to the field without a toothpick to chew on.

By 1904 30-year-old Meredith was City's captain, and scored the only goal of the game in that year's FA Cup final win over Bolton. Meredith was banned for eight months after allegedly attempting to bribe an Aston Villa player before a vital league match in April 1905. He denied the charge and when the ban was lifted he moved across the city to join Manchester United. He helped United to win the FA Cup in 1909 and the Championship in 1910–11. He rejoined Manchester City in 1921 as a player-coach. He finally hung up his boots three years later, when he was four months short of his 50th birthday. His swansong came in City's 1924 FA Cup semi-final defeat by Newcastle. He had played 48 times for Wales between 1895 and 1920, winning the last of his caps when he was 45.

Meredith was at the forefront of a campaign to end the £4 maximum wage that was in force in the early 1900s. That figure was increased to £5 as a result, and the roots of the PFA can be traced back to the Welshman's early efforts to establish a Players' Union. He died in 1958.

Billy Meredith

Jackie Milburn

Born: 11 May 1924
Clubs: Newcastle United
National Team: England

Jackie Milburn's rise from colliery worker to football striker is the stuff of dreams, and it is testament to his playing skill that he is still fondly remembered by Newcastle United fans two decades after his death. 'Wor Jackie' was a Geordie hero for good reason. He had incredible pace and could score from seemingly impossible angles. During the 1950s he was one of the country's foremost strikers. Milburn scored an impressive 178 goals in the eleven years he spent at the Tyneside club. He had joined them as a teenager and led Newcastle to their victories in three FA Cups, in 1951, 1952 and 1955. He scored both the goals in the 2–0 defeat of Blackpool in the 1951 final, and four years later his header in the opening seconds of the final against Manchester City set the Magpies up for their 3–1 win.

In 13 appearances for England, centre-forward Milburn scored 10 goals. He was at the forefront of a footballing dynasty. His brothers were also professionals and his nephews, Bobby and Jackie Charlton, followed him into the England team in the 1960s. Jackie Milburn died in 1988.

Jackie Milburn

Roger Milla

Born: 20 May 1952
Clubs: Éclair de Douala, Leopard de Douala, Valenciennes, Monaco, Bastia, Saint-Etienne, Montpellier, JS Saint-Pierroise
National Team: Cameroon

Roger Milla was the African Footballer of the Year in 1976, 14 years before he shot to global fame in Cameroon's glorious World Cup campaign at Italia '90. His four goals in that tournament, together with his celebratory dance around the corner flag, helped Cameroon reach the quarter-finals, where they were narrowly beaten by England. Milla had played a huge part in helping his country reach their first ever World Cup eight years earlier in Spain, and was still going strong at USA '94, at the age of 42. That campaign was less successful but Milla did grab Cameroon's consolation goal in a 6–1 thrashing by Russia, making him the oldest player ever to score in a World Cup. Milla played most of his club football in France, winning the domestic cup competition in successive seasons with Monaco and Bastia.

Andreas Moller

Born: 2 September 1967
Clubs: Eintracht Frankfurt, Borussia Dortmund, Juventus
National Team: Germany

Many England fans will have all too painful a memory of Andreas Moller. His strutting celebration after converting the penalty which knocked Terry Venables' side out in the semi-finals of Euro '96 marked yet another disappointing chapter in the rivalry between the two countries. Suspension forced Moller to miss the victory over the Czech Republic in the final, but his contribution had been considerable. Moller had been marked out from his early days in junior football as a potential future international playmaker. After spells at Eintracht Frankfurt and Borussia Dortmund, he joined Juventus, whom he helped to win the 1993 UEFA Cup. The Turin club faced Dortmund in the final and trounced them 6–1 over the two legs, with Moller getting one of the goals. Four years later, Moller was back at Dortmund, helping the side to win successive Bundesliga titles in 1995 and 1996. He was also a key figure in Dortmund's 1997 European Cup triumph. The team beat Manchester United in the semis, then avenged the earlier defeat by Juventus by beating the favourites 3–1 in the final. France '98 was Moller's third appearance in a World Cup, although by then he was not an automatic first choice.

Bobby Moore

Born: 12 April 1941
Clubs: West Ham United, Fulham, San Antonio Thunder, Herning FC, Seattle Sounders
National Team: England

Bobby Moore is perhaps best remembered as the captain who led his country to victory in the 1966 World Cup, but there was far more to the inspirational captain of West Ham and England.

Born in Barking, East London, Moore joined the Hammers in 1958, aged 17. He was fiercely loyal to the club, remaining with them until 1974 and making 545 appearances. In 1964, Moore captained the side to their first FA Cup win, over Preston North End, and that same year he was voted England's Player of the Year. The following year they won the European Cup Winners' Cup, beating TSV Munich 1860 2–0.

As an international footballer, he was a superstar. Pele once claimed that Moore was the greatest opponent he had ever faced and many considered him to be the finest defender of all time. Despite criticism that he lacked pace, Moore had an instinctive response and an ability to anticipate, which made him a formidable opponent for a striker. It is telling that during the 1966 World Cup, no goals were scored against England until the semi-final when Eusebio placed a penalty. Capped for the first time in 1962, Moore made 108 full appearances for England, turning out as captain 90 times, equalling Billy Wright's total. He played in the 1962 World Cup when England lost to Brazil in the quarter-finals and in the 1970 World Cup he led the defending champions out at Mexico. England's 1–0 defeat at the hands of Brazil during the group stage is remembered as one of Moore's finest performances. At the end of the game, Moore and Pele embraced in a moment of mutual respect.

His retirement from international football in 1974 also saw him depart West Ham for rivals Fulham. When the team reached the 1975 FA Cup final, they were beaten 2–0, ironically by his former club. After some time spent in the US, Moore briefly entered management. Following a battle with bowel cancer, he died in 1993, aged only 51.

Gerd Müller

Born: 3 November 1945
Clubs: TSV Nordingen, Bayern Munich, Fort Lauderdale Strikers
National Team: West Germany

Gerd Müller's phenomenal goalscoring record puts him in a class of his own in the modern era. Nicknamed 'Der Bomber', Müller scored an incredible 68 goals in just 62 appearances for the national side, including the winner against Holland in the 1974 World Cup final. He spent the majority of his playing career at Bayern Munich, where he hit 365 league goals, a Bundesliga record. Müller was a stocky figure and did not give the appearance of a natural athlete. Yet he was explosive in the box and a consummate predator. In addition to his World Cup winners' medal, Müller helped Germany to European Championship victory in 1972, and there was also a hat-trick of European Cup successes with Bayern in the mid-1970s. His 10 goals in the 1970 World Cup, where Germany reached the semi-final, made him the tournament's top scorer and he was also named European Footballer of the Year.

Gerd Müller

Bobby Moore

Johan Neeskens

Born: 15 September 1951
Clubs: Ajax, Barcelona, New York Cosmos, Fort Lauderdale Strikers, FC Groningen, FC Baar
National Team: Holland

Johan Neeskens scored the first ever penalty in a World Cup final. It came after just two minutes against hosts West Germany in 1974, Neeskens converting from the spot after Cruyff's surging run was ended by Hoeness. Neeskens was a skilful but also combative member of the side that was praised for the 'total football' it played. It was a losers' medal for Neeskens in the 1974 World Cup, and he made it an unhappy double four years later, when Holland went down to Argentina in the final of the next tournament. He won 49 caps between 1970 and 1981, scoring 17 goals. The disappointments on the international stage were at least mitigated by some notable successes at club level. Neeskens broke into the Ajax side as a teenager and played in the brilliant team which won a hat-trick of European Cups in the early 1970s. He moved to Barcelona in 1994, following in Cruyff's footsteps, and played in the side which beat Fortuna Dusseldorf in the 1979 European Cup Winners' Cup final.

Johan Neeskens

Gunter Netzer

Born: 14 September 1944
Clubs: Borussia Moenchengladbach, Real Madrid, Grasshoppers
National Team: West Germany

Gunter Netzer enjoyed a long and successful career in his native Germany, Spain and Switzerland, but he is best remembered for his outstanding performances for his country in the early 1970s. It was Netzer who pulled all the strings when Germany came to Wembley in 1972 and won 3–1, their first ever victory on English soil. The occasion was the quarter-final of the European Championship, which Germany went on to win at a canter. By then Franz Beckenbauer had dropped into the sweeper's role and left the playmaking responsibilities to Netzer. The 1972 side was widely considered even better than the team which won the World Cup two years later. There was to be no double for Netzer, however. He moved to Real Madrid in 1973, ending a 12-year stay at Borussia Moenchengladbach, with whom he won two Bundeliga titles.

By the time the 1974 World Cup came round Netzer found himself marginalised by international team boss Helmut Schoen. He ended his career with just 37 caps, far fewer than his silky skills merited.

Jean-Pierre Papin

Born: 5 November 1963
Clubs: INF Vichy, Valenciennes, Club Brugge, Marseille, AC Milan, Bayern Munich, Bordeaux, Guingamp
National Team: France

AC Milan had to break the bank and set a new world mark of £10 million when they signed Jean-Pierre Papin from Marseille in 1992. Papin had been top scorer in the French league four years running, helping to fire Marseille to four domestic championships. He played in the side which lost in the 1991 European Cup final, Red Star Belgrade winning on penalties after the game ended goalless. For Papin there was the consolation of picking up the European Footballer of the Year award. Fierce competition at Milan meant that he was in and out of the side in his two years with the Serie A club. He came off the substitutes' bench in the 1993 European Cup final, but again finished with a losers' medal. Ironically, the victors were his former club, Marseille. He had a two-year spell at Bayern Munich but failed to find his best form and returned to France with Bordeaux. Papin scored 30 goals in his 54 appearances for France. One of those came against Denmark in the crucial European Championship match in 1992, but France went down 2–1 to the tournament's surprise package.

Daniel Passarella

Born: 25 May 1953
Clubs: Sarmiento, River Plate, Fiorentina, Inter Milan
National Team: Argentina

Daniel Passarella captained Argentina to their first World Cup triumph, on home soil in 1978. A dominant central defender, Passarella was equally effective moving upfield and had a happy knack of scoring vital goals. After winning the Argentinian championship four times with River Plate, Passarella went to Serie A for the latter part of his career. He didn't manage to pick up any silverware in his four years at Fiorentina, or the two seasons he spent at Inter Milan, but he confirmed his reputation as one of the world's outstanding defenders in a league which traditionally produces the best in the business. He returned to River Plate in 1988 and began to turn his thoughts to coaching. He led Argentina at France '98 and also had a spell in charge of Uruguay and has coached club sides around the world.

Jean-Pierre Papin

Pele

Born: 23 October 1940
Clubs: Santos, New York Cosmos
National Team: Brazil

Widely regarded to be the greatest footballer ever, Pele dominated for over two decades. An outstanding player even as a child, Edson Arantes do Nascimento apparently learned to kick a ball in the back streets of Brazil. He began playing for local side Noroeste and his outstanding performances brought him to the attention of Santos, who signed him at only 15 years old. Santos built a whole side around their star and they won the World Club Cup twice, in 1962 and 1963.

Pele first played for Brazil in 1957 when he was only 16. In the 1958 World Cup he came to the attention of the world when he scored six goals, including a hat-trick against France. With Pele on the team, Brazil won three World Cups in twelve years. During the 1966 tournament, he was ruthlessly targeted and Brazil crashed out at the group stages. In protest at his treatment, he declared that he would not play in another World Cup again, but thankfully he did go to Mexico in 1970, where he inspired Brazil to victory yet again, beating Italy in the final 4–1.

Pele's legendary status is well earned. In 1969 he scored his 1000th goal for Santos, sparking carnival on the streets of Rio. During his career, he scored a total of 1,220 goals, bagging five in one game on six occasions, scoring four times in 30 matches and over 90 hat-tricks.

He announced his retirement in 1974, although he continued to play for New York Cosmos until 1977. In the late 1990s he became Brazil's Minister for Sport and in 2000 collected FIFA's Footballer of the Century award.

Pele

Emmanuel Petit

Born: 22 September 1970
Clubs: Argues, Monaco, Arsenal, Barcelona, Chelsea
National Team: France

Even footballers who enjoy long careers have a golden period, when it seems they can do no wrong. For Manu Petit it was the 1997–98 season, his debut campaign in the Premiership with Arsenal. He played a key role in helping the Gunners wrest the championship from Manchester United, forming a brilliant midfield axis with fellow-countryman Patrick Vieira. An FA Cup win over Newcastle followed, and Petit was then part of the France side which lifted the World Cup on home soil. Petit capped a fine tournament by grabbing the third goal in the victory over Brazil. It was all a far cry from the previous year, when Petit struggled to settle after joining Arsenal from Monaco in a £3.5 million deal. Gunners' boss Arsene Wenger knew Petit well, having had him as a young left-back at Monaco. He persuaded the midfielder not to make a hasty decision and he went from strength to strength. The strains began to show in 2000, and this time Petit decided to return to the Continent with a move to Barcelona. Things didn't go well for him in Spain, however, and after just one season he was back in the Premiership with Chelsea. The left foot was as sweet as ever and even on the wrong side of 30 he showed that he was still one of the classiest midfielders in the world. Roman Abramovich's millions allowed Claudio Ranieri to splash out on a number of top midfielders in summer 2003. Petit was given a free transfer in 2004, and after struggling with a knee injury, retired the following year.

Emmanuel Petit

Michel Platini

Born: 21 June 1955
Clubs: Nancy, St Etienne, Juventus
National Team: France

Michel Platini was France's greatest footballer, dominating Europe during the 1980s and helping the French to establish themselves as a top footballing nation. Platini was named European Footballer of the Year three times, in 1983, 1984 and 1985, the only player to win the award on three successive occasions.

He began his career at Nancy where his father was coach and made his international debut in 1976, scoring one goal. At the 1978 World Cup, Platini made a positive impression and moved to St Etienne in 1979. In 1982, his influence was becoming obvious. St Etienne won the domestic championship and at the World Cup finals, France made it into the semi-finals.

As a result of his achievements, Platini was bought by Juventus, who paid £1.2 million for the midfielder. He helped them to a League and Cup Winners' Cup double in 1984. The following year he scored the goal which beat Liverpool in the European Cup final, although the victory was overshadowed by the tragic events at the Heysel Stadium.

When France won the 1984 European Championship on home soil, Platini was not only captain but the top scorer with nine goals, including hat-tricks against Belgium and Yugoslavia and the first goal in the 2–0 victory over Spain in the final. His overall strike record at both club and international level was phenomenal for a midfielder. He hit 68 goals in 147 league games for the Turin club. His 72 appearances for France yielded 41 goals, a return a top striker would have been proud of.

Platini retired following France's exit from the 1986 World Cup in the semi-finals. He became the national manager in 1987, but retired in 1992 following the European Championships. In 2007 Platini was elected president of Uefa, taking over from Lennart Johannson.

Robert Prosinecki

Born: 1 December 1969
Clubs: Dinamo Zagreb, Red Star Belgrade, Real Madrid, Barcelona, Portsmouth, NK Olimpija
National Teams: Yugoslavia, Croatia

One of the most talented midfielders of his era, Robert Prosinecki began his career with Dinamo Zagreb. After joining Red Star Belgrade he won three Yugoslavian championships in four years, and in 1991 the team beat Marseille on penalties to lift the European Cup. By then he was an established international, having made his debut as a 20-year-old in 1989. Prosinecki had won 15 caps before the break-up of the country in the early 1990s, after which he made the first of 49 appearances for Croatia. He helped Croatia reach the knockout stage at Euro '96 and the semi-final of France '98, in what was an excellent World Cup debut for the country. Prosinecki was a 32-year-old veteran at Japan and Korea 2002 and an ageing side went out at the group stage. After leaving Red Star, Prosinecki spent several years in Spain, including spells at both Real Madrid and Barcelona. In August 2001 he joined Portsmouth and in 2002 he transfered to NK Olimpija before returning to Croatia to wind down his career with a lower league club.

Ferenc Puskas

Ferenc Puskas

Born: 2 April 1927
Clubs: Honved, Real Madrid
National Team: Hungary, Spain

In 1953, England played host to Hungary at Wembley. One England player famously remarked, 'Look at that little fat chap. We'll murder this lot.' The 'fat chap' was Hungarian captain Ferenc Puskas, who went on to score two goals in a 6–3 defeat of the home team. England had never been beaten at home before by an overseas team, and Hungary had humiliated them. In the return match, the Hungarians compounded that defeat with a 7–1 drubbing of the visitors. Puskas was indeed short, stocky and overweight, but he was also one of the most powerful footballers of his age and it was thanks to him that Hungary was the most feared team in Europe during the 1950s.

Known as the 'Galloping Major', Puskas had begun playing for his local side Kispest when he was 16. In 1948, the Soviet authorities took control of Kispest, turning them into Honved, a military side and a training team for the national side. Puskas had made his first appearance for Hungary aged 18 in 1945. When the 'Magic Magyars' arrived in Switzerland for the 1954 World Cup, they had been unbeaten for four years and were hot favourites to lift the trophy. Puskas, who was unfit, insisted on playing in the final against West Germany and the Germans won, causing the biggest upset in the tournament's history.

During the 1956 Hungarian uprising, Honved were abroad and Puskas chose to remain in the West. Over 30 years old and overweight, many believed he was past his best, but he went on to play for Spanish giants Real Madrid, who were then managed by former Honved boss, Emil Oestreicher. Forming a deadly partnership with Alfredo di Stefano, Puskas continued to play until he was 39. During that time Real won five successive domestic championships and appeared in three European Cup finals. Puskas scored hat-tricks in two of them, the only player ever to do so. Incredibly, his three goals against Benfica in 1962 weren't enough to win the match; Real went down 5–3. In 1960 he hit four, with di Stefano grabbing three as Real beat Eintracht Frankfurt 7–3 at Hampden Park in one of the greatest matches ever seen.

Puskas took Spanish citizenship and played for Spain in the 1962 World Cup. Although unsuccessful, he was adored in his adopted country for his enormous contribution to Real Madrid's successes. Puskas died in November 2006.

Thomas Ravelli

Thomas Ravelli

Born: 13 August 1959
Clubs: Osters Vaxjo, IFK Gothenburg, Tampa Bay Mutiny
National Team: Sweden

Thomas Ravelli's 138 appearances for Sweden made him the most capped European footballer ever, beating the record set by a fellow 'keeper, England's Peter Shilton. Although Germany's Lothar Matthaus eventually overhauled his tally, Ravelli's record and performances for club and country in the 1980s and 1990s put him in the highest class. After his move to IFK Gothenburg in 1989, the club won six championships in seven years. Ravelli was in top form at the 1994 World Cup, particularly in the quarter-final clash with Romania which went to a penalty shoot-out. His saves helped put Sweden through to meet Brazil for a place in the final. Although they lost 1–0, the Swedes, and Ravelli in particular, won many admirers for their performances.

Frank Rijkaard

Born: 30 September 1962
Clubs: Ajax, Sporting Lisbon, Real Zaragoza, AC Milan, Ajax
National Team: Holland

Along with Marco Van Basten and Ruud Gullit, Frank Rijkaard made up a triumvirate of stars who brought great success to AC Milan and Holland in the 1980s and 1990s. Rijkaard came through the ranks at Ajax in the early 1980s

alongside Van Basten and Dennis Bergkamp. The Amsterdam club won the Championship three times in four years, and in 1987 Rijkaard played in the side which beat Lokomotiv Leipzig 1–0 in the European Cup Winners' Cup final. He fell out with coach Johan Cruyff, and after brief spells in Portugal and Spain he linked up with Van Basten and Gullit at AC Milan. He became a key part of Arrigo Sacchi's all-conquering side, which was bankrolled by media mogul Silvio Berlusconi. Rijkaard played in the 4–0 demolition of Steaua Bucharest in the 1989 European Cup final, and scored the goal which retained the trophy against Benfica a year later. Rijkaard won the first of his 73 caps as a 19-year-old in 1981. The highlight of his 13-year international career came in 1988, when Holland won the European Championship in style. At Italia '90 he was red-carded after a clash with Rudi Voller during Holland's meeting with Germany in the last sixteen. The Dutch lost the game 2–1. Rijkaard scored a superb goal against Denmark in the semi-final of the 1992 European Championship. It brought the Dutch level at 2–2 but Denmark went on to win in a shoot-out. He ended his career on a high note. Having returned to Ajax, 32-year-old Rijkaard helped the team to a European Cup victory over his former team Milan in 1995. In summer 2003 he took over the managerial reins at the Nou Camp, leading the Catalans to the league title two years later and retaining the crown in 2006. That year Rijkaard joined the ranks of those to have won the Champions League as both player and coach.

Frank Rijkaard

Luigi Riva

Born: 7 November 1944
Clubs: Legnano, Cagliari
National Team: Italy

Luigi Riva fought his way up from the lower echelons of Italian football to become the country's top striker. He began his career with Legnano, a Third Division side, before stepping up a rung to join Cagliari in 1963. He helped Cagliari to win promotion to Serie A in his first season, and six years later, 1969–70, the Sardinian club won their first and only championship. Riva was the league's top scorer in that campaign, hitting 21 goals in 28 games. He won 42 caps for Italy, scoring an impressive 35 goals, many with his lethal left foot. His greatest moment came in the 1970 World Cup, when he scored twice in Italy's quarter-final win over Mexico and hit another in the memorable 4–3 semi-final victory over West Germany. He had to be content with a runner-up medal, however, as Italy came up against an irresistible Brazilian side in the final. Riva played on until the mid-1970s, but two broken legs took their toll in the latter days of his career.

Gianni Rivera

Born: 18 August 1943
Clubs: US Alessandria, AC Milan
National Team: Italy

Gianni Rivera was Italian football's golden boy in the 1960s. His performances for his home town club Alessandria in the late 1950s, when he was in his mid-teens, brought AC Milan knocking at his door. He eventually joined the Rossoneri in 1960 and spent the rest of his career there. An elegant inside-forward with great passing ability and a ferocious shot, Rivera twice won the Serie A Championship, and Milan also won the Italian Cup three times during his time at the club. There were also two European Cup victories, over Benfica in the 1963 final and Ajax six years later. 1969 also saw Rivera named European Footballer of the Year. First capped in 1962, Rivera played for his country on 60 occasions over the next twelve years. He never quite managed to recreate his club form at international level, however, and successive managers struggled to get the best out of him. He hit the extra-time winner in the classic 4–3 victory over West Germany in the semi-final of the 1970 World Cup. He then found himself reduced to a late substitute's role for the final, in which Italy went down 4–1.

Roberto Rivelino

Born: 1 January 1946
Clubs: Corinthians, Fluminense, El Hilal
National Team: Brazil

A key member of the great Brazil side which won the 1970 World Cup, Rivelino had both trickery and prodigious power in his feet. His shooting from distance – either direct thunderbolts or banana shots – was legendary. The semi-final clash in Mexico in 1970 saw a Rivelino special, a goal which helped Brazil recover from a goal behind to win 3–1. He didn't get on the scoresheet against Italy in the final but he was involved in some terrific build-up play, notably the move which led to Carlos Alberto's memorable goal which put the icing on a 4–1 victory. Rivelino was one of just three survivors for the disappointing 1974 tournament, and he was a veteran 32 year-old in Argentina in 1978, where Brazil were pipped by the hosts for a place in the final. He ended his international career that year, with 26 goals from his 94 appearances. At club level he spent almost his entire career at just two clubs, Corinthians and Fluminense.

Roberto Rivelino

Bryan Robson

Born: 11 January 1957
Clubs: West Bromwich Albion, Manchester United, Middlesbrough
National Team: England

Bryan Robson was dubbed 'Captain Marvel' for his inspirational performances for Manchester United and England in the 1980s and early 1990s. He was the most complete midfielder in British football and for many years he was arguably England's one world-class player. Some eyebrows were raised when Ron Atkinson paid a record £1.5 million to bring Robson from West Bromwich Albion to Old Trafford in October 1981. But the former West Brom manager knew what he was getting, and it turned into one of the shrewdest deals of the day. Robson won the FA Cup three times and played in the side which overcame Barcelona in the 1991 European Cup Winners' Cup final. When United ended a 26-year drought in winning the inaugural Premiership title in 1993, Robson was coming to the end of his playing days, something which wasn't helped by the catalogue of injuries which had plagued his career. Even with so many enforced lay-offs, Robson still won 90 caps, scoring 26 goals. At the 1982 World Cup in Spain, Robson put England ahead against France after just 27 seconds, the fastest goal ever scored in the tournament. Robson began his management career with Middlesbrough, leading the club to three major finals. He left the Riverside after a torrid 2000–01 season. Robson returned to football with a brief stint as Bradford boss in 2003–04. He took over at the Hawthorns in 2004, but left following a poor start to the 2006–07 campaign. A brief spell in charge of Sheffield United ended in February 2008.

Bryan Robson

Romario

Born: 29 January 1966
Clubs: Olario, Vasco da Gama, PSV Eindhoven, Barcelona, Flamengo, Valencia
National Team: Brazil

Brazil performed so poorly in the run-up to the 2002 World Cup that there was a strong lobby for the inclusion of 36-year-old Romario, the man who had fired the team to victory at USA '94. It all came right for Brazil in Japan and Korea in the end, Rivaldo and Ronaldo providing the firepower which led Brazil to victory, as Romario himself had done eight years earlier. Romario began his career at Vasco da Gama, where he built a reputation as a prodigious if wayward talent. He spent five years at PSV Eindhoven, where he had many run-ins with coaches and players but continued to find the back of the net regularly. In 1993 he joined Johan Cruyff's Barcelona, forming a lethal partnership with Stoichkov. He was recalled by Brazil after a period in the wilderness and scored five goals at USA '94. His performances and goals earned him the 1994 World Footballer of the Year award. In 1995 he returned to Brazil with Flamengo, briefly went back to Spain and a spell at Valencia, then headed home again. After two more years at Flamengo Romario rejoined Vasco da Gama, the club where he first made his name. Injury forced him to miss France '98.

Paolo Rossi

Born: 23 September 1956
Clubs: Prato, Juventus, Como, Lanerossi Vicenza, Perugia, Juventus, AC Milan
National Team: Italy

Paolo Rossi was a rising star in Italian football when he was found guilty of being involved in a match-fixing scandal in 1980. He was handed a lengthy ban but was reprieved after two years, just in time to play in the 1982 World Cup in Spain. He made amends for his misdemeanours with a stunning display in the tournament. His six goals made him the competition's top scorer and carried Italy to victory. His haul included both goals against Poland in the semis and one in the 3–1 win over Germany in the final. But the crowning moment came in the second-round group match against Brazil, when Rossi's hat-trick sent the favourites crashing out. His performances earned him the European Footballer of the Year award. Rossi began his career at Juventus but was loaned out to various clubs because of his susceptibility to injury. After a fine showing in the 1978 World Cup he joined Perugia and it was during his time there that the scandal broke. Juve finally recaptured their former player in 1981, despite the ban that was still hanging over his head. Rossi continued to be dogged by injury, however, and his World Cup exploits in 1982 proved to be the high point of his career. He was forced to retire in 1985 at the age of 29.

Romario

Paolo Rossi

Karl-Heinz Rummenigge

Karl-Heinz Rummenigge

Born: 25 September 1955
Clubs: Bayern Munich, Inter Milan, Servette
National Team: West Germany

In the mid-1970s, when the likes of Beckenbauer and Müller were coming towards the end of their careers, Karl-Heinz Rummenigge assumed the mantle of Germany's star player. Rummenigge featured in Bayern's 1976 European Cup final victory over St Etienne, having joined the club from Lippstadt for just £4,500 two years earlier. He remained at Bayern for ten years, when Inter Milan paid rather more for him – £2 million. Rummenigge hit three goals in West Germany's unimpressive World Cup campaign in Argentina in 1978. He picked up a winners' medal in the European Championship two years later, West Germany beating Belgium in the final in Rome. He was named European Footballer of the Year in both 1980 and 1981, and went to the 1982 World Cup as one of the most feared strikers in the game. He hit five goals as Germany made it to the final, but he was carrying an injury when the team fell to Italy at the final hurdle. He picked up another losers' medal four years later, when injury again prevented him from showing his best form. By the time he retired, prematurely, in 1988 he had won 95 caps, scoring 45 goals. Both of those figures would surely have been higher had he not been dogged by injury.

Ian Rush

Born: 20 October 1961
Clubs: Chester City, Liverpool, Juventus, Liverpool, Leeds United, Newcastle United, Sheffield United, Wrexham
National Team: Wales

Ian Rush played for Liverpool for 16 years and his first touch and pace contributed to an impressive strike-rate that made him a legend with the Kop. He began his career at Chester, and moved to Anfield in 1980 for just £300,000. In the 658 games he played for Liverpool, Rush scored 346 goals. With them he won the championship five times and the FA Cup on three occasions, scoring each time in the Wembley finals. In 1984, Liverpool beat Roma in the European Cup final and Rush, having scored 32 goals during the competition, earned the European Golden Boot. That same year he was also awarded the title of Footballer of the Year. Rush spent one unhappy season at Juventus in 1987–88 and towards the end of his career he played for Leeds, Newcastle and Wrexham. While playing for Wales he scored a record 28 goals in 73 games.

Matthias Sammer

Born: 5 September 1967
Clubs: Dynamo Dresden, Stuttgart, Inter Milan, Borussia Dortmund
National Team: Germany

Matthias Sammer was an elegant, attacking sweeper in the Beckenbauer mould. He was also East Germany's star player in 1990, when the reunification of the country took place. Sammer quickly established himself in the new Germany team and made the move from Dresden to Stuttgart. He joined Inter Milan in 1992 but that proved to be a brief and unhappy sojourn. He returned to the Bundesliga with Borussia Dortmund and

Ian Rush

Matthias Sammer

Hugo Sanchez

Born: 11 June 1958
Clubs: Unam, Atletico Madrid, Real Madrid, America, Royo Vallecano
National Team: Mexico

Hugo Sanchez plied his striker's trade in the Primera Liga for the majority of his career, first with Atletico Madrid and then with city arch rivals Real. Atletico's president Jesus Gil once said that Sanchez was 'as dangerous as a piranha in a bidet'. Atletico was one of the clubs on the receiving end of that threat as Sanchez formed a deadly strike partnership with Emilio Butragueno in the late 1980s. Sanchez's prolific scoring helped Real to five domestic championships in succession between 1986 and 1990. Overall he scored more than 230 goals in Spanish football's top flight, putting him second in the all-time list. Thirty-eight of those came in the 1989–90 season, making Sanchez the joint-winner of the Golden Boot with Hristo Stoichkov. Sanchez won 57 caps for Mexico, hitting 26 goals. The highlight of his international career came at the 1986 World Cup, when he captained the side that went out to West Germany on penalties. In 2006 Sanchez was named as Mexico's coach, having won two domestic titles with UNAM Pumas.

Dejan Savicevic

Born: 15 September 1966
Clubs: Red Star Belgrade, AC Milan, Rapid Vienna
National Team: Yugoslavia

Dejan Savicevic is a member of an elite group of players to have won the European Cup with two different clubs. His four-year spell at Red Star Belgrade included a Champions Cup victory over Marseille on penalties in 1991. The gifted attacking midfielder moved to AC Milan the following year for £4 million. This was one of many high-profile signings as Silvio Berlusconi bankrolled manager Arrigo Saachi as the latter assembled a team of superstars. Milan won a hat-trick of Serie A titles between 1992 and 1994. Savicevic was in top form in the 1994 Champions Cup final, scoring a brilliant goal in Milan's 4–0 demolition of Barcelona. He was outstanding at Italia '90, helping Yugoslavia to reach the quarter-finals, where they went out to Argentina on penalties. His 52 caps also included a cameo appearance at France '98, by which time he was in the veteran class. Savicevic briefly rejoined Red Star in the same year before moving on to Rapid Vienna.

was outstanding as the side won successive league titles, and a famous Champions League victory over Juventus in 1997. Sammer was in imperious form in Germany's Euro '96 triumph, scoring the winner in the quarter-final clash with the Czech Republic. He was named European Footballer of the Year that December, the first player from the former GDR to be thus honoured. Injury prevented him from taking part in France '98 and eventually forced his premature retirement from the game. Sammer coached Borussia Dortmund from 2002–04, and had a season in charge at Stuttgart before taking up a technical director post with the German FA.

Juan Schiaffino

Born: 28 July 1925
Clubs: Penarol, AC Milan, Roma
National Team: Uruguay, Italy

Regarded as Uruguay's greatest ever player, Juan Schiaffino attracted a world record fee of £72,000 when he left Penarol for AC Milan in 1954. He helped Uruguay reach the semi-finals of that year's World Cup, but his greatest moment came in the previous tournament, the first in the postwar era. He hit five goals in the 1950 competition, staged in Brazil, making him joint-second top scorer. Four of those came in an 8–0 thrashing of Bolivia. The fifth was the vital equalizer against favourites Brazil in the final group match, which was effectively the final. Uruguay ran out 2–1 winners. Schiaffino won three championships in his six years with Milan. He also hit a brilliant opening goal in the 1958 European Cup final against Real Madrid, but finished on the losing side. Schiaffino wound down his career with two years at Roma, by which time he was 37. He is also among those players to have been capped by two countries, winning four caps for Italy to add to the 45 he gained with Uruguay. Schiaffino died in 2002.

Enzo Scifo

Born: 19 February 1966
Clubs: Anderlecht, Inter Milan, Bordeaux, Auxerre, Torino
National Team: Belgium

Vicenzo Scifo was born in Belgium of Italian parents. He joined Anderlecht, for whom he made his debut as a 17-year-old. His creative flair and goals helped Anderlecht to a hat-trick of domestic championships between 1985 and 1987. He also played in the team which finished UEFA Cup runners-up to Spurs in 1984, an achievement which was later besmirched by a bribery scandal. Scifo joined Inter Milan in 1987 but his four years at the club included lengthy loan spells at Bordeaux and Auxerre. He was finally sold to Torino, for whom he played in another UEFA Cup final in 1992. It was another runners-up medal, however, as the Italian side went down to Ajax on away goals in the two-legged final. He moved to Monaco in 1993, spending four years there before rejoining Anderlecht. Scifo was first capped just before the 1984 European Championship. He went on to play in the next four World Cups, a semi-final defeat against Argentina in 1986 marking his and Belgium's best achievement.

Peter Schmeichel

Born: 18 November 1963
Clubs: Gladsaxe, Hvidovre, Brondby, Manchester United, Sporting Lisbon, Aston Villa, Manchester City
National Team: Denmark

The outstanding goalkeeper in world football during the 1990s, Peter Schmeichel was surely one of the bargains of the decade. He arrived at Old Trafford from Brondby in August 1991 for a mere £550,000. The following year he was in the Denmark side that gained a last-minute entry into the European Championship, then proceeded to astonish everyone by winning the tournament. His eight years at Manchester United yielded a vast amount of silverware, including the Premiership and FA Cup Double on two occasions. He signed off after the famous European Cup triumph over Bayern Munich in 1999, when he was 36. The man-mountain and shot-stopper supreme headed for Sporting Lisbon, where it seemed he would end his playing days. But after helping the Portuguese club to a first championship in 18 years, Schmeichel returned to the Premiership with Aston Villa and also had a swansong season with Manchester City.

Peter Schmeichel

Enzo Scifo

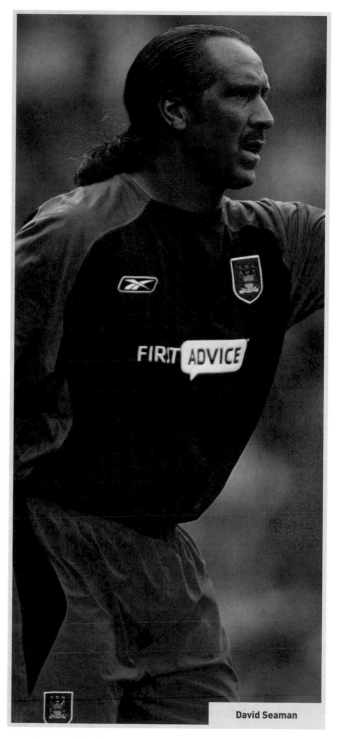

David Seaman

David Seaman

Born: 19 September 1963
Clubs: Leeds United, Peterborough United, Birmingham City, Queen's Park Rangers, Arsenal, Manchester City
National Team: England

As the rock at the heart of a niggardly Arsenal defence for more than a decade, David Seaman did more than enough to earn his 'Safe Hands' tag. Seaman learned his trade as an understudy to John Lukic in the early 1980s. After spells at Peterborough and Birmingham City he joined Queen's Park Rangers, where he began to carve out a big reputation for himself. He made his international debut during his four-year spell at Loftus Road and Arsenal had to pay £1.3 million to acquire his services in May 1990, a record for a British goalkeeper. He has won all the domestic honours, including three Championships. He also picked up a European Cup Winners' Cup Medal when the Gunners beat Parma 1–0 in the 1994 final. A year later, Seaman was left with egg on his face in the final of the same competition, when Nayim's 50-yard lob floated over his head in the last minute of extra-time. Euro '96 saw him at his very best, particularly in the penalty shoot-out against Spain where his saves put England into the semi-final. He was distraught after Ronaldinho's free-kick floated over him as England went down to Brazil in the 2002 World Cup. A year later, David James had taken over as Sven-Goran Eriksson's first-choice 'keeper. In summer 2003 Seaman left Arsenal for Manchester City after Arsene Wenger bought Jens Lehmann from Borussia Dortmund. He retired in January 2004.

Peter Shilton

around. His haul included a hat-trick against Arsenal when he was just 17. Blackburn paid £3.6 million to take him to Ewood Park in 1992, the year he made his international debut. His prolific scoring helped Blackburn to win the Championship in 1995. A year later he was top scorer with five goals at Euro '96 and that year saw him return to Newcastle, this time with a world record £15 million price tag on his head. He suffered a career-threatening injury in 1997, but bounced back to lead England at the following year's World Cup. He retired from international football with 30 goals from 63 games putting him joint fourth in the all-time list of England marksmen. In November 2002 he scored his 100th Premiership goal for Newcastle in a 5–3 defeat at Old Trafford. He thus became the first player to hit a Premiership ton with two different clubs. 2004–05 was to have been Shearer's swansong season, but with Jackie Milburn's record 178 league goals in his sights he agreed to stay on for one more season. His final attempt to bring silverware to St James's Park failed, but he did become the club's all-time leading scorer, with 206 goals. He embarked on a career as a media pundit before being persuaded to return to Newcastle as interim manager in April 2009.

Alan Shearer

Born: 13 August 1970
Clubs: Southampton, Blackburn Rovers, Newcastle United
National Team: England

In the run-up to the 2002 World Cup there was a groundswell of opinion hoping that Alan Shearer would change his mind regarding retirement from international football. Shearer had had another excellent season for Newcastle, and many thought that a Shearer–Owen partnership still represented England's best strike pairing. After another outstanding campaign in 2002–03, Shearer received a special Player of the Decade award to mark ten years of the Premiership.

A Geordie by birth, Shearer took a tortuous route back to his home town club. It was Southampton who took him from under Newcastle's nose. In his four years at The Dell, Shearer proved himself to be one of the hottest young strikers

Peter Shilton

Born: 18 September 1949
Clubs: Leicester City, Stoke City, Nottingham Forest, Southampton, Derby County
National Team: England

Peter Shilton won 125 caps for England, but his tally could have been pushing towards an incredible 200 had successive England managers in the 1970s and early 1980s not alternated between him and Ray Clemence. He began his career at Leicester City in 1966 and became the natural successor to Gordon Banks for both club and country. He played for a number of unfashionable teams, including Stoke and Derby, which wasn't to his advantage as far as winning club honours was concerned. The one exception was his five-year spell at Nottingham Forest, when Brian Clough's side won back-to-back European Cups in 1979 and 1980. At the 1982 World Cup Shilton conceded just one goal in five games, in the 3–1 win over France. Four years later he was beaten by Maradona's infamous 'Hand of God' goal and a wonder strike by the same player. He was over 40 when he went to Italia '90, helping England to a World Cup semi-final clash against Germany. Defeat on penalties meant a third place play-off match against Italy, Shilton's 125th and final appearance in an England shirt.

Allan Simonsen

Born: 15 December 1952
Clubs: Vejle, Borussia Moenchengladbach, Barcelona, Charlton Athletic
National Team: Denmark

Allan Simonsen was the outstanding Danish player of the 1970s and early 1980s. He was a hero and role model to many of the country's talented youngsters, inspiring many of the players who triumphed at the 1992 European Championship. Simonsen began his career at Vejle before having very successful spells at Borussia Moenchengladbach and Barcelona. He helped Moenchengladbach break Bayern Munich's stranglehold on the Bundesliga, winning a hat-trick of titles between 1975 and 1977. The last of those also saw the team reach the European Cup final, when Simonsen scored in the 3–1 defeat by Liverpool. There was consolation for the Dane as he was named European Footballer of the Year. In 1982 he won the European Cup Winners' Cup with Barcelona, once again getting on the scoresheet in the 2–1 win over Standard Liege. Perhaps his most important goal came at Wembley in September 1983, when his penalty gave Denmark their first ever win over England. That helped the country reach the finals of the 1984 European Championship. Unfortunately, Simonsen broke his leg in the opening match against France and he never regained his best form thereafter.

Socrates

Omar Sivori

Born: 2 October 1935
Clubs: River Plate, Juventus, Napoli
National Team: Argentina, Italy

Omar Enrique Savori was one of a number of players who relocated from South America to Italy in the 1950s and 1960s, winning international honours in both continents. In Sivori's case his star performances for River Plate in the mid-1950s persuaded Juventus to break the world record. The Turin club paid £91,000 for Sivori in 1957, beating the fee Milan had paid for Juan Schiaffino three years earlier. The transfer came at a price for this skilful inside-forward, however. Argentina refused to pick him for the national side, regarding the move as an act of disloyalty. Sivori formed a deadly partnership with John Charles at Juve, the duo providing the firepower which brought the club the championship in 1958, 1960 and 1961. He won the 1961 European Footballer of the Year award, and a year later lined up for Italy in what proved to be a disastrous World Cup campaign. Sivori also had a four-year spell at Napoli before returning to his native Argentina. He died in 2005.

Socrates

Born: 19 February 1954
Clubs: Botafogo, Corinthians, Fiorentina, Flamengo, Santos
National Team: Brazil

Socrates Brasileiro Sampaio de Souza Vieira de Oliveira came from an impoverished background, and with his parents' encouragement he studied hard in order to make something of himself. He qualified as a doctor, which gave him a ready nickname on the football field. Socrates was an elegant midfielder. His languid style belied his quick brain and perceptive passing. He came to prominence in the late 1970s playing for Corinthians, with whom he won the Sao Paulo Championship on three occasions. First capped in 1979, he led Brazil at the 1982 and 1986 World Cups. On both occasions they lost in what was thought to be the game of the tournament. In 1982 it was a 3–2 defeat by Italy, the game forever associated with Paolo Rossi's superlative performance. In Mexico four years later Brazil met European champions France in the last eight, a thrilling game worthy of the final. It ended 1–1 and Socrates was one of the unlucky players to miss from the spot in the shoot-out. Socrates won his 60th and final cap that year, ending his international career with a highly creditable 22 goals. Although he was not a World Cup winner, Socrates led a team many regard as one of the finest Brazil has ever produced. He ended his career at Santos in 1990 before joining the medical profession.

Alfredo di Stefano

Born: 4 July 1926
Clubs: River Plate, Millonarios, Barcelona, Real Madrid
National Teams: Argentina, Colombia, Spain

There are those who put Alfredo di Stefano ahead of Pele as the greatest all-round player the game has ever seen. He played in the Real Madrid side which won the European Cup the first five times it was contested, 1956–60, scoring in each of them. Nominally a centre-forward, he also dropped into deep positions to help the defence and to orchestrate the play in midfield. He thus combined individual brilliance with the ability to galvanize the entire team. He was a total footballer long before the term had been coined.

Di Stefano was born in Buenos Aires and began his playing career as a winger with River Plate at the age of 17. Following a players' strike in 1949, di Stefano joined Millonarios of Colombia in a pirate league that was outside FIFA's jurisdiction. Di Stefano was the star player, helping Millonarios to a hat-trick of titles.

It was during a tour that di Stefano came to the attention of Real Madrid and Barcelona, both of whom wanted to sign him. Real cut a deal with Millonarios, their Catalan rivals agreed terms with River Plate. The matter went to court, and in an extraordinary ruling the two clubs were ordered to share the player's services. He duly turned out for Barcelona, but made an indifferent start and the club sold their 50% interest to Real. Four days later, di Stefano hit a hat-trick – against Barcelona. Real went on to win the championship in his debut season, 1953–54. By the time di Stefano left the Bernabeu eleven years later he had helped the club to win the Spanish title eight times. He scored 428 goals in 510 games, including a record 49 in 58 European Cup ties. His crowning moment came in the 1960 final against Eintracht Frankfurt at Hampden Park. Di Stefano hit a hat-trick, while Puskas grabbed four in a stunning 7–3 victory.

Di Stefano played international football for Argentina, Colombia and Spain, but never graced a World Cup. His outstanding performances for Real earned him the European Footballer of the Year award on two occasions, in 1957 and 1959.

Alfredo di Stefano

Hristo Stoichkov

Born: 8 February 1966
Clubs: CSKA Sofia, Barcelona, Parma
National Team: Bulgaria

The temperamental but brilliant Hristo Stoichkov played a huge part in making Bulgaria a very dangerous side in the early 1990s. Having been in the doldrums in international football for many years, Bulgaria reached the semi-final at USA '94. Stoichkov was the tournament's top scorer with six goals. That achievement, together with his outstanding performances for Barcelona in the same season, earned him the 1994 European Footballer of the Year award. Stoichkov had already won a string of domestic honours in his six years with CSKA Sofia. In 1989–90 he hit 38 goals, enough to win him Europe's Golden Boot, an honour he shared with Real Madrid's Hugo Sanchez. He joined Barcelona in 1990 and spent the next eight years at the Catalan club, apart from one season at Parma. He won the Spanish title four times and appeared in two European Cup finals. In 1992 he played in the side which beat Sampdoria 1–0 at Wembley. Stoichkov rejoined CSKA in 1998 and went to the World Cup in France, but neither he nor the team could recreate the success of four years earlier.

Davor Suker

Hristo Stoichkov

Davor Suker

Born: 1 January 1968
Clubs: Osijek, Dinamo Zagreb, Seville, Real Madrid, Arsenal, West Ham, 1860 Munich
National Team: Croatia

France '98 marked Croatia's first appearance in a World Cup finals, and Davor Suker celebrated by firing six goals, helping the country to an excellent third place in the tournament. The World Cup's top scorer was then a 30-year-old veteran, having scored goals at club and international level for well over a decade. He was the Yugoslavian league's top scorer in 1989 when he was playing for Osijek. He made the squad for Italia '90 but didn't play in the team that reached the quarter-finals. In 1991, after two years at Dinamo Zagreb, he moved to Seville. Real Madrid came in for him in 1996, the year when he shone in the European Championship. His chip over Peter Schmeichel in Croatia's 3–0 win over Denmark was sublime. He also scored Croatia's goal in the 2–1 quarter-final defeat by Germany. He won the Spanish league and European Champions Cup with Real Madrid before heading for the Premiership and spells with Arsenal and West Ham.

Hakan Sukur (right)

Hakan Sukur

Born: 1 September 1971
Clubs: Sakaryaspor, Bursaspor, Galatasaray, Torino, Inter Milan, Parma, Blackburn Rovers
National Team: Turkey

It was ironic that Turkey's outstanding showing in the 2002 World Cup came in spite of Hakan Sukur, not because of him. The legendary 'Bull of the Bosphorus' had been earmarked as one of the players who would need to have a good tournament if Turkey were going to do well. In fact, Sukur played poorly throughout, yet Turkey still surprised everyone by making it to the semi-finals. Sukur joined Turkey's top club side, Galatasaray, from Bursaspor in 1992. fifty-four goals in the next three seasons made him the country's hottest striker. He had a spell at Torino but things didn't work out and he was soon back at his beloved Galatasaray. He helped the Turkish club to make the breakthrough in European competition by beating Arsenal in the UEFA Cup final of 2000. That success, together with a fine showing at Euro 2000, persuaded Inter Milan to give him another chance to show what he could do in Serie A. That association proved hardly happier than his first sojourn in Italy, and by the time the 2002 World Cup came round he was in the shop window once again. A move to Parma also turned sour, and in December 2002 Graeme Souness took him to Ewood Park. Souness knew what Sukur could do, having managed him at Galatasaray. However, Sukur struggled with injury and failed to make an impact on the Premiership and returned to Galatasaray in 2003, remaining there until his retirement at the end of the 2007–08 season. Turkey failed to reach the 2006 World Cup, though Hakan did win his hundredth cap in the qualifiers, only the third Turkish player to reach that mark. He is the all-time highest scorer in the Turkish league, with over 240 goals.

Lilian Thuram

Born: 1 January 1972
Clubs: Monaco, Parma, Juventus, Barcelona
National Team: France

Widely regarded as one of the best defenders in the game over the past decade, Lilian Thuram was one of the production line of teenage stars who came through Monaco's ranks in the late 1980s. He missed out on a European Cup Winners' Cup final appearance in 1992, when Monaco lost to Werder Bremen. By 1994 he had won his first cap and soon became a fixture in France's side. At Euro '96 he helped France reach the semi-finals. Shortly afterwards he joined Parma, where he regularly played in central defence. France's strength in that department – with the likes of Blanc, Desailly and Leboeuf – meant that at international level he invariably slotted in at full-back, thus enhancing his reputation as a supremely accomplished all-purpose defender. 1998–99 saw Thuram feature in the Parma side which beat Marseille 3–0 in the UEFA Cup final. The club picked up the Italian Cup in the same season. However, it was at the previous year's World Cup on home soil that Thuram had his finest hour. Outstanding in defence, he also scored both goals in France's 2–1 victory over Croatia in the semi-final. It was his first appearance on the scoresheet in 38 internationals. Thuram moved to Juventus for £29 million in the summer of 2001, thwarting the ambitions of long-time admirer Sir Alex Ferguson to bring the defender to Old Trafford. In his first season he helped Juve reclaim the Serie A title. In his second, 2002–03, the Turin club retained the *scudetto*, although they lost to AC Milan on penalties in the European Champions League final. Thuram came out of international retirement during France's qualifying campaign for the 2006 World Cup. He was in outstanding form during France's run to the final, and during the tournament took over from Marcel Desailly as his country's most capped player. Thuram joined Barcelona that summer, after Juve were stripped of their 2005 and 2006 league titles and relegated to Serie B for their part in a widespread corruption scandal. He announced his retirement at the end of the 2007–08 season after doctors had discovered a problem with his heart.

Lilian Thuram

Jean Tigana

Born: 23 June 1955
Clubs: Toulon, Lyon, Bordeaux, Marseille
National Team: France

Jean Tigana played in the anchor role in France's outstanding midfield of the early and mid-1980s. Alain Giresse and Michel Platini provided the creativity but Tigana's contribution towards making France Europe's most attractive and effective side was vital. Germany dashed the team's hopes at the 1982 World Cup but it all came right in the European Championship two years later. Tigana not only picked up a winners' medal in that tournament but he was also named France's Player of the Year as his club side, Bordeaux, lifted the domestic championship. Tigana, who was born in Mali, played his best football in his late 20s and early 30s. He ended his international career in 1988, by which time he had won over 50 caps. He made an impressive transition into management, notably guiding Monaco to the French Championship in 1997, but failed to make the same impact in the Premiership with Fulham.

Jean Tigana

Tostao

Born: 25 January 1947
Clubs: Cruzeiro, Vasco da Gama
National Team: Brazil

Eduardo Goncalvez Andrade paraded his considerable skills under the name Tostao. In the mid-1960s the teenage centre-forward was dubbed the 'White Pele', a tag he proceeded to live up to in style. He made his international debut in 1966 during Brazil's disappointing World Cup campaign in England. Four years later he was in his prime as a member of the side which not only won the Jules Rimet Trophy in Mexico but which many regard as the greatest of all time. Tostao was top scorer in the qualifiers, hitting nine goals in six games. At the tournament itself the ace goalscorer showed that he was an excellent provider too. In a tight group match against England, which was generally thought to be a rehearsal for the final, Tostao's clever play in the inside-left channel was followed by a deft pass to Pele, who in turn set up Jairzinho for the game's only goal. Tostao retired prematurely, concerned about risking permanent damage to an eye which had sustained a detached retina. In just six years in the famous yellow shirt he won 51 caps, scoring 29 goals.

Carlos Valderrama

Born: 2 September 1961
Clubs: Union Magdalena, Millonarios, Montpellier, Real Vallodolid, Deportiva Independiente Medollin, Atletico Junios, Mutiny
National Team: Colombia

With his mane of frizzy blond hair, Carlos Valderrama was one of the most distinctive figures on the world football stage in the 1980s and 1990s. He was also the driving force in what was regarded as the most talented Colombia side in the country's history. Creative, inventive and with marvellous ball skills, Valderrama was voted South American Player of the Year in 1987, while playing for Atletico Nacional. He moved to Europe the following year but failed to make an impact with either Montpellier or Valladolid and returned to his home country in 1992. Valderrama was first capped in 1985 and was still playing international football thirteen years later at France '98, when he was 37. He helped Colombia reach the second round at Italia '90 and was in sensational form in the run-up to USA '94. He won his second South American Player of the Year award on the strength of his performances, though the team overall disappointed in the tournament. Valderrama was one of the high-profile recruits to Major League Soccer when it got off the ground in 1996.

Marco Van Basten

Carlos Valderrama

Marco Van Basten

Born: 31 October 1964
Clubs: Ajax, AC Milan
National Team: Holland

Marco Van Basten joined a very exclusive club in 1992, becoming the third player to win the European Footballer of the Year award three times. Only Johan Cruyff and Michel Platini had achieved that feat since the inception of the award in 1956. In 1992 he was also named FIFA's World Player of the Year. Van Basten was prevented from adding to a sizeable bank of individual and team honours by an ankle injury, which forced him into premature retirement in 1995. Van Basten began his career at Ajax, making his debut as a substitute for his boyhood hero Johan Cruyff. He scored 128 goals in five years, firing the Amsterdam club to three domestic championships. His 37 goals in 1985–86 won him the golden boot award. Van Basten captained the side and scored the winning goal against Lokomotiv Leipzig in the 1987 Cup Winners' Cup final. A month later he joined AC Milan, where he was part of a powerful Dutch axis with Ruud Gullit and Frank Rijkaard. Milan won the Serie A title in his first season at the club, followed by back-to-back victories in the Champions Cup. Van Basten scored twice in a devastating 4–0 win over Steaua Bucharest in 1989. His 57 appearances for Holland in a nine-year international career yielded 23 goals. The most famous of these came in the final of the 1988 European Championship against the USSR, a stunning volley from an impossible angle in Holland's 2–0 victory. Van Basten took over from Dick Advocaat as Holland coach in 2004, though his first major tournament, Germany 2006, ended in a disappointing 1–0 defeat by Portugal in the last 16. He took the team one round further at Euro 2008 before returning to club management with Ajax.

Gianluca Vialli

Gianluca Vialli

Born: 9 July 1964
Clubs: Cremonese, Sampdoria, Juventus, Chelsea
National Team: Italy

In his 16 years in Italian football Gianluca Vialli established himself as one of the country's all-time greats. He began his career at Cremonese but it was in his eight-year spell at Sampdoria that he really rose to prominence. He formed a potent strike partnership with Roberto Mancini, helping the Genovese club to become the main threat to the mighty AC Milan side of the late 1980s. Sampdoria won the Italian

Cup in 1988 and 1989, then made it to successive European Cup Winners' Cup finals, lifting the trophy in 1990. Vialli hit both goals in a 2–0 win over Anderlecht. Following defeat to Barcelona in the 1992 European Cup final, Vialli moved to Juventus. He picked up a UEFA Cup winners' medal in his first season, Juve beating Borussia Dortmund in the 1993 final. He helped the Turin club to a domestic Double in 1995, then completed his collection of major club honours by captaining Juve to European Cup victory over Ajax the following year. He joined Chelsea the same year. Early in 1998 he became player-manager at Stamford Bridge, following the sacking of Ruud Gullit. Within a matter of weeks he had picked up two trophies, the Coca-Cola Cup and the European Cup Winners' Cup. After leaving Stamford Bridge, he had a season in charge at Watford. Vialli was capped 59 times for Italy, scoring 16 goals.

Rudi Voller

Born: 13 April 1960
Clubs: Kickers, 1860 Munich, Werder Bremen, Roma, Marseilles, Bayer Leverkusen
National Teams: Germany

Rudi Voller's 47 goals in 90 internationals put him joint-second in Germany's all-time list of scorers, behind Gerd Müller. Voller shares second place with Juergen Klinsmann, but his goals-per-game record is far better, his haul coming from 18 fewer games. The 1982–83 season was an important launchpad for the young striker's career. His 23 goals helped Werder Bremen to the Bundesliga title. He was the league's top marksman and picked up the Player of the Year award. He won his first cap, under Jupp Derwall, and went on to play in consecutive World Cup finals during Franz Beckenbauer's tenure as national team boss. In the 1986 final against Argentina a Voller goal helped West Germany recover from a 2–0 deficit before finally going down 3–2. Four years later in Italy he and Holland's Frank Rijkaard were sent off during an ill-tempered clash in the last sixteen. Voller went on to play a key part in West Germany's victory in the final, once again against Argentina. He was brought down by Sensini six minutes from time and Brehme scored from the spot, the only goal of the game. Voller was still there at USA

Rudi Voller

Wenger's Monaco in 1988. He won the domestic championship there in 1991, before moving on to Paris St-Germain the following year. He starred in a team which included David Ginola and Rai in winning the 1994 championship. He moved on to AC Milan for £3.5 million, and even the famously mean Serie A defences couldn't contain his explosive shooting. He won two Italian Championships with Milan before winding down his career at Chelsea and Manchester City.

George Weah

'94. He hit a brace in the 3–2 win over Belgium in the last sixteen but when Germany crashed to Bulgaria in the quarters it finally rang down the curtain on an illustrious career. In 2000 he was appointed Germany's team boss and made an immediate impact, taking an unfancied side to the final of the 2002 World Cup but he was replaced by Klinsmann in 2004.

George Weah

Born: 1 October 1966
Clubs: Tonnerre Yaounde, Monaco, Paris St-Germain, AC Milan, Chelsea, Manchester City
National Team: Liberia

It may not be the greatest accolade to describe George Weah as the greatest footballer that Liberia has ever produced, but in the 1990s he was one of the most feared strikers in the game, and in 1995 won the ultimate individual honour when he was named World Footballer of the Year. In the same year he won his third African Footballer of the Year award, and completed a famous hat-trick by also being named Europe's top player. Weah began to make his mark at the highest level after leaving Cameroon side Tonerre Yaounde to join Arsene

Billy Wright

Born: 6 February 1924
Clubs: Wolverhampton Wanderers
National Team: England

Billy Wright made his debut for Wolves in 1941 and by 1947 he had taken on the captaincy, a role he filled for twelve seasons. The 1950s were the glory years for Wolverhampton Wanderers and Wright was one of their heroes. He led the team to three championships in six years and FA Cup victory in 1949.

The first player to reach the landmark hundred caps for his country, Wright was a true football superstar. He captained England in 90 of his 105 appearances, which included the World Cup tournaments of 1950, 1954 and 1958. When Wolves celebrated their famous victory over the Hungarian superstars Honved, Wright enjoyed a measure of revenge, having been in the England side that was thrashed by the Hungarians 6–3 at Wembley in 1953. In 1959 he married Joy Beverly of the Beverly Sisters, making them the Posh and Becks of their day. Wright retired from league football in 1959 and after a brief spell in management became a broadcaster and pundit. He died in 1994.

Billy Wright

Lev Yashin

Born: 22 October 1929
Clubs: Moscow Dynamo
National Team: Soviet Union

Lev Yashin was the world's premier goalkeeper in the 1950s and 1960s, with only Gordon Banks challenging his supremacy during the latter part of his long illustrious career. Yashin spent his entire career at Moscow Dynamo, whom he joined in 1949. By 1954 he was not only established as the club's first choice 'keeper but had also made the international jersey his own. He played in the Soviet side which won the 1956 Olympic title, and was one of their star performers when the country made its World Cup debut two years later. In the inaugural European Championship in 1960 he picked up a winners' medal as the Soviet Union beat Yugoslavia 2–1 in the final. In 1963 he received the top individual honour in the game at the time, the European Footballer of the Year award. He remains the only goalkeeper ever to receive that honour. Yashin was in the side which made it to the quarter-finals of the 1962 World Cup, and was in outstanding form four years later when the team reached the last four. The USSR went down 2–1 to West Germany but it would have been a much heavier defeat had it not been for Yashin's performance. He was over 40 by the time he retired in 1970, and had a record 78 caps to his name. He died in 1990.

Zico

Zico

Born: 3 March 1953
Clubs: Flamengo, Udinese, Kashmir Antlers
National Team: Brazil

Known as the White Pele, Zico was one of the stars of the great Brazil side of the early 1980s. Most people's favourites to lift the 1982 World Cup in Spain, Brazil went out after a 3–2 defeat by Italy in the second round. Zico had suffered ill-luck four years earlier too. His header from a Nelinho corner would have given Brazil a 2–1 win over Sweden, but referee Clive Thomas blew for full-time before the ball crossed the line. Brazil still progressed to the second round, where they lost to Argentina on goal difference for a place in the final. Zico's third attempt at World Cup success came in 1986, when he missed a penalty in the quarter-final shoot-out against France. Zico spent 20 years at Flamengo, the club he joined as a teenager. The highlight came in 1981, when he hit 11 goals as the club won the Copa Libertadores, South America's premier cup competition. He was outstanding in Flamengo's 3–0 demolition of Liverpool in the World Club Cup in the same year. Zico's only foray into European football came in a spell at Udinese between 1983 and 1985. It was during his time in Italy that he was named World Footballer of the Year. He rounded off his career with Kashima Antlers in Japan, one of the superstars who helped to get the J-League off the ground. He took over from Philippe Troussier as Japan's coach in 2002, but the team failed to win a match at Germany 2006 and Zico was soon on his way to Fenerbahce. He won the domestic league in 2007 and took Fenerbahce to the last eight of the Champions League the following season. After a short spell in Uzbekistan, Zico took over the managerial reins at CSKA Moscow in January 2009.

Zinedine Zidane

Born: 23 June 1972
Clubs: Cannes, Bordeaux, Juventus, Real Madrid
National Team: France

Born in Marseille in 1972, Zinedine Zidane began his career at Cannes as a teenager. He scored his first league goal aged just 17 and that same season Cannes qualified for a place in the UEFA Cup tournament. After an inauspicious second season he decided to move to Bordeaux and while there he came to the attention of the manager of the French national side. His first international game came in 1994, where he scored against the Czech Republic. With Zidane as their striker, Bordeaux qualified for the UEFA Cup, eventually

making it to the final. The success came at a cost to Zidane's international career. Exhausted following the gruelling season, his performance during the European Championships that year was disappointing.

However, Zidane had made an impression on the world and Juventus bought him for £3 million. His artistic flair with the ball flourished at the Italian club and they won the *scudetto* in 1997 and 1998. At the World Cup France 1998, Zidane was outstanding, his performance completely overwriting that of the previous tournament. He headed the two goals that defeated Brazil in the final, sealing victory for France. Two years later the French won the European Championships and Zidane received the accolade of World Footballer of the Year in recognition of those achievements.

Zinedine Zidane

Zidane was naturally coveted by other big-name clubs, and when he expressed an interest in leaving Juventus, the cheque books came out. Juve did not want to lose their star, but when Real Madrid paid an incredible £48 million they were adequately compensated.

In 2002, Real won the European Champions League with a goal by Zidane, but his World Cup performance at Japan and Korea was hampered by injury and France made an early exit.

In 2003 Zidane was again named World Footballer of the Year, the third time he had won the award.

He came out of international retirement to bolster France's flagging Germany 2006 qualifying campaign. Having announced that the tournament would be his swansong, Zidane looked as though he might go out on a high. He scored three goals, including the penalty which put France ahead against Italy in the final. His sorcery had earned him the Golden Ball, awarded to the player of the tournament. It all went horribly wrong as he was red-carded for reacting to a remark by Azzurri defender Marco Materazzi, and had to be content with a runners-up medal as France lost the match on penalties. The rapturous reception he received on returning home showed that the fans were in no mood to condemn a moment of folly; instead they gave their appreciation for the greatest player of his era.

Dino Zoff

Born: 28 February 1942
Clubs: Udinese, Mantova, Napoli, Juventus
National Team: Italy

At the age of 40 Dino Zoff captained Italy in their finest hour of the postwar era, victory over West Germany in the 1982 World Cup final. Paolo Rossi took a lot of the plaudits as Italy memorably saw off favourites Brazil in the second round and West Germany in the final. But the veteran goalkeeper played a huge part in the victorious campaign, the crowning moment of a hugely successful career. Zoff had spells with Udinese and Mantova, but came to prominence when he joined Napoli in 1967. He won his first cap the following year, when Italy won the European Championship. After a move to Juventus in 1972 the silverware began rolling in. Over the next eleven years he won six domestic championships and picked up a UEFA Cup winners' medal in 1977, when Juve beat Atletico Bilbao. In the early 1970s he set a landmark 1143 minutes unbeaten in Italy's goal. Zoff retired in 1983 with 112 caps to his name, a record which was subsequently beaten by Paolo Maldini. He later made a successful transition into management, and came within 20 seconds of leading Italy to victory at Euro 2000.

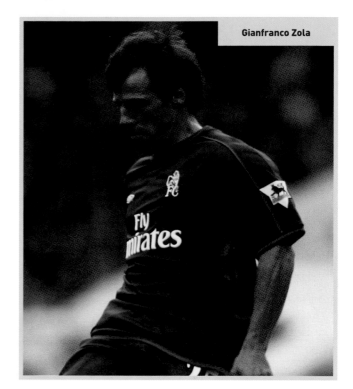
Gianfranco Zola

Dino Zoff

Gianfranco Zola

Born: 5 July 1966
Clubs: Nuorese, Torres, Napoli, Parma, Chelsea, Cagliari
National Team: Italy

In 1996 Chelsea paid Parma £4.5 million to acquire the services of 30-year-old Gianfranco Zola. There was criticism over the number of foreign stars who were coming to the Premiership when they were well past their best. In his seven years at Stamford Bridge Zola proved himself to be one of the glorious exceptions. He graced English football with his exuberant talent, marvellous inventiveness and impeccable behaviour, and his appetite for the game remained undiminished. Even in his mid-30s the little maestro continued to tear around the pitch with the zest of a teenager. Zola was at Napoli in the 1980s when Diego Maradona was the team's – and the world's – undisputed number one player. He emerged from Maradona's shadow when he moved on to Parma, but probably played some of his best football in the Premiership. He picked up the 1997 Footballer of the Year award and a year later came off the bench to score the goal that beat Stuttgart in the European Cup Winners' Cup final. He signed off from Chelsea at the end of the 2002–03 season, and wound down his career back in Italy with Cagliari, retiring in 2005. Zola began his coaching career with Italy's U-21 side, making a sensational return to the Premiership as West Ham boss in September 2008

Heroes
of the
Modern Game

Emmanuel Adebayor

Born: 26 February 1984
Clubs: Metz, AS Monaco, Arsenal
National Team: Togo

Many Arsenal fans tuned in to the 2006 African Cup of Nations to see Arsene Wenger's latest acquisition in action. Togo's star player, Emmanuel Adebayor, had signed from Monaco just before the tournament got under way, though the competition itself was more noteworthy for a public spat with the coach than the player's artistry on the pitch. Adebayor had gained a reputation for being abrasive, having fallen out with Monaco and also left his previous club, Metz, under a cloud. He made his debut for Metz at 17, but came to prominence when he scored 7 goals in 17 matches to help propel Didier Deschamps' Monaco to the 2004 Champions League final. While some of the clubs reportedly tracking his progress may have been deterred, Wenger chose to focus on Adebayor's obvious talent when he paid a fee of around £7 million to get a player admirably equipped to be the long-term successor to Thierry Henry. Evidence of that came six months after his becoming a Gunner, when the tall, rangy Adebayor led the line for Togo in their first ever appearance at the World Cup finals. His 11 goals in the qualifiers made him the Africa zone's sharpest shooter, though he couldn't prevent Togo from being eliminated at the group stage. Over the next year, Adebayor proved himself to be a fine understudy to Henry, though in physique and style he was likened to former Arsenal favourite, Kanu. The Nigerian striker was Adebayor's boyhood hero, and when he signed for Arsenal he opted to take the number 25 shirt that Kanu had worn with such distinction. Following Henry's departure in summer 2007, Adebayor took over the role of Arsenal's number one striker, breaking the 20-goal barrier with three months of the 2007-08 season still to run.

Michael Ballack

Born: 29 September 1976
Clubs: BSG Motor Karl-Marx-Stadt, Chemnitzer FC, Kaiserslautern, Bayer Leverkusen, Bayern Munich, Chelsea
National Team: Germany

Michael Ballack joined Bayern Munich in a fanfare of publicity in the summer of 2002. The hottest property in German football, he had been hugely influential in Bayer Leverkusen's run to the Champions League final, where they went down to Real Madrid. He had also enjoyed an outstanding World Cup, helping an unheralded Germany side to make it to the final. Ballack was seen as the man to pull the strings at Bayern, taking over the mantle of Stefan Effenberg. It didn't quite work out that way, however. The 2001 European champions crashed out of the 2002–03 tournament at the first hurdle. Even so, few doubted Bayern's decision to make Ballack their playmaker. Ballack was born in East Germany and signed for Chemnitz at the age of 14. It was Kaiserslautern who spotted his potential and gave him the chance to play in the Bundesliga. His meteoric rise was briefly halted in 1999 when he fell out with coach Otto Rehhagel. He found himself kicking his heels on the bench all too often. Bayer Leverkusen broke the deadlock by agreeing a £3 million fee with Kaiserslautern. Ballack was close to becoming a free agent under the Bosman rule, but Leverkusen were so keen to get their man that they decided to pay the fee. It proved to be a bargain price. However, even though he was on a long-term contract, a clause allowed other clubs to talk to him if they were prepared to offer £8 million. Bayern did just that. In summer 2006 Ballack became a free agent under the Bosman ruling and Chelsea moved quickly to add another world class midfielder to their squad.

Michael Ballack (right)

Emmanuel Adebayor

David Beckham

Born: 2 May 1975
Clubs: Manchester United, Real Madrid, LA Galaxy, AC Milan (loan)
National Team: England

David Beckham has possibly the most recognised face in football. His image sponsors a multitude of products, his sartorial style sparks controversy and his hair styles influence trends across the globe. However, Beckham is also a talented footballer, whose dedication to his sport has won him honours, admiration and the captaincy of England.

The spotlight first rested on the Leytonstone-born player in 1996. Although Alex Ferguson had signed Beckham as a school boy back in 1992, he wasn't playing for the Manchester United first team properly until 1995. In 1996 Beckham's goal-scoring ability became apparent. He hit the

David Beckham

winner in the FA Cup semi-final against Chelsea in a season when United went on to win the Double. The following season, in a match against Wimbledon, the midfielder scored a spectacular goal from the halfway line, a feat that had eluded even Pele. His performances on the field, combined with his marriage to Victoria 'Posh Spice' Adams, confirmed Beckham's regular appearance in the tabloids, if not always on the back pages.

Beckham's international career began in 1996, when Glenn Hoddle selected him to play against Moldova. Following his disastrous exit from the 1998 World Cup, many believed that his days as an England player were over, but he proved them wrong. His sending off for kicking Diego Simone in the clash with Argentina meant that for a while he was reviled by English fans everywhere, but Beckham continued to play top level football and by the 2002 World Cup he had become England's hero. Beckham's trademark, the curling free-kick, provided the last-minute goal against Greece that assured England of a place at the tournament. Under his leadership, England got to the quarter-finals, only to be beaten by the eventual winners, Brazil. Beckham also finally got his revenge against Argentina by scoring the high-pressure penalty that eventually knocked the South Americans out.

During eleven years with Manchester United, Beckham received a host of medals. He was a key member of the Treble-winning side of 1998–99 and in 2001 was there when United won their third consecutive Championship title. His relationship with United came to an end in 2003, when he signed for Real Madrid amid speculation of a rift with Sir Alex Ferguson.

After leading England to the quarter-finals at Germany 2006, Beckham announced that he was giving up the captaincy, though he insisted he still wanted to further his international career.

New England coach Steve McClaren said Beckham didn't figure in his plans, but the midfielder was recalled to the international fold as England's Euro 2008 campaign faltered. Many thought Beckham's summer 2007 move to MLS side LA Galaxy, a five-year deal worth a reputed £120 million, would signal the end of his international career on 99 caps. Under his former Madrid coach Fabio Capello he not only became the fifth member of the 100 club, but at the beginning of 2009 stood one cap short of Booby Moore's 108 mark, the record for an outfield player. His hopes of overhauling the World Cup-winning captain were boosted by a loan deal to AC Milan in January 2009. Initially a short-term arrangement, the clubs eventually thrashed out a deal by which Beckham would turn out for both through to South Africa 2010.

Dimitar Berbatov

Born: 30 January 1981
Clubs: CSKA Sofia, Bayer Leverkusen, Tottenham Hotspur, Manchester United
National Team: Bulgaria

Following their club's salutary experience with Sergei Rebrov, many Spurs fans probably held their breath when Martin Jol paid Bayer Leverkusen £11 million for another East European striker with a big reputation in July 2006. Their fears soon evaporated, for Dimitar Berbatov scored within minutes of his home debut and quickly established himself as a cult figure at White Hart Lane. It wasn't just the Bulgarian's healthy strike rate they admired – though he would hit the back of the net 46 times at almost a goal every other game over the next two seasons. It was the panache he showed on the pitch, sublime touches that created numerous scoring opportunities for others and an air of unhurried majesty reminiscent of Cantona at his mercurial best.

Berbatov began his career with his local club Pirin Blagoevgrad, the team for which his father Ivan had played. And like his father, Berbatov was soon spotted by CSKA Sofia, making his debut for Bulgaria's premier club side at 18. A prolific start to the 2000–01 campaign persuaded Bayer Leverkusen to open their chequebook in the January transfer window. The following year the Bundesliga side surprised many by reaching the Champions League final, beating Liverpool and Manchester United in the knockout stage before succumbing to Real Madrid in the final. Michael Ballack was Leverkusen's star player at the time, Berbatov having to content himself with a place on the bench for the clash with Zidane and Co. It was the following season when he cemented his place in the side, and in 2003–04 he took the eye with 16 goals from 24 starts. Two further productive seasons in the Bundesliga brought the two-time Bulgarian Footballer of the Year to the attention of a host of European clubs, but Spurs stole a march on the other interested parties by getting his signature. A domestic cup winners' medal gained with CSKA was the sole piece of silverware on Berbatov's mantelpiece when he took his Premiership bow, but he added the League Cup to his haul in 2007–08, scoring from the spot in Spurs 2–1 win over Chelsea. The

partnership he struck up with Robbie Keane was much admired, yet Spurs remained anchored in mid-table. As the campaign drew to a close it became clear that 11th place in the Premiership didn't match Berbatov's ambitions, and his £30.75 million move to Old Trafford that summer was one of football's worst kept secrets. Berbatov is captain of the national side, but the heady days in which Hristo Stoitchkov led the side to the semis of the 1994 World Cup are long gone. In the past decade the only major tournament for which Bulgaria qualified was Euro 2004, and there the team made a swift exit after losing all three group games.

Dimitar Berbatov

Sol Campbell

Born: 18 September 1974
Clubs: Tottenham Hotspur, Arsenal, Portsmouth
National Team: England

Sulzeer Jeremiah Campbell not only starred for England at France '98 and Japan and Korea 2002 but was impressive enough to secure a place in FIFA's 'team of the tournament' on both occasions. Campbell joined Spurs as a 14-year-old, making his league debut at 19, under Terry Venables. It was Venables who brought him into the international fold in 1996, and since then his rock-like performances have earned him over 50 caps. In 1998, during Glenn Hoddle's reign, Campbell became the youngest England captain since Bobby Moore.

For a number of years Campbell was the jewel in the crown of a Spurs side whose trophy cabinet was hardly bursting. There was a Coca Cola Cup victory in 1999, but Campbell's ambitions went beyond that. His decision to move to arch-rivals Arsenal when his contract expired in the spring of 2001 provoked anger among die-hard Spurs fans. Campbell won the Double with the Gunners in his first season, but missed out as Arsenal retained the Cup in 2003, beating Southampton in the final. He had received a four-match ban, following an elbowing incident involving Ole Gunnar Solskjaer. Many put Arsenal's stuttering performances in those three vital league matches — which effectively handed the title back to Manchester United — down to Campbell's absence. He suffered personal problems and loss of form during the 2005–06 season, but scored in the Champions League final defeat against Barcelona and played a part in England's run to the World Cup quarter-finals in Germany. Having become the first English player to feature in six major tournaments, Campbell left Arsenal for a fresh challenge at Portsmouth in summer 2006.

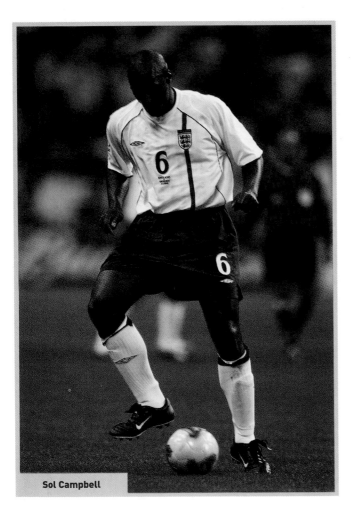

Sol Campbell

Fabio Cannavaro

Born: 13 September 1973
Clubs: Napoli, Parma, Inter Milan, Juventus, Real Madrid
National Team: Italy

2006 was an extraordinary year of highs and lows for Fabio Cannavaro. Having helped Juventus secure back-to-back Serie A titles, he captained Italy to their fourth World Cup success, winning his 100th cap in the shoot-out victory over France in the final. Cannavaro had been impeccable, giving fully committed performances for over 11 hours yet he didn't pick up a single card. He was instrumental in Italy's remarkable record of shipping just two goals in their seven matches. Cannavaro was voted second to Zidane in the Golden Ball awards for player of the tournament, though they were awarded at half-time in the final, before the French maestro's indiscretion.

It was down to earth with a bump as the fall-out from the corruption scandal that rocked Italian football that summer saw Juve stripped of their two most recent scudetti, and the club was also relegated to Serie B. The 'Old Lady' suffered a player exodus which included their outstanding centre-back, who at 33 realized that he could ill afford the time it would take for the club to return to top European action. Cannavaro joined Real Madrid, where he was reunited with former Juventus coach Fabio Capello. By the end of the year he was back on top of the world — literally — as he was named European and World Footballer of the Year. No defender had ever won the Fifa award, and the Uefa honour had been almost exclusively the preserve of midfielders and strikers since its inception in 1956.

Fabio Cannavaro

his seven years there, Parma enjoyed the best spell in its history, finishing runner-up to Juventus in Serie A in 1996–7, and two years later recording a domestic cup-Uefa Cup double. During this period Cannavaro was a rock at the back, his performances recognised by a hat-trick of Migliore Difensore awards, given to the country's top defender. He received that honour again in 2005, his first year at Juventus after a two-season spell at Inter Milan.

First capped in 1997, Cannavaro suffered a string of disappointments on the international stage prior to 2006, notably defeats against France at the 1998 World Cup and in the final of Euro 2000. He took over the Azzurri captaincy from Paolo Maldini after the 2002 World Cup, and currently lies third in the all-time list of capped players, behind Maldini and Dino Zoff.

Roberto Carlos

Born: 10 April 1973
Clubs: Uniao Sao Joao, Palmeiras, Inter Milan, Real Madrid, Fenerbahce
National Team: Brazil

The summer of 2002 saw Roberto Carlos pick up a European Champions League winners medal with Real Madrid, then repeat the achievement with Brazil in the World Cup a few weeks later. During the tournament the speedy, explosive left-back confirmed that he was the best in the world in his position. Roberto Carlos's attacking instincts were formed in his early days at Palmeiras, when he played up front. In 1995 he joined Inter Milan, where he was often played in midfield. He wasn't happy there, and moved to Real Madrid the following year. For a decade he has been a fixture in a Real side which has become synonymous with success and style. In that time he has won the Primera Liga three times, and also picked up three European Champions League winners medals. In 1997 he was narrowly beaten by his international teammate Ronaldo for the World Footballer of the Year award. Roberto Carlos was a 19-year-old fringe player at the 1994 World Cup. He was a fixture in the side four years later, when Brazil disappointed in the final against France. He helped his country put that defeat behind them by winning the 2002 tournament in fine style. Roberto Carlos announced his international retirement after Brazil's defeat by France in the quarter-final of the 2006 World Cup and a year later he joined Fenerbahce, bringing to an end a glittering decade as a Galactico.

Cannavaro began his career with his hometown club Napoli, though in the post-Maradona era they were a rather ordinary mid-table side. Napoli cashed in on one of their bright young stars in 1995, selling Cannavaro to Parma. In

Iker Casillas

Born: 20 May 1981
Clubs: Real Madrid
National Team: Spain

Longevity is not a word commonly associated with the Bernabeu Stadium. Sky-high expectations and impatience for success has often meant a rapid turnover of players and managers. Along with the legendary Raul, one man who has bucked the trend and been a fixture at Real Madrid for a decade is goalkeeper Iker Casillas. The number of managers he has served under runs into double figures, and he is well on the way to reaching the 500-game milestone. And yet because his Bernabeu baptism came when he was still in his teens, Casillas is, arguably, still to reach his peak. He came through the club's youth ranks in the 1990s, and by the end of the decade, aged 18, had relegated Germany international Bodo Illgner to the bench. It was a golden period for the Galacticos, and Casillas had a Champions League winners' medal to his name at the tender age of 19 as Real Madrid routed Valencia in the 2000 final. A dip in form meant he lost his place to Cesar Sanchez during the 2001–02 season, when Real again reached the Champions League final. Injury to Sanchez meant that Casillas got some game time and was able to celebrate the 2–1 victory over Bayer Leverkusen, courtesy of a stunning Zidane volley. As that side was broken up, Real went through a relatively lean time as arch-rivals Barcelona enjoyed a spell in the limelight. But in 2007 Casillas won his third La Liga championship medal, and added another a year later. 2008 was an annus mirabilis for Casillas, who also captained Spain to victory in the European Championship, ending a 44-year run without a major trophy and silencing those who tagged the Iberian giants as the great underachievers of world football.

Petr Cech

Born: 20 May 1982
Clubs: Viktoria Plzen, FK Chmel Blsany, Sparta Prague, Rennes, Chelsea
National Team: Czech Republic

Petr Cech's form in his debut season for Chelsea was a key factor in the club's title-winning campaign of 2004–05. While rivals Manchester United and Arsenal rang the changes between the sticks, none of their four 'keepers looking totally secure, Chelsea were able to field arguably the top shot-stopper in world football. Cech conceded just 15 goals in the Premiership, beating Arsenal's Premiership record, and going one better than Liverpool's postwar mark of 16, although that was in the 42-match era. The two goals Cech picked out of the back of the net in the 2–2 draw at Highbury on 12 December 2004 were the last until 5 March, Leon McKenzie scoring in Chelsea's 3–1 win over Norwich. Cech had gone 1025 minutes without conceding, a new Premiership best. Cech began his career at his home-town club, Viktoria Plzen, and also had a spell with FK Chmel Blsany, for whom he made his debut as a 17-year-old. But it was at Sparta Prague, whom he joined for £460,000 in 2001, where he made his name. He set a new national record, going 855 minutes without conceding, and also began his Champions League career by shutting out holders Bayern Munich. After just one season at Sparta his

Petr Cech

value increased to £3.3 million, the fee Rennes paid in July 2002. The French club was not challenging for top honours in his two seasons there, but Cech helped a struggling team to mid-table respectability, and to the semi-final of the domestic cup. On the international front, Cech starred in the Czech side which won the UEFA U-21 championship in 2002. He kept a clean sheet against a dangerous France team in the final, then saved twice in the shoot-out. He made his debut for the senior side the same year. With four more clean sheets in the eight Euro 2004 qualifiers, Cech made an important contribution as the Czech Republic topped a group including Holland. In Portugal the team surprisingly went down to Greece in the semis, but Cech's performances earned him a place in UEFA's squad of the tournament. His £7 million move to Chelsea was sealed early in 2004, though he didn't move to Stamford Bridge until the end of the season. In Carlo Cudicini Chelsea already had one of the top Premiership 'keepers, but Cech's form in back-to-back title-winning campaigns showed that he had the potential to dominate between the sticks in a way not seen since the Peter Schmeichel era at Manchester United. Cech suffered a fractured skull in a game at Reading early in the 2006–07 season, which sidelined him for three months. Since then, he has worn a rugby-style headguard, making him a distinctive as well as distinguished figure in the modern game.

Hernan Crespo

Hernan Crespo

Born: 5 July 1975
Clubs: River Plate, Parma, Lazio, Inter Milan, Chelsea, AC Milan (loan), Inter Milan (loan), Inter Milan
National Team: Argentina

Hernan Crespo is one one of the most prolific marksmen of the modern era, averaging a goal every other game in a career which has seen him ply his finishing skills in Argentina, Italy and the Premiership. Crespo started out at River Plate, with whom he won the national championship and the coveted Copa Libertadores, South America's equivalent of the Champions League. He scored both goals in the 2–1 aggregate victory over America de Cali in the final of the latter competition. That was in 1996, by which time he was keen to test himself in a top European league. He joined Parma, winning the UEFA Cup and the Coppa Italia in his two seasons at the club. He opened the scoring in the final of the former competition, Parma running out 3–0 winners over Marseille. Lazio paid a world record £36 million to acquire his services in 2000, and Crespo repaid the club by hitting 26 goals, making him Serie A's top scorer. After a season at Inter Milan, where he replaced Real Madrid-bound Ronaldo, Crespo became one of Chelsea's high-profile recruits. He hit 12 goals, but failed to settle in London and new Chelsea boss Jose Mourinho allowed him to return to Italy in a season-long loan deal with AC Milan.

Crespo was in fine form in 2004–05, and when he scored twice in the first half of the Champions League final against Liverpool, he must have thought he had added another piece of silverware to his haul. The Steven Gerrard-inspired comeback robbed him of that, but Crespo had confirmed his reputation as one of the game's best poachers, and Chelsea welcomed him back with open arms. He showed better form in his second stint in English football, helping Chelsea to retain their Premiership crown though he was allowed to return to Italy in another loan deal, this time with Inter. That deal was made permanent after Chelsea released him in summer 2008. Crespo was first capped in 1995, Germany 2006 marking his third appearance in the World Cup finals.

Deco

Born: 27 August 1977
Clubs: Nacional, Corinthians, Benfica, Alverca (loan), Salgueiros, Porto, Barcelona, Chelsea
National Team: Portugal

Deco pulled all the strings in Porto's 3–2 victory over Glasgow Celtic in the 2003 UEFA Cup final. A year later he picked up a Champions League winners medal as Porto beat Monaco 3–0, the team having put out Manchester United en route to the final. Deco – or 'Magico' as he was dubbed by the fans – was one of the stars of the side, coveted by many of Europe's top clubs. He was rumoured to be on his way to Stamford Bridge, along with his manager Jose Mourinho, but Barcelona eventually won the race for his signature. Fears that the Catalan team could not accommodate both his and Ronaldinho's extravagant playmaking skills, and that he might be overshadowed by the Brazilian ace, proved unfounded as Barca went on to win back-to-back Primera Liga titles. Deco and Ronaldinho might also have been international teammates, had Brazil not allowed the pocket-sized schemer to slip through the net. He played for Brazilian sides Nacional and Corinthians before joining Benfica as a 19-year-old. The Lisbon club loaned him out to second division side Alverca, and on his return there was a contractual dispute which resulted in a move to Salgueiros. His performances there took the eye of Porto, who signed him in the winter transfer window of 1998–99. He eventually became eligible for Portugal under the residence rule, though there were some dissenting voices when he made his international debut in 2003, Luis Figo among them. Ironically, Brazil provided the opposition when he won his first cap, and it must have given him extra satisfaction when he came off the bench and hit the winner from a 25-yard free kick. Having won league titles in Portugal and Spain, the UEFA Cup and Champions League, with both Porto and Barcelona, Deco has already accumulated an impressive medal haul, though he and Portugal did have to settle for the runners-up spot when the team went down to Greece in the Euro 2004 final. New Chelsea boss Luiz Felipe Scolari showed how highly he rated the player he coached during his time in charge of Portugal by making Deco his first acquisition when he took over at Stamford Bridge in summer 2008.

Deco

Alessandro del Piero

Born: 9 November 1974

Clubs: Padova, Juventus

National Team: Italy

In the mid-1990s Alessandro del Piero took over Roberto Baggio's mantle as the golden boy of Italian football. He began his career at Padova, moving to Juventus in 1993. He has now notched up 15 years at the Turin club, a marvellous achievement in an era more noted for rapid turnover and lack of loyalty. In 1995, when he was still just 20, he inspired Juve to a League and Cup double. A glorious Treble proved a hurdle too far as Juve went down to Parma in the UEFA Cup final. Del Piero became Juve's undisputed star player. There were two more Serie A titles and a European Champions League triumph over Ajax in 1996. Juve also reached the final of the European Champions League in the following two years, but lost out to Borussia Dortmund and Real Madrid respectively. Del Piero made his international debut in 1995 during the qualifying series for Euro '96. Hampered by injury, he struggled at France '98, and although Italy finished runners-up at Euro 2000, del Piero himself had a forgettable tournament. Italy was strongly fancied at Japan and Korea in 2002 but crashed out in the second round, their cause not helped by some dubious refereeing decisions. In 2005–06 del Piero became Juve's all-time record goalscorer, though coach Fabio Capello tended to use the veteran striker as an impact player. Marcello Lippi also used him sparingly and to potent effect in Italy's victorious Germany 2006 World Cup campaign.

Juve lost a number of stars after being relegated to Serie B in 2006–07 for its part in the corruption scandal, but del Piero pledged his future to the club until 2010. His goals helped Juve bounce back to Serie A at the first attempt, and in 2007–08 he netted 21 times to become the premier division's top marksman. Early in the 2008-09 season Del Piero passed the 250-goal mark for Juve, while his 27 goals for Italy put him fourth in the all-time list.

Alessandro del Piero

Didier Drogba

Born: 11 March 1978
Clubs: Le Mans, Guingamp, Marseille, Chelsea
National Team: Ivory Coast

Didier Drogba

Didier Drogba's power and pace made him Jose Mourinho's number one choice for Chelsea's central striking position in two title-winning campaigns. Drogba terrorises defenders and creates space and opportunities for the likes of Lampard, Robben and Cole to exploit. Drogba started out as a defender, and his early career was steady rather than spectacular. He spent four years at Le Mans, in France's second division. Since his move to Championnat strugglers Guingamp in January 2002, Drogba has gone from strength to strength. In his one full season with the club, he scored 17 goals at the magical rate of one in two, something all strikers strive for. That earned him a move to Marseille, where he fell just one short of equalling that prodigious strike rate. His goals fired Marseille to the UEFA Cup final, and although the team went down to Valencia, Drogba was named France's Player of the Year, and Mourinho came knocking on the door waving a £24 million cheque. Drogba hit both goals in the 2–1 victory over Arsenal in the 2005–06 curtain-raiser. With a Carling Cup success also under his belt, it meant that Drogba had garnered four winners medals from just two seasons in English football. Drogba played a key role in helping Ivory Coast reach the 2006 World Cup, the country's first appearance in the finals. The team warmed up for the historic event by reaching African Cup of Nations final in February 2006, though they went down to hosts Egypt on penalties. Drogba missed from the spot in the shoot-out, though he had scored the decisive goals against Cameroon and Nigeria in the previous two rounds.

He was in scintillating form in 2006–07. By March he had hit 28 goals in all competitions, topping the hotshot list in both the Premiership and the Champions League. He was the Premiership's top marksman with 20 goals, and found the net 33 times in all competitions. His clinical finishing earned him the African Footballer of the Year award.

Michael Essien

Born: 3 December 1982
Clubs: Liberty Professionals, SC Bastia, Olympique Lyonnais, Chelsea
National Team: Ghana

Chelsea's pursuit of Michael Essien in the summer of 2005 was one of the longest-running transfer sagas of the close season. The midfielder threatened to go on strike if Lyon did not allow him to move to Stamford Bridge, and in the end Gerard Houllier, the boss of the French champions, bowed to the inevitable; Jose Mourinho got his man, at a cost of £24 million.

The powerful, combative Essien starred for Ghana in the world U-17 championship in 1999. The following year he moved from Ghanaian side Liberty Professionals to Bastia, with whom he reached France's domestic cup final in 2002. He made his debut for the senior national team that year, helping Ghana reach the quarter-final of the African Cup of Nations.

By the summer of 2003, Essien was a target for several big clubs, reigning champions Lyon eventually getting his signature. Essien helped Lyon win two more championships, establishing himself as one of Europe's top midfielders. Although regarded primarily as a holding player, Essien hit five goals in 10 Champions League matches during Lyon's impressive 2004–05 campaign. He did miss from the spot in the quarter-final shoot-out defeat by PSV, but his form that

Michael Essien

season earned him the country's Player of the Year award. Little wonder that Mourinho was so assiduous in his pursuit of the player.

Essien took time to settle into the pace of the Premiership, and some rugged tackling earned him a 'hard man' tag in his first season. But in 2006–07 he showed his true class – and his adaptability, for he was also pressed into service at full-back and in central defence, where he was equally outstanding. He also enhanced his reputation by helping Ghana qualify for the knockout stage at Germany 2006, though he was sidelined by suspension as the Black Stars went down 3–0 to Brazil.

Samuel Eto'o

Born: 10 March 1981
Clubs: Real Madrid, Real Mallorca, Barcelona
National Team: Cameroon

Cameroon's surprise failure to reach Germany 2006 deprived Samuel Eto'o of a third appearance in the finals. He was a fringe player when he went to France '98 as a 17-year-old, but played in all three games in Japan and Korea, where Cameroon finished behind Germany and the Republic of Ireland at the group stage. If the World Cup hasn't yet been a happy hunting ground for this powerful, gifted striker, he has more than made up for it in other competitions. In 2000 he helped Cameroon take Olympic gold in Sydney, and victory in the African Cup of Nations. Two years later, Cameroon retained their CAF crown, beating Senegal in the final. There was no hat-trick in Egypt 2006, Cameroon going out in the quarters, though Eto'o had the consolation of being the tournament's hotshot with five goals. Eto'o signed for Real Madrid at 16, though the majority of his six years on the Bernabeu's books was spent on loan to Real Mallorca. The deal was eventually made permanent, though Real Madrid retained a 50 per cent stake in the player. The club's decision to relinquish their interest and allow Eto'o to join Catalan rivals Barcelona in 2004 backfired somewhat. For while Real's form dipped, a new-look Barca hit top form, with Eto'o leading the attack. In 2006 the team made it back-to-back La Liga titles, Eto'o hitting 25 goals in 33 games. In 2005 he received his third successive African Player of the Year award, setting a new record. At the 2008 African Cup of Nations Eto'o reached another milestone, notching his 16th goal to become the tournament's all-time record marksman.

Francesc Fabregas

Born: 4 May 1987
Clubs: Arsenal
National Team: Spain

The mercurial midfield skills of Cesc Fabregas

would grace any side, and in the current market deep pockets would be needed to acquire a playmaker of his quality. How galling, therefore, for Barcelona, who had Fàbregas on their books but allowed him to slip through their fingers. The signs were there as Fàbregas starred for Spain in the Fifa U-17 tournament in 2003, picking up both the Golden Ball and Golden Boot awards in the team's march to the final. But at club level Fabregas never got further than the second team, and that same year Arsene Wenger snapped up yet another stellar young talent. Barca's loss was Arsenal's gain.

Fàbregas was carefully groomed, his first team appearances restricted to League Cup matches in 2003–04. When he turned out against Rotherham United in October

Samuel Eto'o

Cesc Fàbregas

Rio Ferdinand

Born: 7 November 1978
Clubs: West Ham United, Leeds United, Manchester United
National Team: England

Since the glory days of the World Cup-winning triumvirate and the astute tutelage of Ron Greenwood, Upton Park has been lauded for a youth development programme that has produced a wealth of star players. Rio Ferdinand was one of the shining lights in West Ham's academy in the early 1990s, though the club had plenty of competition when it came to signing the wiry Peckham-born youngster. Ferdinand often played in midfield as a junior but his Upton Park mentors saw his potential as an elegant, ball-playing centre-back in the Bobby Moore mould. He made his first-team debut at the back end of the 1995–96 season, when he was just 17, and quickly established himself as a regular in the senior side. Ferdinand's emergence was a major plus as the Hammers narrowly avoided relegation in 1996–97, and even though they finished in the top half of the table the following term and took fifth spot in 1998–99, the question of how long the club could hang on to Rio became a regular feature on the back pages. The answer was just one more full season, for in November 2000 West Ham accepted an £18 million offer from Leeds United, who were then riding high prior to a cataclysmic fall. It was a British transfer record, and a new world mark for a defender. When Leeds finished out of the Champions League places that season, the house of cards quickly collapsed and Ferdinand was on the move again. Manchester United swooped to take him to Old Trafford in summer 2002, though his stock had risen further in his 18-month stint at Elland Road and Sir Alex Ferguson had to pay £30 million to get his man. Ferdinand picked up a championship medal in his first season with United, and when the team finished third the following term, many felt that Rio's enforced absence for missing a drugs test was a major factor. He has since added two more league titles to his personal haul, and won the Carling Cup, but no doubt his proudest moment was leading the team to victory against Chelsea in the dramatic Champions League final of 2007–08. The opposing captain that day was John Terry, with whom Ferdinand has formed a formidable axis at the heart of the England defence. Rio won his first cap under Glenn Hoddle in November 1997, a 2–0 victory over Cameroon at Wembley. He started 2009 with 72 caps to his name, putting him in the top 20 in the all-time list in terms of England appearances

of that season, he became the Gunners' youngest ever senior player, at 16 years and 177 days. He made his first Premiership start at the beginning of the 2004–05 campaign, and in only his third match he got on the scoresheet, his strike against Blackburn in August giving him another place in the Arsenal record book, as youngest ever scorer.

It was after Patrick Vieira's departure at the end of the 2004–05 season that Fabregas really grew in stature. He became a fixture in the team and took the responsibility of midfield generalship on his young shoulders. He was outstanding in Arsenal's run to the Champions League final, notably in the high-octane clashes with Real Madrid and Juventus in the knockout stages. Ironically, in the latter encounter he came up against Vieira, who had gone to Turin in a £14 million deal. Fabregas was still just 18, but it was a case of the pupil besting the master.

He won his first senior cap in March 2006, becoming Spain's youngest international for 80 years. He featured in all four of Spain's matches at Germany 2006, a run which ended in a 3–1 defeat by France in the second round.

Luis Figo (left)

control, had purchased him from Sporting Lisbon, his first team. Figo was instrumental in bringing the Barcelona two domestic championships, two Spanish Cups and, in 1997, the European Cup Winners' Cup.

His move to Real Madrid enraged Barcelona fans and he remains deeply unpopular with them despite his former success at the club. In his first season, he helped Real to win the Primera Liga and reach the semi-final of the European Champions League. In 2001–02 they went one better and Real were crowned champions of Europe, beating Bayer Leverkusen in the final. In 2001, Figo also received an individual honour, being given FIFA's World Footballer of the Year award.

Figo earned his first full international cap in 1991 aged 19. He led his country to the

Luis Figo

Born: 4 November 1972
Clubs: Sporting Lisbon, Barcelona, Real Madrid, Inter Milan
National Team: Portugal

Luis Figo is a hero in both his native Portugal and Spain, where he has played for the two giants of Spanish football, Barcelona and Real Madrid. In 2000, the year he was named European Footballer of the Year, he caused one of the biggest upsets in the game by defecting from the Catalan side to their arch-rivals Real in a deal worth £40 million.

Figo had joined FC Barcelona in 1995, when Johan Cruyff, impressed by his aggressive dribbling and stylish ball

quarter-finals of Euro '96, and four years later to the semi-finals of the European Championships. Both Figo and Portugal disappointed at the 1998 World Cup, for which they failed to qualify, and Japan and Korea 2002, where they were eliminated at the group stage. However, Figo was named in Fifa's squad of the tournament for Germany 2006, following his contribution towards getting Portugal to the semi-finals, equalling the country's best showing in the tournament.

By then, Figo was an Inter Milan player. He joined the Serie A giants in summer 2005, after falling out of favour at Real. He was a regular starter as Inter won the *scudetto* in 2006 and 2007, the first of those titles by default after Juventus and AC Milan were docked points for match-fixing.

Steven Gerrard

Born: 30 May 1980
Clubs: Liverpool
National Team: England

By common consent Steven Gerrard is one of England's few world-class players. Unfortunately for Gerrard and England, injury forced him to miss the 2002 World Cup. Although Nicky Butt played superbly, Gerrard was sorely missed. He has been a fixture in the international side since Kevin Keegan handed him his first cap in 2000, and for three years didn't taste defeat while playing for England. Gerrard showed glimpses of his attacking form at Germany 2006, notably a stunning left-foot drive which flew past Trinidad and Tobago's Shaka Hislop, and a power header against Sweden in the group decider. However, most pundits felt the midfield balance was awry, and that it ought to be constructed round the Liverpool maestro.

A boyhood Liverpool fan, Gerrard joined the club at the age of eight and came through the youth ranks. He made his debut in 1998, but suffered a succession of fitness problems early in his career, something that was put down to growth spurts. By 2001 he was looking more and more accomplished in midfield, although with his tenacious tackling and excellent reading of the game he was equally adept at full-back. Gerrard was named the 2001 PFA Young Player of the Year after accomplished performances both in midfield and full-back. He soon became the driving force in the Liverpool side, but by the summer of 2004 his desire for silverware prompted speculation that he might follow Michael Owen out of Anfield. The following May he hoisted the Champions Cup aloft after an inspirational display against AC Milan in the final in Istanbul.

Gerrard's two goals in Liverpool's dramatic victory over West Ham in the 2006 FA Cup Final landed him a unique quadruple: he became the only player to have scored in the final of both domestic cup competitions, the Uefa Cup and the Champions League.

Steven Gerrard

Ryan Giggs

Born: 29 November 1973
Clubs: Manchester United
National Team: Wales

Ryan Giggs

Ryan Giggs burst onto the scene in 1991, the first of Manchester United's brilliant youth side to become a regular in the first team. His speed, marvellous control and breathtaking dribbling immediately invited comparisons with the great George Best. Giggs preferred to do his talking on the pitch, and in the past 15 years has helped United to dominate the domestic scene, including the Double on three occasions. One of those came in 1999, when United also finally ended a 30-year drought by lifting the European Champions League.

Giggs became Wales' youngest ever international when he won his first cap, at the age of 17 years 332 days. For a long time he was the star player in a rather ordinary side, and was criticised for putting club before country as he withdrew from rather too many international squads. Even so, he turned out for his country 64 times over a 16-year period, and was captain of the side when he retired in 2007 to focus his energies on club football.

In March 2007 Giggs chalked up his 700th appearance for United, putting him second in the all-time list behind Bobby Charlton. In May 2008 Giggs picked up his 10th Premier League winners' medal. No other player in the history of the game has won so many league championships. Moreover, he had scored in every Premiership campaign since its inception in 1992, a record matched only by Gary Speed.

Thierry Henry

Born: 17 August 1977
Clubs: Monaco, Juventus, Arsenal, Barcelona
National Team: France

In summer 2007, Thierry Henry brought an illustrious eight-year spell with Arsenal to an end when he signed for Barcelona in a £16 million deal. After joining the Gunners in 1999, Henry embarked on a scoring spree that would make him the club's all-time League goal-scorer with 174 goals, and also their top marksman in European competition, with 42 goals. During this period, he was twice runner-up in the FIFA World Player of the Year awards, and was the European Golden Boot winner in 2004 and 2005, the first player to retain the honour.

Arsene Wenger bought Henry from Juventus for £11 million. He had seen his talent first hand when he was coaching at Monaco, Henry's first club. His impressive pace and deft ball skills made him indispensable at Arsenal, where Wenger placed him in a central position. Although he had previously been a winger, Henry soon proved to be one of the deadliest central strikers in the world, and in his first season at Arsenal he scored 26 goals in only 47 appearances. He was named Player of the Year in 2003 and his 32 goals made him England's top goal-scorer that year.

Although Henry has not won any international trophies at club level, with his national side he lifted the Euro 2000 trophy, following their victory over Italy. Henry was unfortunate to miss out on a starting place in the 1998 World Cup final which France won, but he had scored three goals in the group matches. At the 2002 World Cup, his red card during the Uruguay match completed a forgettable tournament for both Henry and France, but he was in good form in his country's run to the final of Germany 2006, scoring a blistering volley which beat favourites Brazil in the last eight and winning the penalty that beat Portugal in the semi-final. In 2007 Henry passed Michel Platini's record of 41 international goals, and the following year became only the sixth player to reach the 100-cap mark for France.

Filippo Inzaghi

Born: 9 August 1973
Clubs: Piacenza, Leffe, Piacenza, Parma, Atalanta, Juventus, AC Milan
National Team: Italy

Filippo Inzaghi became the all-time leading scorer in Uefa competition when he netted his 63rd goal in December 2007, during AC Milan's bid to retain the Champions League trophy. It put him ahead of the great Gerd Muller, whose record had stood for over 30 years. Two of Inzaghi's European goals came in the 2006–07 Champions League final, where he earned the man-of-the-match award for the brace that gave Milan a 2–1 victory over Liverpool. Inzaghi's boyhood hero was Paolo Rossi. He was often pushed into playing in goal as a youngster but always wanted to be a striker. He found that he had all the attributes of a forward, in particular an instinctive eye for goal, and was soon scoring freely in the lower divisions of Italian football. Parma gave him his first taste of Serie A, but he was plagued with injury and soon moved on to Atalanta. They were a struggling side at the time, which made his 24-goal haul all the more impressive. It was enough to win him the Capocannoniere – the coveted award for the league's top striker. It also earned him a £9 million move to Juventus in 1997. Inzaghi spent four years in Turin, hitting a creditable 57 goals for the club. A dip in form in 2001 put him behind Trezeguet in the pecking order and AC Milan paid £26 million to take him to the San Siro. The 2003 European Champions League final pitted Inzaghi against the club that sold him. He didn't manage to get on the scoresheet but helped Milan to pick up the trophy for the sixth time. Inzaghi hit 15 goals in his first 32 games for Italy, the best record of the current crop of Italian internationals. Even so he was not an automatic choice in Trapattoni's side which underperformed at the 2002 World Cup. He played only a cameo role at Germany 2006, too, though he did get on the scoresheet in Italy's victorious campaign.

Filippo Inzaghi

Kaka

Born: 22 April 1982
Clubs: Sao Paulo, AC Milan
National Team: Brazil

Kaka

Kaka's brother is said to have given the AC Milan and Brazil star his footballing moniker, the result of the truncated efforts of the younger sibling to get his tongue around the name 'Ricardo'. Kaka's rise to the top came at a dizzying speed. Barely a year after making his debut for Sao Paulo, he was named Brazil's top player and drafted into the international squad. That was in January 2002. Although he made only a cameo appearance at that summer's World Cup – in the 5–2 group stage win over Costa Rica – the 20-year-old was fiercely proud of being a member of the victorious squad. Since then, he has been rather more than a bit-part player, helping Brazil to win the 2004 Copa America, and the Confederations Cup in 2005. By then, this classy attacking midfielder was an AC Milan player, the Italian giants having won the race for his signature in 2003. Milan won the Serie A title in Kaka's first season with the club, though in his second campaign he suffered a dual blow as the team ceded the championship to Juventus and had a Champions League victory snatched away by Liverpool. He was named the tournament's best midfielder that season and in December 2007 he picked up both the European and World Footballer of the Year awards. A committed Christian, Kaka's goal celebration consists of pointing skywards, in acknowledgment of the great gift God has bestowed upon him. His faith has been one of the central pillars of his life since he recovered from a career-threatening broken back, the result of a diving-board accident. In January 2009 Kaka was the subject of a reported £100 million bid from Manchester City, prompting howls of protest from Milan fans. The deal fell through, but the very fact that an offer doubling the world record transfer fee was mooted is a reflection of his special talent.

Frank Lampard

Born: 20 June 1978
Clubs: West Ham United, Chelsea
National Team: England

Fittingly, it was Frank Lampard who scored both Chelsea goals in the 2–0 win at Bolton which sealed the 2004–05 Premiership title for Chelsea, ending the club's 50-year wait for the championship. He ended the campaign with 13 goals, an excellent return for a midfielder. Lampard had not only featured in every game, but notched over 140 consecutive appearances, a remarkable achievement for any box-to-box player; even more so in a Stamford Bridge era spanning Claudio Ranieri's celebrated rotation system and the revised all-star squad assembled by Jose Mourinho. After leaving school Lampard joined West Ham, where his father had had an illustrious career as a full-back. His league debut came during a loan spell at Swansea City, in October 1995, Lampard making his first Premiership start for the Hammers early the following year. Over the next two seasons he established himself in the first team, and also earned a call-up to Peter Taylor's England U-21 side, which he went on to captain. Ranieri paid £11 million to bring Lampard to Stamford Bridge in June 2001. He made a steady but unspectacular start; it took him almost half a season to open his account for his new club. But he matured into one of the country's most effective and consistent midfielders. Lampard won his first England cap in a friendly against Belgium in 1999 but missed out on both Euro 2000 and the World Cup two years later. By the time Euro 2004 came round he was a certain starter, the only question mark being whether both he and England's other world class attacking midfielder Steven Gerrard could be accommodated in the same line-up. Lampard scored three goals in England's run to the quarter-finals in Portugal. He was named in UEFA's squad of the tournament, and England fans also voted him their player of the year. In 2004–05 Lampard's outstanding contribution towards Chelsea's title-winning campaign won him the Football Writers Player of the Year award, while teammate John Terry pipped him in the PFA poll. In November 2005 he was named runner-up in the European and World Footballer of the Year awards, losing out to Ronaldinho in both polls.

Lampard was below par at the 2006 World Cup, one of three men who missed from the spot in the quarter-final shoot-out defeat by Portugal, but he remains one of the most influential players in Chelsea and England's midfield. In February 2008 Lampard notched his 100th goal for Chelsea. His century came in less than seven years, an extraordinary achievement for a midfielder.

Lionel Messi

Born: 24 June 1987
Clubs: Barcelona
National Team: Argentina

Over the past twenty years many players have been burdened with the tag 'the new Maradona', but in Lionel Messi Argentina finally seem to have unearthed the real deal. Messi was a precociously gifted youngster who was on the books of Newell's Old Boys between the ages of eight and thirteen. His ball skills were prodigious, but his diminutive frame was a concern. At just 1m 40cm, Messi needed a growth spurt if he was to cope with the physical demands of the professional game. A hormone deficiency was diagnosed, and when the family moved to Spain, Barcelona was only too glad to pick up the tab for the medical bills. He soon began to fill out. It is said that when the club's U-14 coach saw Messi in action, he grabbed the nearest thing to hand to commit the youngster to the club – a serviette! Messi progressed through the junior ranks in record time, making his first-team appearance aged 16. His debut in a competitive match came in October 2004, when he was 17 years 4

months, and before that championship-winning campaign was over he had notched his first league goal, becoming the youngest Barca player to get on the scoresheet. The Spanish FA was keen to draft Messi into the international fold, but he had set his sights on playing for the country of his birth. He didn't have long to wait. Summer 2005 saw him star in Argentina's victorious U-20 World Cup campaign. Six goals in seven games won him the Golden Boot, and he was also named Player of the Tournament. Chelsea have special reason to remember Messi, for it was his tormenting runs at Stamford Bridge in the knockout stage of the 2005–06 Champions League that provoked Asier del Horno's reckless challenge, resulting in a red card which Jose Mourinho highlighted as the turning point of the tie. Barca went on to beat Arsenal in the final, and Messi helped the team secure another La Liga title. If anyone still had doubts about comparing Messi to Maradona, the young wizard surely quashed them in a cup match with Getafe in 2007. He took possession just inside his own half and beat six players, including the 'keeper, before slotting home. It was a wonder goal eerily reminiscent of Maradona's mesmerising solo effort against England in the 1986 World Cup.

Lionel Messi

Michael Owen

Born: 14 December 1979
Clubs: Liverpool, Real Madrid, Newcastle United
National Team: England

Michael Owen marked his professional debut with a goal for Liverpool in 1997, when he was 17, and in the past decade he has established himself as one of the game's most potent strikers. Lightning pace, agility and a deadly eye for goal marked him out in the schoolboy ranks, and he was snapped up for the Anfield academy. Twenty one goals in his debut season earned him the PFA Young Player of the Year award and ended speculation that his diminutive frame might not withstand the rigours of the Premiership.

Owen's England debut came against Chile in a warm-up game for the World Cup. At 18 years and 59 days old, he became the youngest player to turn out for England. It was during France '98, his first tournament as an international player, that Owen burst onto the world stage with a sensational goal against Argentina. Although England suffered disappointment in France, Owen had proved himself a vital force to be reckoned with. Despite persistent hamstring problems, he was back on form for the 2001 World Cup qualifiers. Owen repeated Geoff Hurst's achievement of scoring a hat-trick against Germany when England beat them in Munich 5–1. That performance helped him to win the coveted European Footballer of the Year award, the first British player to do so since Kevin Keegan in 1979.

With Liverpool, he collected a number of honours. In 2001 he was instrumental in their victory over Arsenal in the FA Cup final. Owen's two late goals secured the win and the tie has since been dubbed the 'Michael Owen final'. That same season he scored his 100th goal for the Reds against West Ham, aged only 21.

Michael Own left Anfield for the Bernabeu in summer 2004. Although he struggled to command a regular first-team place at Real Madrid in his debut season, Owen's goals-per-minute-on-the-pitch record was better than any other player. He joined Newcastle United for a club record £17 million in summer 2005, making a blistering start to the new season with seven goals in

Michael Owen

11 games. A broken metatarsal kept him out of action for four months, then a cruciate ligament injury sustained in the World Cup group game against Sweden meant the 2006–07 season was a write-off.

Going into 2009 Owen's international record stood at 40 goals in 89 appearances, putting him fourth behind Bobby Charlton, Gary Lineker and Jimmy Greaves in the all-time list. The fact that his 40th goal came in September 2007, and that he didn't seem to figure in coach Fabio Capello's plans, suggested that Charlton's record of 49 might be safe for a while longer.

Sergio Ramos

Sergio Ramos

Born: 30 March 1986
Clubs: Sevilla, Real Madrid
National Team: Spain

Sergio Ramos's flowing mane has made him a distinctive figure in the Real Madrid and Spain line-ups in recent years. His style of play is equally distinctive, for he is a rock-like defender who likes nothing better than to be relieved of his core duties and make marauding forays into the opposition's half. He has earned a reputation for his happy knack of popping up with useful goals, bagging five in each of Real's championship-winning campaigns of 2006–07 and 2007–08. Ramos was a product of Sevilla's acclaimed youth system, making his first-team debut a month short of his 18th birthday. He was soon a fixture in a side that was on the up under Joaquin Caparros, but after helping the team secure a top-six finish in 2004–05, Ramos was lured to the Bernabeu in a big-money deal. The Madrid giants singled him out as a long-term replacement for the legendary Fernando Hierro, for Ramos was equally comfortable at the heart of the defence and raiding down the flanks. The transfer did mean that he missed out on back-to-back Uefa Cup successes with Sevilla, but Ramos was soon a firm favourite with the fervent Bernabeu fans, who warmed to his drive and determination as well as his ball skills. He is a natural leader on the pitch, tipped by many to be handed the armband for both club and country one day. Ramos already has two major international tournaments under his belt, having played for Spain in the 2006 World Cup and in the victorious Euro 2008 campaign. He won his first cap in March 2005, a few days before he turned 19. It made him Spain's youngest international for over half a century, a record later beaten by Arsenal's Cesc Fabregas.

Franck Ribery

Born: April 1 1983
Clubs: Boulogne, Olympique, Alès, Stade Brest, Metz, Galatasaray, Marseille, Bayern Munich
National Team: France

Franck Ribéry

Ribery's searing pace and bewitching footwork marked him out as an outstanding player from an early age, but he believes a childhood automobile accident played an important part in his journey to the top. At the age of two he was thrown through the windscreen of the family car, suffering horrific facial injuries. The long road to recovery gave him a steely resolve which he went on to apply in his footballing endeavours. Ribery served his apprenticeship in the lower leagues of his native country, earning a move to top-division side Metz in 2004. A run-in with the club's hierarchy led to a move to Galatasaray early the following year. He was an instant hit with the Turkish club's fans, who dubbed him 'FerraRibery' because of his blistering pace. He helped Gala win the domestic cup before a row over unpaid wages precipitated a move back to France, this time to Marseille. He took over the star player mantle from the departing Didier Drogba, his performances earning him a call-up to the France side just before the 2006 World Cup. After showing his class on the biggest stage, Ribery was on the wish list of several top European clubs, though Marseille managed to hold on to him for another season before bowing to the inevitable. Ribery starred in his swansong season with Marseille, helping the club to finish runners-up to perennial champions Olympique Lyonnais before joining Bayern Munich in a club record £15 million deal. Ribery had a hard act to follow, taking over the No. 7 shirt of the recently retired Mehmet Scholl, who had become a legend in Bavarian football circles in his 15 years with Bayern. But Ribery was an immediate success yet again, which was hardly surprising as no less a figure than Thierry Henry has said that Ribery is peerless in his ability to accelerate with the ball at his feet.

Juan Roman Riquelme

Born: 26 June 1978
Clubs: Argentinos Juniors, Boca Juniors, Barcelona, Villareal, Boca Juniors
National Team: Argentina

Juan Roman Riquelme cut an abject figure when he missed from the spot in the 88th minute of Villareal's Champions League semi-final against Arsenal in April 2006. It brought to an end a remarkable run, though Riquelme had no reason to reproach himself. It was his outstanding form in the Primera Liga in 2004–05 which had helped Villareal reach Europe's top club competition for the first time. En route to the defeat by the Gunners, Villareal had beaten Everton in the qualifiers, topped a group including Manchester United and put out Rangers in the knockout stage. Riquelme established himself as a rising star with Argentinos Juniors. Boca Juniors, the club he supported as a boy, beat River Plate to his signature in 1995, and over the next seven years he built his reputation as one of the silkiest playmakers in South America. He was twice a winner of the Copa Libertadores with Boca, in 2000 and 2001, picking up the continent's Player of the Year award in the latter season. He joined Barcelona the following year, but the Catalan giants were struggling at the time, putting added pressure on their star recruit. Riquelme suffered a dip in confidence and form, lost his place and was allowed to go on loan to Villareal after just one season at the Nou Camp. His form over the past three years suggests that Barcelona acted somewhat hastily. Riquelme won the World U-20 championship with Argentina in 1997. Pekerman saw Riquelme as his side's Zinedine Zidane – someone who would provide artistry with end product – and he showed both facets at Germany 2006. Many felt the decision to substitute Riquelme against the hosts in the quarter-finals cost Argentina the game – and Pekerman his job. A fall-out between Riquelme and Villareal's coach saw him return to Boca on loan early in 2007, a deal subsequently made permanent after he helped the Argentine club win the Copa Libertadores.

Rivaldo

Born: 19 April 1972
Clubs: Paulista, Santa Cruz, Corinthians, Palmeiras, Deportivo La Coruna, Barcelona, AC Milan, Cruzeiro, Olympiakos, AEK, FC Bunyodkor
National Team: Brazil

Louis van Gaal surprised many when he agreed to let Rivaldo leave Barcelona for AC Milan in the summer of 2002. It was the second time Rivaldo had played under the Dutch coach. He joined Barca from Deportivo La Coruna in 1997, the year van Gaal arrived for his first stint in charge at the Nou Camp. Back then he was the big-name replacement for his compatriot Ronaldo, who was on his way to Inter Milan. The peak of Rivaldo's five years at Barca came in 1999, when he was named both European and World Footballer of the Year. His lethal left foot helped Barca win back-to-back Primera Liga titles in 1998 and 1999. Despite his excellent form for Brazil in the victorious World Cup campaign in Japan and Korea, van Gaal decided it was time to freshen things up at Barcelona. AC Milan snapped Rivaldo up, and with Shevchenko and Inzaghi already on the San Siro books, coach Carlo Ancellotti had some of the most exciting firepower in

Europe at his disposal. Rivaldo's glittering career and millionaire lifestyle was a far cry from the slums of Recife where he grew up. He played for several Brazilian clubs before joining Deportivo in 1996. He hit 21 goals in just 41 games in his one season at Deportivo before Barcelona bought out his contract. First capped in 1993, Rivaldo played in all seven of Brazil's matches at France '98, scoring three goals. He put the disappointment of defeat in that year's final behind him in Japan and Korea. He was on top form, as England found to their cost in the quarter-final. He drilled a superb equaliser past Seaman from Ronaldinho's pass. In 2003 AC Milan beat Juventus in the European Champions League final, but Rivaldo was left on the bench. His contract was cancelled early the following season, and after a brief spell with Cruzeiro, Rivaldo joined Olympiakos in summer 2004. After three years with the Athens club, Rivaldo moved across the city to join rivals AEK. At AEK he averaged a goal every other game, as he had for the majority of his career, but stunned his employers by moving on after just one season. He accepted a lucrative offer from Uzbekistan side FC Bunyodkor, who decided that even at 36, Rivaldo was still a potent striker, not to mention a massive draw.

Rivaldo

Arjen Robben

Born: 23 January 1984
Clubs: Bedum, FC Groningen, PSV Eindhoven, Chelsea, Real Madrid
National Team: Holland

Had it not been for injury, Arjen Robben would certainly have challenged teammates Lampard and Terry for the honours handed out by the PFA and Football Writers at the end of Chelsea's 2004–05 title-winning campaign. The only person who must have been galled by his dazzling wing play was Sir Alex Ferguson. Manchester United had been tracking the young star at PSV Eindhoven, but when the club wouldn't match the Dutch side's valuation, Chelsea stepped in and paid the £12 million asking price, snatching the young star from under their rival's nose.

Robben started his career with his local club Bedum, but it was during his spell with FC Groningen that it became clear that here was a rare talent. He made his senior debut as a 16-year-old in December 2000, turning in a dazzling display in a victory over league leaders Feyenoord. He was named the club's player of the year, and at the end of that season a deal was struck to take him to PSV, though the move was deferred for a year to enable Robben to gain more experience. In 2002–03, his first campaign with PSV, he missed just one match as the team regained the title from

Robinho

Born: 25 January 1984
Clubs: Santos, Real Madrid, Manchester City
National Team: Brazil

Arjen Robben

If Manchester City fans needed any reassurance that their club's new Abu Dhabi owners were prepared to spend big in order to build a team capable of chasing top honours, it came on 1 September 2008 with the £32 million acquisition of Robinho. The fact that City had snatched Real Madrid's ace striker from under Chelsea's noses was a major coup, particularly as the erstwhile wunderkind had expressed a desire to join the established Premiership giants in the capital. The Eastlands faithful were soon being treated to the full array of flicks, tricks and deft touches that have become the hallmark of players from his native land. All Brazilian magicians are inevitably compared to Pele, and while that may be premature, the paths of master and pupil did cross during Robinho's formative years. He came through the ranks at Santos at a time when the youth development programme was being overseen by the country's greatest footballing son. In his debut season with Santos 18-year-old Robinho helped the club win the Brazilian championship. He scored in the 5-2 aggregate win over Corinthians in the play-off final, as did future City teammate Elano. Santos repeated the achievement in 2004, by which time some of Europe's big fishes were courting the young star. The club managed to hold on to him for one more year before accepting an offer from Real Madrid, who had just finished runners-up to Barcelona in La Liga. Spain's big two finished in the same positions in Robinho's debut season but Real Madrid then won back-to-back titles to extend their lead over Barca in the all-time list. It wasn't all plain sailing for Robinho during his three years in Spain, and he warmed the bench for a lengthy period when he fell out with coach Fabio Capello during the 2006–07 campaign. Even so, when he arrived in Manchester, the 24-year-old already had four championship medals from two of the most glamorous leagues in world football. He won his first cap in 2003, but with the likes of Ronaldo, Ronaldinho, Kaka and Adriano in the mix, it took some time to establish himself in the national side. He was still a fringe player when the 2006 World Cup came round, but a year later he was the star of the show in Brazil's Copa America victory. He took the Golden Shoe with six goals as Brazil swept to glory, beating Argentina 3–0 in the final.

Ajax. Robben weighed in with 12 goals in 33 games and won the country's Young Player of the Year award.

He made his senior international debut towards the end of that season, and scored his first goal at the top level in a Euro 2004 qualifier against Moldova. Holland manager Dick Advocaat bemused fans by his decision to take Robben off in the country's second group match in Portugal, against the Czech Republic. The Dutch led 2–0 but went down 3–2. Robben was on top form in the 3–0 win over Latvia, then hit the winning penalty in the quarter-final shoot-out against Sweden. Although the team lost in the semis against hosts Portugal, Robben emerged with his reputation hugely enhanced, while Advocaat was soon out of a job. He went to Germany 2006 with another Premiership winners medal under his belt, and showed flashes of dazzling wing play until Holland's run was ended in an explosive second-round clash with Portugal. Summer 2007 saw Robben move to Real Madrid in a £24 million deal. In his first season at the Bernabeu he helped Real win yet another La Liga crown, which gave him four championship winners' medals in three different countries at the age of 24.

Ronaldinho

Born: 21 March 1980
Clubs: Gremio, Paris St-Germain, Barcelona, AC Milan
National Team: Brazil

Ronaldo de Assis Moreira – better known as Ronaldinho ('Little Ronaldo') – was confirmed as the best footballer on the planet in November 2004, when he topped the FIFA poll of international team coaches and captains. He won by some distance, from Thierry Henry and Andriy Shevchenko. Further endorsement of the buck-toothed genius's talent came from two unimpeachable sources: Pele, who acclaimed the greatest ball artist of the current Brazil era, and Diego Maradona, who said that Ronaldinho played on a different level to everyone else. Ronaldinho joined Gremio as a 7-year-old. His consummate natural skill was matched by an indefatigable work ethic. His tireless practising of tricks and feints resulted in a vast repertoire of ways to beat an opponent. One such came against Venezuela during Brazil's run to the Copa America final in 1999. He took the ball at full tilt, lobbed it over a defender, rounded him and controlled it on the full – a trick called 'the sombrero' – then back-heeled the ball over his own head to beat a second defender before firing in from a tight angle. England's Ashley Cole was on the receiving end of another of Ronaldinho's favourite party pieces in the 2002 World Cup quarter-final. In the blistering run which set up Rivaldo's equaliser he used 'the elastico' – where he feints to go right, then rolls his foot over the ball and brings it the other way, all done at bewildering speed. The 40-yard free kick which sailed over David Seaman's head and put Brazil into the semis was quite intentional, Ronaldinho insisted. A red card against England could have kept him out of the final, but common sense prevailed and he duly picked up his winners medal after the 2–0 win over Germany. Ronaldinho moved to Paris St Germain 2001, but in his two seasons there the best the club could manage was a domestic cup final defeat by Auxerre. 2003 saw PSG in the wrong

half of the table, and Ronaldinho keen for a bigger stage. His move to Barcelona that summer prompted a revival for the Catalan club. He was a regular on the scoresheet in his first La Liga campaign, helping the team to the runner-up spot behind Valencia. In 2004–05 Barca won their first title for six years. Coach Frank Rijkaard paid tribute to his star player, to whom he gives no instructions other than to go onto the field and do what comes naturally. In November 2005 he was named European and World Footballer of the Year, those honours bestowed during a campaign which saw Ronaldinho spearhead Barca's charge to another domestic title and Champions League glory. After an injury-hit 2007–08 season, Ronaldinho ended a stellar five-year career at the Nou Camp and joined AC Milan, who were more than happy to have the 28-year-old superstar aboard as they sought to wrest the Serie A title from city rivals Inter.

Ronaldinho

Ronaldo

Born: 22 September 1976
Clubs: Cruzeiro, PSV Eindhoven, Barcelona, Inter Milan, Real Madrid AC Milan, Corinthians
National Team: Brazil

Brazil's biggest football hero since Pele, Ronaldo is arguably the best player of the nineties and promises to be the first 'great' of the 21st century. Luis Nazario de Lima was born in Rio de Janeiro in 1976 and by the time he was 17 years old, his playing name, Ronaldo, was known throughout the world. He had begun his career at Cruzeiro and was so impressive that he was picked for Brazil's World Cup squad in 1994. PSV Eindhoven bought Ronaldo that same year and in his first season in Europe he scored 35 goals. Two years later, he joined Barcelona and 34 goals in that season made him not only the Primera Liga's hotshot but also won him the golden boot. He also put away the goal which beat Paris St-Germain in the European Cup Winners' Cup final. That same year he won the first of three World Footballer of the Year awards, the second coming the following year.

The 1998 World Cup presented high expectations for the 22-year-old striker and his inexplicably disappointing performance in the final cost Brazil the trophy. Four years later, Ronaldo demonstrated just how dangerous he was by scoring eight goals in the tournament, including the two against Germany that won Brazil the Jules Rimet trophy.

After a spell at Inter Milan during which they won the 1997–98 UEFA Cup, Ronaldo moved to Real Madrid. Impressed by his performance in Japan and Korea, Vicente del Bosque paid Inter £30 million to bring Ronaldo to the Bernabeu. Ronaldo finished a memorable year by scoring one of Real's goals in the 2–0 victory over Olimpia in the World Club Cup in December 2002. Ronaldo has twice been named European Footballer of the Year, and his three World Footballer of the Year awards set a record which has been matched only by Zinedine Zidane. Three goals in Brazil's run to the quarter-finals of Germany 2006 made Ronaldo the top scorer in World Cup history, his career haul of 15 overtaking the legendary Gerd Muller. Ronaldo returned to Serie A in January 2007, joining AC Milan. A goal against Inter meant that he had scored for both Milan sides in the city Derby, a unique achievement, but his eighteen-month stay at the San Siro was not a happy one. Injury problems, allied to his well-documented weight issues, curtailed his opportunities and Milan released him in summer 2008. At the end of the year the 32-year-old returned to his homeland, signing a one-year contract to play for Corinthians.

Ronaldo

Cristiano Ronaldo

Cristiano Ronaldo

Born: 5 February 1985
Clubs: Nacional, Sporting Lisbon, Manchester United
National Team: Portugal

For Manchester United fans the loss of David Beckham and Juan Sebastian Veron in the summer of 2003 was mitigated by the arrival of one of the hottest properties in world football. Cristiano Ronaldo may not have been a household name in Manchester, but after an electrifying 30-minute debut appearance as substitute against Bolton Wanderers his name was on all the United fans' lips.

Ronaldo was born in Madeira and played for local side Nacional before being snapped up by Sporting Lisbon. He made his debut for the Portuguese club in September 2002 as a 17-year-old. Sir Alex Ferguson was soon tracking his progress and in the summer of 2003 his positive assessment was reinforced by his own players. That came after United had been on the receiving end of some Ronaldo magic in a pre-season friendly between United and Sporting to mark the opening of the latter's new stadium. The £12 million deal was soon completed, making Ronaldo the most expensive teenager in British transfer history. Already a full international, Ronaldo looked set to become the second player of that name to take the footballing world by storm.

In the early part of his Old Trafford career too often the dazzling footwork wasn't matched by the end product, but by the 2006–07 season his tally of goals and assists increased dramatically, making him the most potent weapon in United's armoury. In 2007–08 Ronaldo had the Midas touch in front of goal, banging in 42 in all competitions to fire United to yet another championship and claim Europe's Golden Shoe award. His 42nd goal came in the Champions League final against Chelsea, and even though he missed from the spot in the shoot-out, he left Moscow with a winners' medal. His superb performances earned him the European Footballer of the Year award, the first United player to be thus honoured since Law, Charlton and Best

picked up the laurels in a five-year period in the sixties. It was no surprise when the World Footballer of the Year award followed, Ronaldo becoming the first player from an English club side to claim Fifa's top individual prize.

Wayne Rooney

Born: 24 October 1985
Clubs: Everton, Manchester United
National Team: England

After Arsene Wenger had just watched Wayne Rooney score a brilliant winner against his side in October 2002 – ending Arsenal's 30-match unbeaten run in the Premiership – the Gunners' boss declared the 16-year-old the most exciting young talent he had seen in his six years in English football. Rooney followed it up with a superb strike which accounted

Wayne Rooney

for Leeds United. Those who had monitored his development at Goodison Park had long known that here was a star in the making. An Evertonian to the core, Rooney's family home is just 3 miles from Goodison. He was spotted by a club scout while playing in a local junior league when he was nine years old. Everton snapped him up for their academy and by the time he was 15 the powerfully built striker was turning out for the Under-19s. He became Everton's youngest ever scorer – a record previously held by Tommy Lawton – when he hit two against Wrexham in a Worthington Cup tie. Inevitably there have been comparisons with Michael Owen. Rooney has already eclipsed the Liverpool player in one respect: his goal against Arsenal made him the Premiership's youngest ever scorer, a record previously held by Owen. Sven-Goran Eriksson wasted little time in drafting Rooney into the international set-up, and the youngster quickly showed that he was at home on the bigger stage. His four goals and outstanding performances at Euro 2004 brought comparison with the impact Pele made in the 1958 World Cup. Two months later 'Roonaldo' moved to Manchester United in a £27 million deal.

Much of England's hopes for Germany 2006 were pinned on Rooney's young shoulders. Although he made a remarkable recovery from a broken metatarsal to help England qualify from their group, Rooney's World Cup ended on a sour note, with a red card against Portugal in the quarter-final.

Paul Scholes

Born: 16 November 1974
Clubs: Manchester United
National Team: England

Quiet and unassuming, Paul Scholes may not enjoy the celebrity status of some of his United teammates. But insiders and aficionados alike regard this combative midfielder as a gem of a player. He would be invaluable just for his excellent technique, vision and passing. The fact that he has the knack of timing his forward runs to perfection and unlocking tight defences has made Scholes priceless in the modern game. He made his first team debut in September 1994, grabbing both of United's goals in a 3–2 defeat by Ipswich. Since then he has won a string of honours, including eight Premiership winners' medals. Unfortunately, suspension forced him to miss United's European Champions League victory over Bayern Munich in 1999.

Scholes won his first cap in the Le Tournoi tournament in 1997. He was soon an automatic choice for England and a regular on the scoresheet. He hit a blistering goal in England's World Cup opener against Tunisia at France '98, and grabbed a hat-trick against Poland in a Euro 2000 qualifier. In the play-off against Scotland it was Scholes' brace at Hampden Park which effectively booked England's place at the Holland and Belgium tournament. He ended a three-year drought for England with a goal against Croatia at Euro 2004. It was to be his last, 29-year-old Scholes announcing his retirement from international football following that tournament. His 2005–06 season was curtailed when he began to suffer from blurred vision, a condition which threatened to bring the curtain down on an illustrious career.

Scholes' return to prime form in 2006–07 was key to United's push for yet another Premiership title, and led many pundits to declare that England's best player was in self-imposed international exile. It was a trademark Scholes strike that beat Barcelona in the Champions League semi-final in 2007-08, and this time he made it onto the pitch for the showpiece in Moscow, a game that ended in a glorious shoot-out victory over Chelsea.

Clarence Seedorf

Clarence Seedorf

Born: 1 April 1976
Clubs: Ajax, Sampdoria, Real Madrid, Inter Milan, AC Milan
National Team: Holland

Clarence Seedorf made history in the 2003 European Champions League final, in which his AC Milan side took on Juventus. Seedorf missed from the spot in the shoot-out, but that didn't prove costly as Milan went on to win the trophy. Seedorf thus picked up his fourth winners' medal in the competition. Other players had done that but Seedorf became the first player to be a European Champions League winner with three different clubs.

He came to prominence with Louis van Gaal's prodigiously talented crop of young players at Ajax in the early 1990s. He won the Dutch championship in 1994 and 1995, and in the latter year picked up his first European Champions League winners medal as Ajax beat AC Milan 1–0. After a spell at Sampdoria, Seedorf joined Real Madrid, with whom he also won a domestic championship and European Champions League. His four years at the Bernabeu included a second European Champions League victory, over Valencia in 2000. He then returned to Serie A with Inter Milan, but it was after moving to their city rivals that he claimed his record-breaking fourth European Champions League winners' medal. First capped in 1994, Seedorf has played more than 50 times for Holland. He missed a vital spot-kick in the Euro '96 quarter-final penalty shoot-out against France, and was also part of the squad which made it to the semi-final of France '98.

European Champions League hotshot with eleven goals, and was instrumental in Kiev's run to the semi-final, where they lost 4–3 on aggregate to Bayern Munich. Having been named European Footballer of the Year in 2004, Shevchenko led Ukraine to their first major tournament, Germany 2006, where the team performed beyond expectations in reaching the last eight. In summer 2006 Shevchenko moved to Stamford Bridge in a £30 million deal, but Chelsea fans saw only occasional glimpses of the true 'Sheva' magic in his two years at the club. In August 2008 he returned to AC Milan, where he was a cult hero for the 173 goals he scored in his first spell at the San Siro.

Andriy Shevchenko

Born: 29 August 1976
Clubs: Dynamo Kiev, AC Milan, Chelsea
National Team: Ukraine

In the autumn of 2002 Andriy Shevchenko's stellar career seemed to have stalled for the first time. He had suffered a series of niggling injuries over the previous year, and even after regaining full fitness he had slipped behind Filippo Inzaghi in the pecking order as No. 1 striker at AC Milan. There were rumours that he might be on his way out of the San Siro. A brilliant winner against Real Madrid in a European Champions League group match put paid to that, and the Ukrainian was soon back to his very best. He scored the goal which beat city rivals Inter in the semi-final, then struck the decisive penalty in the shoot-out against Juventus in the final. His goals put him hot on the heels of Raul in the all-time list of European Champions League scorers. Shevchenko came through the ranks at Dynamo Kiev, under the watchful eye of master coach Valeri Lobanovski. He won the domestic championship five times, forming a devastating strike partnership with Sergei Rebrov. In 1997–98 Shevchenko hit a hat-trick against Barcelona in a 4–0 win at the Nou Camp. The following year he was the

Andriy Shevchenko

John Terry

Born: 7 December 1980
Clubs: Chelsea
National Team: England

John Terry

John Terry capped an outstanding 2004–05 season, in which he led Chelsea to their first championship in 50 years, by being named the Player of the Year by his fellow professionals in the PFA awards. It was the first time a defender had taken that honour since Paul McGrath in 1993. Jose Mourinho hailed him as the country's top defender, the 'perfect player', and put a valuation of £50 million on his man – adding that he was not for sale. It was high praise for a player who a year earlier had feared for his place in the side when the new Portuguese broom had swept into Stamford Bridge. As a Chelsea junior Terry played in midfield, filling in at centre-back for the youth team on one occasion. He had the talent and temperament to play in that position, and when he matured physically it became his natural home. He made his debut under Gianluca Vialli in October 1998, and won the club's Young Player of the Year award that season. But it was during the Ranieri era that he established himself as a first-team regular, eventually ousting France's World Cup winner Frank Leboeuf from the side. In 2000–01 Terry captained the England U-21 side and was named Chelsea's Player of the Year. The following season he showed his talent for scoring as well as stopping goals, finding the net in both the quarter-final and semi-final of the FA Cup, Chelsea going down to double-winners Arsenal in the final. In the run-up to Japan and Korea a place in the World Cup squad looked a distinct possibility, but that disappeared with an affray charge over an incident in a London club hanging over his head. Terry was subsequently cleared of all charges, and in the past three seasons he has matured into a model professional as well as a model of consistency. Terry made his England debut as a substitute against Serbia and Montenegro in June 2003, making his first start two months later, in a friendly against Croatia. There was nothing friendly about the match in Turkey which clinched England's place at Euro 2004, a game in which Terry gave a faultless performance. At the finals in Portugal Rio Ferdinand's suspension paved the way for a Terry-Campbell partnership at the heart of the defence, and despite the fact that he was carrying an injury, Terry gave three sure-footed performances. By the time the Chelsea man lifted the Premiership trophy a year later, it was no longer a question of him breaking up the Campbell-Ferdinand pairing; now it appeared to be a battle between those two and any other contenders for the right to play alongside the inspirational Chelsea leader. Germany 2006 ended in quarter-final disappointment, though Terry had the consolation of being the sole England player to be named in Fifa's squad of the tournament.

Terry's rock-solid performances, inspiring play and leadership qualities made him a natural choice for the England captaincy when David Beckham stood down after Germany 2006. His total commitment to the cause was encapsulated in the 2007 Carling Cup final against Arsenal, when he put his head in the thick of flying boots and was knocked unconscious. Chelsea won the game and Terry left hospital to join the celebrations. By contrast, 2007–08 was a season of disappointment as Chelsea finished runners-up in three competitions, including the Champions League, where Terry was inconsolable after missing the penalty that would have won the trophy.

Luca Toni

Born: 26 May 1977

Clubs: Modena, Empoli, Fiorenzuola, Lodigiani, Treviso, Vicenza, Brescia, Palermo, Fiorentina, Bayern Munich

National Team: Italy

Luca Toni came to the fore in Italy's World Cup campaign of 2006, in which the Azzurri swept all before them to record their fourth tournament victory. Toni netted twice against Ukraine in the quarters, and was unlucky not to get on the scoresheet in the final against France, hitting the bar and having a goal disallowed. However, this was no young tyro making a name for himself; Toni was a 29-year-old veteran who had served a long apprenticeship in the lower reaches of Italian football before taking his place in the spotlight.

Toni began his professional career in 1994 with Modena, the club he had joined in his early teens. Over the next eleven years he changed clubs at a dizzying speed, scoring goals at a decent rate wherever he went. Among his long list of employers was Vicenza, which gave him his first taste of Serie A in 2000–01. His return dipped to single figures, showing that goals weren't so easy to come by in the top flight. He had two seasons with Brescia, playing alongside former golden boy Roberto Baggio, then in the twilight of his career. Again, his goal stats were steady rather than spectacular, but that was about to change. He returned to Serie B with Palermo, firing 30 goals in a promotion-winning campaign, and the following term netted 20 times, his best effort thus far in the top division. His goals helped Palermo to a sixth-place finish and Uefa Cup qualification, and it was during this prolific spell that Toni won his first senior cap.

In 2005 he joined a Fiorentina side that had only just avoided relegation, and it proved to be £7 million well spent for a club trying to rebuild after being declared bankrupt and demoted to Serie C three years earlier. Toni scored 31 goals in 2005–06, helping Fiorentina to fourth place and Champions League qualification. Although that performance was tarnished when the club was subsequently implicated in a match-fixing scandal, Toni retained the coveted individual honour of the Capocannonieri, awarded to Serie A's sharpest shooter. He became the first player to top 30 goals for a season since 1959. Toni weighed in with 16 more goals in an injury-hit 2006–07, when Fiorentina had to contend with a 15-point deficit as part of their punishment. He signed off by helping the club qualify for the Uefa Cup despite the handicap, joining Bayern Munich in summer 2007. He was the Bundesliga's top marksman in 2007–08, netting 24 goals, while his brace in the cup final helped Bayern to a 2–1 win over Borussia Dortmund and yet another domestic double.

Luca Toni

Fernando Torres

Fernando Torres

Born: 20 March 1984
Clubs: Atletico Madrid, Liverpool
National Team: Spain

Fernando Torres' eye for goal marked him out from a very early age. He scored Spain's winner in the final of the 2001 Uefa U-16 Championship and the 2002 U-19 Championship, picking up the golden boot in both tournaments. He became Atletico Madrid's youngest ever scorer, after making his debut in 2001 for the club he supported as a boy and joined at the age of 11. Such prowess in one so young earned him the nickname 'El Nino' – the child. Atletico were then in Spanish football's second tier, and it wasn't until 2002-03 that he took his bow in the top flight, when he hit 13 goals in 29 starts. The following season he met the benchmark of all top strikers by scoring a goal every other game, and at the age of 19 he was handed the captain's armband, a mark of his maturity as well as his influence on the pitch.

Torres made his international tournament debut at Euro 2004, where he confirmed his reputation as one of the hottest properties on the Continent. Transfer speculation was rife by the time Torres went to the 2006 World Cup, where he hit three goals in helping Spain reach the Second Round.

He curbed his ambition to join one of Europe's elite clubs for one more season, when Liverpool's offer of £20 million plus Luis Garcia proved too tempting for Atletico. Torres quickly became a favourite of the Anfield terraces, and some fans criticized Rafael Benitez's rotation policy when it left the mercurial striker kicking his heels on the bench. Even so, some former Reds legends had seen enough to comment that Torres had all the attributes to make him an Anfield legend to be mentioned in the same breath as Keegan, Rush and Dalglish. He set about living up to the billing immediately, scoring 24 goals in his first Premiership campaign. It was the first time since the days of Robbie Fowler at his peak that a Liverpool striker had topped the 20-goal mark in the league. Torres rounded off a memorable season by scoring the goal that beat Germany in the Euro 2008 final, ending Spain's 44-year barren spell in the international arena.

Francesco Totti

Born: 27 September 1976
Clubs: Roma
National Team: Italy

Roma's playmaker took over Italy's golden boy tag from Roberto Baggio and Alessandro del Piero. A Roman through and through, Totti made his debut for the club in 1993, aged 16. His rise to the top wasn't without its trials, however. A couple of the managers he played under in the early days were unsure about him and he even considered leaving the club at one point. But under Fabio Capello he mastered the art of playing in the floating role between the midfield and the strikers. He was outstanding in the 2000–01 season, when Roma won their first *scudetto* for 18 years. The following season the club failed to retain their crown by a single point. Totti cemented his place in the national side at Euro 2000. He went into the 2002 World Cup with a huge weight of expectation on his shoulders, coach Giovanni Trapattoni believing he could have the same impact that Zidane had had four years earlier. It went badly, both for Totti personally and for Italy. Euro 2004 was another disaster: a spitting incident earned Totti a ban until the knock-out stage, but that proved academic as Italy failed to progress from their group. Totti recovered from a broken leg just in time for Germany 2006, playing a vital role in Italy's fourth World Cup triumph. His last-gasp penalty which beat Australia in the second round will live long in the memory of Azzurri fans. During the 2007–08 season, his 16th with Roma, Totti notched his 200th goal for the club, and also picked up his fifth Italian Player of the Year award.

Francesco Totti

Ruud Van Nistelrooy

Born: 1 July 1976
Clubs: Den Bosch, Heerenveen, PSV Eindhoven, Manchester United, Real Madrid
National Team: Holland

Ruud van Nistelrooy is one of Europe's most prolific marksmen. Only Raul has scored more European Cup/Champions League goals, and in April 2006 he chalked up his 150th goal for Manchester United, plundered from barely 200 games.

It wasn't always that way. Ruud van Nistelrooy's four-year spell at Den Bosch, then a Division Two side in the Dutch league, yielded only a goal every four games. When he moved to top-flight side Heerenveen, it was by no means certain that the 21-year-old had what it took. A year later, on his 22nd birthday, Bobby Robson paid £4.2 million to take him to PSV Eindhoven. Robson's predecessor, Dick Advocaat, had also taken a look at Van Nistelrooy but had seen some flaws. He missed too many chances, something that the player himself learnt to correct by letting instinct take over instead of trying too hard. He ended his first season at PSV as the Dutch league's top scorer with 31 goals,

enough to make him runner-up to Mario Jardel for the golden boot award. He carried on in the same rich vein the following season, and early in 2000 Manchester United were keen to sign him. A cruciate ligament injury deferred the deal for just over a year, but in April 2001 United got their man for £19 million. Thirty-six goals in his debut season in the Premiership was a personal triumph, although United ended the campaign empty-handed. He was in scorching form again in 2002–03 and this time he picked up a Premiership winners' medal. Van Nistelrooy also scored twice in United's European Champions League quarter-final clash with Real Madrid but still finished on the losing side.

He fell from favour with Sir Alex Ferguson during the 2005–06 campaign, regularly finding himself warming the bench despite showing the kind of form which made him the Premiership's second top scorer. It was no surprise when he left to join Real Madrid in a £10 million deal that summer. He was La Liga's top scorer in his first season, his 25 goals goals in 2006–07 helping to wrest the La Liga crown from Barcelona. He bagged another 20 the following term as Real retained the championship, but the 2008–09 season came to an abrupt end when he was sidelined with a serious knee injury just before Christmas.

Ruud Van Nistelrooy

Patrick Vieira

Patrick Vieira

Born: 23 June 1976
Clubs: Cannes, AC Milan, Arsenal, Juventus, Inter Milan
National Team: France

Patrick Vieira has been one of the world's outstanding midfield players of the last decade. He has graced the Premiership, Serie A and the Championnat with his elegant passing, combative ball-winning with inspirational leadership. Senegalese by birth, Vieira grew up in France. He made his league debut for Cannes in 1993, when he was 17 years old. Two years later, he was made captain, the youngest player to skipper a French first division side. AC Milan paid £3.5 million for him in 1995, but he could not be guaranteed a regular first team place at the Serie A club. He became one of Wenger's first signings when the latter took over at Highbury. Gunners fans may have shrugged at a £3 million fee for a relatively unknown 20-years-old. Seven years on it must go down as one of the deals of the decade, as Vieira formed a near-impregnable midfield axis with compatriot Emanuel Petit. Their partnership was key to Arsenal's

Double-winning campaign of 1997–98. He capped a memorable season by joining up with the national squad for their World Cup triumph on home soil. Didier Deschamps' presence meant that his opportunities were somewhat limited, although he did come on as substitute in the final, setting up Petit for France's third goal against Brazil. Since then Vieira has been a key member of the France side, one of only six players to reach 100 caps. In 2002–03 Vieira was at the heart of the side whose early form led Wenger to speculate whether they could go through the season unbeaten. The Gunners faded that year, but Vieira captained the team in an historic unbeaten league campaign in 2003–04. Two months after scoring the decisive penalty in the shoot-out against Manchester United in the 2005 FA Cup final, Vieira joined Juventus in a £14 million deal. He spent just one season in Turin, moving to Inter after Juve were stripped of their title and relegated to serie B following a match-fixing scandal. Vieira added several bona fide Serie A winners medals to his collection following Inter's success in recent seasons.

Christian Vieri

Born: 12 July 1973
Clubs: Prato, Torino, Pisa, Ravenna, Venezia, Atalanta, Juventus, Atletico Madrid, Lazio, Inter Milan, AC Milan, Monaco, Fiorentina
National Team: Italy

A much-travelled striker who once bore the burden of being the world's most expensive player, Christian Vieri has proved that a powerhouse centre-forward in the traditional mould can score heavily in Serie A. Vieri went to the 2002 World Cup as Italy's top striker, ahead of the likes of Inzaghi and del Piero. He was one of those to suffer at the hands of some dubious refereeing decisions in Japan and Korea, but at least returned home with his personal reputation enhanced. Vieri was born in Bologna but grew up in Australia until the age of 14, when the family returned to Italy. He burst onto the footballing scene as an 18-year-old with Torino. Between 1993 and 1999 he had six different clubs, spending just one season with each. The 1996–97 season at Juventus was a turning point. The coaches at the Turin club smoothed out the rough edges to his game and improved his all-round performance considerably. Atletico Madrid certainly thought so, for they paid £12 million to take him to Spain. Vieri repaid them with 24 goals, making him the club's top marksman, before a disagreement with the coaching staff meant that he was on his travels yet again. Lazio paid £18 million for him in 1998, and in the same year he was Italy's top scorer at the World Cup with five goals. In his one season at Lazio he again topped the scoring charts, and was on target in the 2–1 win over Real Mallorca in the European Cup Winners' Cup final. He joined Inter Milan shortly afterwards for a new world record fee of £31 million. The personal highlight of his six years at the club came in

2002–03, when he topped the list of Serie A marksmen with 24 goals. After a brief spell with rivals AC Milan in 2005, Vieri moved to Monaco for regular first team football and thus a better chance of making the Azzurri squad for Germany 2006.

A knee injury ended that hope, and when he regained full fitness Vieri was on his travels again, back to Atalanta. The chairman of the Serie A club put the veteran striker on a modest basic wage but offered a reputed 100,000 euros per goal scored. It didn't prove expensive as Vieri netted just twice in seven appearances, and in summer 2007 he moved on to Fiorentina. After just one season in Florence, Vieri returned to Atalanta for a third spell at the age of 35.

Christian Vieri (left)

David Villa

Born: 3 December 1981
Clubs: Sporting de Gijon, Real Zaragoza, Valencia
National Team: Spain

The formidable strike partnership of David Villa and Fernando Torres spearheaded Spain's triumphant Euro 2008 campaign, a tournament which saw the country shake off the 'perennial underachievers' tag in style. Torres may have grabbed the goal that beat Germany in the final, but it was Villa who took the Golden Shoe with four goals, a fine haul considering he missed two games through injury. Following on from the three goals he plundered from Spain's four games at the 2006 World Cup, it showed that the Valencia striker was adept at finding the net at the very highest level. Indeed, he went into 2009 with 24 international goals from just 41 games, putting him in the top five in the all-time list of Spain's marksmen at just 27 years of age. Villa's story is one of endeavour and belief. Overlooked by Real Oviedo, the biggest footballing name in the Asturias region where he grew up, Villa joined second-division side Sporting de Gijon. After three fruitful years there, he joined Real Zaragoza in 2003 for his first taste of top-flight football. In his two seasons at Zaragoza the club was firmly anchored in mid-table, but Villa made a telling contribution in a terrific run in the Spanish Cup in 2003–04. He nervelessly scored from the spot at the Nou Camp in Zaragoza's 2–1 aggregate victory over Barcelona, and fired another penalty in the 3–2 win over Real Madrid in the final. Valencia paid £8 million for Villa's services in the summer of 2005, and he began repaying the club immediately by hitting 25 goals, one behind Barcelona's Samuel Eto'o in that season's hot-shots table. Valencia finished third that term, one point adrift of Real Madrid and three behind champions Barca. Villa was again Valencia's top striker the following year with 16 goals, and even when the team dipped to finish halfway in La Liga in 2007–08, he still netted 18 times in 27 appearances to finish fourth in the division's list of top marksmen. That represented over one-third of Valencia's league goals, and Villa also helped the club win the Copa del Rey, his second winner's medal in that competition. Valencia will be hoping to keep its chief asset for the duration of his long-term contract, but a player with a career record of a goal every other game is bound to attract the attention of clubs with deep pockets and high ambitions.

David Villa (right)

The
Managers

Enzo Bearzot

Born: 26 September 1927
Management Career: Prato, Italy
Major Honours: World Cup 1982

In the run-up to the 1982 World Cup even the most ardent Azzurri fans had little confidence that Enzo Bearzot would be able to bring the country their third success in the tournament. Italy's form during the qualifiers had been patchy and Bearzot had been the subject of some vitriolic criticism in the press. The group matches did little to change public opinion as Italy drew all their games and squeezed through on goal difference at Cameroon's expense. Thereafter, however, the team got better and better. The exuberant talent that Bearzot knew his side possessed came to the fore just at the right time. The undoubted star was Paolo Rossi, with whom Bearzot kept faith despite the fact that his two-year ban for match fixing had expired just two months earlier. Rossi's hat-trick against favourite's Brazil in the second round, and a brace against Poland in the semis, put Italy into the final. A 3-1 win over West Germany meant that Bearzot had delivered what no other Italy manager had done since the the legendary Vittorio Pozzo in the 1930s. A third tournament win also put Italy level with Brazil in the all-time list.

Franz Beckenbauer

Franz Beckenbauer

Born: 11 September 1945
Management Career: West Germany, Olympique Marseille, Bayern Munich
Major Honours: World Cup 1990; UEFA Cup 1996

In 1984 Franz Beckenbauer got the job as West Germany's manager on the strength of his outstanding achievements as a player over the previous 20 years. No one doubted the Kaiser's ability on the field, but with no track record as a manager, others were less sure about his appointment as boss of the national team. In the next six years the selectors were vindicated in their decision. Beckenbauer led West Germany in two World Cup campaigns, reaching the final of both. At Mexico '86 his team included Rummenigge, Matthaus and Voller, but they went down 3-2 to an Argentina side inspired by Maradona. Many of the same personnel were on show four years later at Italia '90, when the same two teams contested the final. This time an Andy Brehme penalty gave the West Germans victory, and also earned Beckenbauer a unique place in the record books as the first man to captain and manage a World Cup-winning side. Beckenbauer stepped down soon after this historic achievement. He went into club management with a brief spell at Marseille, before returning to his beloved Bayern Munich. He led the Bavarian side to the Bundesliga title in 1994, and a resounding 5–1 aggregate victory over Bordeaux in the UEFA Cup final two years later. He later moved upstairs, becoming president of the club for whom he had made his debut in 1964.

Rafael Benitez

Born: 16 April 1960
Management Career: Valladolid, Osasuna, Extremadura, Tenerife, Valencia, Liverpool
Major Honours: Uefa Cup 2004; Champions League 2005

Benitez came to Liverpool in 2004 on the back of a hugely successful three-year spell at Valencia, where he had broken the Real Madrid-Barcelona axis by winning La Liga twice in three years, the club's first championship successes since 1971. In the second of those title-winning campaigns, 2003–04, Benitez steered Valencia to a famous double as the team also lifted the Uefa Cup with a 2–0 victory over Marseille.

     Benitez never made it to the top as a top player, his career cut short by injury. He showed an interest in coaching from an early age, though his first step on the managerial ladder, with Valladolid in 1995–96, ended in the sack following a disastrous run of results. After a similar experience with Second Division side Osasuna, Benitez won promotion with Extremadura and Tenerife, both Division Two clubs, achievements which earned him a contract at Valencia in 2001. He inherited a fine side from predecessor Hector Cuper, including the talents of Roberto Ayala, Rubén Baraja and Pablo Aimar, and wasted no time in getting the best out of his stars. In 2002 Benítez was named Spain's Manager of the Year as he led Valencia to their first La Liga title in thirty-one years. After a blip the following season, Valencia were top of the pile again, clinching the title with three games to spare. Benitez fell out with the club's hierarchy and quit that summer, moving to Liverpool. The Anfield faithful celebrated their fifth European Cup success in Benítez's first season with a famous victory over AC Milan, the Reds overturning a 3–0 half-time deficit to win on penalties. There was more drama as Liverpool came from behind to beat West Ham in the 2006 FA Cup final, though their luck ran out a year later in Athens, when AC Milan exacted revenge as the clubs again contested the Champions League final. There were rumblings of discontent as 2007–08 saw the Reds once again off the Premiership pace, despite the signing of star striker Fernando Torres. Many pundits criticized Benítez's rotation policy, which had been successful in cup competitions but had failed to deliver the coveted Premiership title.

Matt Busby

Born: 26 May 1909
Management Career: Manchester United
Major Honours: European Cup 1968

When Matt Busby took over at Manchester United in 1945 their stadium was a bombed-out wreck and the club was bankrupt. Busby had been expected to coach Liverpool, the side he had played for, but the Scot had also played for Manchester City, and perhaps due to his fondness for Manchester, it was United that he chose. That decision was the turning point in United's history. During Busby's 26-year reign at Old Trafford they won five Championships and were runners-up seven times, were victors in two FA Cup finals and lifted the European Cup once, having been at four European Cup semi-finals.

Busby had insisted he be given absolute control over the playing side, including picking the team. The first side he built beat Blackpool in the 1948 FA Cup final and then took the Championship title in 1952. As that side aged, Busby began to scour the country in search of raw young talent. The side he created in the mid-50s was one which many believed would be the best in Europe. The

'Busby Babes' as they became known had already started to dominate English football winning the Championship in 1956 and 1957. They had already made it to two European Cup semi-finals, when following a successful quarter-final return match against Red Star Belgrade, the team was wiped out in an air crash at Munich. Eight players lost their lives on 6 February 1958 and Busby was so badly injured that he received the last rites.

Busby did recover, and by the mid-60s had built another winning side, with the likes of Denis Law and George Best joining survivors Bill Foulkes and Bobby Charlton. In 1963, despite finishing fourth from bottom in the league, United beat Leicester City in the FA Cup final. The following year they were league runners-up, then winners in 1965 and 1967. However, Busby's most heartfelt victory came in 1968, when ten years after the Munich disaster his brilliant side beat Benfica 4–1 at Wembley to lift the European Cup. Manchester United became the first English team to win that trophy and Busby only the second British manager to lift a cup in Europe. He was knighted that same year. Sir Matt Busby died in 1994.

Matt Busby

Fabio Capello

Born: 18 June 1946
Management Career: AC Milan, Real Madrid, Roma, Juventus, Real Madrid, England
Major Honours: European Champions League 1994

When former international midfielder Fabio Capello hung up his boots, he joined the coaching staff at AC Milan, one of his former clubs. He took over the top job in 1991, following Arrigo Sacchi's departure. Capello built on Sacchi's successes, guiding Milan to four Serie A titles between 1992 and 1996. He also led the club to their fifth European Cup success, with a 4–0 rout of Barcelona in 1994. Capello joined Real Madrid in 1996, and in just one season in charge he took the team to a 27th Primera Liga title. He then returned to Italy, leaving his successor Jupp Heynckes an outstanding team which would go on to win the 1997–98 Champions League Cup. Capello was back at AC Milan by then. Things didn't go so well second time around, particularly the 1998 Italian Cup final, when Lazio came from behind to beat Milan 3–2. Capello was soon on his way again, this time to Roma. In 2000 he signed Gabriel Batistuta from Fiorentina in a £23 million deal. It proved to be money well spent as 'Batigol' helped Roma win their first Serie A title for 18 years. Capello brought the scudetto to Juve in 2005 and 2006, though both titles were expunged from the record books in the wake of the match-fixing scandal that rocked Italian football during the latter campaign. Capello returned to Real Madrid in summer 2006, and although he succeeded in wresting the La Liga title back from Barcelona, he was on his way again after a single season at the Bernabeu. Nine league titles in 16 years, managing in the hothouse conditions of Italy and Spain, impressed the FA enough to offer Capello the England job after the team failed to reach Euro 2008 under Steve McClaren.

Fabio Capello

Herbert Chapman

Born: 19 January 1878
Management Career: Leeds City, Huddersfield Town, Arsenal

Herbert Chapman was the most successful manager of the 1920s and early 1930s, his influence on the game continuing long after his death in 1934. He had had an undistinguished playing career at Northampton, Sheffield United and Spurs, standing out more for his trademark yellow boots than for the quality of his play. He made his name during the First World War as manager of Leeds City, but in 1919 he was suspended over financial irregularities. He took over an ailing Huddersfield Town side in 1920 and within four years he transformed the club into championship winners. After retaining the title, Chapman moved to Highbury in 1925. Along with veteran inside-forward Charlie Buchan, Chapman reacted to a change in the offside law by replacing the rigid 2-3-5 formation with a revolutionary 3-3-4 formation.

Chapman had an uncanny knack for spotting potential. He signed Cliff Bastin and paid a world record £10,890 for David Jack. Alex James was acquired for slightly less than Jack, but it was his arrival from Preston in 1929 that sparked a phenomenal run of success.

With James, Arsenal went on to win the championship three times in four years, and finished runners-up to Everton in 1931–32. There was also an FA Cup victory over Chapman's former club, Huddersfield, in 1930.

Chapman died just before Arsenal confirmed their third championship, but all the pieces were in place for

Jack Charlton

further success. The Gunners' League titles of 1935 and 1938, together with another FA Cup victory in 1936, also owed much to the groundwork Chapman had laid. His influence also spread to the international side, notably when England beat Italy in November 1934. Chapman's Arsenal provided seven of the players who beat the reigning world champions 3–2.

Jack Charlton

Born: 8 May 1935
Management Career: Middlesbrough, Sheffield Wednesday, Newcastle United, Republic of Ireland

Jack Charlton made the transition from player to manager in 1973, when he was 37. He took over at Middlesbrough, then a struggling Division Two side. Under Charlton's guidance Boro romped to promotion in 1973–74, finishing 15 points clear at the top of the table. The following season he took the team to a creditable seventh place in the top flight. Charlton also had spells at Sheffield Wednesday and Newcastle United before taking over as Republic of Ireland manager in 1986. He led the team to the European Championship League finals in 1988, the country's first appearance in a major tournament. They acquitted themselves well, most memorably with a 1–0 win over England. Two glorious World Cup campaigns followed. At Italia '90 the Republic reached the last eight, where they went down 1–0 to the hosts. Four years later in the USA, Charlton got the Republic out of a difficult group. They qualified at the expense of both Italy and Norway before going down to Holland in the second round. Charlton stepped down after the team failed to qualify for Euro '96. Charlton's teams were invariably well organised and difficult to break down, though they were sometimes criticised for being unadventurous and lacking in flair. However, he presided over the most successful period in the Republic's history.

Brian Clough

Born: 21 March 1935
Management Career: Hartlepool, Derby County, Brighton &
Hove Albion, Leeds United, Nottingham Forest
Major Honours: European Cup 1979, 1980

When Brian Clough took over the management
of Hartlepool in 1965, he became the youngest
manager in the country, aged just 29. Known for
his no-nonsense, outspoken approach, Clough
was the England manager that never was. Adored
by players and fans but feared by the footballing
establishment, he was never chosen for the top
job, despite his outstanding credentials.

Clough had enjoyed a brief but highly
successful playing career. Before it was cut short
through injury, he had played for Middlesbrough
and Sunderland, scoring a total of 251 goals in
274 games. He managed Hartlepool for just two
years, moving on to Second Division Derby
County and it was there that he established his
reputation. The Rams were second division
champions in 1969 and within three years they
had become League champions for the first time
in their history. In 1973, Derby reached the
semi-final of the European Cup, eventually
losing 3–1 to Juventus. Clough left Derby that
same year following disagreements with the
board, moving first to Brighton & Hove Albion
and then to Leeds. His position with the
Yorkshire club lasted for only 44 days, and
Clough then joined another Second Division
club, Nottingham Forest.

Brian Clough and Nottingham Forest were
together for 18 years, in a relationship that
earned Clough a place in history and Forest
promotion, League Championship and a host of
trophies. Within two years of his taking the job,
Forest won promotion to the First Division,
winning the championship at the first time of
asking in 1977–78. In 1979, they won the
European Cup, beating Malmo 1–0. The goal
scorer was Trevor Francis, whom Clough had
signed for a record £1 million. They retained the
cup, beating Hamburg the following year. Forest
also won the League Cup four times, but never
won the FA Cup, reaching the final in 1991 but
losing to Spurs. Relegation in 1993 marked the
end of Clough's career; he retired at the end of
that season. Clough died in September 2004.

Brian Clough

Johan Cruyff

Born: 25 April 1947
Management Career: Ajax, Barcelona
Major Honours: European Cup 1992;
European Cup Winners' Cup 1987, 1989;
European Super Cup 1992

Johan Cruyff's achievements as a coach came at two of the clubs he had graced as a player: Ajax and Barcelona. Like his illustrious contemporary, Franz Beckenbauer, Cruyff had no formal coaching qualifications. But after ending his playing days at Feyenoord, he took over the reins at the club where he first made his name 20 years earlier. He took Ajax to the European Cup Winners' Cup final in 1987 with a side which included Van Basten, Rijkaard and teenage sensation Dennis Bergkamp. Van Basten hit the goal which beat Lokomotive Leipzig in the final, the scoreline hardly reflecting Ajax's supremacy. Cruyff moved on to Barcelona the following season, the start of a nine-year reign at the Nou Camp. He led the side to Cup Winners' Cup victory in 1989, Barca beating Sampdoria 2–0 in the final. Between 1991 and 1994 he steered the Catalan club to four successive Primera Liga titles, ending a period of domination by arch-rivals Real Madrid. In 1992 he brought Barcelona their first European Cup success. His side boasted the attacking flair of Romario and Stoichkov, but in the final it was defender Ronald Koeman who hit the only goal of the game in extra-time. Sampdoria were once again on the receiving end. Two years later, Barcelona reached the final again, but this time suffered a resounding 4–0 defeat at the hands of AC Milan. Cruyff was ousted from his job following an internal power struggle in the spring of 1996.

Johan Cruyff

Hector Cuper

Born: 16 November 1955
Management Career: Huracan, Atletico Lanus, Real Mallorca, Valencia, Inter Milan, Real Mallorca, Real Betis, Parma, Georgia

In his playing days Hector Cuper won eight caps for Argentina. He began his coaching career with Huracan, his last club, and also had a spell with Atletico Lanus before Real Mallorca offered him his first coaching job in Europe in 1997. He led Mallorca to the Cup Winners' Cup final in 1999, and although the team went down 2–1 to Lazio, Cuper had impressed enough to be given the job at Valencia, following the departure of Claudio Ranieri. The team didn't perform well, and halfway through Cuper's first season in charge there were already calls for his head. That all changed as Valencia went on a dazzling run in the Champions League, culminating in a first appearance in the final. Valencia had been outstanding against Lazio and Barcelona in the quarters and semis, but the final against Real Madrid proved to be a hurdle too far, Madrid winning 3–0. Valencia were runners-up the following season too, Bayern Munich proving to be the stumbling block this time. Cuper moved on to Inter Milan and his exciting side were Serie A front-runners in the early stages of the 2002–03 season. With Hernan Crespo, Christian Vieri and Alvaro Recoba providing the firepower, Inter were on course to bring the club their first championship since 1989. However, they eventually had to settle for the runners-up spot behind Juventus. Cuper also led Inter to the semi-final of the 2002–03 Champions League, where they went out to eventual winners AC Milan. Despite making another good start in the 2003–04 Champions League campaign, Inter's indifferent league form cost Cuper his job early in the season. Real Mallorca was pleased to welcome him back but he stepped down in February 2006, with Mallorca anchored at the foot of La Liga. There followed a brief spell at Real Betis, which ended in 2007 when that club, too, was battling relegation. After a brief spell in charge of Parma, Cuper was appointed coach to the Georgia national team in summer 2008.

Hector Cuper

Kenny Dalglish

Born: 4 March 1951
Management Career: Liverpool, Blackburn Rovers, Newcastle United

Having enjoyed a successful playing career at Liverpool, Kenny Dalglish was selected by the club to become its new manager on the retirement of Joe Fagan. However, Dalglish was to begin his stint as player manager under appalling circumstances. The day before he officially took the job,

Kenny Dalglish

Liverpool's role in the Heysel tragedy resulted in English clubs being banned from European football. In addition to that, the club was trailing behind Mersyside rivals Everton in the English league. Yet on the last game of Dalglish's first season in charge, they needed to beat Chelsea away to secure the Championship. It was Dalglish who scored the game's only goal and when Liverpool went on to win the FA Cup, he could celebrate a Double. Two more Championship titles followed, in 1988 and 1990, along with another victory in the FA Cup in 1989. Yet tragedy was to strike Liverpool again, when 95 fans died at Hillsborough. His time at the club marked by both success and disaster, Dalglish left Anfield in 1991 citing pressure as a reason.

In October that year, he took a position as manager at Blackburn Rovers. At the end of the 1991–92 season, Rovers were promoted to the Premiership and they consolidated their position there by finishing fourth the following season. Dalglish had Jack Walker's fortune at his disposal and he spent the money wisely, building a team that won the title in 1995; it was the club's first Championship since 1914.

He stepped down at the end of that season, but returned to management in 1997, succeeding Kevin Keegan at Newcastle United. Although they reached the FA Cup final in 1998, the title went to Arsenal and Dalglish was sacked from the club at the start of the following season.

Vicente Del Bosque

Vicente Del Bosque

Born: 23 December 1950
Management Career: Real Madrid, Besiktas, Spain
Major Honours: European Champions League 2000, 2002; World Club Cup 2002; European Super Cup 2002

Vicente Del Bosque was a Real Madrid man through and through. In 2002 he notched up 34 years at the Bernebeu, having joined the club as a teenager. His midfield skills also won him 18 caps for Spain. Del Bosque joined the coaching staff when his playing days ended, and was catapulted into the top job in 1999, following the sacking of John Toshack. Few expected Del Bosque to survive long, as Real had gone through a string of coaches during the previous five years. An outstanding display in the 2000 European Champions League final, in which Real beat Valencia 3–0, raised his stock considerably. Just as importantly, new club president Florentino Perez decided that a period of stability was needed. Real won the Primera Liga in 2001, their first championship for four years. In 2002 Del Bosque steered Real to their third

European Champions League victory in five years with a 2–1 win over Bayer Leverkusen. With the likes of Zidane, Roberto Carlos, Raul, Luis Figo and Ronaldo in the side, Del Bosque was regarded as a coach with an embarrassment of riches at his disposal. In 2002–03 Del Bosque delivered the domestic championship yet again — the 29th in the club's history. This wasn't enough to prevent him from losing his job, Real having lost to Juventus in the semi-final of the European Champions League. Del Bosque took over at Turkish club Besiktas in summer 2004, but with the team struggling in the league he was shown the door midway through the season. After a spell on the sidelines, Del Bosque took over from Luis Aragones as coach of a high-flying Spain side that had just triumphed at Euro 2008.

Sven-Goran Eriksson

Born: 5 February 1948
Management Career: IFK Gothenburg, Benfica, Roma, Fiorentina, Benfica, Sampdoria, Lazio, England, Manchester City, Mexico
Major Honours: UEFA Cup 1982

When Sven-Goran Eriksson became the England manager in 2001, the decision sparked controversy across the nation. Eriksson was the first foreign manager to be given the top job and many were angry at the FA's decision. However, the England team had suffered from a rapid turnover of managers and Swede Eriksson, a highly experienced and successful manager, appeared to be the best choice.

Eriksson had first demonstrated his tactical acumen with IFK Gothenburg, who reached the 1982 UEFA Cup final and became the first Swedish team to win a European trophy. He then moved to Benfica, who during his two years in charge won the Portuguese championship twice, the domestic cup and reached the UEFA Cup final. He left Portugal in 1984 for Italy, spending time at Roma and Fiorentina, then in 1989 returned to Benfica, taking them to the European Cup final of 1990, where they lost to AC Milan. It was back to Italy and league success with Sampdoria

in 1992. In 1997 Eriksson moved to Lazio, who went on to top Serie A for the first time in 26 years in 2000.

It was this record of success that made Eriksson the ideal candidate for the England job. At his appointment, they were in a precarious position in the World Cup qualifiers, and desperately in need of stability following the departure of Kevin Keegan. Eriksson's business-like approach galvanized the team and they eventually qualified for the 2002 tournament at the top of their group with some fine performances, including the stunning 5–1 win in Germany. Although the team was knocked out of the finals by eventual winners Brazil, they had fought an impressive campaign.

At both Euro 2004 and Germany 2006 Eriksson's team went out to Portugal on penalties. There were mixed views regarding three successive quarter-final appearances but Eriksson's tenure wasn't an issue, for it had already been announced that he would be stepping down after the 2006 World Cup. After a season on the sidelines, Eriksson made a dramatic return to club football with Manchester City, his new-look side making an immediate impression on the Premiership. Ninth place wasn't enough to keep his job, and after leaving Eastlands in June 2008 Eriksson had a short spell as coach of Mexico's national side.

Sven-Goran Eriksson

Alex Ferguson

Born: 31 December 1941
Management Career: East Stirlingshire, St Mirren, Aberdeen, Scotland, Manchester United
Major Honours: European Cup Winners' Cup 1983, 1991; European Champions League 1999, 2008

Sir Alex Ferguson is the most successful manager in the history of English football. With Manchester United, he has won a host of domestic trophies, including two Doubles and an incredible Treble in 1999, when United added the European Champions League Cup to their League and FA trophies.

Ferguson began his managerial career in 1974 with East Stirlingshire, but it was with St Mirren that he began collecting trophies, starting with the Scottish First Division Championship in 1977. In 1978 he joined Aberdeen and for eight years he transformed the club. They broke the 'Old Firm' stranglehold on Scottish football, winning three League titles, four Scottish cups and the Scottish League Cup. Then, in 1983, Aberdeen enjoyed a famous victory over Real Madrid in the European Cup Winners' Cup final. A brief spell as Scotland manager followed and then Ferguson opted to move south of the border to restore some of their former glory to Manchester United.

United hadn't won the Championship for 20 years and Ferguson was under pressure to garner some silverware. It took three years for his influence on the club to bear fruit; United won the FA Cup in 1990, then the following year they beat Barcelona in the European Cup Winners' Cup.

Ferguson had invested in a youth system at Manchester that eventually began to produce great players such as Giggs, Scholes, the Neville brothers and Beckham. Some astute signings, including those of Peter Schmeichel and Eric Cantona, completed a powerhouse team which began to dominate the new Premier League. They won the inaugural Premiership title in 1993, following that with the Double in 1994 and again in 1996. Ferguson's greatest moment came when, in 1999, United won the historic Treble. His inspired management at the end of the Champions League Cup final, when Bayern Munich looked set to enjoy a 1–0 win, secured United's victory. He brought on substitutes Teddy Sheringham and Ole Gunnar Solskjaer and in the closing seconds each of them scored.

Ferguson flirted with retirement in 2002 but stayed on to build yet another all-conquering side. In 2004 United won the FA Cup for the fifth time during his tenure and

2008 saw a second Champions League success, following a dramatic shoot-out victory over Chelsea. Victory in the 2008–09 Carling Cup brought United's haul to 21 major trophies in the Ferguson era. 2009 made it 11 Premiership titles in 17 years, putting the club level with Liverpool in the all-time list.

Louis van Gaal

Born: 8 August 1951
Management Career: Ajax, Barcelona, Holland, Barcelona, AZ Alkmaar
Major Honours: UEFA Cup 1992; European Champions League 1995; World Club Cup 1995; European Super Cup 1995

Louis van Gaal made his name as a coach at Ajax, for whom he had played in the 1970s. He took over at the Amsterdam club in 1991, promoted from youth team coach after Leo Beenhakker left to join Real Madrid. Within a year he had delivered the UEFA Cup. His exciting young side, including Frank de Boer, Dennis Bergkamp and Bryan Roy, put out Genoa in the semis and beat Torino in the final on away goals. Van Gaal steered the club to a hat-trick of domestic titles between 1994 and 1996. In 1995 he took Ajax to the top of European football when his team overcame an all-star AC Milan team in the European Champions League final. The Ajax squad included two 18-year old substitutes, Nwankwo Kanu and Patrick Kluivert, and it was the latter who came on to score the only goal of the game five minutes from time. Ajax reached the final again in 1996, but this time the side, hampered by injuries, lost to Juventus on penalties.

The break-up of the team, and van Gaal's departure to Barcelona, followed at a dizzying speed. Van Gaal took over from Bobby Robson at the Nou Camp in 1997. He won the domestic double in his first season, helped by several of his former Ajax players, whom he paid big money to bring with him. Barca retained the championship in 1999, but thereafter the lustre soon wore off.

His decision to quit in 2000 was met with much approval by the fans. Van Gaal took over as Holland coach but failed to make it to the 2002 World Cup, Portugal and the Republic of Ireland going through at the expense of the Dutch. He returned to Barcelona in the summer of 2002, but although the team was in sparkling form in the early stages of the European Champions League, they were at the wrong end of the Primera Liga. Van Gaal paid the price in January 2003. After a spell back at Ajax as technical director, van Gaal took over at AZ Alkmaar in 2005.

Alex Ferguson

Ernst Happel

Born: 25 June 1929
Management Career: Wacker Innsbruck, Feyenoord, Den Haag, Club Brugge, Holland, Hamburg, FC Swarovski Tirol, Austria
Major Honours: European Cup 1970, 1983; World Club Cup 1970

Ernst Happel is a legendary figure in Austrian football. He was a skilful defender, winning 51 caps for his country before going on to become one of Europe's top coaches. He began his career in management with Feyenoord, guiding the team to European Cup victory in 1970. Ajax went on to dominate the competition for the following three years, but it was Happel who first brought to the European Cup to Holland, playing his own brand of 'total football'. Eight years later, he took Bruges to the final of the same competition, but this time finished on the losing side as a Kenny Dalglish goal gave Liverpool their second successive victory. That same year he took Holland to the World Cup final, with a side including many of the stars who had fallen at the last hurdle in 1974. They put out West Germany and Italy in the second round to reach the final, but there they went down 3–1 to hosts Argentina. His final spell in club management took him to Hamburg, whom he guided to the European Cup final in 1983. The opposition was Giovanni Trapattoni's star-studded Juventus, who were expected to run out easy victors. But despite having a much less impressive side on paper, the master tactician orchestrated a brilliant 1–0 victory. After Happel's death in 1992, Vienna's Prater Stadium was renamed in honour of Austria's greatest footballing son.

Sepp Herberger

Born: 28 March 1897
Management Career: Germany, West Germany
Major Honours: World Cup 1954

Sepp Herberger was a clever inside-forward with Mannheim in the 1920s. A decade later he took his cerebral approach to the game into his role as a coach. In 1932 he was appointed assistant to Otto Nerz, who was then in charge of Germany's national team. Four years later, Herberger was given the top job. He led the team to the 1938 World Cup, Germany going out to Switzerland in a tournament which was organised on a straight knockout basis. Sixteen years later, at the 1954 World Cup in Switzerland, 57-year-old Herberger had his greatest triumph, masterminding a victory over the great Hungarian side. Herberger cleverly fielded a weakened side when the two teams met at the group stage. Hungary ran out 8–3 winners, but West Germany also got through to the knockout stage, following a play-off victory over Turkey. When the two teams met again in the final, few gave West Germany a hope. Herberger's unheralded side went 2–0 down but fought back brilliantly for a famous 3–2 victory. Helmut Schoen became Herberger's number two for the last eight years of his tenure, and the success that West Germany enjoyed in the 1960s and 1970s was in no small part down to the footballing wisdom that Herberger imparted to Schoen. He died in 1977.

Happel's Bruges play Liverpool in the 1978 European Cup final.

Helenio Herrera

Born: 17 April 1917
Management Career: Puteaux, Red Star 93, Stade Francais, Atletico Madrid, Malaga, Valladolid, Sevilla, Barcelona, Italy, Spain, Inter Milan, Roma
Major Honours: European Cup 1964, 1965; World Club Cup 1964, 1965

Helenio Herrera was a controversial figure in the footballing world but his credentials were impeccable. His trophy haul with club sides in Spain and Italy was hugely impressive. He was also one of the chief architects of the ultra-defensive 'catenaccio' system which pervaded Italian football in the 1960s. It was not pretty to watch but Herrera refined it into an art form which yielded enormous success. Argentinian by birth, Herrera began his coaching career in France before moving on to Atletico Madrid, Valladolid and Seville. In the mid-1950s he took over at Barcelona, where he deployed the skills of Hungarian stars Kocsis, Kubala and Czibor with devastating effect. When he joined Inter Milan he decided that an expansive game was too risky and developed the 'catenaccio' system. It brought Inter three Serie A titles in four years and the European Cup in 1964 and 1965. Herrera also had spells as manager of the Spanish and Italian national sides. He took Spain to the 1962 World Cup in Chile. The team went out at the first hurdle, although the 2–1 defeat by eventual winners Brazil which ended their hopes was regarded as one of the games of the tournament.

side to European Cup victory two years later, beating Benfica on penalties in the final. After a spell in Spain with Valencia, Hiddink was appointed manager of Holland. He was somewhat fortunate in taking the side to the quarter-finals of Euro '96. Patrick Kluivert's consolation goal in a 4–1 hammering by England proved crucial in getting Holland into the last eight, where they went out on penalties to France. Hiddink's side also went out on penalties at France '98, this time against Brazil at the semi-final stage. He returned to Spain thereafter, and had spells at Real Madrid and Real Betis before agreeing to lead South Korea into the 2002 World Cup. He resigned after taking the joint-hosts to the semi-finals, the South Korean football association renaming the Gwangju stadium in his honour. He returned to PSV, combining that job with leading Australia to only their second World Cup appearance. The Socceroos impressed before going down narrowly to eventual winners Italy in the second round. After the tournament, Hiddink took over as coach of Russia, steering the side to the semi-finals at Euro 2008. In February 2009 he replaced Luiz Felipe Scolari at Chelsea, insisting it was a short-term appointment that would run in tandem with his efforts to reach the 2010 World Cup with Russia.

Guus Hiddink

Born: 8 November 1946
Management Career: De Graafschap, PSV Eindhoven, Fenerbahce, Valencia, Holland, Real Madrid, Real Betis, South Korea, PSV Eindhoven/Australia, Russia/ Chelsea
Major Honours: European Cup 1988

Guus Hiddink could have run for any post he wanted in South Korea following the 2002 World Cup. He had not only guided the country to an astonishing semi-final place in the tournament, but his side had played with flair and style. Hiddink spent a long apprenticeship learning the game. He was a journeyman player in his native Holland and also had a spell in the North American Soccer League in the 1970s. After a stint as youth coach at De Graafschap, he became assistant at PSV Eindhoven, both of which clubs he had been with in his playing days. He took over the top job at PSV in 1986 and led the

Guus Hiddink

Ottmar Hitzfeld

Born: 12 January 1949
Management Career: Zug, Aarau, Grasshoppers Zurich, Borussia Dortmund, Bayern Munich, Switzerland
Major Honours: European Champions League 1997, 2001

After taking over from Trapattoni at Bayern Munich in 1998, Ottmar Hitzfeld continued to build on his reputation as one of the outstanding coaches of the modern era. He led Bayern to the Bundesliga title in 1999 and 2000, and to European Champions League victory in 2001. But in the autumn of 2002 the picture was very different, Bayern crashing out of the European Champions League in the first round of group matches. New signings, including Michael Ballack and Ze Roberto, failed to ignite as Bayern took just one point from their first four games. Hitzfeld and Bayern parted company in 2004. Hitzfeld began his coaching career in Switzerland, but it was after joining Borussia Dortmund in 1991 that he made a name for himself. He built a side which brought Dortmund successive championships in 1995 and 1996, something the club hadn't achieved since the 1960s. He then masterminded the side's famous 3–1 victory over hot favourites Juventus in the 1997 Champions Cup final. After two years on the sidelines, Hitzfeld made a surprise return to Bayern in January 2007, following the sacking of Felix Magath. Midway through the 2007–08 campaign, with Bayern leading the Bundesliga, Hitzfeld announced that he would be leaving the club at the end of the season. Midway through the 2007–08 season, with Bayern on their way to yet another championship, Hitzfeld announced that he would be leaving the club at the end of the season. That summer he took over as coach of Switzerland, where he had enjoyed considerable success at club level in his early managerial career.

Ottmar Hitzfeld

Aime Jacquet

Born: 27 November 1941
Management Career: Lyon, Bordeaux, Montpellier, Nancy, France
Major Honours: World Cup 1998

Aime Jacquet enjoyed great success as Bordeaux manager in the 1980s. He joined the national team's coaching staff in 1992, and took over the top job from Gerard Houllier the following year, after France's failure to qualify for USA '94. Jacquet led France to the semi-finals of Euro '96, where they lost on penalties to the Czech Republic. That meant that expectations were high two years later when France enjoyed home advantage in the World Cup. In the run-up to the tournament Jacquet came in for a lot of criticism for his team selection and tactics, but as the tournament unfolded all Jacquet's decisions were vindicated and all his star players hit top form. The team eased through the group stage with maximum points. It took a Laurent Blanc golden goal to beat Paraguay in the second round and a penalty shoot-out to dispose of Italy in the quarters. After beating an excellent Croatia side 2–1, Jacquet's men lined up against holders Brazil. What should have been a titanic struggle turned out to be a routine victory. France were outstanding, Brazil completely out of sorts. France celebrated in style after their 3–0 victory and Jacquet was lionized for bringing home the trophy for the first time in its 68-year history. He was awarded the Legion d'Honneur for his achievement but even that couldn't alter his decision to step down from the job.

Marcello Lippi

Marcello Lippi

Born: 12 April 1948
Management Career: Sampdoria, Pontedera, Siena, Pistoiese, Carrarese, Cesena, Lucchese, Atalanta, Napoli, Juventus, Inter Milan, Juventus, Italy
Major Honours: World Cup 2006; European Champions League 1996, World Club Cup 1996, European Super Cup 1996

Marcello Lippi ended a nine-year barren spell for Juventus when he won the Serie A title in 1995, his first season in charge. Lippi had had a string of appointments with some of Italian football's lesser lights, and spells at both Napoli and Atalanta. But it was after he joined the Turin club in 1994 that he began racking up the silverware. The 1995 championship was Lippi's first major honour as a coach, but thereafter they came thick and fast. He won the Coppa Italia in 1995, and nearly made it an astonishing hat-trick when Juventus reached the UEFA Cup final. Parma spoiled the party, winning 2–1 on aggregate. That defeat was erased the following year as Lippi led Juve to the European Champions League cup final, where they faced holders Ajax. The game

ended 1–1, with Juve winning the penalty shoot-out. Lippi's third season at the club yielded another Serie A title and victory over the River Plate in the World Club Cup. They were favourites to retain the European Cup too, but went down unexpectedly to Borussia Dortmund. 1997–98 saw Lippi steer Juventus to a third championship in four years, but the team once again fell at the last hurdle in the European Cup, going down 1–0 to Real Madrid. Lippi left to take over at Inter Milan in 1999 but he returned to Juve in the summer of 2001. He added two more domestic championships to his trophy haul, in 2002 and 2003. In the latter campaign Juve put out holders Real Madrid in the semi-final of the European Champions League. But once again Lippi's side fell at the final hurdle, AC Milan winning the match on penalties. Lippi took over from Trapattoni as the Italian national coach in 2004, leading the Azzurri to a fourth World Cup triumph at Germany 2006. He left the post a national hero, only to make a dramatic return two years later, following Italy's disappointing showing at Euro 2008 under Roberto Donadoni.

Valeri Lobanovski

Born: 6 January 1939

Management Career: Dnepr Dnepropetrovsk, Dynamo Kiev, Soviet Union, United Arab Emirates, Kuwait, Ukraine

Major Honours: European Cup Winners' Cup 1975, 1986

Valeri Lobanovski took over the reins at Dynamo Kiev in 1973. He had played for the club and won two caps for the Soviet Union, but it was as a coach that he made his mark. Under Lobanovski Kiev became the country's outstanding side of the 1970s and 1980s. They won the Cup Winners' Cup in 1975, easily overcoming Ferencvaros 3–0 in the final. Having become the first Soviet side to land a major honour, Kiev followed it up with a superb 3–0 aggregate win over Bayern Munich in the European Super Cup. Oleg Blokhin scored all three goals, and his technical excellence encapsulated the quality Lobanovski instilled into the side. Blokhin was still there eleven years later, when Kiev won the Cup Winners' Cup for the second time. Atletico Madrid were on the receiving end of a 3–0 scoreline this time round. Lobanovski also led the USSR at the 1986 World Cup and Euro '88. In the former tournament his team topped their group before going out to Belgium in a 4–3 thriller in the second round. Two years later his side reached the final of the European Championship. Having beaten Holland at the group stage, the USSR faced the same opposition in the final, this time going down 2–0. In the early 1990s Lobanovski had spells coaching the national sides of Kuwait and the United Arab Emirates, returning to Dynamo Kiev in 1997. In his first season back in charge he took Kiev to the quarter-final of the European Champions League, where they lost to Juventus. Their results at the group stage included a 4–0 thrashing of Barcelona at the Nou Camp. Lobanovski died in May 2002 and a new cup competition was introduced in his honour.

Valeri Lobanovski

Steve McClaren

Born: 3 May 1961

Management Career: Manchester United, Middlesborough, England, FC Twente

When injury brought Steve McClaren's modest playing career to a premature end, he turned to coaching with one of his former clubs, Oxford United. It was during his spell with Derby, another team for whom he had paraded his midfield skills, that he made his name as one of the best young coaches in England. As Jim Smith's number two, McClaren played a key role in helping the Rams gain promotion to the Premiership in 1995–96 and consolidate their place in the top flight over the next two seasons. These achievements made him Alex Ferguson's choice as his right-hand man after Brian Kidd departed to take the top job at Blackburn. McClaren's first season at Old Trafford ended with United landing the historic treble, raising his stock still further. After helping the club to a hat-trick of Premiership titles, McClaren took over at Middlesbrough in 2001. Boro beat Bolton in the 2003–04 Carling Cup final to land their first silverware since the club was formed in 1876. That gave Boro a first taste of European football, and although Sporting Lisbon ended the club's UEFA Cup run in the last 16, seventh place in the Premiership meant another crack at the competition in 2005–06. This time Boro went all the way, overturning three-goal deficits against Basel and Steaua Bucharest en route to the final. The fairytale run came to a crashing end in Eindhoven, Boro comprehensively beaten 4–0 by Juande Ramos's Sevilla side, but McClaren had enhanced his cv by taking an unheralded club to a European final. McClaren was drafted into the England coaching set up in 2000, in the interregnum prior to Sven-Goran Eriksson's appointment. After his move to Teesside, McClaren continued in his dual role as club manager and coach to the international team. He was appointed Eriksson's successor in May 2006, but his tenure lasted barely a year as England crashed out of Euro 2008 at the qualifying stage. In summer 2008 McLaren was appointed coach of Eredivisie side FC Twente. His new side lost to Arsenal in a Champions League qualifier, but then went on a fine run. Going into the final third of the season Twente were second in the league, heading both PSV and Ajax, and also reached the knockout stage of the Uefa Cup, the club's best European performance since the 1970s.

Hugo Meisl

Born: 16 November 1881
Management Career: Amateure, Austria

Hugo Meisl was an influential figure in the 1920s, when football moved into the professional era. It was he who had a vision of a knockout tournament between clubs throughout Europe, an idea which came to fruition with the inaugural Mitropa Cup in 1927. This was to be a hugely prestigious tournament in the interwar years and survived until 1991, Meisl had played inside-forward for F K Austria before moving into management with Admira Wacker. He went on to become secretary of the Austrian Football Federation, a post he held for over 30 years. He also coached the brilliant national side, which was dubbed the 'Wunderteam' in the 1920s and early 1930s. Meisl drafted in former Bolton Wanderers player Jimmy Hogan as his assistant and the two masterminded a brilliantly successful period for Austrian football. When the team lost to England 4–3 in December 1932, it was their first defeat in 18 matches. The 'Wunderteam' went into the 1934 World Cup as favourites, along with Vittorio Pozzo's Italy. The two countries met at the semi-final stage, where the skilful Austrians failed to cope with the heavy conditions and lost 1–0. Meisl died in 1937.

Cesar Menotti

Born: 5 November 1938
Management Career: Huracan, Argentina, Barcelona, Penarol, Boca Juniors, River Plate, Mexico, Atletico Madrid, Independiente, Sampdoria, Valencia, Rosario Central, Independiente
Major Honours: World Cup 1978

Cesar Menotti masterminded Argentina's first World Cup triumph in 1978, 48 years after the country had lost in the final of the inaugural tournament. Chain-smoking Menotti was appointed in October 1974, having guided Huracan to the league championship the previous year. In 1978 he was under severe pressure from the passionate home supporters, who wanted him to arrest a long period of under-achievement. Menotti opted to play an expansive game, which some thought was a mistake. He also surprised everyone by refusing to select a single player from Boca Juniors, the country's premier club and reigning league champions. That decision meant there was no place for the teenage prodigy Diego Maradona. But it all came right in the end, and in the final his side got the better of Holland, regarded as the most talented team of the day. Menotti went on to manage a host of clubs, including Barcelona, Atletico Madrid and Sampdoria. He also had a spell in charge of the Mexico national team. In 2002, aged 63, Menotti's career turned full circle when he took over at Rosario Central. This was Menotti's home town club, which he had supported as a boy and which had given him his first professional contract as a player. In 2005 he had a brief spell back at Independiente and has since been coaching club sides in Mexico.

Rinus Michels

Rinus Michels

Born: 9 February 1928
Management Career: Ajax, Barcelona, Holland, Ajax (technical director), Barcelona, Los Angeles Aztecs, Koln, Holland (technical director) Holland, Bayer Leverkusen, Holland
Major Honours: European Cup 1971; European Championship 1988

It was Rinus Michels who formulated the concept of Total Football in the late 1960s, then unleashed it on the world with devastating effect during his six-year tenure as manager of Ajax. The idea was simple enough: a fluid system of play in which all players were comfortable on the ball and could pop up in all areas of the pitch. Obviously, he needed the personnel to be able to put theory into practice, and Michels was fortunate in having the likes of Cruyff, Neeskens, Krol and Rep at his disposal. English fans got a taste of what was to come when Ajax humbled Liverpool 5–1 in a European Cup tie in 1967. Four years later, the Dutch side won the first of a hat-trick of European Cups. Michels moved to Barcelona in 1971, and two years later paid his former club a world record £922,000 to renew his partnership with Cruyff. Michels led Holland at the 1974 World Cup, where his all-star team was undone by West Germany in the final. He had spells at Bayer Leverkusen and the Los Angeles Aztecs, then returned as coach of the national side before the 1988 European Championship. The team, including Gullit, Rijkaard and Van Basten, had all the hallmarks of a Michels side and won the tournament in style, beating the Soviet Union 2–0 in the final. Michels died in March 2005.

Bora Milutinovic

Born: 7 September 1944
Management Career: Pumas UNAM, Mexico, San Lorenzo, Almagro, Costa Rica, Udinese, USA, Mexico, Nigeria, MetroStars, Peru, China, Honduras, Al-Sadd, Jamaica
Major Honours: CONCACAF Championship 1989; Gold Cup 1991, 1996

In Japan and Korea 2002, Bora Milutinovic notched up a remarkable achievement. In leading China to their first ever World Cup finals he made it five tournaments in a row as a coach, all with different countries. A former Partizan Belgrade player, Milutinovic wound down his playing career in Mexico. It was there that he took up coaching, and it was Mexico who gave him his first national team appointment. On home soil his side reach the World Cup quarter-finals in 1986. Four years later he took Costa Rica to the second round, and he nearly managed to get the USA to the same stage in 1994, the side going out narrowly on goal difference. His Nigeria team topped their group at France '98 before crashing to Denmark in the second round. Although 2002 was a disappointment, Milutinovic was unfortunate in his China side being grouped with eventual winners Brazil and surprise semi-finalists Turkey. He stepped down after the tournament, and his next port of call was the Honduras national team. They were progressing well in their bid to qualify for the 2006 World Cup from the CONCACAF group when Milutinovic stepped down in July 2004. He had a brief stint with Qatar side Al-Sadd, and took charge of Jamaica's national team until the axe fell in 2007 following a run of poor results.

Jose Mourinho

Born: 26 January 1963
Management Career: Benfica, Uniao de Leiria, Porto, Chelsea, Inter Milan
Major Honours: UEFA Cup 2003, European Champions League 2004

In June 2004 Jose Mourinho took over a Chelsea side that had finished runner-up in the Premiership and reached the semi-finals of the Champions League. He had just successfully defended the Portuguese championship with Porto, and steered the side to a 3–0 Champions League victory over Monaco. Manchester United were among Porto's scalps en route to being crowned European champions, Mourinho memorably dancing down the Old Trafford touchline as his men secured a last-gasp winner. Now Mourinho was coming to England aiming to break the United–Arsenal stranglehold. The son of a top-level goalkeeper, Mourinho played for his home-town club,

Bora Milutinovic

championship. He also gave the club its third League Cup success, Chelsea beating Liverpool in the final. He delivered the Premiership title in the 35th game of the season and although his men went down to Liverpool in the last four of the Champions Cup, it still left the star coach with an impressive tally of seven major trophies in three years. Chelsea continued their success, defending their Premiership crown in 2006 and winning both domestic cup competitions in 2006–07. The much-publicised tense relationship between Mourinho and Chelsea owner Roman Abramovich was strained to breaking point as the team made a faltering start to the 2007–08 season. Mourinho left Stamford Bridge in September 2007, having won six trophies in his three years at the club. Nine months later, he took over the reins of an Inter Milan side that had won three successive scudettos. By March 2009 the team was on course to make it four in a row, adding yet another championship to Mourinho's impressive cv.

Miguel Munoz

Born: 15 September 1924
Management Career: Plus Ultra, Real Madrid, Hercules, Seville, Las Palmas, Spain
Major Honours: European Cup 1960, 1966

Miguel Munoz had joined Real in 1948, and captained the side in the first two campaigns. He actually scored the goal which began Real's outstanding run of success, against Servette in September 1955. It wasn't until 21 ties later – 39 matches in total – that Real finally tasted defeat, against Barcelona in the 1960–61 season. Munoz moved straight into management with Real when he decided to hang up his boots, following the 1959 victory over Reims. It was a hard act to follow, but Munoz guided the side to what is regarded as the greatest display ever seen by a club side. After disposing of Helenio Herrera's Barcelona 6–2 on aggregate in the last four of the 1959–60 competition, Real met Eintracht Frankfurt in the final, staged in Glasgow. The German side had put 12 goals past Rangers in the semis but in front of 130,000 fans Munoz's side gave a dazzling display in a 7–3 victory. Munoz guided Real to three more European Cup finals in the 1960s, notching another victory in 1966, over Partizan Belgrade. There was also a run of eight Spanish championships in nine years in the 1960s. Munoz later led the national team to the runners-up spot in the 1984 European Championship and to the quarter-final of the World Cup two years later. He died in 1990.

Setubal, but never made it in the professional ranks. From an early age he set his sights on coaching, former Scotland boss Andy Roxburgh guiding him through some of the UEFA courses. His shrewdness, attention to detail and tactical awareness were immediately apparent. He was also a great communicator, his facility with languages being an obvious asset in an era of multi-lingual dressing-rooms.

Indeed, it was as a translator that he got his first big break, working under Bobby Robson at Sporting Lisbon in the early 1990s. He moved to Porto with Robson in 1993, becoming increasingly involved in the coaching side. After winning two championships in three years, the two went to Barcelona. Robson departed after bring the Cup Winners' Cup to the Nou Camp; incoming coach Louis van Gaal retained Mourinho as his No. 2, and Barca won successive La Liga titles, in 1998 and 1999. It wasn't until 2000 that he finally got his first top job, at Benfica. A boardroom row meant his tenure lasted just nine games. He then worked his magic with Portuguese minnows Uniao de Leiria, guiding them to fifth in the league and a UEFA Cup spot. It was back to Porto midway through the 2001–02 season. He halted a nightmare run, and the following season led Porto to a remarkable treble: the domestic double, followed by a UEFA Cup victory over Celtic.

In his first Premiership campaign Mourinho broke Manchester United and Arsenal's 10-year grip on the

Bill Nicholson

Born: 26 January 1919
Management Career: Tottenham Hotspur
Major Honours: European Cup Winners' Cup 1963; UEFA Cup 1972

Bill Nicholson was with Tottenham Hotspur as both man and boy. He began playing for Spurs when he was 16, became a coach in 1955 and took over as manager in 1959. He managed the side for 16 years, becoming the longest-serving manager in the club's history, and under him Spurs won eight major trophies.

The team that Nicholson assembled in 1959 included players like Danny Blanchflower and Dave Mackay. His first game in charge was a 10–4 defeat of Everton, a sign of what was to come. In the 1960–61 season the team won 31 of their 42 league games with 115 goals scored, taking the Championship with eight points to spare. They then became the first 20th-century side to achieve the Double when they beat Leicester City in the FA Cup final.

Spurs won the FA Cup twice more, in 1962 and 1967, bringing the trophy to White Hart Lane three times in seven years. In 1963, Nicholson became the first British manager to win a European trophy when Spurs beat Atletico Madrid 5–1 in the Cup Winners' Cup final. In 1971 and 1973 they won the League Cup and in 1972 they were winners of the UEFA Cup. Nicholson retired following the 1974–75 season but remained associated with the club. He died in October 2004.

Bill Nicholson

Bob Paisley

Born: 23 January 1919
Management Career: Liverpool
Major Honours: UEFA Cup 1976; European Cup 1977, 1978, 1981

For many, Bob Paisley is the greatest manager to have worked in British football; he has certainly surpassed the achievements of any other manager in the game. During the nine years that he managed Liverpool, he amassed an incredible number of honours, including six League Championships, three League Cups, the 1976 UEFA Cup and the European Cups of 1977, 1978 and 1981. He was also six times voted Manager of the Year by the FA.

Paisley's connection with Liverpool reached back to 1939, when he had signed with the club as a player, although the war had delayed his debut. He was a member of the title-winning side of 1947 and had captained the team in the early 1950s. Paisley had remained with the club as a coach following his retirement, and became Bill Shankly's number one man in the boot room. When Shankly announced his retirement in 1974, Paisley was the obvious and popular choice to replace him.

Despite reigning in the great man's shadow, Paisley

took Liverpool on from strength to strength, with canny signings that helped to make them the most feared club in Europe. In 1977 he became the first English-born manager to lift a European Cup when the Reds beat Borussia Moenchengladbach 3–1 in Rome; they had already secured the English Championship title for that year. Bruges were beaten in the final the following year and in 1981 it was Real Madrid who were put to the sword.

Paisley announced his retirement in 1983, and when Liverpool won the League Cup that year, captain Graeme Souness led his boss up the famous Wembley steps in an unprecedented move to collect the trophy. He died in 1996.

Bob Paisley

Vittorio Pozzo

Born: 2 March 1886
Management Career: Torino, Italy
Major Honours: World Cup 1934, 1938, Olympics 1936

Vittorio Pozzo was the undisputed giant of Italian football in the first half of the 20th century. He fell in love with the game during his time as a student in Edwardian England. He led the Italy side at the 1912 Olympic Games, held in Stockholm. He couldn't prevent England from successfully defending their Olympic title, but he did meet another legendary manager, Austria's Hugo Meisl, with whom he would cross swords in a World Cup semi-final 22 years later. Pozzo had a long association with Torino, but it was for his period as national team coach that he became best known. Italy lost just seven games in the 1930s under his guidance.

Pozzo's men lifted the World Cup on home soil in 1934, although they rode their luck at times. Pozzo had taken his squad to a training camp for six weeks before the finals and the players were in peak condition, which proved to be a vital factor in the team's success. After squeezing past Meisl's Austria in the semis, Italy beat Czechoslovakia in extra time. The players paid tribute to their manager, hoisting him aloft at the final whistle. Pozzo led a very different side in France four years later and this time they were worthy champions. Between these two victories Pozzo also guided Italy to Olympic victory in Berlin in 1936, beating arch-rivals Austria in the final. He died in 1968.

10 June 1934, Pozzo talks to the Italian team during the World Cup final against Czechoslovakia.

Alf Ramsey

Born: 21 January 1920
Management Career: Ipswich Town,
England, Birmingham City
Major Honours: World Cup 1966

When Alf Ramsey was offered the England job in 1963, it was as a replacement for Walter Winterbottom, who had run the team for 16 years. Ramsey had been the manager at Ipswich Town, taking them from the Third Division to the First in just two seasons. His impressive achievement in East Anglia boded well for an England team that were not expected to do well at the next World Cup tournament, despite home advantage. Ramsey insisted that he be given absolute responsibility for selection, a freedom that Winterbottom had not enjoyed. A humiliating defeat by France marked his first game in charge, yet just three years later Ramsey's side were to enjoy the accolade of being world champions, and he, the pleasure of being right after confidently predicting their success back in 1963. He was knighted the following year.

Ramsey had been a player himself. He had joined Spurs in 1949 and with them won the Division Two title in 1950, then the League Championship the following year. He had also been capped for England 32 times and it was perhaps as a result of his playing background that Ramsey displayed a fierce loyalty to his own players.

Sir Alf Ramsey

Ramsey's England did not repeat their 1966 success. They went out of the 1968 European Championship at the semi-final stage and, despite having an apparently stronger squad for the 1970 World Cup, they lost to West Germany in the quarter-final. Ramsey came in for some criticism after that game, as many believed his decision to take off Charlton and Peters was instrumental in West Germany's come-back from 2–0 down to win by 3 goals to 2. Germany was to take revenge on Ramsey yet again in the 1972 European Championships, knocking England out in the quarter-finals. However, England's failure to qualify for the 1974 World Cup resulted in Ramsey's dismissal and he retired from management in 1977, having ended his career at Birmingham City. Sir Alf Ramsey died in 1999.

Alf Ramsey with the England squad

Otto Rehhagel

Born: 9 August 1938
Management Career: Werder Bremen, Bayern Munich, Kaiserslautern, Greece
Major Honours: European Cup Winners' Cup 1992, European Championship 2004

Otto Rehhagel was a much-travelled player and coach in his native Germany before he joined Werder Bremen in 1981. In 1988 he broke Bayern Munich's stranglehold on the champion-ship, and lifted the title again five years later. He also won the domestic cup competition twice, and his side beat Monaco 2–0 in the 1992 European Cup Winners' Cup final. In 1995 he moved to Bayern but after less than a season in charge, he was sacked, becoming coach of Kaiserslautern. Relegated in 1996, Kaiserslautern bounced straight back with Rehhagel at the helm. Then, to everyone's surprise, he took the team to the championship, the first promoted side to achieve this in the Bundesliga. His team held off Bayern Munich by a single point to secure the title. Rehhagel took over as manager of Greece's national side in 2001, winning plaudits for getting the team to Euro 2004 and dubbed 'King Otto' for taking the 80–1 outsiders all the way, beating hosts Portugal in the final. Greece failed to reach Germany 2006 but Rehhagel made sure the country would defend its title as European champions with an impressive qualification campaign for Euro 2008. The tournament itself was a disappointment, Greece crashing out at the group stage after losing all three matches.

Otto Rehhagel

Bobby Robson

Bobby Robson

Born: 18 February 1933
Management Career: Fulham, Ipswich Town, England, PSV Eindhoven, Sporting Lisbon, Porto, Barcelona, Newcastle United
Major Honours: UEFA Cup 1981, European Cup Winners' Cup 1997

Many were of the opinion that the knighthood awarded to Bobby Robson in 2002 was long overdue. An outstanding club manager for 30 years and the man who led England to the semi-final at Italia '90, Robson's appetite for the game was undiminished as he approached his 70th birthday. Robson had an excellent playing career, making the England squad for the 1958 and 1962 World Cups. It was with Ipswich in the 1970s that he made his reputation as a coach. Like Alf Ramsey before him, he turned an unfashionable club into an outstanding side capable of competing with the likes of Liverpool and Arsenal. His team didn't quite manage to win the Championship, finishing runners-up in 1981 and 1982, but he led the side to FA Cup victory over Arsenal in 1978. There was also a famous UEFA Cup final victory in 1981, Ipswich beating AZ Alkmaar 5–4 over the two legs. He took over as England boss in 1982. His team went out to Argentina in the quarter-final of the 1986 World Cup, the

infamous 'hand of God' game. He went one better at Italia '90, England going down on penalties to Germany in the semis. Robson then returned to club management, winning championships in Holland and Portugal, with PSV Eindhoven and Porto respectively. In 1996 he moved to Barcelona and won European Cup Winners Cup in his first season, beating Paris St. Germain in the final. He had a second spell at PSV before returning to St. James's Park. Robson built an exciting side which was soon challenging for top honours again. His young team reached the second stage of the 2002–03 Champions League, and finished third in the Premiership to earn yet another crack at Europe's premier club competition. The team crashed out at the first stage and thus gained entry to the UEFA cup. An injury-hit side went down to Marseille in the semis, Newcastle's best performance in Europe for 35 years. Robson was sacked in August 2004, after Newcastle's faltering start to the new season. In January 2006 he took up a consultancy position, assisting the new Republic of Ireland boss Steve Staunton, though that association ended when the Republic failed to qualify for Euro 2008.

Arrigo Sacchi

Born: 1 April 1946
Management Career: Rimini, Parma, AC Milan, Italy, AC Milan, Atletico Madrid, Parma
Major Honours: European Cup 1989, 1990; World Club Cup 1989/90

Arrigo Sacchi

Arrigo Sacchi had been only an average player, but after he turned to coaching in the late 1970s he proved that success on the field was not a prerequisite for success in the dugout. He did well at Rimini and Parma, both struggling in the lower divisions when he took over. In 1987 he was chosen by media mogul Silvio Berlusconi as the man to bring the glory days back to AC Milan. The following year Sacchi delivered the Serie A title, the club's first championship for nine years. In 1989 Milan were crowned European champions. Dutch superstars Gullit and Van Basten hit two each as Milan thrashed Steaua Bucharest 4–0 in the final. They defended their crown the following year, this time the other member of Milan's triumvirate of Dutch masters – Frank Rijkaard – hitting the goal which beat Benfica. Sacchi departed in 1991 to take over as Italy's coach. The country failed to reach Euro '92 but Sacchi took the team to the World Cup final two years later. After a goalless 120 minutes against Brazil, Roberto Baggio missed the vital penalty and Italy had to settle for the runners-up spot. Sacchi stepped down after Italy limped out of Euro '96 at the group stage. He returned to Milan, but this time he lasted just six months. In December 2004 Sacchi left Parma to become technical director at Real Madrid but stepped down after a run of poor results which saw manager Vanderlei Luxemburgo sacked in December 2005.

Tele Santana

Tele Santana

Born: 26 June 1931
Management Career: Atlético Mineiro, Grêmio, Palmeiras, Brazil, Al-Ahli, Brazil, Flamengo, São Paulo
Major Honours: World Club Cup 1992, 1993

Brazil's 1982 side went into that year's World Cup in Spain as the favourites to lift the trophy. It was a fluid attacking team, its style moulded by coach Tele Santana. Brazil lost 3–2 to eventual winners Italy in the second round. Four years later, Santana took another side full of flair to Mexico. Once again they were favourites, but again it proved a fruitless campaign as Brazil went out to France on penalties at the quarter-final stage. Santana's record was put into stark relief in 1994, when a much less impressive Brazil side lifted the trophy. By then Santana was back in club management, with Sao Paulo. There he showed that stylish football and silverware could go hand in hand. He revived Sao Paulo's flagging fortunes, leading the team to the World Club Cup in 1992 and 1993, beating Barcelona and AC Milan respectively. He died in 2006.

Helmut Schoen

Born: 15 September 1915
Management Career: Saarland, West Germany
Major Honours: European Championship 1972; World Cup 1974

Helmut Schoen's own international career was foreshortened by the Second World War. Even so he managed 17 goals in just 16 games for Germany between 1937 and 1941. By the time he was 40 he was assistant coach of the national side, under the inspirational Sepp Herberger. Schoen took over from Herberger in 1963, and over the next 15 years he guided West Germany in a period of unparalleled success. His side finished runners-up to England in the 1966 World Cup, then lost a thrilling semi-final to Italy four years later. The side he created which won the European Championship in 1972 was regarded as one of the best ever seen. In 1974 it was still an outstanding outfit, boasting the likes of Beckenbauer, Breitner and Müller, yet most people's favourites to win that year's World Cup was Holland. Despite going behind to an early penalty, Schoen's men lifted the trophy on home soil. It was another runners-up spot in the European Championship of 1976, West Germany going down to Czechoslovakia in the final. Schoen finally called it a day after his side went out in the second round at the 1978 World Cup. He died in 1996.

Luiz Felipe Scolari

Born : 9 November 1948
Management career: CSA, Juventude, Brasil de Pelotas, Al-Shabab, Gremio, Goias, Al-Qadsia, Kuwait, Criciuma, Al Ahli, Jublio Iwata, Palmerias, Cruzeiro, Brazil, Portugal, Chelsea
Major Honours: Copa Libertadores 1995, 1999; World Cup 2002

'Big Phil' Scolari served a long managerial apprenticeship in his native Brazil before becoming a household name as coach of the national side that lifted the 2002 World Cup. He took charge of a succession of smaller clubs in the 1980s after calling time on a modest playing career, but his breakthrough came in 1991, when he won the Brazilian Cup with an unheralded Criciuma side. It brought him to the attention of the bigger clubs, including Gremio, for whom he had played in the '70s. Scolari delivered the domestic cup in 1994, his first season in charge, and followed it up with a 4–2 aggregate victory over Colombia's Atletico Nacional in the Copa Libertadores. A Brazilian championship in 1996 kept up the average of

winning at least one trophy a season. In the late 1990s he enjoyed a three-year spell with Palmeiras, whom he also guided to Copa Libertadores victory, beating another Colombian side, Deportivo Cali, in the final. That success also brought him the first of his South American Coach of the Year awards. After a brief spell at Cruzeiro, he took over the reins of the national side from Emerson Leao. A quarter-final defeat to Honduras in the 2001 Copa America tournament got his reign off to a disastrous start, and Brazil was also struggling in the World Cup qualifiers. Yet a year later Scolari sat on top of the pile as his team hit 18 goals on their way to beating Germany in the final. Prior to that campaign Scolari had resisted the clamour to include the legendary Romario in his squad, showing that he was both strong-willed and no respecter of reputations. He stepped down after Brazil's triumph, which brought him a second award as South America's top coach. His next challenge was to try to make a disciplined, battle-hardened team from the gifted individuals at Portugal's disposal. He took the team to its first major final, on home soil in Euro 2004, and although Greece spoiled the party, Scolari's stock rose still further. So much so that the FA began wooing Big Phil in the run-up to Germany 2006, after it was announced that Sven-Goran Eriksson was leaving his post after the World Cup. Scolari ended the brief courtship, and proceeded to get the better of

Helmut Schoen

England and Eriksson for the third tournament running at the quarter-final stage. A controversial Zidane penalty ended Portugal's run in the semis, and brought forth a typical touchline display of animated histrionics from the coach. Scolari returned to club management with Chelsea after guiding Portugal to the quarter-finals at Euro 2008. Under his watch Chelsea's four-year unbeaten home record in league matches came to an end, and with Champions League qualification hanging in the balance, Scolari was sacked in February 2009.

Gusztav Sebes

Born: 21 June 1906
Management Career: Hungary, Ujpest Doza

Gusztav Sebes enjoyed a successful playing career with Vasas and MTK Budapest in the 1920s, but it was for the part he played in creating the Magic Magyars in the late 1940s and 1950s that he is best known. Sebes was Deputy Sports Minister in 1949 when Hungary crashed 5–2 to Czechoslovakia. He decided to concentrate all the country's talent into two clubs, the army side Honved and Red Banner. He also dispensed with the traditional assignment of rigid roles to players. Sebes encouraged a fluid system in which players could turn up virtually anywhere on the pitch, a precursor to the 'total football' concept which Holland reinterpreted nearly 20 years later. Of course, Sebes needed quality personnel to be able to put these ideas into practice and he was fortunate in having the likes of Puskas, Hidegkuti, Kocsis and Czibor at his disposal. Between June 1950 and November 1955 Hungary lost just once in 48 internationals. They scored 210 goals, averaging more than four per game. The only reverse came in the 1954 World Cup final, when the Magyars went down to West Germany. Sebes resigned after many of his players fled the country in the wake of the 1956 uprising. He died in 1986.

Bill Shankly

Born: 2 September 1913
Management Career: Carlisle United, Grimsby Town, Workington, Huddersfield Town, Liverpool
Major Honours: UEFA Cup 1973

During the 1970s and 80s, Liverpool were arguably the best football team in England, dominating the league and driving a path through Europe. That success was in no small way due to the legacy of Bill Shankly. Shankly joined the Reds at the end of 1959 when they were languishing in the Second Division. By his retirement in 1974, Liverpool had won three League titles, two FA Cup finals and the 1973 UEFA Cup.

Born in Ayrshire, Shankly started out as a player, first with Carlisle, then Preston North End. He won seven caps for Scotland before the Second World War ended his playing career. He managed a succession of clubs, including Carlisle and Huddersfield, before being asked to take on Liverpool following the inglorious departure of Phil Taylor.

Liverpool were prepared to invest in the club and Shankly was able to build a stronger team, resulting in promotion in 1961–62 followed by League Championship in 1964. They beat Leeds United to win the FA Cup in 1965, winning it for a second time under Shankly in 1974, beating Newcastle United. In 1973, Shankly lifted the UEFA Cup when Liverpool beat Borussia Moenchengladbach 3–2 on aggregate, with star players such as Kevin Keegan and John Toshack leading the field.

Shankly retired in 1974. Revered by both players and fans his name adorns the gates at the entrance to Anfield and his statue stands in the Kop. He died of a heart attack in 1981.

Bill Shankly

Jock Stein

Born: 1 October 1922
Management Career: Dunfermline Athletic, Hibernian, Celtic, Leeds United, Scotland
Major Honours: European Cup 1967

Jock Stein was a giant of British football, a leading light in the procession of great Scottish managers who dominated the domestic game in the 1960s and 1970s. He beat all his contemporaries to the greatest prize in club football, leading Celtic to European Cup victory in 1967. Stein had been an average player, first with Albion Rovers and then in the Welsh League with Llanelli. Celtic signed him as cover for their regular centre-half, and an injury crisis catapulted him into first team action. He captained the side to a League and Cup double in 1954, but injury ended his playing days the following year. He began his coaching career at the Glasgow club, left to take up the reins at Dunfermline and Hibernian, then returned to Celtic in 1965. The team which beat Inter Milan in the European Cup final two years later was assembled for next to nothing. Stein also led the club to nine Championships in a row before stepping down in 1977. He came out of retirement to take over at Leeds, but his reign at Elland Road was brief as he responded to the call for him to manage Scotland following the team's disappointing showing in the 1978 World Cup. Stein died after suffering a heart attack at Ninian Park on 10 September 1985. He had just watched his side draw 1–1 with Wales in a World Cup qualifier, a result which helped to take the country to the finals in Mexico.

Jock Stein

Giovanni Trapattoni

Born: 17 March 1939
Management Career: AC Milan, Juventus, Inter Milan, Bayern Munich, Cagliari, Bayern Munich, Fiorentina, Italy, Benfica, Stuttgart, Red Bull Salzburg, Republic of Ireland
Major Honours: UEFA Cup 1977, 1991; European Cup Winners' Cup 1984; European Super Cup 1984; European Cup 1985; World Club Cup 1985

Giovanni Trapattoni was probably the most frustrated coach at the 2002 World Cup. His Italy side went into the tournament as one of the favourites, and by common consent they were on the receiving end of some poor officials' decisions. Italy crashing out in the second round to co-hosts South Korea. Trapattoni was a distinguished defensive midfielder in the 1950s and 1960s. He played in the AC Milan side which beat Benfica in the 1963 European Cup final, although he was outstripped by Eusebio for the Portuguese side's goal. He picked up another winners' medal in the same competition six years later, before moving onto the coaching staff at the club. However, it was his decade at

Juventus, whom he joined in 1976, that made his name. With a mixture of top Italian players, such as Rossi and Zoff, together with overseas stars including Platini and Boniek, Juve became the first team to win all three European competitions. Trapattoni also won six Serie A titles before moving on to Internazionale. He won the championship in 1989 with Inter, and the UEFA Cup two years later. He had two spells at Bayern Munich, becoming the first overseas coach to win the Bundesliga title in 1997. At the start of the 2002–03 season Trapattoni came in for a lot of criticism after Italy took just one point from six at the start of their European Championship campaign. The 2–1 defeat against Wales was Italy's fifth in ten games over an eight-month period, and Trapattoni's position as national team coach was looking increasingly under threat. Trapattoni's contract was up after Euro 2004, and another disappointing tournament for the Azzurri did nothing to alter that arrangement. He returned to club football with Benfica, guiding the Lisbon giants to the 2004–05 championship, their first since 1994. It was back to the Bundesliga with Stuttgart next, but he was sacked in February 2006, after less than a season in charge. Austria was the next port of call, Trapattoni teaming up with Lothar Matthaus in a title-winning campaign with Red Bull Salzburg, the rebranded Austria Salzburg. In February 2008 Trapattoni announced he would be leaving the club at the end of the season to take over as Republic of Ireland coach.

Giovanni Trapattoni

Terry Venables

Born: 6 January 1943
Management Career: Crystal Palace, Queen's Park Rangers, Barcelona, Tottenham Hotspur, England, Australia, Leeds United

Terry Venables was a footballing prodigy, playing for England at every level. His career took him to Chelsea, Spurs, QPR and Crystal Palace, where he distinguished himself as a clever inside-forward. He cut his managerial teeth at Palace and QPR before landing one of the highest profile jobs in the game: coach at Barcelona. He brought the championship to the Nou Camp in 1985, the club's first Primera Liga success for eleven years. He nearly delivered the European Cup the following year, but after beating holders Juventus in the quarter-finals, Barcelona surprisingly went down on penalties to Steaua Bucharest in the final. In the summer of 1986 Venables paid Everton £4 million for Gary Lineker, who had just finished as the World Cup's top marksman. Two years later, 'El Tel' was back in English football, at White Hart Lane. He won the 1991 FA Cup but his stormy relationship with chairman Alan Sugar saw him depart to take over the England job in January 1994. His one tournament in the top job, Euro 96, enhanced his reputation further as England played attractive football in reaching the semi-finals. After resigning from the job, Venables coached Australia, just failing to take the country to France 98. He had an executive role at Portsmouth and also had another spell at Palace. He seemed to have settled for a pundit's role when, in summer 2002, he returned to the Premiership fray with Leeds following David O'Leary's dismissal. The Leeds slump continued and he was sacked midway through the season, although he wasn't helped by the fact that the club was forced to sell some of its top stars. One of Steve McClaren's first actions as new England coach in summer 2006 was to appoint Venables as his assistant but the team's failure to reach the Euro 2008 finals cost both men their jobs.

Terry Venables

Arsene Wenger

Born: 22 October 1949
Management Career: Cannes and Nancy, Monaco, Grampus Eight, Arsenal

When Arsene Wenger took over from Bruce Rioch at Arsenal in 1996, he was already an experienced and well-respected coach. He had begun his management career with Cannes and Nancy before moving on to Monaco, the club where his reputation was made. Monaco won the French league in 1988 with a team that included players such as Glenn Hoddle and Chris Waddle.

The Frenchman was relatively unknown at the north London club. Wenger quickly silenced the sceptics at Highbury, when just two years after his arrival Arsenal won the League and FA Cup Double. Although Arsenal lacked the financial resources to poach prized players, Wenger's wise purchasing of French stars such as Thierry Henry, Sylvain Wiltord, Robert Pires and Emmanuel Petit resulted in a highly successful side who won the Double again in 2001–02 and their third FA Cup in 2003. The Gunners were finally challenging Manchester United's tournament – as a player at Sweden '58 – and his last, as coach at France '98. The left-winger followed up the success in Sweden with another winners' medal in Chile four years later. He took over as national team coach after Brazil's poor showing at the 1966 World Cup. At Mexico four years later, he led what is often described as the greatest team ever to victory. The 4–1 win over Italy in the final made Zagallo the first man to win the trophy as both player and coach. He stepped down from the job after the 1974 tournament, when Brazil finished fourth. He managed both the Kuwait and United Arab Emirates national sides, before taking centre stage again in the 1990s, when he was over 60. He was assistant to Carlos Alberto Perreira in the victorious USA '94 tournament. At France '98 he was in sole charge yet again. Brazil's poor performance against the hosts in the final meant there was to be no fifth victory for Zagallo, but his record remains unsurpassed. He retired in 2001, after a spell at Flamengo, but was sensationally recalled to take charge of Brazil in the autumn of 2002 on an interim basis until a successor to Luiz Felipe Scolari could be appointed.

Arsene Wenger (right)

domination of the Premiership, finishing runners-up in the Premiership whenever they failed to win it and reaching the FA Cup final four times in six years. In 2003–04 Wenger led Arsenal to a third Premiership title, this time the Gunners went through the entire league programme unbeaten. The 2005–06 season saw Arsenal finish outside the top two in the Premiership for the first time since Wenger's arrival, though his exciting young side progressed to the final of the Champions' League. Over the next two seasons, Wenger's new-look side was praised for its style, though the Gunners failed to add any silverware to the trophy cabinet.

Mario Zagallo

Born: 9 August 1931
Management Career: Botafogo, Brazil, Fluminese, Flamengo, Brazil, Kuwait, Saudi Arabia, United Arab Emirates, Brazil, Portuguesa de Desportes, Flamengo, Brazil (technical director)
Major Honours: World Cup 1970, 1994 (technical co-ordinator); Copa America 1997

Brazil's Mario Zagallo has the longest World Cup pedigree of all, some 40 years separating his first appearance in the

Mario Zagallo

Great Clubs

Aberdeen Scotland

Founded: 1903
Colours: Red; red; red
Honours: 4 League titles; 7 Scottish Cups; European Cup Winners' Cup 1983; European Super Cup 1983

When Aberdeen won the Scottish championship in 1980, it broke the stranglehold of the two big Glasgow clubs stretching back to the mid-1960s. It was Alex Ferguson who masterminded Aberdeen's rise to the top. He delivered what was the club's second League Championship in only his second season in charge. He then proved it was no fluke by bringing the title to Pittodrie twice more in the following five years. Aberdeen also won the Scottish Cup four times in five years, but the greatest triumph came in 1983, when the Dons beat Real Madrid to lift the Cup Winners' Cup. An extra-time goal by John Hewitt gave Aberdeen a famous 2–1 victory over the Spanish giants in Gothenburg. Aberdeen went on to lift the European Super Cup, beating Champions Cup winners SV Hamburg 2–0 on aggregate. Aberdeen's success inevitably made Ferguson a prime target, and since his departure in 1986 the Dons have failed to reach the same heights.

Ajax Holland

Founded: 1900
Colours: Red/white; white; red/white
Honours: 29 League titles; 17 Dutch Cups; European Champions 1971, 1972, 1973, 1995; UEFA Cup 1992; European Cup Winners' Cup 1987; European Super Cup 1972, 1973, 1995; World Club Cup 1972, 1995

Ajax has been a veritable production line of outstanding players over the past 40 years. The club's famed youth academy has produced some of the greatest names of the modern era. The Amsterdam club has enjoyed considerable success in this period, including six major European trophies. But too often the club has lost its stars to the glamour clubs of Italy and Spain.

Formed at the dawn of the 20th century by a small group of businessmen, Ajax won promotion to the country's top division in 1911. The club won its first championship in 1918, and defended the title the following year. After a barren spell in the 1920s, the following decade saw Ajax win the championship five times. The next 25 years brought intermittent success both in the league and cup competitions. It was when former player Rinus Michels took over in 1964 that the club hit new heights. Michels developed the concept of 'total football', a fluid system in

Patrick Kluivert pictured playing for Ajax.

Baum (left) of Locomotive Leipzig and Van Basten (right) of Ajax watch the referee flick a coin before the European Cup Winners' Cup final in 1987.

which all players were comfortable in all positions and interchanged with devastating effect. Technical excellence was needed to implement such a system and Michels nurtured a crop of gifted players – the greatest of these was undoubtedly Johan Cruyff. Ajax won the league six times between 1966 and 1973. The team reached its first European Cup final in 1969, and although they went down 4–1 to AC Milan, success was not far away. Ajax beat Panathinaikos in the final of the same competition two years later, then defeated Inter Milan and Juventus in the following two years. It was the first hat-trick in the competition since the days of Real Madrid's dominance in the 1950s. Cruyff left for Barcelona after the 1973 European Cup final, and Johan Neeskens followed shortly afterwards. Ajax continued to pick up domestic honours in the 1970s and 1980s but success in European competition proved elusive. The production line then went into overdrive as players such as Frank Rijkaard, Marco Van Basten, Dennis Bergkamp, Clarence Seedorf,

Patrick Kluivert and the de Boer twins came through the ranks. With Cruyff back at the club as coach, Ajax beat Lokomotiv Leipzig in the 1987 European Cup Winners' Cup final, then lifted the UEFA Cup in 1992, beating Torino over two legs. The latter victory meant that Ajax followed Juventus into the record books as the only clubs to have won all three major European trophies. A Patrick Kluivert goal gave Ajax a Champions League victory over AC Milan in 1995. Since 2002 the club has added two more league titles, and finished runners-up to PSV on four occasions. A cup victory over champions PSV in 2006 couldn't save coach Danny Blind. The legendary former captain was sacked as Ajax trailed in fourth in the Eredivisie, 24 points behind PSV, the club's worst league showing for 40 years.

Hopes that Ajax would regain domestic supremacy and once again be a force in European football were raised when Marco Van Basten arrived, fresh from guiding the national team to the quarter-finals at Euro 2008.

Anderlecht Belgium

Founded: 1908
Colours: White/purple; white/purple; white
Honours: 29 League titles; 9 Belgian Cups; European Cup Winners' Cup 1976, 1978; UEFA Cup 1983; European Super Cup 1976, 1978

Anderlecht is by some distance the most famous name in Belgian football, and the most successful by some margin. Standard Liege, FC Bruges and Antwerp have all enjoyed domestic success and won through to European finals, but the record of each pales beside that of Anderlecht. The club was formed in 1908, reaching Belgium's top flight in 1935. It was another twelve years before the club claimed its first championship. Since then, however, Anderlecht have dominated the domestic game, including a spell in the 1980s and 1990s when they took the League crown nine times in eleven years.

In 1970 Anderlecht became the first Belgian club to contest a European final when they went down 4–3 to Arsenal in the Fairs Cup. In 1976 the club went one better, beating West Ham 4–2 in the Cup Winners' Cup final. Rob Rensenbrink and Frankie van der Elst hit two goals each to bring a major trophy to Belgium for the first time. The club nearly became the first to defend that trophy successfully but under-performed against Hamburg and lost 2–0. Anderlecht were back again in 1978 and this time made no mistake in a

resounding 4–0 win over FK Austria. Dutch star Rensenbrink again grabbed a brace.

In 1983 and 1984 Anderlecht made back-to-back appearances in the UEFA Cup final. First they unexpectedly beat a Benfica side coached by Sven-Goran Eriksson 2–1 on aggregate. A year later the team went down on penalties to Tottenham Hotspur. In the late 1990s it was revealed that the club had been involved in bribing the referee in the semi-final victory over Nottingham Forest. A UEFA inquiry resulted in Anderlecht being handed a one-year ban from European competition.

Arsenal England

Founded: 1886
Colours: Red/white; white; red/white
Honours: 13 League titles; 10 FA Cups; UEFA Cup 1970; European Cup Winners' Cup 1994

2005 saw Arsenal finish runners-up in the Premiership and lift the FA Cup for the 10th time with a shoot-out victory over arch rivals Manchester United. It meant that in Arsene Wenger's eight full seasons in charge, the Gunners had never finished outside the top two in the league, and won the FA Cup on four occasions. In 1998 and 2002 the club completed the coveted Double, while in 2003–04 Arsenal went through

Tony Adams holds the FA Cup aloft in 1998.

Henry and Pires celebrate a European Champions' League goal.

their league programme unbeaten, a feat not achieved since Preston North End's 'Invincibles' won the inaugural championship in 1888–89. In the Wenger era the Gunners have been feted for their stylish football, though results in European campaigns haven't matched the successes on the domestic front. Many thought 2003–04 would see Arsenal win its third European trophy, but the team went down to Chelsea in the Champions League quarter-final.

The club took its name from the Royal Arsenal at Woolwich, whose workers formed the club in 1886. This also gave Arsenal their nickname, despite the fact that the Woolwich connection disappeared when the club relocated to north London in 1913.

It wasn't until Herbert Chapman took over the manager's reins in 1925 that Arsenal began a period of dominance. With players of the stature of Charlie Buchan, Alex James, David Jack and Cliff Bastin, Arsenal won the Championship five times and the FA Cup twice. The team also formed the backbone of the international side. Chapman died in 1934 but his influence contributed towards the club's success for several years after his passing.

Arsenal added further Championships in 1948 and 1953, but the next great achievement came in 1971, when Bertie Mee's side won the Double.

Arsenal appeared in a hat-trick of FA Cup finals between 1978 and 1980, a dramatic 3–2 victory over Manchester United sandwiched between two defeats. It wasn't until the late 1980s, with former player George Graham in charge, that the club won the Championship again. Arsenal went to Anfield needing a 2–0 win to secure the title. Michael Thomas provided the second goal with almost the last kick of the match, and the Gunners took the title by virtue of having scored eight more goals than Liverpool, their records identical in every other respect.

Graham was sensationally dismissed in 1995 for receiving illegal payments during transfer deals. Bruce Rioch had a brief spell in charge and it was he who signed Dennis Bergkamp from Inter Milan. But it was after Wenger's arrival in 1996 that Arsenal began a new successful era and finally shook off the 'boring' tag. A new-look young side suffered 11 league defeats in 2005–06, just pipping Spurs for fourth place in the Premiership. The Gunners saved their best form for the Champions League, eliminating Real Madrid and Juventus en route to meeting Barcelona in the final. An early red card for Jens Lehmann made the task even harder, but the ten men took the lead through a Sol Campbell header. Chances to score a vital second goal were squandered, and Barca struck two late goals to snatch victory.

The 2006–07 season saw the Gunners relocate to the Emirates Stadium, ending a 93-year association with Highbury. Wenger's third Arsenal side is still under construction and has failed to land any silverware since moving to the Emirates, though it continues to receive plaudits for its eye-catching style of play.

Aston Villa England

Founded: 1874
Colours: Claret/blue; white; claret/blue
Honours: 7 League titles; 7 FA Cups; European Champions 1982

One of the founder-members of the Football League, Aston Villa have a proud record of winning major honours. The club has won the Championship and FA Cup seven times each. Unfortunately, most of those successes came in the first 25 years of Villa's existence. They won the league title five times in seven seasons between 1894 and 1900. When they took their fifth championship they hit 77 goals, making them also Division One's top scorers for the sixth season running. Three of Villa's FA Cup triumphs also came before the dawn of the 20th century. Their 1897 victory over Everton gave Villa the prestigious Double, a feat that would not be repeated until 1961.

Another Championship was delivered in 1909–10,

when the team finished with 53 points, equalling the existing record. Success became harder to come by thereafter. There have been just three FA Cup wins since then, in 1913, 1920 and 1957. The last of those, a 2–1 win over Manchester United, made Villa the competition's most successful club. It came in controversial circumstances as Peter McParland flattened United 'keeper Ray Wood with a challenge early in the game. In an era before substitutes United, that season's champions, struggled as they tried to reorganise.

Villa were relegated twice in four years in the late 1960s but were back in the top flight by the 1975–76 season. Just five years later, in 1981, Villa won their first Championship for 71 years. Ron Saunders' side was captained by Dennis Mortimer and included Peter Withe and Gary Shaw up front, and midfield maestro Gordon Cowans. A year later the team, by now managed by Tony Barton, brought the European Cup back to England for the sixth successive year. Withe hit the goal which beat Bayern Munich in Rotterdam.

Later in the 1980s Villa had another brief spell in Division Two but bounced back under Graham Taylor to finish runners-up to Liverpool in 1989–90. Taylor departed to take over the England job on the strength of his achievements. His successor, Ron Atkinson, also took Villa to second place in 1992–93, the inaugural season of the Premiership. They also won the League Cup under Atkinson, but the club has found success elusive in recent years. Graham Taylor returned for a second stint in charge, replacing John Gregory in 2001. This time he lasted barely a season as Villa struggled yet again.

Summer 2006 saw big changes at Villa Park. Martin O'Neill replaced David O'Leary in the manager's hotseat, and Chairman Doug Ellis finally let go of the reins, selling out to American tycoon Randy Lerner in a £62 million deal. By 2007–08, an exciting side including England squad regulars Gabriel Agbonlahor, Ashley Young and Gareth Barry threatened to break the Big Four's long-standing stranglehold on the Premier League.

Darius Vassell playing for Aston Villa.

Atletico Madrid Spain

Founded: 1903
Colours: Red/white; blue; white
Honours: 9 League titles; 9 Spanish Cups; World Club Cup 1974; European Cup Winners' Cup 1962

For most of their history Atletico Madrid have had to live in the shadow of neighbours Real and Catalan giants Barcelona. The club has enjoyed sporadic success in the domestic League and Cup competitions and also lifted one European trophy, but has never been able to dominate its domestic rivals for long.

Formed in 1903, Atletico's first championship came in 1940. The country was still recovering from civil war and Atletico found themselves in such straitened circumstances that they had to merge with the Air Force club to ensure survival. Thus the 1940 title appears in the record books as 'Atletico Aviacion'. The club retained the title under the same name the following year. Exactly ten years later Atletico achieved another Championship Double, this time under their own name. But after the second of those titles, in 1951, the club would win just four championships in the next 40 years. That period did bring European glory, however. Atletico won through to the final of the Cup Winners' Cup in 1962, only the second year of the competition's existence. The Spanish side met defending champions Fiorentina, and after a 1–1 draw at Hampden Park Atletico beat the Italian side 3–0. Incredibly, there was nearly a four-month hiatus between the two games. Atletico also reached the final the following year but were crushed 5–1 by Spurs.

After winning the 1973 Championship Atletico reached the European Cup final the following season. A Luis Aragon free-kick in extra time almost gave the club victory over Bayern Munich but the German side equalized in the dying seconds before running out 4–0 winners in the replay.

When tycoon Jesus Gil took over as Atletico's president in 1987 he vowed to bring sustained success to the club. He pumped in millions of pounds and brought in coaches of the stature of Cesar Menotti and Ron Atkinson. But it was Raddy Antic who worked the oracle. Appointed in 1995, Antic brought the club an historic League and Cup Double in his first season. The Yugoslav departed in 1998, returning two years later in a vain attempt to prevent Atletico from being relegated. The club spent two seasons out of the top flight, winning promotion back to the Primera Liga in 2002.

Nano of Atletico Madrid (right) in action against Seville.

Auxerre France

Founded: 1905
Colours: White; white; white
Honours: 1 League title; 4 French Cups

Few jobs are more precarious than that of a football coach, but Guy Roux bucked that trend in some style. When he left Auxerre after the team's victory over Sedan in the 2005 French Cup final, he ended a 44-year managerial reign. Auxerre was a small amateur club when Roux took charge in 1961. Thirty-five years later, in 1996, he steered the team to a famous League and Cup Double. This represented three trophies in two years, Auxerre having also won the French Cup in 1994.

Roux has always been known for bringing on talented youngsters. Djibril Cisse's move to Anfield in 2004 was the latest in a long line of young stars nurtured by Auxerre and sold on in big-money transfers. Roux also showed great foresight when he signed Khalilou Fadiga in 2000. Fadiga was one of the stars of Senegal's outstanding run in the 2002 World Cup. Auxerre topped their Champions League group in 1996–97 before going out to eventual winners Borussia Dortmund in the quarter-finals. The following season the club reached the same stage in the UEFA Cup, where they lost to Lazio.

Gary Lineker (right) and Lopez Rekarte embrace after Barcelona's victory in the European Cup Winners' Cup final in 1989.

Barcelona Spain

Founded: 1899
Colours: Dark blue/red; dark blue/red; dark blue/red
Honours: 19 League titles; 25 Spanish Cups; European Champions 1992, 2006 2009; European Cup Winners' Cup 1979, 1982, 1989, 1997; Fairs Cup 1958, 1960, 1966; European Super Cup 1992, 1997

The passionate Catalan supporters who turn up at the Nou Camp in droves are members as well as fans, for Barcelona continues to operate as a private club, not a publicly-quoted company. The club was formed in 1899 by Swiss businessman Hans Gamper. The birth of one of the most famous and richest clubs in the world began with a modest advertisement for players in a local newspaper. The club won the inaugural domestic championship in 1929, but it wasn't until 20 years later that they were regularly among the honours. Between 1948 and 1960 Barca won the League six times and the Cup on five occasions, yet still found themselves in the shadow of their rivals Real Madrid, who dominated the early years of the European Cup. Barcelona did become the first winners of the Inter-Cities Fairs Cup: a side including Luis

Suarez and Evaristo beat a select London XI in the final. Barca retained the same trophy in 1960, this time the competition being completed in just two years rather than three!

In 1957 the club relocated from their original home, Les Corts, to the famous Nou Camp. Four years later, Barca reached their first European Cup final but went down to Benfica 3–2. It would be another 30 years before the club would actually lift Europe's premier trophy. That victory, a 1–0 win over Sampdoria in 1992, came during Johan Cruyff's tenure as coach. Eighteen years earlier Barca had paid a world-record £922,000 to bring Cruyff from Ajax. But it was when he returned to manage the club that they had one of their most successful spells. Apart from the European Cup triumph, Barca won the the Primera Liga four times in a row from 1991. The team crashed 4–0 to AC Milan in the 1994 European Champions League final, however, and Cruyff's days were numbered. The other European competitions have proved more fruitful for Barcelona. They lifted the Fairs Cup for a third time in 1966

and have won the Cup Winners' Cup on four occasions. The most recent of those came in 1997, when a Ronaldo goal beat Paris St-Germain in the final. That victory came during Bobby Robson's brief reign at the Nou Camp. His replacement, Louis van Gaal, delivered two more championships before falling from favour in 2000. At the start of the 2002–03 season van Gaal was reappointed. The team performed brilliantly in the group stage of the Champions League but woefully in La Liga. He was shown the door before the season was over. Frank Rijkaard was charged with bringing success back to the Nou Camp, and with the World Footballer of the Year Ronaldinho in the side, Barcelona took their first Primera Liga title for six years in 2004–05. Barca retained the domestic crown in 2006, and came from behind to beat Arsenal 2–1 in the Champions League final.

After two trophyless seasons the Rijkaard era came to an end and the talismanic Ronaldinho departed to AC Milan as new coach, former Barca star Pep Guardiola, set about rebuilding the team.

Barcelona's Brazilian Ronaldinho (right) fights for the ball with Seville's Marti.

Volborn of Bayer Leverkusen holds the UEFA Cup after victory against Espanol in 1988.

Bayer Leverkusen Germany

Founded: 1904
Colours: Red; black; red
Honours: 1 German Cup; UEFA Cup 1988

Bayer Leverkusen were the surprise package in the 2001–02 Champions League. They marched all the way to the final, beating both Liverpool and Manchester United along the way. Although the team couldn't prevent Real Madrid from claiming their third European Champions League in five years, it showed that Leverkusen were a force to be reckoned with. The club also reached the last 16 in 2002–03, but having lost playmaker Michael Ballack and Ze Roberto to Bayern Munich in the summer, Leverkusen didn't look quite so formidable, and their Bundesliga form had slumped dramatically. Runners-up in 2002, Leverkusen narrowly avoided relegation the following season, by which time coach Klaus Toppmoller had already been shown the door.

Leverkusen, who are sponsored and funded by the huge Bayer chemical company, tasted victory in a major final when they lifted the UEFA Cup in 1988. Having put out Barcelona and Werder Bremen along the way, the team came back from a 3–0 away defeat against Espanol in the final. The German side matched that score in the home leg, then took the trophy on penalties. Leverkusen won the German Cup in 1993, but it was in the 1997–98 season that they caught the

eye. Having finished runners-up in the Bundesliga the season before, the club won through to the quarter-finals of the Champions League, where they went down to eventual winners Real Madrid 4–1 on aggregate.

Bayern Munich Germany

Founded: 1900
Colours: Blue/red; blue/red; blue/red
Honours: 21 League titles, 14 German Cups; World Club Cup 1976; European Champions 1974, 1975, 1976, 2001; European Cup Winners' Cup 1967; UEFA Cup 1996

Bayern Munich is the only German club to have won all three major European trophies. The hat-trick was achieved in 1996 with a UEFA Cup victory over Bordeaux, Bayern joining Juventus and Ajax as the only clubs to have achieved that prestigious Treble.

Between the club's formation in 1900 and the foundation of the Bundesliga in 1963, Bayern achieved just one national title and cup victory. Their track record was such that the club didn't feature in the new elite group of league clubs, although Bayern did gain promotion to the top flight in 1965. The following year the club finished third in the league and won the German Cup, thus qualifying for the 1966–67 Cup Winners' Cup. A team including Sepp Maier, Franz Beckenbauer and Gerd Muller won through to the

Bayern Munich with the Champions League trophy in 2001.

final, where they beat Rangers 1–0, the club's first European trophy. In 1969 Bayern won the domestic double, but it was in the following decade that the team reached its peak. A hat-trick of Bundesliga titles was achieved between 1972 and 1974, and the club provided the nucleus of the Germany team which won the European Championship and World Cup in 1972 and 1974 respectively. 1974 also saw Bayern demolish Atletico Madrid 4–0 in the final of the European Cup. After drawing the first game 1–1, Bayern made no mistake in the replay, Uli Hoeness and Gerd Muller hitting two goals each. Bayern went on to beat Leeds United the following year to retain the trophy, then completed a hat-trick with a 1–0 win over St Etienne in 1976.

This great side then broke up, but Bayern re-emerged in the 1980s with another impressive line-up, including Karl-Heinz Rummenigge and Lothar Matthaus. Bayern added six more Bundesliga titles in that decade, and also reached the European Cup final twice, beaten by Aston Villa in 1982 and Porto five years later.

Matthaus and Rummenigge both departed to Italy, but the former returned to the club in the mid-1990s as a veteran sweeper. He inspired Bayern's 1996 UEFA Cup triumph over Bordeaux. After an outstanding performance to beat Barcelona in the semis, Bayern ran out comfortable winners against a Bordeaux side that included a young Zinedine Zidane. Two years later Bayern won the German Cup and lost the championship to Kaiserslautern by a single point, yet this achievement wasn't enough to prevent the departure of coach Giovanni Trapattoni. He was replaced by Ottmar Hitzfeld, who brought European Champions League glory to Munich within three years. A victory over Valencia in the 2001 final ended a 25-year wait for the club to be crowned kings of Europe once again. When playmaker Michael Ballack arrived from Bayer Leverkusen in the summer of 2002, it was thought that he would be the architect of further success. Ballack didn't settle immediately, and Bayern crashed out of the 2002–03 Champions League at the first hurdle. Even so, they went on to wrap up yet another championship, finishing 16 points clear of Stuttgart. In 2005–06 Bayern left the Olympic Stadium for a new home at the Allianz Arena, and celebrated the move by completing the domestic double for the seventh time. The team was off the pace in 2006–07, however, and midway through the season Ottmar Hitzfeld was reappointed as manager, replacing Felix Magath.

Hitzfeld had restored Bayern to the top of the table when he announced he was stepping down at the end of the 2007–08 season. Former national team coach Jurgen Klinsmann was named as his successor.

Michael Ballack playing for Bayern Munich challenges David Beckham of Real Madrid.

Benfica Portugal

Founded: 1904
Colours: Red; white; red
Honours: 31 League titles; 27 Portuguese Cups; European Champions 1961, 1962

Benfica's Eusebio

Benfica was the club which ended Real Madrid's domination of the European Cup in the early 1960s. They met Barcelona – Real's conquerors – in the 1961 final, running out 3–2 winners. Real bounced back the following year and met the defending champions in the final. The Spanish side went 3–1 up, but Benfica, inspired by their new Mozambique-born acquisition Eusebio, won the game 5–3.

Benfica featured in three more finals in the next six years but finished on the losing side each time. However, five appearances in the final of the premier European competition, not to mention eight domestic championships, made the Portuguese club one of the great sides of the 1960s.

Benfica was founded in 1904. From the 1930s to the 1950s the club shared the domestic honours almost exclusively with city rivals Sporting and FC Porto. The club relocated to the famous Estadio da Luz – Stadium of Light – in 1954. Hungarian coach Bela Guttman arrived at the end of that decade and created the side which enjoyed unprecedented success. His policy of bringing in gifted players from countries that were then Portuguese colonies, such as Angola and Mozambique, was inspired. Mario Coluna and Jose Aguas arrived via this route, as well as the great Eusebio.

After losing to Manchester United in the 1968 European Cup final, Benfica were less successful at the highest level, though the club continued to dominate at home. The 1980s brought a revival as Benfica widened the net in the search for new players. As the former colonies gained independence the club's long-standing route for acquiring talent dried up. In 1978 Benfica decided to sanction buying players from other countries, breaking a long-established tradition. The club reached three European finals in the 1980s. In 1983, with Sven-Goran Eriksson in charge, the team reached the UEFA Cup final but lost 2–1 to Anderlecht on aggregate. 1988 saw Benfica reach their first European Cup final for 20 years. Their opponents, PSV, took the trophy on penalties after the game ended goalless. Benfica also made it to the final two years later, but a Frank Rijkaard goal for AC Milan consigned the Portuguese side to the runners-up spot for the fifth time. Benfica has had to play second fiddle to Porto in recent seasons, but ended an 11-year barren run by winning the championship in 2004–05.

Blackburn Rovers England

Founded: 1875
Colours: Blue/white; white; blue/white
Honours: 3 League titles; 6 FA Cups

Blackburn Rovers were formed in 1875 and were one of the founder members of the Football League. In the first 50 years of its existence the club enjoyed considerable success. Rovers achieved a hat-trick of FA Cup successes in the 1880s and added to their trophy haul with back-to-back victories in 1890 and 1891. In 1890, the year the club moved to Ewood Park, Blackburn enjoyed a 6–1 victory over Sheffield Wednesday in the FA Cup final. Winger William Townley became the first player to score a hat-trick in the showpiece of the footballing calendar. Blackburn won their first Championship in 1911–12, and finished seven points clear of Aston Villa to lift the title again two years later. But after notching a sixth FA Cup win in 1928, Blackburn's fortunes slumped. It wasn't until 1995 when the club, backed by industrialist Jack Walker's resources, claimed a third Championship. Kenny Dalglish's side pipped Manchester United by a single point. Just four years later Blackburn were relegated though they bounced back in 2001, re-established as a Premiership outfit under Graeme Souness. Former Wales coach Mark Hughes established Rovers as a top-half Premiership side during his four-year tenure, but results dried up under Paul Ince in 2008-09. Ince lasted just half a season, replaced by former Bolton and Newcastle boss Sam Allardyce.

Boca Juniors Argentina

Founded: 1905
Colours: Blue/gold; blue; blue/gold
Honours: 23 League titles; World Club Cup 1977, 2000; 2003 Copa Libertadores
1977, 1978, 2000, 2001, 2003, 2007; Super Cup 1989

It was in 1905 that the inhabitants of the predominantly
Italian Boca district of Buenos Aires decided to form their
own club, with a little help from an Irishman named Patrick
MacCarthy. Boca won their first championship in 1919, and

repeated that achievement three times before 1931, when a
professional league was established. Boca and River Plate
emerged as the dominant forces, although the picture was
clouded by the fact that there were two versions of the
Argentine championship during the 1920s and early 1930s.

In the 1950s Boca played second fiddle to River Plate
and Racing Club. The early 1960s saw a resurgence, and Boca
not only won the domestic title three times in four years but
also reached the final of the Copa Libertadores for the first
time. They came up against holders Santos, a side which
included Pele. Boca's star was striker Jose
Sanfilippo, who hit three goals in the two-
legged final, but Santos ran out 5–3
winners.

Boca had to wait another 14 years
before finally being crowned South
American Champions. The team took the
honours in 1977 with a victory on penalties
over Brazilian side Cruzeiro. They followed
it up with a victory over Borussia
Moenchengladbach in the World Club Cup,
drawing 2–2 in Buenos Aires then winning
3–0 in Germany. Boca retained the Copa
Libertadores by beating Colombia's
Deportivo Cali in 1978, and made it a hat-
trick of final appearances the following year,
although this time they went down to
Olimpia of Paraguay. In 1980 Boca signed
Maradona from Argentinos Juniors, but the
following year sold him to Barcelona for £5
million, five times the amount they had
paid. The next 15 years was a lean time for
Boca. But having lost the 1998
championship to River Plate by a single
point, they won the title in 1999. Boca went
on to win the Copa Libertadores in both
2000 and 2001, and in 2003 made it three
wins in four years with a resounding 5–1
aggregate victory over Santos in the
final. Future Manchester United star Carlos
Tevez was one of the young stars of the
2003 side. An even more emphatic 5–0
aggregate win over Gremio in the 2007
Copa Libertadores made Boca the most
successful club in the competition's recent
history, and second only to Independiente in
the all-time list.

**Matias Abel Donnet
of Boca Juniors battles with Seedorf
of AC Milan.**

Borussia Dortmund Germany

Founded: 1909

Colours: Yellow/black; black; yellow/black

Honours: 6 League titles; 2 German Cups; European Cup Winners' Cup 1966; World Club Cup 1997; European Champions 1997

Borussia Dortmund have fallen just short of joining an elite group of clubs to have won all three major European trophies. In 1966 Dortmund became the first German club to win one of Europe's top honours when they beat favourites Liverpool in the Cup Winners' Cup final. An extra-time goal from Reinhard Libuda secured a 2–1 win over Bill Shankly's side at Hampden Park. It proved to be a false dawn for Dortmund, however, for while Liverpool went on to enjoy extraordinary domestic and European success, the German club had a fallow period. Over the next 25 years Dortmund won just one piece of silverware, the German Cup in 1989. The 1990s proved to be much more fruitful. The club reached the UEFA Cup final in 1993 but crashed 6–1 over two legs against Juventus. By the mid-1990s Dortmund were a force to be reckoned with. Fielding stars of the calibre of Matthias Sammer, Karl-Heinz Riedle and

Andreas Moller, Dortmund won successive Bundesliga titles in 1995 and 1996. These were the club's first championships since 1963, when the Bundesliga was in its infancy. In 1997 Ottmar Hitzfeld's side were crowned kings of Europe. Dortmund surprised many by overcoming Manchester United in the semis, and were also the underdogs when they faced the superstars of Juventus in the Champions League final at the Olympic Stadium in Munich. But two headed goals from Riedle helped the team to a 3–1 victory and sweet revenge for the UEFA Cup thrashing of four years earlier. Dortmund went on to beat Cruzeiro in the World Club Cup, Germany's first success since Bayern Munich beat the same opposition 21 years earlier. The following season proved to be an anticlimax. Paulo Sousa and Paul Lambert were among the players who departed, while injury ended Sammer's career. Since winning their most recent Bundesliga title in 2001-02, Dortmund has been on the slide, while the club's finances have been in a parlous state. The sale of star player Tomas Rosicky to Arsenal in summer 2006 helped balance the books but did nothing for the team's fortunes, and in 2007–08 Dortmund finished just above the relegation zone.

Borussia Moenchengladbach Germany

Founded: 1900

Colours: White; white; white

Honours: 5 League titles; 3 German Cups; UEFA Cup 1975, 1979

Borussia Moenchengladbach enjoyed a spell of success in the 1970s in which they outshone Bayern Munich, winning five Bundesliga titles in eight years. The club also lifted the UEFA Cup twice, in 1975 and 1979. The first of those triumphs saw them take on Twente Enschede in the final. After a goalless first leg in Dusseldorf, Moenchengladbach went to Holland and won 5–1. The team featured German internationals Netzer, Stielike, Vogts, Bonhof and Heynckes, along with Danish star Allan Simonsen. Heynckes hit a hat-trick, with Simonsen grabbing the other two goals. The team reached two other European finals during the decade, the UEFA Cup in 1973 and the European Cup in 1977, but on both occasions Liverpool proved to be the stumbling block. The man who masterminded the club's success was the acclaimed coach and master tactician Hennes Weisweiler. Moenchengladbach were, arguably, the team of the decade. Apart from a cup victory in 1995, the last 20 years has been

Hausweiler of Borussia Moenchengladbach and Ebbe Sand.

a fallow period. The club has suffered relegation twice in the past decade, though on each occasion it quickly regained its top-flight status.

Brondby Denmark

Founded: 1964
Colours: Yellow; blue; yellow
Honours: 10 League titles; 6 Danish Cups

Brondby didn't win its first Danish championship until 1985, but in the next 13 years the club captured the title a further seven times, making it the country's most successful team of the modern era. Brondby players formed the backbone of Denmark's brilliant victory in the 1992 European Championships. One of those was Peter Schmeichel, although he had moved to Old Trafford the previous summer for a bargain £550,000. Since winning the double in 2004–05 under one of the club's greatest footballing sons, Michael Laudrup, Brondby has been off the pace in the league, though it scored a sixth cup victory in 2007–08.

FC Bruges Belgium

Founded: 1894
Colours: Black/blue; black; black
Honours: 13 League titles; 10 Belgian Cups

Bruges enjoyed its most successful period in the 1970s. The club emerged from the shadow of Anderlecht and Standard Liege to claim the Belgian championship five times in eight years, including the Double in 1977. Bruges reached the UEFA Cup final in 1976 and the European Cup final two years later. On both occasions Liverpool were the victors. In the first of the encounters Bruges took a 2–0 lead at Anfield but lost 3–2. A 1–1 draw in Belgium was enough for Liverpool to lift the trophy. In the 1978 European Cup campaign Ernst Happel's side put out Atletico Madrid and Juventus but lost to a Kenny Dalglish goal in the final. The 1980s proved to be a thin time for Bruges, but a championship win in 2004–05 completed a decade in which the club never finished out of the top two. A tenth domestic cup success in 2006–07 extended Bruges' lead at the top of the all-time list in that competition.

Brondby legend Michael Laudrup.

Cardiff City Wales

Founded: 1899
Colours: Blue; white; white
Honours: 1 FA Cup

Cardiff City is the only team to have taken the FA Cup out of England. With a side containing just one Englishman, Cardiff took on mighty Arsenal in 1927. Hughie Ferguson scored the only goal of the game, Arsenal 'keeper Dan Lewis fumbling his shot and allowing the ball to cross the line. Ironically, Lewis was a Welsh international 'keeper. Three years earlier, in 1923–24, Cardiff failed to win the Championship by the slenderest of margins. They and Huddersfield each finished on 57 points and both also had a goal difference of 27. But at the time goal average was the decisive factor and Huddersfield took the title. The 1920s remains the most successful period in the club's history, though the team did reach the FA Cup final in 2007–08, going down 1–0 to Portsmouth.

Celtic Scotland

Founded: 1887
Colours: Green/white; white; green/white
Honours: 42 League titles; 34 Scottish Cups; European Champions 1967

Celtic was formed in 1887 at the behest of Brother Walfrid, of the Roman Catholic order of Marist Brothers. Its original aim was to raise funds for the needy offspring of Irish immigrants, who were often subjected to discrimination. The sectarian allegiance survives to the present day, although Celtic sides down the ages have included many illustrious Protestant players. 'The Bhoys', as Celtic came to be known, won their first Championship in 1893, and have since formed a virtual duopoly over Scottish football with rivals Rangers.

Celtic became the first British club to win the European Cup, lifting the trophy in 1967, a year before Manchester United's triumph. The club was then in the early stages of an amazing period of domination of Scottish

Henrik Larsson of Celtic is beaten to the ball by Porto's Jorge Costa in the UEFA Cup final in 2003.

football. Celtic won the Championship in 1966, their first title for twelve years. Under legendary manager Jock Stein, who had joined the club in 1965, Celtic proceeded to win the Scottish League for the next eight seasons too. They also won the cup eight times in 13 seasons between 1965 and 1977. But the greatest moment unquestionably came in the European Cup final in Lisbon in 1967, in which Stein's side faced Inter Milan. Celtic recovered from an early penalty by Sandro Mazzola to win the game 2–1 with goals from Tommy Gemmill and Steve Chalmers. Incredibly, the entire Celtic side consisted of players born within a 30-mile radius of Glasgow. Celtic reached the final of the same competition in 1970, but went down 2–1 to Feyenoord in a match that went to extra time.

More recently the balance of power shifted to rivals Rangers. Between 1989 and 1997 Rangers equalled Celtic's record nine successive Championships. Wim Jansen prevented Rangers from making it ten in a row by leading Celtic to the title in 1998. He subsequently left in acrimonious circumstances, but with Martin O'Neill's arrival Celtic once again found themselves top of the tree in Scottish football, winning the title in 2001 and 2002. Celtic lost 3–2 to Porto in the 2003 UEFA Cup final, but bounced back the following season to record their eighth domestic double. In 2005 Celtic came within three minutes of making it four championships in five years, but two late Motherwell goals meant that the title went to Ibrox. When O'Neill stepped down for personal reasons, Gordon Strachan took over and, after a stuttering start, the team cruised to the 2005–06 SPL title. In 2006–07 Celtic reached the knockout stage of the Champions League for the first time, beating Manchester United in the group stage. They faced AC Milan in the last 16, an extra-time winner from Kaka at the San Siro deciding the tie after both games finished goalless. There was consolation as the Hoops claimed yet another domestic double. Celtic chalked up a 42nd league success in 2007–08, completing the club's first hat-trick of titles since the Jock Stein era.

Chelsea England

Founded: 1905
Colours: Blue; blue; blue
Honours: 3 League titles; 5 FA Cups; European Cup Winners' Cup 1971, 1998

Under successive managers in the 1990s Chelsea re-established itself as the glamour club of the capital. Glenn Hoddle, Ruud Gullit and Gianluca Vialli all contributed towards making the team increasingly cosmopolitan, and Chelsea became synonymous with stylish and attractive

The Chelsea team celebrate after receiving the Barclays Premiership trophy in 2005.

football. The club also won its first silverware for a generation. Roberto di Matteo scored the goal which won the 1997 FA Cup final, during Gullit's reign at Stamford Bridge. Less than a year later the Dutchman had been replaced by Vialli. Within four months of taking over, in February 1998, Vialli had picked up the League Cup, then followed it up with a victory in the European Cup Winners' Cup final. Gianfranco Zola came off the bench to score the goal which beat Stuttgart in Stockholm. Chelsea won the FA Cup again in 2000 but Vialli found himself surplus to requirements soon afterwards. Claudio Ranieri was brought in to make Chelsea title challengers as well as a good Cup side.

Chelsea legend Peter Osgood, who died in 2006

Chelsea's only Championship to date came in 1954–55, exactly 50 years after the club came into existence. Chelsea failed to build on that success and the following years found them languishing in mid-table. The 1955 Championship did earn Chelsea an invitation to participate in the inaugural European Cup, but the club declined after taking advice from the Football League. In the 1960s, under Tommy Docherty, Chelsea was the fashionable club to follow and players such as Peter Osgood, Terry Venables and Charlie Cooke made the team exciting to watch. Third place was their highest league finish, however. An FA Cup victory in 1970 came after a titanic struggle with Leeds. The following year Chelsea notched their first European success, beating Real Madrid in the Cup Winners' Cup final. This victory was followed by a 26-year barren spell.

In 2003 Ranieri steered Chelsea to third in the Premiership, then found himself with virtually unlimited funds following the purchase of the club by Russian oil billionaire Roman Abramovich. The shopping spree brought Veron, Duff, Crespo, Mutu and Cole to the Bridge, and they helped the side to finish runners-up in the league and reach the semi-final of the Champions League. It wasn't enough to save Ranieri, who was replaced by Jose Mourinho, the man who had led Porto to UEFA Cup and Champions League victories in successive seasons. His signings included Drogba, Robben and the outstanding Rennes 'keeper Petr Cech, though it was two men already on the books, John Terry and Frank Lampard, who were the top performers in 2004–05. Chelsea lost just once on their way to the Premiership title, and also won the Carling Cup, though the team they beat in the final, Liverpool, gained their revenge in the Champions League semi-final. Mourinho's men set the pace all season to retain the crown in 2005–06. Chelsea thus matched Manchester United's feat in the Premiership era, and became the first London club since the 1930s to win back-to-back championships. Chelsea claimed both domestic cups in 2006–07 and finished runners-up in the Premiership, but that wasn't enough to save Mourinho from the axe in September that year, the club's recently-appointed Director of Football Avram Grant taking over management duties at the Bridge. He led Chelsea to the runner-up spot in three competitions, including the Champions League, where the team came within a post width of beating Manchester United on penalties. Grant was soon on his way, replaced by World Cup-winning manager Luiz Felipe Scolari. He lasted until February 2009, when Chelsea were flirting with losing their coveted top-four status in the Premier League. Russia coach Guus Hiddink was brought in as a stopgap appointment, guiding the club to a fifth FA Cup success before making way for former AC Milan boss Carlo Ancelotti.

Colo-Colo Chile

Founded: 1925
Colours: White; black; black
Honours: 28 League titles; 10 Chilean Cups; Copa Libertadores 1991; South American Recopa 1991; Interamerican Cup 1992

Colo-Colo has been Chile's top club side in recent years by some margin. Between 1979 and 1998 they won the domestic championship on ten occasions, including a hat-trick of titles between 1989 and 1991. The latter was a particularly significant year, for Colo-Colo also became South American Champions, the first Chilean side to achieve that honour since inception of the competition in 1960. In the final Colo-Colo faced Olimpia of Paraguay and won the match with a 3–0 home victory, having earlier fought out a goalless draw in Asuncion.

Colo-Colo was founded in 1925 by a breakaway faction from another Chilean club, Magallanes. The rebel group named the new club after the local slang term for 'wildcat'. Both Magallanes and Colo-Colo were among the founding members of the country's professional league in 1933. Magallanes opened with a hat-trick of titles, but after Colo-Colo took the championship in 1937 the club slowly established itself as the premier outfit. After winning the 1972 championship Colo-Colo made it to the final of the Copa Libertadores but lost to Independiente in a play-off. The Chilean league season is split into two separate tournaments, the Apertura and Clausura championships. Colo-Colo claimed both crowns in 2006 and 2007, and took the Clausura title in 2008 to take the club's tally to 28 championships in its 82-year history.

Mark Viduka (left) in a friendly match between Leeds United and Colo-Colo in Melbourne, 2002.

Deportivo la Coruna Spain

Founded: 1906
Colours: Blue/white; blue; blue
Honours: 1 League title; 2 Spanish Cups

It took Deportivo almost a century to make their mark on Spanish and European football. A Cup victory over Valencia in 1995 was the club's first silverware, and that success was repeated in 2001, with a 2–1 victory over Real Madrid at the Bernebeu. There have also been some notable European campaigns. In 1996, under John Toshack, Deportivo made it to the semis of the Cup Winners' Cup. In 2001–02 Deportivo beat Manchester United home and away in the Champions League group stage before losing to Alex Ferguson's side in the quarter-finals. The highlight came in 2000, when Deportivo won La Liga, finishing five points ahead of Barcelona to become only the ninth Spanish club to win the championship.

It was in 1902 that Jose Maria Abalo returned to his home town of La Coruna, after a period spent studying in England. He and a group of friends enthusiastically took up the game, and the club was formed in 1906. Deportivo failed to qualify for the top division when La Liga was established in 1928. The club finally made it into the top flight in 1941, but it wasn't until the 1950s that it enjoyed a sustained period of success. Future European Footballer of the Year Luis Suarez was the club's star player, but Deportivo couldn't hang onto him when Barcelona came knocking at the door. The 1970s and 1980s were fallow years. After suffering relegation in 1973 Deportivo struggled in the lower divisions, and often found itself in straitened circumstances. The late 1980s ushered in a new era. Top-flight status returned in 1991, and with players of the stature of Brazil's Bebeto and Mauro Silva, the club's fortunes quickly improved. Deportivo's first European campaign came in the 1993–94 UEFA Cup, when they beat Aston Villa before going out to Eintracht Frankfurt. The club also finished runners-up in La Liga in 1994 and 1995. A major factor in the club's recent successes has been the strike partnership of Diego Tristan and Roy Makaay, but that was broken up in the summer of 2003 when Bayern Munich paid £18 million for the Dutch marksman, making him the German club's record signing.

Dinamo Tbilisi Georgia

Founded: 1925
Colours: White/blue; white; white
Honours: 15 League titles (2 Soviet and 13 Georgian); 2 Soviet Cups; 8 Georgian Cups; CIS Cup 2004; European Cup Winners' Cup 1981

Georgia withdrew from the Soviet federation in 1989, and since then Dinamo Tbilisi, the country's most famous club, has dominated domestic football. Tbilisi also won two Soviet championships, in 1964 and 1978. The latter came in the middle of a three-year spell in which the club also won the Soviet Cup competition on two occasions, making it the most successful period in the club's history. The crowning moment came in 1981, when this technically excellent side won through to the European Cup Winners' Cup final.

Goce Sedloski of Dinamo Zagreb.

Dinamo fell behind to Carl Zeiss Jena but hit back with goals from Gutsayer and Daraselia for a famous victory. The team looked a good bet to retain the trophy the following year but went down to Standard Liege in the semi-final. Dinamo's cause wasn't helped by the fact that six of their players were called up for a friendly in Argentina. They didn't arrive home until 48 hours before the second leg, which the Belgian side won 1–0. In 2004 Tbilisi beat Skonto Riga to claim their only success to date in the CIS Cup, the competition introduced in 1993 for the champions of the former Soviet Republics and Baltic states.

Dinamo Zagreb Croatia

Founded: 1945
Colours: Blue/white; blue; blue
Honours: 14 League title (4 Yugoslav and 10 Croatian); 7 Yugoslav Cups, 9 Croatian Cups; Fairs Cup 1967

In the 1960s Red Star Belgrade was probably Yugoslavia's most famous club, and Partizan Belgrade made it to the 1966 European Cup final. But it was Dinamo Zagreb who became the country's first club side to lift a European trophy. Dinamo's success came in the 1967 Inter-Cities Fairs Cup. The club had reached the final four years earlier, becoming the first Eastern European side to contest a major final. On that occasion their run included victories over Bayern Munich and Ferencvaros. But they came unstuck against an excellent Valencia team in the final, going down 4–1 on aggregate. Four years later Dinamo overturned a 3–0 first-leg defeat by Eintracht Frankfurt in the semi-final, winning the return match 4–0. Dinamo faced a powerful Leeds United side in the final, and after winning 2–0 at home they took the trophy with a goalless draw at Elland Road. Between that success and the break-up of Yugoslavia, Dinamo won just one domestic championship, in 1982. The team changed its name to FC Croatia when Croatia became an independent state once again in 1990, a return to the situation that existed in the 1940s. Since then, the club has shared most of the domestic honours with Hajduk Split, the country's other best-known team.

Dukla Prague Czech Republic

Colours: Brown/yellow; yellow; red
Honours: 11 Czechoslovakian League titles, 8 Czechoslovakian Cups

Dukla Prague was one of several army clubs that came into

existence in Eastern European countries in the postwar era. Many players from Slavia Prague and Sparta Prague – the clubs which had dominated Czech football before the Second World War – were conscripted into the new side. Unsurprisingly, Dukla soon began to accumulate honours including seven championships between 1956 and 1967. Domestic success meant that the club featured regularly in European Cup campaigns. They lost 3–1 to Manchester United in 1957–58, one of the last appearances by Matt Busby's famous side before the Munich air crash. The club went down to England's Double winners Tottenham Hotspur at the quarter-final stage in 1961–62. And in 1966–67 Dukla lost to eventual winners Celtic. After the fall of the Iron Curtain and foundation of the Czech Republic, Dukla struggled for success and in 1996 was reconstituted as FK Pribram following a merger with a rival club.

Dynamo Kiev Ukraine

Founded: 1927
Colours: Purple/white; purple; white
Honours: 12 Ukrainian League titles; 13 Soviet League titles; 9 Ukrainian Cups; 9 Soviet Cups; CIS Cup 1996, 1997, 1998, 2002; European Cup Winners' Cup 1975, 1986; European Super Cup 1975

Dynamo Kiev was the most successful club in the history of the Soviet Union. It took the Ukraine club 34 years to capture its first championship, in 1961, but from then until the collapse of the Soviet system Kiev enjoyed considerable success. The club added twelve more championships in that 30-year period. Under coach Valeri Lobanovski, a former Kiev player, Kiev concentrated on technical excellence instead of the rugged, physical style that many Eastern bloc teams were noted for. It brought the club two European Cup Winners' Cup victories, in 1975 and 1986. The first of those saw Kiev beat Ferencvaros comprehensively 3–0 in the final. Oleg Blokhin was outstanding, capping a virtuoso display by scoring the third goal. Blokhin was still at the heart of the team which won the same trophy eleven years later. He was on target too, as Kiev won 3–0, Atletico Madrid on the receiving end this time. The team also included star striker Igor Belanov, who became only the third Soviet player to win the European Footballer of the Year award, following in the footsteps of Blokhin and Yashin.

Kiev has dominated the Ukraine league since its formation in 1992. The team has also enjoyed some excellent Champions League campaigns. In 1997–98 a team spearheaded by Shevchenko and Rebrov reached the quarter-finals of the competition. Results at the group stage included a 3–0 win over Barcelona at home and a 4–0 victory at the Nou Camp. Having earned a 1–1 draw against quarter-final opponents Juventus in Turin, the team slumped to a 4–1 home defeat. Kiev reached the last eight the following year too, going down to eventual runners-up Bayern Munich.

Anatoli Demianenko of Dynamo Kiev with the Cup Winners' Cup in 1986.

Eintracht Frankfurt Germany

Founded: 1899
Colours: Red; black/red; black
Honours: 1 League title; 4 German Cups; UEFA Cup 1980

Eintracht Frankfurt will forever be associated with a famous defeat: the 7–3 demolition at the hands of Real Madrid in the 1960 European Cup final, regarded by many as the greatest club match ever seen. It ended with Madrid lifting the trophy for the fifth successive year. Eintracht contributed hugely, however, and actually opened the scoring. They had also put twelve goals past Rangers in the previous round.

Formed in 1899, Eintracht Frankfurt was among the founding members of the Bundesliga in 1963. The club's only championship had come four years earlier. Since then silverware has proved hard to come by. Eintracht did win the German cup four times between 1974 and 1988, however. And in 1980 they captured the UEFA Cup, the club's only European success to date. Remarkably, all four semi-finalists hailed from Germany. Eintracht thrashed Bayern Munich 5–3, then came through narrowly in the final, beating Borussia Moenchengladbach on away goals. The mid-1980s regularly turned into a relegation dogfight for Eintracht. Although a new regime and new players led to a recovery in the early 1990s, it proved to be short-lived and in 1996 the club was relegated for the first time in its history. Promotion back to the top flight soon followed but Eintracht has been something of a yo-yo club ever since.

Estudiantes Argentina

Founded: 1905
Colours: Red/white; white; red/white
Honours: 4 League titles; Copa Libertadores 1968, 1969, 1970; World Club Cup 1968; Interamerican Cup 1969

Estudiantes won only one Argentine championship in the 1960s, in 1967, but that paved the way for a hat-trick of Copa Libertadores victories. Based at the small town of La Plata, near Buenos Aires, Estudiantes temporarily eclipsed the capital's big-name clubs, River Plate and Boca Juniors.

The 1967 championship earned Estudiantes entry into the following season's Copa Libertadores, where they beat Palmeiras of Brazil in a play-off. The club defended the trophy by beating Nacional the following year, and completed a hat-trick with a 1–0 aggregate win over Penarol in 1970. The second leg in Montevideo included a mass brawl. Estudiantes were famous for cynical fouling and gamesmanship during this era, and although they picked up a lot of silverware, they won few friends.

The Copa Libertadores victories meant that Estudiantes appeared in three successive World Club Cup finals from 1968. They won the first, a bruising encounter with Manchester United. The ill feeling from the World Cup clash between Argentina and England two years earlier spilled over into some disgraceful challenges on the pitch. The Argentine side was up to its usual tricks against AC Milan and Penarol in the following two finals but lost both.

Four Estudiantes players were jailed after the Milan game. The era came to an end when Uruguayan side Nacional prevented Estudiantes from winning a fourth successive Copa Libertadores, beating them in a play-off in the 1971 final. In 2002 the club hailed a returning hero, Argentina's 1986 World Cup-winning coach Carlos Bilardo, but he had gone by the time the club won the 2006 Apertura championship, its first title for 23 years. Former star Juan Veron, on loan from Chelsea, played a part in that success.

Estudiantes v Manchester United in 1968.

Everton England

Founded: 1878
Colours: Blue; white; blue
Honours: 9 League titles; 5 FA Cups; European Cup Winners' Cup 1985

Everton was formed in 1878, an offshoot of St Domingo's Sunday School. Indeed, for the first year it was known as St Domingo's FC, the club being renamed in 1879. One of the founder-members of the Football League, Everton's original home was Anfield. A dispute saw the club relocate to Goodison Park in 1892, leaving a new club, Liverpool FC, to fill the void left behind.

The first of Everton's nine championships came in 1890–91, the second on the eve of the First World War. In 1927–28 Everton already had the title sewn up when Arsenal came to Goodison on 5 May, but 48,000 fans turned up to see their star centre-forward, Billy 'Dixie' Dean, get the hat-trick he needed to record a magical 60 League goals for the season. Dean remains Everton's most prolific marksman, hitting 349 goals in his twelve years at the club. After winning two more Championships in the 1930s, Everton had a barren spell until Harry Catterick brought further success in the 1960s. His 'school of science' approach brought two Championships and, in 1966, a third FA Cup victory. The famous Kendall-Harvey-Ball midfield trio was generally regarded as the finest of its day.

It was when Howard Kendall returned as manager in the 1980s that the club managed to get the better of Liverpool, a rarity in the modern era. Not only did his side relegate the Reds to runners-up spot in 1985 and 1987, but they also won the FA Cup in 1984 and lifted the European Cup Winners' Cup the following season. The 3–1 win over Rapid Vienna was the club's first European trophy. Unfortunately, the five-year ban imposed on English clubs following events at the Heysel Stadium denied Everton the chance to add to that tally.

The 1990s saw Everton often in the wrong half of the table, even flirting dangerously with going out of the top flight for the first time since 1954. There was a fifth FA Cup win, over Manchester United, in 1995, but a tenth Championship looked a distant possibility. David Moyes' arrival from Preston North End to replace Walter Smith in 2002 had an immediate impact. Everton finished seventh in the Premiership in his first season, and in 2004-05 surprised many by securing a Champions League place, despite selling star players Wayne Rooney and Thomas Gravesen.

Rooney and Carragher clash in a Merseyside derby.

Ferencvaros Hungary

Founded: 1899
Colours: Green/white; white; white
Honours: 28 League titles; 20 Hungarian Cups; Fairs Cup 1965

Ferencvaros is Hungary's most successful club by some distance. Since claiming a first championship in 1903 – four years after its formation – Ferencvaros has regularly been in the honours. The only decade in which the club failed to win the championship was the 1950s, when Honved was the country's top side. Ferencvaros put ten goals past Rapid Wien in winning the 1928 Mitropa Cup final. The club repeated this success in 1937 with a 9–6 aggregate victory over Lazio. Ferencvaros has also featured in three major postwar finals.

The first of those, the 1964–65 Fairs Cup, made the Budapest-based club the first from Eastern Europe to win any of the three major trophies. They put out Manchester United in the semis, a game which needed a play-off after the teams finished 3–3 over the two legs. In the final they faced Juventus in Turin, lifting the trophy with a 1–0 victory. The team reached the final again three years later but lost to Leeds United 1–0. That side featured the great Florian Albert, who had won the 1967 European Footballer of the Year award, the only Hungarian player to be thus honoured. Ferencvaros also featured in the 1975 Cup Winners' Cup final but went down 3–0 against Dynamo Kiev.

Feyenoord Holland

Founded: 1908
Colours: Red/white; black; red
Honours: 14 League titles; 11 Dutch Cups; World Club Cup 1970; European Champions 1970; UEFA Cup 1974, 2002

Although Ajax took Europe by storm in the early 1970s, winning a hat-trick of European Cups, it was Feyenoord who first brought the trophy back to Holland. The Rotterdam club were crowned European champions in 1970, a year ahead of their Amsterdam rivals, beating Celtic 2–1 in a game that went to extra-time. The club was formed in 1908, largely thanks to wealthy benefactor CRJ Kieboom. A first domestic championship came in 1924, but the club enjoyed only sporadic success for the next 35 years. It was in the 1960s, particularly under Ernst Happel's guiding hand, that Feyenoord became a consistent force. The team won the championship five times in eleven years between 1961 and 1971, and lifted the cup twice during the same period. Happel imposed his own brand of 'total football' on the side, which brought considerable success and won many admirers before Ajax took over as the country's outstanding side.

Feyenoord's last championship for a decade came in 1974, and the club reached

Jovic (left) of Ferencvaros and Tamasi of FC Ujpest fight for the ball.

the UEFA Cup final in the same year. They drew 2–2 with Tottenham Hotspur at White Hart Lane, then completed the victory with a 2–0 win at home.

The 1984 title was inspired by the veteran Johan Cruyff and young prodigy Ruud Gullit. Both soon departed and it wasn't until former player Wim Jansen returned as manager in the early 1990s that Feyenoord once again scaled the heights. He took the club to the title in 1993, and Leo Beenhakker brought the championship to Rotterdam again in 1999. In 2002 Feyenoord lifted the UEFA Cup, beating Borussia Dortmund 3–2 in the final, but domestic trophies have been thin on the ground in recent years. An eleventh Cup win in 2008 was the club's first silverware for a decade on the home front.

Fiorentina Italy

Founded: 1936
Colours: Purple; purple; purple
Honours: 2 League titles; 6 Italian Cups;
European Cup Winners' Cup 1961

Fiorentina's fall from grace over recent seasons has been dramatic. In 2000 the club was battling with Manchester United and Valencia for a place in the Champions League quarter-finals, and in Gabriel Batistuta boasted one of the most prolific strikers in world football. Fiorentina would soon be doing battle with Serie C sides, having been demoted over a financial scandal. 2002–03 saw Fiorentina back in Serie B, and the following year the club returned to the top division via the play-offs.

In 1956 Fiorentina broke the stranglehold on Italian football held by the clubs from Turin and Milan. The club's first title came 20 years after it was founded and was based on a steely defence. The following year Fiorentina reached the European Cup final but couldn't prevent Real Madrid from retaining the trophy, their cause not helped by having to play the final at the Bernebeu Stadium. Four years later Fiorentina became the first Italian club to win a major European trophy. It came in the newly instituted Cup Winners' Cup, which had attracted an entry of ten clubs. Fiorentina beat Dinamo Zagreb in the semis, then met Rangers in the final. They won 2–0 at Ibrox and comfortably protected their lead in the return leg. Fiorentina also reached the final the following year, by which time the two-legged format had been dropped. They drew 1–1 with Atletico Madrid at Hampden Park before going down 3–0 in the replay.

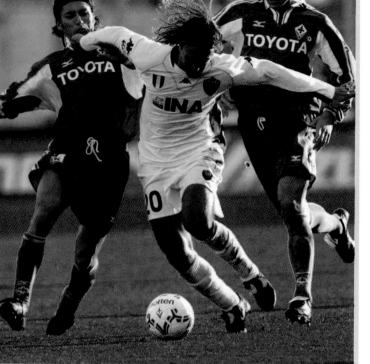

Roma's Batistuta outruns the Fiorentina defence during their Serie A match in 2002.

The 'Viola', as the Florentine club is known, won its only other Serie A title in 1969. Apart from a Coppa Italia victory in 1975, Fiorentina made little impact in the next 20 years. They reached a third major final in 1990 when they faced Juventus in the UEFA Cup. Juve won the match 3–1, and within days the Fiorentina fans suffered a second blow: the sale of their star player Roberto Baggio – to Juventus. A world record £8 million failed to assuage them. Florence soon had a new hero, Gabriel Batistuta. The Argentine's prolific scoring, together with his decision to remain when the club was relegated in 1993, elevated him to legendary status. It was Batistuta's goals which helped Fiorentina beat Atalanta in the 1996 Italian Cup final. It was the club's only success of the decade and their first trophy for 21 years.

In June 2006, while star striker Luca Toni was helping Italy win the World Cup for the fourth time in Germany, his club was docked 15 points and thrown out of the 2006–07 Champions League for its part in the corruption scandal rocking Italian football. The Viola still managed to finish in a Uefa Cup spot, and was placed 4th in 2007–08, despite selling Toni to Bayern Munich.

Flamengo Brazil

Founded: 1911
Colours: Black/red; white; white
Honours: 5 Brazilian championships; 30 Rio State championships; 1 Rio–Sao Paulo title; World Club Cup 1981; Copa Libertadores 1981; Copa Mercosur 1999

Flamengo started life as a sailing club in 1895. It wasn't until 1911, when a number of dissidents from neighbouring football team Fluminense joined the club, that Flamengo began their illustrious association with the round ball game. For some 60 years Flamengo contested the Rio de Janeiro state championship, the geography of Brazil making a countrywide competition impractical. Thus began a long rivalry with Rio's other big clubs, Fluminense, Botafogo and Vasco da Gama. By the time the national championship was finally established in 1971, Flamengo had won the state title on 16 occasions. The club was finally crowned champions of Brazil at the tenth attempt, in 1980, and went on to take the title three times in four years. The star man in this period was Zico, who was top scorer in both 1980 and 1982. In 1981 he hit all four of Flamengo's goals against Chilean side Cobreloa in the final of the Copa Libertadores, which went to a play-off after two drawn matches. Zico was also outstanding as Flamengo went on to beat Liverpool 3–0 in the World Club Cup final in December of the same year. Flamengo have added two more national titles since, in 1987 and 1992, but in the last decade the club has played second fiddle to the likes of Palmeiras, Corinthians and Gremio.

Edilson (right) of Flamengo and Marco of Fluminense in action during the Havelange Cup, 2000.

Fluminense Brazil

Founded: 1902
Colours: Red; green/white; white
Honours: 1 Brazilian championship; 30 Rio State championships; 2 Rio–Sao Paulo titles

One of Rio de Janeiro's top club sides, Fluminense was founded by an Englishman, Arthur Cox, in 1902. The team won five of the first six Rio state championships after the competition was instituted in 1906. Despite these early successes, Fluminense were hammered 10–1 by a touring Corinthians side in 1910, an indication that European football was far more tactically advanced at this time. Fluminense became a professional club in 1932, the first Brazilian side to take such a step. This ushered in another period of dominance, including a hat-trick of titles between 1936 and 1938. In the 30 years up to 1971, when the national championship was established, success was more sporadic. However, the club did provide some famous players for the Brazil side over the years, including Didi, Carlos Alberto and Felix. Fluminense have only won the Brazilian championship once, in 1984, when their star player was Paraguay's Romerito, who was voted South America Footballer of the Year in 1985. In 2002 Fluminense reached the semi-final of the Brazilian championship, helped by goals from the veteran striker Romario. In 2008 the club reached its first Copa Libertadores final, but went down to Ecuadorian side LDU Quito on penalties. Clashes with Flamengo are particularly intense affairs, the rivalry between the two sets of supporters broadly falling along class lines. Fluminense are dubbed the aristocrats, while Flamengo is noted as the people's club.

Galatasaray Turkey

Founded: 1905
Colours: Yellow; red; black
Honours: 17 League titles; 14 Turkish Cups; UEFA Cup 2000; Super Cup 2000

Turkey surprised many by reaching the semi-finals of the 2002 World Cup, but it was perhaps a landmark match two years earlier that signalled a significant breakthrough in Turkish football. That was when the country's premier club side, Galatasaray, finally turned domination of the domestic scene into a first European triumph. The club overcame Leeds United in the semi-final of the 2000 UEFA Cup, then lifted the trophy with a penalty shoot-out victory over Arsenal. Galatasaray went on to beat the Galacticos of Real Madrid 2-1 in the European Super Cup, and added a domestic double to make it the most memorable year in the club's history. Gala have regularly featured in the Champions League in recent years. They reached the semi-final in 1989, losing to Steaua Bucharest. Five years later the club enjoyed a fine victory over Manchester United, after scoring three goals at Old Trafford. Galatasaray hasn't done quite so well in recent years, and indeed the triumphant UEFA Cup campaign began with an early exit from the Champions League.

Galatasaray's Hasan Sas (left) pursues Barcelona forward, Javier Saviola.

SV Hamburg Germany

Founded: 1887
Colours: White; red; red
Honours: 6 League titles; 3 German Cups; European Champions 1983; European Cup Winners' Cup 1977

Hamburg has not enjoyed much good fortune in recent years, yet remains one of Germany's most successful club sides. The golden era was in the late 1970s and early 1980s, when the team boasted the double-European Footballer of the Year in Kevin Keegan. Hamburg not only won the Bundesliga three times in five years but also appeared in four European finals. Having beaten Real Madrid in the semi-final of the 1980 European Cup, Hamburg surprisingly went down to Nottingham Forest in the final. Three years later it was Hamburg's turn to be triumphant underdogs when they beat a Juventus side including Michel Platini. Felix Magath, one of Hamburg's greatest ever players, scored the goal which won the trophy. Magath had also scored in the 2–0 win over Anderlecht in the 1977 European Cup Winners' Cup final. A great era came to an end with a shock 4–0 aggregate defeat by IFK Gothenburg in the 1982 UEFA Cup final. Victory in the German League Cup in 2003, along with a couple of Intertoto Cup successes, have been the highlights in the last decade, though under ex-Spurs boss Martin Jol, Hamburg were in the shake-up for domestic honours in 2008–09.

Honved Hungary

Founded: 1909
Colours: Red/black; black; black
Honours: 13 Hungarian league titles; 6 Hungarian cups

This famous Hungarian club was originally known as Kispest and enjoyed modest success in the first 30 years of its existence. The glory days came after the renamed club became the de facto national side in Communist Hungary of the postwar era. Honved was able to recruit the best young

Hamburg's golden boy, Kevin Keegan.

talent in the country, but even allowing for that luxury the team of the late 1940s and early 1950s was outstanding.

Ferenc Puskas, the team's star player, was the league's top scorer for four seasons. He formed a deadly partnership with Sandor 'Golden Head' Kocsis for both club and country. By 1954 Honved was regarded as the best club side in the world. When they came to Molineux and lost 3–2 to Wolves, the media were quick to dub the Midlanders the uncrowned champions of Europe. It was this boast that led to the introduction of the European Cup. Honved lost in the first round of the inaugural competition, in 1955–56. After the Soviet Union suppressed an uprising in 1956 there was an exodus of players, including Puskas and Kocsis, and the club went into decline. Ujpest Doza and Ferencvaros dominated Hungarian football for many years, although Honved did enjoy great success in the 1980s, winning the league six times. In 2003 a new club, Budapest Honved FC, was formed from the ashes of the old as part of a deal to wipe the slate clean after an insolvency crisis.

IFK Gothenburg Sweden

Founded: 1904
Colours: Blue/white; blue; blue
Honours: 18 League titles; 5 Swedish Cups; UEFA Cup 1982, 1987

IFK Gothenburg has been Sweden's most successful club side of the modern era, though their 2007 league title was the first for 11 years. Their haul of domestic championships included a run of six titles in seven years in the 1990s. The club also became the first from that country to win major European honours. Under Sven-Goran Eriksson IFK beat Valencia and Kaiserslautern en route to the 1982 UEFA Cup final, where they faced Hamburg. The Swedes took a slender one-goal advantage to Germany for the second leg, then surprised everyone by winning there too, 3–0 the score. The pattern was much the same five years later when IFK reached the final again. They only beat Dundee United 1–0 at home and the Scottish club was strongly fancied to emerge victorious. But the game ended 1–1 and IFK lifted the trophy for the second time.

Jimmy Svensson of IFK Gothenburg heads the ball in front of Orgryte's Marek.

Independiente Argentina

Founded: 1905

Colours: Red/blue; blue; black

Honours: 14 League titles; World Club Cup 1973, 1984; Copa Libertadores 1964, 1965, 1972–75, 1984; Inter-American Cup 1973, 1974, 1976; Super Cup 1994, 1995

In 1905 a group of Italian employees from the British store, City of London, decided to leave their employer's sports club and form one of their own. It was independence they wanted and so, fittingly, named their new club Independiente. The team won Argentina's championship in 1922, and the fans were soon hailing their first superstar: Raimundo Orsi. A flying winger, Orsi played for Argentina in the 1928 Olympic final before being lured away to Juventus the following year. The next decade produced a new hero, Arsenio Erico, whose prolific scoring helped bring Independiente the championship in 1938 and 1939. It wasn't until the 1960s that Independiente enjoyed their next period of sustained success. In 1964 Independiente became the first Argentine team to win the Copa Libertadores, the continent's club championship. They retained the title the following year but on each occasion fell to Inter Milan in the World Club Cup. The 1964 match was a particularly ugly affair, setting a trend for some ill-tempered encounters between club sides from the two continents.

Independiente were South America's club champions four times in a row between 1972 and 1975, an unprecedented run of success. In 1973 they finally lifted the World Club Cup. They faced European Cup runners-up Juventus, who insisted on a one-off match staged in Italy. Independiente agreed to the terms, went to the Olympic Stadium in Rome and won 1–0.

In 1984 Independiente became South American champions for the seventh time. Star player Jorge Burruchaga scored the only goal of the two-legged clash with holders Gremio of Brazil. Burruchaga would go on to score the winner for Argentina against West Germany in the World Cup two years later. That December Independiente faced the true European champions, Liverpool, beating them 1–0 in Tokyo to take the World Club Cup for a second time. In 2002–03 Independiente defied all the odds to win the Apertura, the country's opening championship (the season being divided into two mini-championships since 1992). This marked the club's first domestic title for a decade. Diego Forlan's star performances for the the club prompted Sir Alex Ferguson to pay £7 million to bring the striker to Old Trafford.

Dennis Bergkamp lifts the UEFA Cup after Inter Milan defeated Salzburg in the 1994 final.

Inter Milan Italy

Founded: 1908
Colours: Black/blue; black; black
Honours: 17 League titles; 5 Italian Cups; World Club Cup 1964, 1965; European Champions 1964, 1965; UEFA Cup 1991, 1994, 1998

Internazionale was formed in 1908 following a rift within the ranks of AC Milan. A breakaway faction created a new Milan club and thus began one of the great city rivalries in world football. Inter were champions in 1910 and 1920 but the Mussolini regime took a dim view of the club's open recruitment policy. It was even forced into a name change: Internationale thus became Ambrosiana, a state of affairs which lasted until after the Second World War. Under coach Alfredo Foni, Inter won the championship in 1953 and 1954, their hallmark being an impregnable defence. But it was during Helenio Herrera's period in charge that the club reached new heights. Apart from winning the league three times in four years in the mid-1960s, Inter were also crowned champions of Europe in 1964 and 1965. The side included some legendary names: Facchetti in defence, Luis Suarez in midfield and Sandro Mazzola up front. In 1967 Celtic ended Inter's hopes of a hat-trick of European Cups, and five years later they lost again, to an outstanding Ajax side including Johan Cruyff. In the next 17 years Inter won

Serie A just once, in 1980, when a restriction on foreign players was lifted. In the 1980s and 1990s Inter invested heavily in some big-name overseas stars – the likes of Liam Brady, Lothar Matthaus, Juergen Klinsmann and Dennis Bergkamp. In the past ten years Juventus and arch-rivals AC Milan have fared better, both domestically and in European competition. Inter did win the UEFA Cup three times in the 1990s, though. The club missed out on the 2001–02 *scudetto* on the last day of the season. Despite letting star player Ronaldo depart to Real Madrid they were runners-up again in 2002–03, and also reached the semi-finals of the Champions League. Inter claimed a 14th *scudetto* in 2005–06, despite finishing only third in the league. Inter were awarded the title after Juventus and AC Milan were penalised for their part in a match-fixing scandal. Inter retained the *scudetto* in 2007, though the league was weakened by the punishments handed out to its main rivals.

Inter completed a league hat-trick in 2007–08, yet that wasn't enough to save coach Roberto Mancini. He was replaced by Jose Mourinho, who was seen as the man to take the club to the top of the European pile, something the blue-and-black half of Milan hadn't achieved for over 40 years. The 'Special One' performed no better than Mancini in his first season, Inter going down to Manchester United in the last 16.

Inter Milan's striker Christian Vieri (right) with teammate Adriano.

Ipswich Town England

Founded: 1887
Colours: Blue; white; blue
Honours: 1 League title; 1 FA Cup; UEFA Cup 1981

Since Ipswich Town FC came into being in 1887, the club's successes have been confined to two relatively short periods, both masterminded by future England managers. Alf Ramsey took over in the mid-1950s, when the club was in the Third Division (South). In 1960–61 Ipswich won promotion to the top flight, scoring 100 goals on the way to the Division Two championship. The following season Ramsey led the East Anglian side to the League title. The decline was very rapid thereafter, however, and it wasn't until Bobby Robson took over that Ipswich embarked on its next great era. By the mid-1970s Ipswich were regularly a top six side. Although a second Championship proved elusive, Robson did deliver the club's first FA Cup success, with a victory over Arsenal in 1978. Three years later the club won the UEFA Cup, its only European trophy to date. Ipswich beat Dutch champions AZ 67 Alkmaar 5–4 on aggregate in the two-legged final. When John Wark scored a vital goal in the away tie it was his 14th of the campaign, equalling the existing record.

Once again the club was unable to build on its success after Robson departed to take over as England boss. The side broke up and relegation followed in 1986. In the late 1990s former player George Burley built a side which not only won promotion to the Premiership but also enjoyed an impressive UEFA Cup campaign. The 2002–03 season saw Ipswich back in Division One.

Terry Butcher playing for Ipswich Town.

Juventus Italy

Founded: 1897
Colours: Black/white; white; black/white
Honours: 27 League titles; 9 Italian Cups; World Club Cup 1985, 1996; European Champions 1985, 1996; European Cup Winners' Cup 1984; UEFA Cup 1977, 1990, 1993

Juventus has won more domestic honours than any Italian club, and is among the elite few to have won every major European trophy. Formed in 1897 by a group of students, Juventus played in red for the first six years. In 1903 a club official went on a trip to England and saw Notts County play. He was taken by the black-and-white kit, took a set of shirts back home with him and the rest is history.

A first championship came in 1905, but it was during the 1930s that the Turin club enjoyed its first era of dominance, helped by the backing of the Fiat Motor Company. One of the stars of a glittering line-up was striker Raimundo Orsi. Juve had paid the Argentine star a £1400 signing-on fee in 1928, an early indication that the club was prepared to pay big money to get the best. It proved to be a sound investment as they won five championships in a row between 1931 and 1935.

In the 1950s Juventus continued to scour the world for

John Charles (right) who joined Juventus in 1957

In 1990 Juve won the UEFA Cup again, beating Fiorentina 3–1 in the final. Within days they compounded the Florence club's misery by purchasing their star player Roberto Baggio. Baggio, together with Vialli, Deschamps and del Piero, helped to bring further success. Marcello Lippi took over in 1994 and won the Serie A title in his first season. There followed a hat-trick of European Champions League final appearances. Juventus won in 1996, beating Ajax on penalties. They were favourites against Borussia Dortmund and Real Madrid in the following two seasons but lost on both occasions. Lippi was sacked soon after the latter defeat and Carlo Ancellotti took over. He couldn't reproduce Lippi's success and the latter was reappointed. Juventus won the scudetto in 2002 and 2003, in the latter season also finishing runners-up in the Champions League.

Fabio Capello took over in 2004 and immediately steered the club to its 28th Serie A title. That success was tarnished a year later, as Juve clinched top domestic honours yet again. In May 2006 the board resigned en masse over allegations that club officials had influenced the appointment of referees during the 2004–05 campaign. The 'Old Lady' was stripped of her 2005 and 2006 titles and relegated to Serie B, the only time in the club's history it has not featured in the top flight. Juve gained promotion back to Serie A at the first attempt, and began the quest for further honours under former Chelsea boss Claudio Ranieri.

talent. Danes John and Karl Hansen, Argentina's Omar Sivori and Welshman John Charles helped bring further honours to the club. Five more championships were added between 1950 and 1961. In 1971 the club reached the final of the last ever Inter-Cities Fairs Cup, losing to Leeds United on away goals. A first European trophy came in 1977, when an outstanding side created by Giovanni Trapattoni beat Atletico Bilbao in the UEFA Cup final. Zoff, Gentile, Tardelli, Scirea, Boninsegna and Bettega formed the nucleus of both the Juve and national team. Bettega's goal in Spain proved decisive, winning Juve the trophy on away goals.

In the 1980s imported stars including Boniek and, in particular, Platini, made Juventus one of the most formidable sides in Europe. The club added four more League titles in six years, and completed the set of major honours by winning the Cup Winners' Cup in 1984 and the European Cup the following year. In the former they were far too good for Porto, the 2–1 scoreline not reflecting their superiority. The 1985 European Cup final against Liverpool was won with a Platini penalty, but the victory was overshadowed by the tragic events that occurred at the Heysel Stadium.

Juventus' Alessandro del Piero (left) runs with the ball followed by Zaccardo of Bologna.

Lazio Italy

Founded: 1900
Colours: Blue; white; white
Honours: 2 League titles; 5 Italian Cups; European Cup Winners' Cup 1999;
Super Cup 1999

As Lazio approached its centenary in 2000, the trophy haul from the first 99 years was hardly impressive: a domestic Cup victory in 1958, another 40 years later and an isolated Serie A title in 1974. Lazio missed out on a European Cup appearance in 1974–75 after a ban for crowd trouble. There was further misery for the club in 1980 when it was relegated for its part in a bribery scandal. The 1980s was a fallow period. But during the following decade, under the presidency of Sergio Cragnotti, Lazio invested heavily and drafted in many overseas stars, including Paul Gascoigne, Marcelo Salas, Karl-Heinz Riedle and Alen Boksic. In 1998,

as well as winning the Coppa Italia, Lazio made it to the UEFA Cup final, with Inter Milan the opponents. Hampered by the loss of Boksic through injury, Lazio crashed to a 3–0 defeat. The following season brought another major final and a first European success. Under Sven-Goran Eriksson Lazio reached the Cup Winners' Cup final, where they faced Real Mallorca. Christian Vieri opened the scoring, Dani equalized for Mallorca and Nedved hit the winner. Lazio's Nesta became the last captain to hold the trophy aloft, as the competition was in its final season. Lazio sold Vieri to Inter Milan shortly afterwards for a world record £31 million, yet the club went from strength to strength in the 1999–2000 season, winning the domestic Double. A win over Juventus in the 2004 Coppa Italia final marks Lazio's most recent success. Lazio lost its place in the 2006-07 Uefa Cup competition as punishment for its part in a corruption scandal.

Lazio's Signori (left) takes on Kohler of Juventus.

Leeds United England

Founded: 1919
Colours: White; white; white
Honours: 3 League titles; 1 FA Cup; Fairs Cup 1968, 1971

Leeds United came into existence in 1919, following the demise of Leeds City, who were expelled from the League after being found guilty of making illegal payments to players. In its first 40 years the club won nothing. It was after Don Revie was appointed manager in 1961 that Leeds became a force to be reckoned with. The club won promotion as Division Two champions in 1964, then made an immediate impact on the top flight. Over the next decade Leeds may have won the championship just twice, in 1969 and 1974, but they were runners-up on no fewer than five occasions. There was also an FA Cup victory over Arsenal in 1972, courtesy of an Allan Clarke goal. But once again Leeds often fell at the final hurdle, losing in three other finals.

Under Revie Leeds didn't always endear themselves to their rivals. There was certainly a steely quality and ruthless efficiency, but with players such as Gray, Giles, Lorimer and Bremner in the side there was plenty of artistry too. Leeds won the Fairs Cup in 1968 and 1971, beating Ferencvaros and Juventus respectively. Yet even in Europe it was all too often the case of being nearly men. In 1967 they lost to Dinamo Zagreb in the final of the same competition; were beaten by AC Milan in the 1973 Cup Winners' Cup final; and suffered a 2–0 defeat at the hands of Bayern Munich in the 1975 European Cup final. By then Revie had left to take over as England manager. When that outstanding team finally broke up, the club went into a period of decline, culminating in relegation in 1982. It was eight years before Howard Wilkinson brought top-flight football back to Elland Road. And in 1992 Leeds became the last winners of the old Division One title. The team beat Manchester United by four points to take the Championship, but in the following seasons it was United who dominated the new Premiership, while Leeds embarked on a period of fluctuating fortunes. Since Wilkinson's sacking in 1996, George Graham, David O'Leary and Terry Venables have all tried to bring the glory days back to Elland Road. O'Leary led a side which had been assembled at enormous cost to the semi-finals of the Champions League. But no silverware was forthcoming, and in a dramatically short space of time it emerged that the club had overstretched itself. Venables, Peter Reid and former star player Eddie Gray all attempted to halt Leeds' slide. All were hampered by the sale of top players as the club tried to balance the books. Relegation in 2004 precipitated the loss of even more prized assets, including Paul Robinson, Mark Viduka and Alan Smith.

Things went from bad to worse in 2006–07 when, facing relegation once again, Leeds went into voluntary administration, incurring an automatic 10-point penalty which saw the club fall into English football's third tier for the first time in its history. Leeds started the 2007–08 campaign with a further 15-point deficit for breaking League rules, but manager Dennis Wise steered the side into a play-off place before departing to St James's Park. Former Elland Road favourite Gary McAllister was appointed to carry forward the revival but he was sacked after less than a year in the hot seat.

Billy Bremner (left), Alan Clarke, Eddie Gray, Johnny Giles and Leeds manager Don Revie after losing the 1973 FA Cup final against Sunderland.

Liverpool England

Founded: 1892

Colours: Red; red; red

Honours: 18 League titles; 7 FA Cups; European Champions 1977, 1978, 1981, 1984, 2005; UEFA Cup 1973, 1976, 2001; Super Cup 1977, 2001, 2005

Liverpool is the most successful club in the history of English football. Liverpool FC was formed in 1892 as a breakaway faction from Everton, the city's premier club at the time. After an indifferent start, Liverpool won their first Championship in 1901, by which time the famous red strip had been adopted. The rollercoaster continued as Liverpool were relegated in 1904, then bounced back immediately to take their second League title. A first FA Cup appearance on the eve of the First World War was the only other highlight of the club's first 25 years in existence.

A new-look side claimed back-to-back Championships in 1922 and 1923, but Liverpool failed to build on the success and the rest of the interwar years proved to be a barren spell. The club claimed their fifth title in 1946–47, the first postwar season. The team featured flying winger Billy

Liddell, one of the club's most famous sons, and a certain Bob Paisley, who had joined the club in 1939. Years of decline followed, culminating in relegation in 1954. Liverpool were still struggling at the start of the 1959–60 season, and the directors targeted Huddersfield boss Bill Shankly as the man to restore Anfield's pride. It heralded the start of a glorious era. Shankly's side took the Division Two title in 1961–62, and became League champions two years later. In Shankly's 15-year reign Liverpool became one of the top sides in the land. The club also claimed its first European trophy, the UEFA Cup, won in 1973. But it was after Shankly stepped down the following year, after winning the FA Cup for the second time, that the club reached new heights. With Bob Paisley now at the helm, the Liverpool machine went into overdrive. Paisley won 13 major trophies in just nine years, including three European Cups. Joe Fagan was appointed from the famous 'boot room' to take over, and in his first season Liverpool claimed yet another Championship and the European Cup for the fourth time. Fagan's second and final season in charge ended in tragedy as 39 fans died at the Heysel Stadium as Liverpool lined up against Juventus in yet

Dalglish holds aloft the Milk Cup trophy, 1984.

Liverpool pose for a picture after winning the European Champions League final against AC Milan on 25 May 2005

another European Cup final. Kenny Dalglish, who had taken over Kevin Keegan's famous No. 7 shirt in 1977 and established himself as a legend at the club, took over as player-manager. He won the Double in his first season in charge and brought the club two more Championships during his five-year reign. His tenure also included the Hillsborough disaster, when 96 Liverpool fans lost their lives. Liverpool beat Nottingham Forest in the rearranged FA Cup semi-final and went on to win the trophy.

In the 1990s Liverpool lost their pre-eminence, neither Graeme Souness nor Roy Evans managing to build a side capable of challenging for top honours. Former France coach Gerard Houllier, brought in to assist Evans in 1998, soon found himself in sole charge. In 2001 Liverpool won both domestic cups and also lifted the UEFA trophy after a thrilling 5–4 victory over Alaves in the final. The Reds remained off the pace in the Premiership, however, runners-up to Arsenal in 2002 being their best showing for a decade. In 2005 Liverpool trailed in fifth, but Rafael Benitez's first

season in charge saw the team go on a Champions League run which belied their league form. Having put out Juventus and Chelsea, the Reds came back from a 3–0 deficit to AC Milan in the final to win on penalties. No team had ever staged such a comeback to lift a European trophy. The club's fifth victory in the competition meant it retained the trophy. Liverpool were comeback kings once again in the 2006 FA Cup final against West Ham. The Hammers led 2–0, and 3–2 with seconds to go. A Gerrard thunderbolt took the game into extra time, and the Reds won their seventh FA Cup in another dramatic shootout.

Liverpool had been looking for a new backer with deep pockets for some time, and in February 2007 the club followed Chelsea, Manchester United and Aston Villa when it was sold to American partners George Gillett Jr and Tom Hicks in a deal worth £450 million. Their relationship soon unravelled and rumours of a resale abounded, though the fans were more concerned with Benitez turning his Midas touch in cup competitions into a first league title since 1990.

Malmo Sweden

Founded: 1899
Colours: Sky-blue; white; white
Honours: 15 League titles; 14 Swedish Cups

Malmo won a hat-trick of Swedish championships between 1949 and 1951, but it was in the 1970s, under English coach Bob Houghton, that the club enjoyed its most successful period. Having accumulated five more titles during that decade, Malmo won through to the 1979 European Cup final, the first Swedish club to do so. They went down to Nottingham Forest, Brian Clough's recent million-pound acquisition Trevor Francis heading the only goal of the game. Malmo has struggled to scale the heights in recent years, taking the league title just once in the past two decades. But it has been a breeding ground for young talent, numbering Inter Milan star Zlatan Ibrahimovic among its graduates.

Manchester City England

Founded: 1880
Colours: Light blue; white; light blue
Honours: 2 League titles; 4 FA Cup; European Cup Winners' Cup 1970

Manchester City was formed in 1880 but the club enjoyed its most successful spell in the late 1960s and early 1970s, under Joe Mercer and Malcolm Allison. An outstanding team including Francis Lee, Mike Summerbee and Colin Bell beat neighbours United into the runners-up spot in the 1967–68 title race. It was the club's second Championship, the first having been achieved in 1936–37. City went on to win the FA Cup in 1969, a fourth victory in the competition. City lifted both the League Cup and Cup Winners' Cup the following season. In the latter competition they met Gornik Zabrze in the final, which was played in Vienna. Neil Young and Francis Lee hit the goals in City's 2–1 victory.

Since then, apart from another League Cup success in 1976, City has had to live in the shadow of neighbours and rivals, Manchester United. It looked as if the club had hit rock bottom in 1995–96, when it suffered relegation. But worse was to come as the club found itself in Division Three two years later. Kevin Keegan's arrival sparked a major revival. City won promotion back to Division One, then returned to the Premiership as champions in 2001–02. Keegan attracted some big-name players, including Nicolas Anelka, Robbie Fowler and Steve McManaman. 2003–04 saw the opening of the new City of Manchester Stadium, ending the club's 80-year residence at Maine Road. Keegan stepped down midway through the 2004–05 season, assistant coach Stuart Pearce taking over the top job.

After two seasons in charge, Pearce paid the price for setting an unwanted top-flight record, the fewest goals scored at home in a season. In came Sven-Goran Eriksson, returning to club football a year after leaving the England job. His new-look side impressed as it established itself in the top half of the table in 2007–08, though not quite impressive enough for the new owners, an Abu Dhabi-based group whose vast resources made City one of the world's richest clubs. Their intent was signalled on transfer deadline day, when new manager Mark Hughes broke the British transfer record in paying £32 million for Real Madrid's Brazilian ace Robinho.

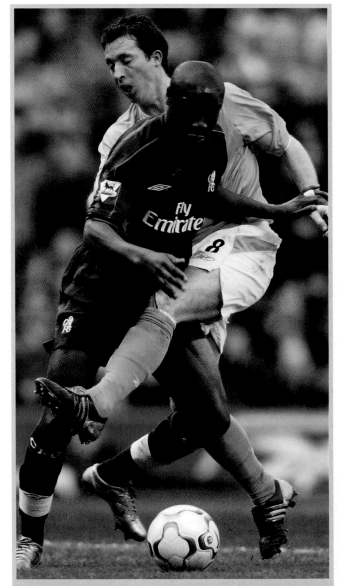

Robbie Fowler playing for Manchester City clashes with Chelsea's Gallas in 2004.

Manchester United England

Founded: 1902

Colours: Red; white; black

Honours: 18 League titles; 11 FA Cups; World Club Cup 1999, 2008; European Champions 1968, 1999, 2008; European Cup Winners' Cup 1991; European Super Cup 1991

Manchester United is one of the most famous clubs in the world, with legions of supporters in every corner of the globe. It is also in the elite as far as the commercial side of the game is concerned. United is a lucrative blue-chip brand name as well as a footballing powerhouse.

Formed in 1902 from the ashes of the defunct Newton Heath, United won the League in 1911 but didn't really set the footballing world alight until the arrival of Matt Busby at the end of the Second World War. Over the next 24 years Busby built three outstanding sides. The first brought the FA Cup to Old Trafford in 1948 and the Championship four years later. It was an ageing team by then, and Busby set about building an exciting new young side. He scoured the country for the most talented youngsters, players of the calibre of Jackie Blanchflower, Roger Byrne, Bobby Charlton and Duncan Edwards. The young stars, dubbed the 'Busby Babes', won the Youth Cup in 1953 and retained it for the following four years. Slowly they were drafted into the senior side, and United won successive championships in 1956 and 1957. The team looked as if it would dominate the English game for years to come, but it was decimated before reaching its prime. Eight players lost their lives in the 1958 Munich air crash, while survivors Johnny Berry and Jackie

Nobby Stiles, George Best and Bobby Charlton pose at Old Trafford in 1968, two months after helping Manchester United win the European Cup.

Blanchflower never played at the top level again. Busby himself was not expected to survive and was given the last rites.

As the 1960s dawned, the United boss set about creating yet another Championship-winning side. Munich survivors Charlton and Bill Foulkes were still there, Denis Law was bought from Torino and a 15-year-old from Belfast named George Best came for a trial. Busby's third great side won the Championship in 1965 and 1967, and in 1968 he finally fulfilled his dream of winning the European Cup when United beat Benfica 4–1 in the final, staged at Wembley. After Busby stepped down and the team broke up, United had a lean spell, culminating in relegation in 1974. The team bounced straight back and won the FA Cup in 1977, under Tommy Docherty. Ron Atkinson also led United to Cup glory in the 1980s, but it was not until well into Alex Ferguson's tenure as manager that United once again scaled the heights. After lifting the European Cup Winners' Cup in 1991, Ferguson brought the Championship back to Old Trafford two years later, ending a 26-year drought. With a blend of outstanding home-grown talent, including Giggs, Beckham and Scholes, and astute signings including Cantona, Keane and Schmeichel, Ferguson's team won the League and Cup Double in 1994 and 1996. The crowning moment came in 1999, when United lifted the

Bryan Robson and Eric Cantona celebrate with the Premiership trophy in 1993.

Celebrating a goal against Juventus.

European Champions League after a dramatic last-gasp victory over Bayern Munich. In 2002–03 United ended the season strongly to regain the Championship they had lost to Arsenal the previous season. It was the club's eighth title in eleven years and fifteenth overall, putting the club just three behind Liverpool in the all-time list.

In 2003–04 the team boasted £12 million teenage sensation Cristiano Ronaldo, who starred in the 3–0 win over Millwall in the FA Cup final. United returned to Cardiff in 2005 in the wake of Malcolm Glazer's take-over of the club. Far from being unsettled, Ferguson's men dominated opponents Arsenal but lost on penalties. Wayne Rooney's first season at Old Trafford ended without silverware, only the fourth time in 15 years that United had failed to land a trophy.

There was further disappointment in 2005–06 as United finished bottom of their Champions League group, the first time in a decade that the team had failed to progress to the second phase. But there was a Carling Cup victory and United finished runners-up to Chelsea in the Premiership. Those positions were reversed a year later as United claimed their first title for four years and 16th overall. The arrival of Nani, Anderson, Carlos Tevez and Owen Hargreaves that summer made the champions' squad even more formidable. Another league title duly followed, and United were crowned European champions for the third time after overcoming Chelsea on penalties in Moscow. The team won a record-equalling 18th championship in 2008–09, adding the World Club Championship and League Cup to the trophy cabinet, but went down to Barcelona in the Champions League final.

Ruud van Nistelrooy strikes the ball for Manchester United.

Marseille France

Founded: 1898

Colours: White, white, white

Honours: 8 League titles (1993 title revoked); 10 French Cups; European Champions 1993

In the summer of 1993 Marseille was basking in the glory of having won the European Champions League, beating an outstanding AC Milan side in the final. It was an historic victory, for no French club had ever won a major European trophy. The celebrations were short-lived, however, as the club was rocked by a match-fixing scandal within a matter of weeks. The consequences included Marseille being stripped the League championship. The club was also relegated to France's second division and president Bernard Tapie was later imprisoned for his part in the affair. Between 1898, the year Marseille was formed, and Tapie's arrival in 1985, successes had been few and far between. The club won just four League titles, the last of those back in 1972. But with an injection of cash and acquisition of some star players, fortunes quickly improved. The likes of Chris Waddle, Didier Deschamps, Marcel Desailly and Jean-Pierre Papin helped Marseille to win four successive championships between 1989 and 1992, equalling their record of the previous 89 years. They reached the semi-final of the 1990 European Cup, losing on away goals to Benfica. The following year they went through to the final, but after a dour, goalless 90 minutes it was opponents Red Star Belgrade who lifted the trophy.

Recovery from the corruption scandal began in 1996 when, under new owners, Marseille regained top-flight status in France. Three years later they were back in a major final, the UEFA Cup, but went down 3–2 to Parma. Marseille lost to Valencia in the 2003-04 UEFA Cup final, and shortly afterwards lost star striker Didier Drogba, who moved to Chelsea in a £24 million deal.

Alen Boksic of Marseille is congratulated by his teammates in 1993.

Carlo Ancelotti, Frank Rijkaard, Marco Van Basten and
Ruud Gullit of AC Milan line up in a wall during 1989.

AC Milan Italy

Founded: 1899

Colours: Red/black, white, white

Honours: 17 League titles; 5 Italian Cups; World Club Cup 1969, 1989, 1990, 2007; European Champions 1963, 1969, 1989, 1990, 1994, 2003, 2007; European Cup Winners' Cup 1968, 1973; European Super Cup 1989, 1990, 1994, 2003, 2007

When Milan went 3-0 up against Liverpool in the 2005 Champions League final, the club's seventh victory in the competition seemed assured. An extraordinary comeback prevented that, Milan losing on penalties, but with six successes in Europe's premier club competition the Italian giants lie second only to Real Madrid in the all-time list. Three of those victories came between 1989 and 1995, and Milan were also twice losing finalists in this period. During this extraordinarily successful spell, Milan fielded players of the stature of Maldini, Baresi, Desailly and Costacurta, along with Dutch trio Gullit, Rijkaard and Van Basten. The two men responsible for making Milan the powerhouse of European football were media magnate Silvio Berlusconi and coach Arrigo Sacchi. After arriving at Milan in 1986, Berlusconi injected huge amounts of capital. It saved a club that was reeling from a bribery scandal which had seen them relegated to Serie B. Sacchi used the money well, building one of the best club sides in the game's history. He departed in 1991 to take over as national team boss but under new coach Fabio Capello Milan continued to flourish. They won four Serie A titles between 1992 and 1996. Capello also presided over the team's resounding 4–0 demolition of Barcelona in the 1994 European Champions League final.

Milan had been among the founding members of the Italian League in 1899. A first title came in 1901 but the achievement was repeated just twice more in the next 40 years, when the club regularly found itself in the shadows of city rivals Inter. In the postwar period Milan embraced the idea of bringing in talent from around the world, Uruguay's Juan Schiaffino foremost among their expensive imports. The team went down 3–2 to Real Madrid in the 1958 European Cup final. Five years later Milan were crowned champions of Europe, the first Italian side to win the trophy. The line-up included two future coaches of the national team, Giovanni Trapattoni and Cesare Maldini, Paolo's father. There was also Gianni Rivera, the golden boy of Italian football, and Brazilian Jose Altafini, who scored both goals in a 2–1 victory over Benfica. Milan beat Hamburg 2–0 to lift the European Cup Winners' Cup in 1968 and the following year saw a second

European Cup victory, the team crushing a burgeoning Ajax side 4–1. From then until Berlusconi's arrival some 17 years later Milan had a relatively lean spell. The club did add another European Cup Winners' Cup to its trophy haul, however, with a 1–0 win over Leeds United in 1973.

In summer 2006, while Andrea Pirlo and Gennaro Gattuso were among the Milan players starring in Italy's World Cup triumph, the club learned its punishment for its part in the match-fixing scandal that rocked Serie A. Milan was hit with a retrospective points ban for 2005–06, where they had finished runners-up, and had to go into the next campaign with an eight-point deficit. That damaged their title hopes, but Carlo Ancellotti's team swept to Champions League victory, gaining revenge over Liverpool in a repeat of the 2005 final.

AC Milan's Kaka is tackled by Siena midfielder Argilli.

Millonarios Colombia

Founded: 1938
Colours: Blue; white; white
Honours: 13 League titles; Copa Merconorte 2001

Millonarios played a prominent role in introducing professionalism into Colombian football. Originally formed as amateur side Deportivo Municipal in 1938, Millonarios was at the forefront of the pirate league that operated in the country in the late 1940s and early 1950s. It was around this time that a journalist remarked that the club was now more about 'millionaires' than 'municipal', and the name change stuck. It was run outside FIFA's jurisdiction and attracted many star players from other countries. Most famous among these was Alfredo di Stefano, whom Millonarios attracted amid the turmoil of a players' strike in Argentina. Di Stefano steered Millonarios to a hat-trick of championships in the early 1950s before departing to scale even greater heights in Spain. Millonarios won nine of their 13 League titles between 1949 and 1964. In the past decade the club's best performances came in 1994 and 1996, when they were runners-up in the domestic championship.

Glenn Hoddle in action for Monaco in 1987.

Monaco France

Founded: 1924
Colours: Red/white; red; white
Honours: 7 League titles; 5 French Cups

Monaco is one of the footballing world's glamour clubs, not least because of its setting and its long association with the principality's royal family. Between 1960 and the mid-1980s Monaco won five championships. The team Arsene Wenger built, including Glenn Hoddle, made it League title number five in 1988. Four years later, Monaco reached the European Cup Winners' Cup final, where they faced Werder Bremen. Neither club had won a major European honour. The Monaco line-up included George Weah and a young Emmanuel Petit, but Bremen ran out 2–0 winners. In the last ten years Monaco have continued to be consistent performers, adding further championships in 1997 and 2000. In 2003-04 coach Didier Deschamps steered Monaco to the Champions League final, where they went down to Porto 3–0.

Moscow Dynamo Russia

Founded: 1923
Colours: Blue; blue; white
Honours: 11 Soviet League titles; 6 Soviet Cups; 1 Russian Cup

Moscow rivals Spartak have enjoyed much greater success in recent years, but Dynamo remains Russia's most illustrious club. Its origins go back to the late 19th century, when British cotton mill owners the Charnock brothers introduced football into the country. The team was known as Morozovotsky, but renamed Moscow Dynamo after the Russian Revolution. Dynamo enjoyed considerable success, but this was restricted to regional competition until 1936, when the national league was formed. Dynamo won the inaugural championship. 1945 saw the club lift its third title and in the same year the team embarked on a ground-breaking tour of Britain and Scandinavia. Results included a 4–3 win over Arsenal and a 10–1 thrashing of Cardiff City. The 1950s saw the emergence of Dynamo's greatest ever player, Lev Yashin. The famous 'keeper picked up the European Footballer of the Year award in 1963, the first Soviet player to receive that honour. In 1972 Dynamo became the first Soviet side to appear in a major European final. Facing Rangers in the Cup Winners' Cup at the Nou Camp, Dynamo fell 3–0 behind. Two second-half goals made the score respectable but Dynamo had to be content with the runner-up spot.

Moscow Dynamo's Vitaly Grishin chases Amoruso of Rangers.

Nacional Uruguay

Founded: 1899
Colours: White; blue; white
Honours: 41 League titles; World Club Cup 1971, 1980, 1988; Copa Libertadores 1971, 1980, 1988; South American Recopa 1989; Inter-American Cup 1972, 1989

Along with Penarol, Nacional is Uruguay's top club side. Nacional was formed in 1899, some eight years after their great rivals. However, it is the oldest club to be founded by the indigenous population, Penarol having its roots in the British expatriate community. Penarol won the country's first two League titles, in 1900 and 1901, and Nacional replied with the next two championships. That set the pattern for the rest of the 20th century as the two clubs vied for domestic supremacy. Between 1932, when the game went professional, and 1975, Nacional won the country's championship on 20 occasions, Penarol the other 23. Nacional's best run of success was five successive League titles between 1939 and 1943, which the club still regards as its golden era. Penarol stole a march when the Copa Libertadores was instituted in 1960, winning it in the first two years. Nacional were runners-up three times in the competition in the 1960s. The club was finally crowned South American Club Champions in 1971, ending Estudiantes' run of three victories in a row. Their Argentine international Luis Artime scored one of the goals in the play-off, which ended 2–0. He then hit all of Nacional's goals in a 3–2 win over Panathinaikos in the World Club Cup. Nacional's victory over PSV Eindhoven on penalties in the 1988 World Club Cup was the last time that a Uruguayan side has featured in the final. In 1994 Uruguay's domestic season was split into two mini-championships, with the winners of each playing off for the title. In 2002 Nacional completed a hat-trick of league titles for the fourth time in the club's history, and collected its 41st and most recent championship in 2005-06.

Napoli Italy

Founded: 1904
Colours: Blue; white; blue
Honours: 2 League titles; 3 Italian Cups; UEFA Cup 1989

Napoli didn't set the footballing world alight in its first 80 years. There were two isolated Cup victories, in 1962 and 1976, but there were many years spent flitting between the top two divisions. That all changed in 1984 when the club paid Barcelona a world-record £5 million to acquire the services of Diego Maradona. Napoli began recouping the fee immediately as Maradona's presence ensured sell-out crowds and merchandising income. More importantly, he galvanized Napoli to success on the pitch. The club won the Double in 1987 and added a second *scudetto* three years later. 1989 saw the club win their only European trophy. It came in the UEFA Cup, when Napoli put out Bayern Munich in the semis, then beat Stuttgart in the final. Maradona and Brazilian star Careca scored to give Napoli a narrow 2–1 lead to take to Germany. Napoli went 3–1 up in the second leg and although Stuttgart hit two late goals it wasn't enough to prevent Napoli lifting the trophy 5–4 on aggregate.

When Maradona tested positive for drugs in 1991, it signalled the end of Napoli's brief reign at the top of Italian football. After the great man's departure other stars were sold to pay off the club's huge debts and performances on the pitch inevitably suffered. The decline was rapid and culminated in relegation to Serie B in 1998. Napoli has recently recovered from bankruptcy and relegation to Serie C, winning promotion back to the top flight in 2007.

Diego Maradona playing for Napoli in 1988.

Newcastle United England

Founded: 1882
Colours: Black/white; black; black
Honours: 4 League titles; 6 FA Cups; Fairs Cup 1969

The 1990s saw an extraordinary Tyneside revival, sparked initially by the arrival of Kevin Keegan as manager in 1992, and funded by chairman Sir John Hall. In 1991–92 Newcastle finished 20th in Division Two. They stormed back to win that league the following season, and then finished third in their first campaign back in the top flight. Keegan's exciting attacking side twice finished runners-up to Manchester United, in 1996 and 1997. The spending continued, including a world-record £15 million to bring Alan Shearer from Blackburn in July 1996. Having not quite managed to deliver any silverware, Keegan resigned in January 1997. Kenny Dalglish and Ruud Gullit each had a

spell in charge but neither could bring a long-awaited trophy to St James's Park. Even worse, the team was no longer playing in the style that the passionate 'Toon Army' had come to expect. By the late 1990s Newcastle were languishing in mid-table. Bobby Robson's appointment as boss of the club he supported as a boy was warmly greeted on Tyneside. He immediately set about the task of restoring some of the club's dented pride. In 2002 Newcastle finished fourth and the following season they went one better, mounting the only serious challenge to Manchester United and Arsenal. 2002–03 also saw the club reach the last sixteen in the Champions League. A poor start to the 2004–05 season resulted in Robson's sacking, but his successor Graeme Souness lasted barely a year as Christmas 2005 saw the team languishing at the wrong end of the table. Newcastle staged a brief revival under former Tyneside favourite Glenn Roeder, but his tenure lasted barely a year. Sam Allardyce spent even less time at St James's, overseeing just 24 games before his departure in January 2008. The Toon Army hailed the return of the messiah as Kevin Keegan rejoined the club he had left 11 years earlier. The revered saviour quit after eight months, citing a lack of autonomy regarding player acquisitions. Joe Kinnear was brought in as stopgap for the 2008-09 season, in which Newcastle found themselves at the wrong end of the table. He stepped aside for health reasons, but not even the arrival of Alan Shearer as interim manager could save Newcastle from the drop. It leaves Newcastle still searching to add to its four League Championships. Three of those came in a five-year spell in the early 1900s, the last in 1927, when Hughie Gallacher established himself as a Tyneside legend. By the 1950s the fans had another hero at centre-forward, Jackie Milburn. The club lifted the FA Cup in 1951, 1952 and 1955, adding to three victories in the competition earlier in the century. Newcastle's only other major honour came in 1969 when they won the Inter-Cities Fairs Cup.

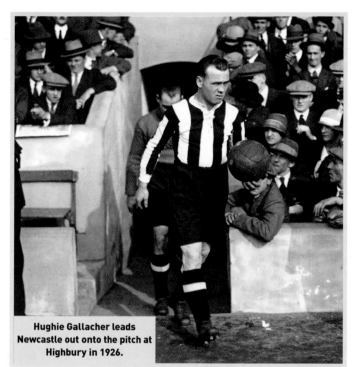

Hughie Gallacher leads Newcastle out onto the pitch at Highbury in 1926.

Alan Shearer celebrates scoring for Newcastle in 2003.

Notts County England

Founded: 1862
Colours: Black/white, white, black
Honours: 1 FA Cup

Despite a dearth of honours, Notts County's place in the history books is secure as the oldest surviving professional club in the world. Founded in 1862, Notts County was one of the twelve original members of the Football League when it was formed in April 1888. The club's only piece of silverware remains an FA Cup victory in 1894. County, a Division Two outfit at the time, beat Bolton Wanderers 4–1 in the final.

Nottingham Forest England

Founded: 1865
Colours: Red; white; red
Honours: 1 League title; 2 FA Cups; European Champions 1979, 1980; Super Cup 1979

Nottingham Forest pulled off a major achievement in winning the European Cup at the first time of asking in 1979. The East Midlands club then proved it was no fluke by retaining the trophy the following year, thereby joining a select group of clubs to have been crowned champions of Europe in successive seasons. Forest's achievement was all the more notable since just four years before the first of those famous victories the club had been languishing in the Second Division. The remarkable turnaround was down to the arrival of Brian Clough. Having taken unfashionable Derby County to the top of English football, he proceeded to do the same at Forest. Before Clough's arrival, the club had two FA Cup victories, in 1898 and 1959, in its 110-year history. Forest won promotion to the top flight in 1976–77, then took the Championship the following season, beating European Cup holders Liverpool into second place by a 7-point margin. In February 1979 Clough made Trevor Francis Britain's first £1 million player. The former Birmingham City striker repaid a lot of the fee by scoring the goal which beat Malmo in the European Cup final three months later. The following season John Robertson scored the goal which beat a Hamburg side including Kevin Keegan. Forest had to work very hard to keep the German side at bay. It was a tactical triumph for Clough and his assistant, Peter Taylor, and they were helped by the fact that 'keeper Peter Shilton was in top form. Forest went on to lift the League Cup four times in Clough's 18-year reign at the City Ground, which came to an end after the club was relegated in 1993. The slide continued, culminating in relegation from the Championship in 2005.

Trevor Francis playing for Nottingham Forest in 1980.

Panathinaikos Greece

Founded: 1899
Colours: Green; white; green
Honours: 19 League titles; 16 Greek Cups

In 2004 Panathinaikos halted Olympiakos' run of seven successive championships, and also beat their arch-rivals in the cup final to notch the club's seventh domestic double. Panathinaikos also has the better pedigree in European competition. It remains the only Greek club to have reached a major European final. With Ferenc Puskas as coach, Panathinaikos lost 2–0 to Ajax in the 1971 European Cup final. The two sides met in the same competition in 1996, this time at the semi-final stage. Having topped a group including Porto and Nantes, Panathinaikos beat Legia Warsaw in the quarter-final before going down 3–1 on aggregate to the Dutch side. Thanks largely to a formidable home record Panathinaikos reached the quarter-finals of the Champions League in 2001–02, losing to Barcelona 3–2 on aggregate. The following season saw Pana reach the same stage of the UEFA Cup, where they lost to eventual winners Porto.

Panathinaikos' Dimitris Papadopoulos is tackled by Nicky Butt playing for Manchester United.

Paris St-Germain France

Founded: 1970
Colours: Blue/red; blue; blue
Honours: 2 League titles; 7 French Cups; European Cup Winners' Cup 1996

Paris St-Germain has only won the French championship twice, although it has to be remembered that the club only came into existence in 1970 and didn't become fully professional until 1973. PSG quickly established itself as the fashionable club for Parisians to follow. They won their first silverware, the domestic Cup competition, in 1982, retaining the trophy the following year. In 1986 the championship came to the capital for the first time in 50 years. Gerard Houllier was the man in charge for this landmark moment. Houllier was subsequently lured away, and the club also suffered financial problems. French television station Canal Plus invested heavily, and with stars of the calibre of David Ginola, George Weah and Brazil's Rai, the club enjoyed considerable success in the 1990s. There was only one championship, in 1994, but the club reached the semi-final stage of European competition four years running. Three of those ended in defeat: by Juventus in the 1993 UEFA Cup, by Arsenal in the 1994 Cup Winners' Cup, and by AC Milan in the 1995 European Champions League. Victory finally came in 1996. PSG overcame Deportivo la Coruna in the Cup Winners' Cup semi-final, then beat Rapid Vienna 1–0 in the final. As Marseille's 1993 European Champions League victory was rescinded, PSG can thus be credited with being the first French club to win a European trophy. The team nearly broke the European Cup Winners' Cup holders hoodoo by retaining the trophy. But having overcome Liverpool in the semis, they went down to Barcelona, who won the game with a Ronaldo penalty.

Gianfranco Zola in action for Parma in 1995.

Parma Italy

Founded: 1913
Colours: White/yellow; white/yellow; white
Honours: 3 Italian Cups; European Cup Winners' Cup 1993, UEFA Cup 1995, 1999; European Super Cup 1993

Parma was founded in 1913, but the first 50 years of the club's existence was spent struggling in the lower reaches of Italian football. After 1968, when Parma had to merge with another club in order to ensure its survival, things went much better. By the 1980s, Parma finally began to make a name for itself on the pitch, and was no longer known just for its connections with composer Verdi and the famous ham that bears its name.

In the late 1980s, under Arrigo Sacchi, the club made huge strides, and in 1990 made it into Serie A for the first time. In 1992 the club beat Juventus in the Italian Cup to claim their first major honour. That gave Parma entry into the 1993 Cup Winners' Cup, and under new coach, Nevio Scala, the club ran out comfortable 3–1 winners over Royal Antwerp. No club had ever retained the trophy but Parma came close the following year when they faced Arsenal in the final. Swedish star Tomas Brolin failed to convert a couple of

golden opportunities early on and Alan Smith's goal gave Arsenal victory. In 1995 Parma reached the UEFA Cup final, an all-Italian affair involving Juventus. Midfielder Dino Baggio scored in both legs to give Parma a 2–1 aggregate victory. Four years later Parma won the trophy again. By then the UEFA Cup final was a single-legged affair and Parma overran Marseille 3–0. The team boasted the likes of Buffon, Thuram, Crespo and Veron, an indication that with the backing of the Parmalat dairy company, Parma could attract big-name stars. The club entered a turbulent period when it was revealed in 2003 that Parmalat was embroiled in a fraud scandal. Despite the sale of many top players, the club maintained its status in the elite division until 2007–08, when it finally suffered relegation to Serie B.

Penarol Uruguay

Founded: 1893
Colours: Black/yellow; black; black
Honours: 45 League titles; World Club Cup 1961, 1966, 1982; Copa Libertadores 1960, 1961, 1966, 1982, 1987; Inter-American Cup 1969

Penarol is Uruguay's oldest club. Its roots lie in the Central Uruguayan Railway Cricket Club, formed by a handful of British workers in 1891. Waning British influence led to the

Penarol's Garcia (l) and Hernandez fight for the ball with Blanco of CF America of Mexico in the 2004 Copa Libertadores.

club being renamed Penarol in 1913, after the district where the marshalling yards were situated. Penarol won ten championships between 1900 and 1931, with 1905 in particular a red-letter campaign: the club was not only undefeated but didn't even concede a goal! Penarol also took the title in 1932, the first of the professional era. Since then Penarol has shared the domestic honours with arch-rivals Nacional, a virtual duopoly which has been broken on very few occasions.

Penarol provided many of the players who helped Uruguay win the inaugural World Cup in 1930, and the first postwar tournament in 1950. The star of the latter era was Juan Schiaffino, who scored one of the goals in Uruguay's 2–1 win over Brazil in the 1950 World Cup final. Penarol sold him to AC Milan for a record £72,000 in 1954.

Penarol became the first winners of the Copa Libertadores in 1960. One of the goals in the 2–1 aggregate victory over Olimpia of Paraguay was scored by Ecuador's Alberto 'Pedro' Spencer, who was the competition's top scorer that year. Spencer was also on target in the following year's final, when Penarol retained the title with a victory over Palmeiras. He went on to hit a record 50 goals in the tournament over his career. After beating Palmeiras, Penarol went on to thrash Benfica 5–1 in the World Club Cup, helping to erase the memory of the previous year, when Real

Madrid hammered them by the same score. Another Copa Libertadores-World Club Cup double came in 1966. Penarol added two more South American club championships in the 1980s. After the first of those, in 1982, Penarol beat European Cup winners Aston Villa 2–0 to become the first club to win the World Club Cup on three occasions. In 1997 Penarol completed the 'quinquenio' – five championships in a row, although since then Nacional have had the upper hand.

Porto Portugal

Founded: 1893
Colours: Blue/white; blue; white
Honours: 24 League titles; 18 Portuguese Cups; World Club Cup 1987, 2004; European Champions 1987, 2004; UEFA Cup 2003; European Super Cup 1987

Until the mid-1980s Porto had enjoyed only sporadic success in Portuguese football, remaining in the shadow of Sporting Lisbon and Benfica for decades. The pendulum swung when Porto reached the final of the 1984 European Cup Winners' Cup, then took the domestic championship in the following two seasons. The pinnacle was reached in 1987, when Porto lifted the European Cup. They met Bayern Munich in the final, staged at Vienna's Prater Stadium. Bayern were not the powerhouse of the 1970s but remained a dangerous outfit and took the lead. Porto hit back for a deserved 2–1 victory, giving Portugal its first European trophy for 25 years. Paulo Futre was the homegrown star, though the line-up was cosmopolitan. This was apposite, as 50 years earlier Porto had been pioneers in the international transfer market. The club brought in two Yugoslav players to help them win successive championships in the late 1930s. Following their European Cup victory, Porto built on their success in the 1990s, lifting the domestic title eight times. In 2003 the club beat Celtic to win the UEFA Cup, and a year later Jose Mourinho led the side to a 3–0 Champions League final victory over Monaco before departing for Stamford Bridge. Porto added another domestic title in 2007–08, the club's fifth championship in six seasons.

Porto celebrate after winning the UEFA Cup in 2003.

Preston North End England

Founded: 1881
Colours: White/navy; navy; navy
Honours: 2 League titles; 2 FA Cups

Preston North End won the inaugural League Championship in 1888–89, remaining undefeated in the 22-game programme. The club also won the FA Cup, without conceding a goal. They thus became the first Double winners and earned the nickname 'The Invincibles'. The club, which had been formed in 1881, retained the title the following year and then finished runners-up for the next three seasons. Preston had a long wait for their next piece of silverware, a second FA Cup triumph in 1938. The victory came thanks to a penalty in the last minute of extra time. George Mutch converted the first spot-kick to be awarded in a Wembley final. Preston's greatest player was Tom Finney, who spent his entire career at Deepdale, from 1946 to 1960.

PSV Eindhoven Holland

Founded: 1913
Colours: Red/white, black, black
Honours: 21 League titles; 8 Dutch Cups; European Champions 1988; UEFA Cup 1978

Philips Sports Verein is the sporting arm of the electronics giant. The stadium bears the Philips name and a significant proportion of the Eindhoven population is employed by the company. The link goes back to 1913, when the club came into being. Up to the 1970s, PSV won the occasional piece of silverware but were well behind Ajax and Feyenoord in the country's pecking order. That changed with three championships in four years between 1975 and 1978. The last of those saw PSV add a UEFA Cup victory to their roll of honour. A team including the van der Kerkhof twins put Barcelona out in the semis before running out comfortable 3–0 winners over Corsican side Bastia in the final.

By the mid-1980s PSV was Holland's undisputed top side, winning six championships in seven years. The acquisition of Ruud Gullit from Feyenoord in 1985 was a major factor, but he had moved on to AC Milan by the time the club reached its pinnacle. That came in 1988, when PSV won the domestic Double, then went on to beat Benfica in the European Cup final. The match ended goalless, PSV winning on penalties to become the third Dutch side to be crowned kings of Europe. Several of

the players, including Ronald Koeman and 'keeper Hans van Breukelen, went on to win the European Championship with Holland in the same year.

Brazilian stars Romario and Ronaldo starred for PSV in the 1990s before moving on to bigger stages. The club also sold players of the calibre of Jaap Stam and Ruud van Nistelrooy, both to Manchester United. PSV reached the knockout stage of the Champions League for the first time in 2005, going down to AC Milan in the semis. In 2007 the club continued its recent dominance of the Eredivisie by pipping Ajax on goal difference to clinch a sixth title in eight years, and retained the title in 2008 to make it seven championships in nine years.

Mateja Kezman and Mark Van Bommel celebrate PSV's league championship win in 2003.

Queen's Park Scotland

Founded: 1867
Colours: White/black; white; white/black
Honours: 10 Scottish Cups

When Queen's Park beat Celtic 2–1 in the 1893 Scottish Cup final, it was the club's tenth victory in the competition in 20 seasons. It was also to be the last major honour to date for the club whose home is the famous Hampden Park stadium. Queen's Park also holds a special place in the record books by dint of their early sorties south of the border to contest the FA Cup. The club competed in the very first competition, in 1871–72, and received a bye to the semi-final! They fought out a goalless draw with the Wanderers but couldn't afford to return for the replay. Queen's Park did go one better in both 1884 and 1885, but went down to Blackburn Rovers in each of those finals.

Rangers Scotland

Founded: 1873
Colours: Blue; white; blue
Honours: 51 League titles; 32 Scottish Cups; European Cup Winners' Cup 1972

Along with arch-rivals Celtic, Rangers have dominated Scottish football for a century. Between 1989 and 2000 Rangers won the Championship every year bar one. Celtic's 1998 success was significant for the passionate Old Firm fans, for it meant that Rangers missed out on a record ten successive titles. Rangers had to settle for nine championships in a row, equalling Celtic's achievements of the 1960s and 1970s.

Rangers have failed to translate long periods of domestic success into victories in Europe. The relative lack of depth and competitiveness of the Scottish League has been blamed for the fact that Rangers' regular forays into Europe have frequently ended in disappointment. The one exception was in the 1972 European Cup Winners' Cup final, when the team beat Moscow Dynamo 3–2. Rangers had lost in two previous finals of the same competition, but this time it all came right. A Colin Stein strike and a brace from Willie Johnston put Rangers 3–0 up before Dynamo hit back twice to make it a nervy last few minutes. Appalling behaviour from Rangers' fans meant that the club was prevented from defending the title the following year. This blow came on the heels of one of the worst tragedies in footballing history. The previous year 66 people died when crash barriers gave way at a New Year fixture between Rangers and Celtic at Ibrox.

1985 marked a watershed in Rangers' fortunes and ushered in a hugely successful spell lasting 15 years. Graeme Souness was appointed player-manager and he brought in many quality English players, including Terry Butcher, Mark Hateley and Trevor Steven. With backing from new owner David Murray, Souness also broke the club's unwritten rule of signing only Protestant players when he brought ex-Celtic striker Maurice Johnston to Ibrox in 1989. The club had to play second fiddle to a resurgent Celtic under Martin O'Neill in 2001 and 2002, but Alex McLeish guided Rangers to a clean sweep of domestic trophies in 2002–03. The championship went to Ibrox for the 51st time in 2005, but a poor start to the 2005–06 campaign cost McLeish his job. Paul le Guen failed to reproduce the success he had enjoyed at Lyon, and in January 2007 Rangers coaxed national team boss Walter Smith back to Ibrox. Smith had led Rangers to seven successive titles after taking over from Souness in 1991. He took the team to the 2007–08 Uefa Cup final, where they went down to a Zenit St Petersburg side coached by former Rangers boss Dick Advocaat.

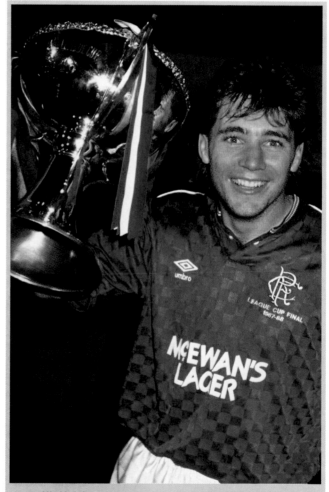

Ally McCoist celebrates after winning the 1987 Skol Cup.

Rapid Vienna Austria

Founded: 1899
Colours: Green/white; white; white
Honours: 32 League titles; 14 Austrian Cups

Rapid Vienna was formed in 1899 under the name of First Workers Football Club. By 1912, when the country's inaugural championship was held, the club had adopted the name which it now bears. Rapid won the title that year, and on another 13 occasions before the end of the Second World War. The club also featured regularly in the Mitropa Cup, winning the competition in 1930. The backbone of Hugo Meisl's outstanding national team of the 1930s came from Rapid. Austria was subsumed into a greater Germany in 1938 and Rapid found itself in a much more competitive environment. Even so, Rapid beat Frankfurt to win the cup in 1938, then lifted the championship in 1941. Rapid were regularly among the honours in the postwar period, but at the end of the 1960s suffered a lean spell which lasted more than a decade. Star striker Hans Krankl led the side which ended the drought in 1982, when Rapid added yet another championship to their tally. Krankl had a spell at Barcelona but was back at Rapid for their first appearance in a major final, the European Cup Winners' Cup in 1985. Krankl scored against opponents Everton but Rapid lost the game 3–1. They reached the final of the same competition in 1996 but again finished on the losing side, Paris St-Germain winning the game more comfortably than the 1–0 scoreline suggested.

Alfred di Stefano (centre) backheels the ball past Manchester United's goalkeeper, Harry Gregg, in 1959.

Real Madrid Spain

Founded: 1902
Honours: 31 League titles; 17 Spanish Cups; European Champions 1956–1960, 1966, 1998, 2000, 2002; UEFA Cup 1985, 1986
Colours: White; white; white

Real Madrid were crowned kings of Europe three times between 1998 and 2002, making it nine wins in all Uefa's premier competition, a record unmatched by any other club. The blend of home-grown talent such as Raul and Casillas, together with imported stars including Ronaldo, Zidane and Figo set the standard for performance with style. The last seven years have been leaner, particularly on the European front, yet the 'Galacticos' have an aura which is not solely dependent on silverware.

Real Madrid celebrate with the trophy after the European Champions League final against Juventus in 1998.

David Beckham, Luis Figo, Javier Portillo and Brazilian Ronaldo celebrate a goal in 2004.

The club was formed in 1902 as Madrid FC, the Real (royal) prefix added 18 years later, a dispensation from King Alfonso XIII. Madrid won their first championship in 1932, but it was not until the 1950s that the club established itself as a giant in both domestic and European competition. The person most responsible for raising Real to its position of pre-eminence was Santiago Bernebeu. A former player and coach, Bernebeu became president of the club in 1943. He was the driving force behind the construction of the famous stadium which bears his name today, a replacement for the former ground which was destroyed during the Spanish Civil War. Bernebeu also masterminded the creation of the team which won the inaugural European Cup in 1956, then proceeded to defend it four years running. The all-star line-up included some of the game's legendary names: Gento, Puskas, Kopa and di Stefano. Real's 7–3 victory over Eintracht Frankfurt at Hampden Park in the 1960 European Cup final is still widely regarded as the greatest ever display by a club side. Real dominated on the domestic front too. Between 1954 and 1969 the club won the Spanish championship on 12 occasions. Real appeared in three more European Cup finals in the 1960s, adding a sixth success in the competition in 1966 with a 2–1 victory over Partizan Belgrade. The club had to wait 32 years to be crowned champions of Europe again. In that time Real regularly

added to its haul of domestic trophies and also enjoyed successive UEFA Cup victories in 1985 and 1986. But the passionate Madrid supporters demanded the top honours for the club's vast outlay. Fabio Capello, who had coached the all-conquering AC Milan side of the early 1990s, was appointed in 1996. He only remained for one year, but in that time he laid the foundations for the club's future success. Heynckes inherited an excellent team and guided Real to Champions League victory, beating Juventus in the 1998 final. Real demolished Valencia two years later, and were far too good for Bayer Leverkusen in 2002, Zidane scoring a wonder goal in the final. 2002–03 saw Real win the Primera Liga for the 29th time, and reach the semi-final of the Champions League. This wasn't enough to prevent del Bosque from being axed and replaced by Carlos Queiroz, who had been No. 2 to Sir Alex Ferguson at Manchester United. 2003–04 was a poor season by Real's standards: the club fell at the quarter-final stage in the Champions League, were runner-up in the Spanish Cup and saw Valencia take the Primera Liga title. Under Wanderley Luxemburgo, Real's third coach in a year, the club finished runners-up to rivals Barcelona in 2004–05. He was soon dispensed with, but it made little difference as Real finished the 2005–06 campaign empty handed, the club's third successive barren season.

The Real Madrid team before playing Manchester United in the 1957 European Cup semi final.

Fabio Capello returned for the 2006–07 campaign and led Real to a 30th La Liga title by a wafer-thin margin. The team finished level on points with Barcelona, and although Barca had a superior goal difference, Real took the title by virtue of a better head-to-head record. It didn't earn Capello another term, however. Former Germany international Bernd Schuster — an ex-Real and Barca player — was appointed in July 2007. Under his stewardship Real made it back-to-back championships for the first time since 1990, yet he, too, was soon on his way, ex-Sevilla and Spurs boss Juande Ramos becoming the club's 14th manager in 20 years.

Luis Figo and Raul celebrate with the trophy after the Real Madrid v Feyenoord 2002 UEFA Super Cup at the Stade Louis II in Monaco. Real Madrid won the match 3-1.

Red Star Belgrade Serbia

Founded: 1945
Colours: Red/white; red; red/white
Honours: 25 League titles; 22 Yugoslavian Cups; European Champions 1991; World Club Cup 1991

Red Star Belgrade were acclaimed European champions in 1991, after beating Marseille on penalties in the final. It was the crowning moment for a club which only came into existence in 1945. An all-star line-up, including players of the calibre of Robert Prosinecki and Dejan Savicevic, went on to beat Chile's Colo Colo 3–0 in the World Club Cup, the first Eastern European side to win the trophy. The outbreak of civil war in Yugoslavia in 1992 and subsequent fragmentation of the country precipitated the break-up of this outstanding team. Although Red Star has continued to accumulate domestic honours since then, the club has struggled to make an impact on the bigger stage.

By the mid-1950s, a decade after its formation, Red Star was both dominant at home and a force to be reckoned with in the newly instituted European Cup. The team reached the semi-final in 1956–57, losing 1–0 to Fiorentina over the two legs. The following season they lost a thrilling quarter-final to Manchester United. It was during the return trip from Belgrade that the United side was all but wiped out in the Munich air crash. In 1971 Red Star beat Panathinaikos 4–1 in the first leg of the semi-final but suffered a 3–0 defeat by Puskas's team in the return fixture to miss out on a final appearance on away goals. Eight years later it was Red Star who profited from an away goal, in a UEFA Cup semi-final clash with Hertha Berlin. It meant a first appearance in a major final, but an Allan Simonsen penalty in Dusseldorf sealed victory for Borussia Moenchengladbach, the two sides having drawn 1–1 in Belgrade. Following the break-up of Yugoslavia, Red Star competed in the Serbia and Montenegro league until 2006, when a new Serbian League was formed. Red Star won the double in 2006–07, its inaugural season.

Robert Prosinecki in action for Red Star Belgrade in 1991.

Reims France

Founded: 1931
Colours: Red/white; white; white
Honours: 6 League titles; 2 French Cups

The 1950s was undoubtedly Stade de Reims' golden era. The club lifted the French championship six times and the French Cup twice between 1949 and 1962. The 1955 title earned Reims an invitation into the following season's inaugural European Cup, and the club won through to the final. Reims went 2–0 up against Real Madrid after 11 minutes, and also led 3–2 before finally going down 4–3. Reims not only had to endure defeat but also the loss of their star player Raymond Kopa, who joined Real shortly afterwards. The two clubs met again in the 1959 final, in Stuttgart. Reims couldn't prevent Real making it four victories in a row, however, di Stefano and Mateos scoring without reply. The last of Reims' six championships came in 1962, since when the club has had a barren spell.

River Plate Argentina

Founded: 1901
Colours: White/red; black; white/black/red
Honours: 33 League titles; World Club Cup 1986; Copa Libertadores 1986, 1996; Inter-American Cup 1986; Super Cup 1997

River Plate's rivalry with their Buenos Aires neighbours Boca Juniors is one of the most intense in world football. Formed in an affluent area of the city in 1901, River's traditional image as a wealthy club polarizes the passionate local support still further. River Plate was at the forefront of the campaign to introduce a professional league in Argentina, something that was eventually achieved in 1931. River won the championship seven times in the first 17 years, and in that time produced a crop of outstanding players. The club's forward line in the 1940s was known as 'La Maquina' – 'The Machine' – for the devastating way it ripped defences apart. The most famous of these was Alfredo di Stefano, who made his debut in 1944, aged 18. Following a loan spell at Huracan, di Stefano returned to the club in 1947, helping them to win the league.

River lost twice in the final of the Copa Libertadores, to Penarol in 1966 and Cruzeiro ten years later. Both matches went to play-offs after a victory apiece. Against Penarol, River let a two-goal lead slip and eventually lost 4–2 after extra time. River were finally crowned South American Club Champions in 1986, beating America Cali both home and away in the final. The team went on to beat Steaua Bucharest in the World Club Cup, capping a great year for both River and Argentina, who lifted the World Cup that year. In 1996 River won the Copa Libertadores for the second time, once again beating America Cali in the final. The team boasted the talents of Francescoli, Salas and Ortega, but couldn't repeat their World Club Cup success, a del Piero goal winning the game for Juventus.

River Plate's Maschemano (left) vies with Helguera of Real Madrid during a friendly match in 2003.

Since 1991, each domestic season has been divided into two mini-championships. In that time River have picked up twelve titles, comfortably better than arch-rivals Boca Juniors, although in the same period Boca have won the South American Club Championship four times to River Plate's once.

Roma Italy

Founded: 1927
Colours: Red/yellow; red/yellow; red/yellow
Honours: 3 League titles; 9 Italian Cups; Fairs Cup 1961

Up to 2000 Roma had only won Serie A twice in their 73-year history, putting the club a long way behind the Milan and Turin sides in terms of domestic success. That year the club prised Gabriel Batistuta away from Fiorentina and he, together with the likes of playmaker Francesco Totti and outstanding Brazilian full-back Cafu, helped them win their third *scudetto*. The following season Roma came within a point of retaining their crown.

Roma was the first Italian team to win a European trophy. Their new Argentine striker Pedro Manfredini provided the firepower which took them to the Inter-Cities Fairs Cup in 1961, in which they overcame Birmingham City 4–2 on aggregate. It was another 20 years before Roma enjoyed a sustained period of success. Most of the honours came in the Coppa Italia, which the club won four times in seven years between 1980 and 1986. In 1983 they lifted the championship for only the second time in their history, the first *scudetto* having been won back in 1942. In 1984 they won through to the European Cup final, where they enjoyed home advantage for their clash with Liverpool. Coached by Nils Liedholm, the side boasted Bruno Conti and Francesco Graziani, plus the Brazilian pair Falcao and Cerezo. The game ended 1–1 and went to a penalty shoot-out, the first in the competition's history. Bruce Grobbelaar played the clown in

Totti of Roma (left) and Legrottaglie of Juventus in action in 2004.

Liverpool's goal and it was the Roma players whose nerve went. Conti and Graziani both missed, while Falcao refused to even take a spot-kick. Liverpool won the game 4–2. Since then the nearest Roma have come to landing a major European trophy was in 1991, when they went down to Inter Milan in the UEFA Cup final. Amazingly, Roma faced the same opposition in four successive Coppa Italia finals between 2005 and 2008. Inter got the better of the first two, but Roma took the trophy with a 7–4 aggregate victory in 2007, then scored a ninth success in the competition in the single-match 2008 final to draw level with Juventus in the all-time list.

Di Bartolomei (left) captain of Roma, and Graham Souness of Liverpool at the start of the 1984 European Cup final.

Rosenborg Norway

Founded: 1917
Colours: White; black; black
Honours: 20 League titles; 9 Norwegian Cups

Rosenborg has enjoyed a virtual monopoly of success in Norwegian football in recent years. In 2004 the club secured its thirteenth successive championship, with coach Nils Arne Eggen at the helm almost throughout that period. Rosenborg's success has been achieved despite a regular exodus of players to bigger clubs. Harald Brattbakk, Steffen Iversen and Stig-Inge Bjornebye are among the players who first made their names at the Trondheim-based club. Domestic success has paved the way for several Champions League campaigns, the highlight being a quarter-final appearance in 1996–97. The team beat AC Milan in the San Siro at the group stage before going out to Juventus in the last eight. In 1999–2000 Rosenborg topped a group including Feyenoord, Borussia Dortmund and Boavista but were eliminated at the second group stage.

St Etienne France

Founded: 1920
Colours: Green; white; green
Honours: 10 League titles; 6 French Cups

St Etienne has had a lean time in the past 20 years, a period in which Marseille, Bordeaux, Lens, Auxerre and Monaco, not to mention the club's chief rivals Lyon, have all enjoyed much greater success. But in the 1960s and 1970s St Etienne dominated French football. Between 1964 and 1981 the club won nine championships and five Cups, including the Double on four occasions. In 1976 the team reached the European Cup final, facing Bayern Munich, the team that had beaten them at the semi-final stage the previous year. St Etienne dominated the match at Hampden Park for long periods but a second-half goal from Franz Roth made it a hat-trick of European Cups for Bayern. There was further disappointment the following season, when St Etienne met Liverpool in the European Cup quarter-final. The French champions took a 1–0 lead to Anfield and came within eight minutes of winning the tie. David Fairclough came off the bench to score the crucial goal which gave Liverpool a 3–2 victory on aggregate.

Michel Platini in action for St Etienne in 1980.

Sampdoria Italy

Founded: 1946
Colours: Blue; white; blue
Honours: 1 League title; 4 Italian Cups; European Cup Winners' Cup 1990

Sampdoria came into being in 1946 following a merger between two Genovese clubs, Sampierdaranese and Andrea Doria. The next 30 years brought little success, but when tycoon Paolo Mantovani took over the presidency in 1979 he steered Sampdoria on a path which would make the club one of the top sides in Europe. Mantovani's deep pockets allowed the club to make many high-profile signings, including Trevor Francis, Graeme Souness and Liam Brady. Sampdoria won the Italian Cup in 1985 and repeated the achievement three times in the following nine years. In 1991 the club finally took the Serie A title, and the following year reached the European Cup final. On that occasion an extra-time goal by Ronald Koeman gave Barcelona victory. Sampdoria had also lost to the Spanish club in the final of the 1989 European Cup Winners' Cup. However, the Genovese side lifted the trophy in 1990, Gianluca Vialli scoring twice against Anderlecht in extra time after a goalless 90 minutes. Since the heady days of the late 1980s and early 1990s Sampdoria has found success hard to come by.

Santos Brazil

Founded: 1912
Colours: White/black; white; white
Honours: 17 Sao Paulo League titles; 2 Brazilian Championships; 5 Rio-Sao Paulo titles; World Club Cup 1962, 1963; Copa Libertadores 1962, 1963

The history of Santos is inextricably linked with that of the world's greatest ever player, Pele. Pele was in Santos's first team at the age of 15 and played his last game for the club 18 years later, in 1974. In that time he scored 1281 goals in 1363 appearances.

In 44 years between the founding of the club, in 1912, and Pele's arrival, Santos's achievements were modest. They entered the Sao Paulo state championship in 1916 but didn't win the title until 1935. Santos had turned professional two years earlier, the second Brazilian club to do so, following Fluminese. The club did little of note for the next 20 years, but the mid-1950s saw the team begin a long period of domination. Santos won the state championship 11 times between 1955 and 1969. As well as Pele, the team boasted the likes of Gilmar, Zito and Mauro, all of whom won World Cup winners' medals. Santos embarked on a series of lucrative overseas tours as they became the most glamorous

The world's most famous Number 10, Pele plays his final match for Santos in 1974.

side in world football. That didn't stop them winning the Copa Libertadores in both 1962 and 1963. The first of those marked their debut in the tournament, and they beat Penarol 3–0 in a play-off. Pele scored twice, and Coutinho – the man dubbed his 'twin' for the near-telepathic relationship they had on the pitch – grabbing the other. Santos retained the South American club Championship the following year by beating Boca Juniors home and away. Santos followed up each of these victories by winning the World Club Cup, beating Benfica and AC Milan respectively. After Pele departed for the NASL in 1974, Santos struggled for success. But in 2002, under coach Emerson Leao, the club rolled back the years to become Brazilian champions with an exciting young side including teenage striking sensation Robinho. It was Santos's first success since winning the Sao Paulo state championship in 1984.

Sao Paulo Brazil

Founded: 1935

Colours: White/red/black; white; white

Honours: 21 Sao Paulo League titles; 6 Brazilian Championships; 1 Rio-Sao Paulo title; World Club Cup 1992, 1993, 2005; Copa Libertadores 1992, 1993, 2005; Super Cup 1993; Interamerican Cup 1998

Sao Paulo only came into existence in 1935, long after the likes of Flamengo and Fluminese established themselves as leading lights in Brazilian football. Yet the club's rise to prominence was swift, and it won five Sao Paulo state championships in the 1940s. After the last of those successes, in 1949, Sao Paulo played second fiddle to Corinthians, Palmeiras and, in particular, Santos. The club reached its first Copa Libertadores final in 1974 but went down to an Independiente side which dominated the competition four years running. It was not until the arrival of former Brazil coach Tele Santana in the late 1980s that Sao Paulo enjoyed their most successful period. The club captured the state title three times in four years, and was crowned champions of Brazil in 1991. The following year they finally won the South American Club Championship, beating Newell's Old Boys of Argentina in the final. The side included internationals of the calibre of Cafu and Rai, and went on to win the the trophy again in 1993. A 5–1 home win against Chile's Universidad Catolica in the first leg virtually sealed the tie, and Sao Paulo became the first side to retain the cup since Boca Juniors in the late 1970s. The team added the World Club Cup in both years, beating Barcelona and AC Milan respectively. Sao Paulo hasn't managed to reproduce that kind of success since, but hit the headlines in 1998 when they sold Denilson to Real Betis for a world-record £21 million. Supporters had high hopes for Kaka, a new star who emerged in 2002, but he was soon lured to AC Milan. Sao Paulo beat Liverpool in the final of the 2005 Fifa Club World Cup, and in 2007 claimed a record fifth Brazilian championship, which saw the club awarded the trophy outright. It went on to retain the title in 2008.

Kaka of Sao Paulo and Assuncao of Palmeiras in action in 2002.

Sheffield FC England

Founded: 1855
Colours: Red; black; black
Honours: None

Formed in 1855, Sheffield FC has the honour of being the oldest club in the world. Its players had come through the public school and university system, where the modern game has its roots. Sheffield won the FA Amateur Cup in 1903–04 but today it is a minor league club playing its fixtures at the Don Valley Stadium.

Sporting Lisbon Portugal

Founded: 1906
Colours: Green/white; white; white
Honours: 18 League titles; 19 Portuguese Cups, European Cup Winners' Cup 1964

Sporting Lisbon is one of Portugal's big three clubs, along with city rivals Benfica and Porto. These three, together with Belenenses, were the only clubs to have won the domestic championship from its inception in 1935 until 2001, when Boavista made a surprise breakthrough. Sporting have won the title on 18 occasions, including a run of seven championships in eight years in the late 1940s and early 1950s. However, after winning the Double in 1982 the club had to wait until 2000 before being crowned Portuguese champions again.

Sporting have enjoyed many European campaigns but have won just one trophy. That came in 1964, when the club lifted the European Cup Winners' Cup. In the quarter-final they crashed 4–1 to Manchester United at Old Trafford but turned the tie around with a 5–0 scoreline in Lisbon, Osvaldo Silva hitting a hat-trick. They needed a play-off to get past Olympique Lyon in the semis, after the clubs were locked at 1–1 on aggregate. A single goal put them into the final, where they faced MTK Budapest. A see-saw match at the Heysel Stadium ended in a 3–3 draw and Sporting again came out on top in the replay. Morais scored the only goal of the game direct from a corner. Their hold on the trophy was relinquished early the following season when they went down ignominiously to Cardiff City, who were then a Division Two side. Sporting's best performance since came in 2004–05, when the team went down to CSKA Moscow in the Uefa Cup final, despite the advantage of the match taking place in Lisbon.

Sporting Lisbon's Joao Pinto in action during the 2002–03 season.

Steaua Bucharest Romania

Founded: 1947
Colours: Red/blue; red/blue; red/blue
Honours: 23 League titles; 20 Romanian Cups; European Champions 1986

Eastern European club sides have long had the reputation for technical excellence but lacking the ability to win at the highest level. Steaua Bucharest helped to dispel that notion in 1986. After eliminating the likes of Anderlecht and Rangers in that year's European Cup, Steaua beat a glamorous Barcelona side to be crowned European champions. They held Terry Venables' side to a goalless draw before running out 2–0 winners on penalties. Steaua also reached the final three years later, but this time suffered a thumping 4–0 defeat at the hands of AC Milan. Steaua were also in the middle of an extraordinary run of domestic success which yielded eleven championships and seven cups in the the 14 years between 1985 and 1998. Like Honved, Dukla Prague and CSKA Sofia, Steaua did have the advantage of being the country's army side. The club also had the patronage of dictator Nicolae Ceaucescu. When that regime collapsed in 1989, many thought Steaua's period of dominance would wane. However, with stars of the quality of Marius Lacatus and Gheorghe Hagi the club continued to flourish. Even when the top players departed, Steaua's stranglehold on Romanian football continued, though they have been unable to make further inroads into the major European competitions.

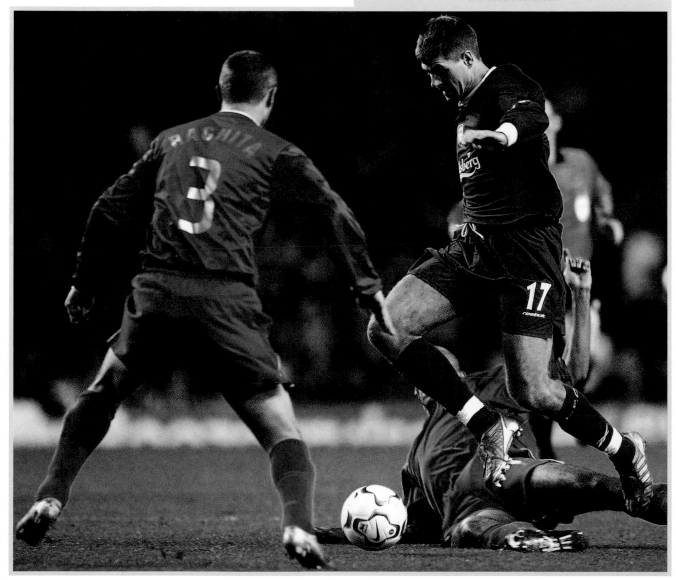

Steven Gerrard of Liverpool and Valeriu Rachita of Steaua Bucharest.

Sunderland England

Founded: 1879
Colours: Red/white; black; red
Honours: 6 League titles; 2 FA Cups

A famous FA Cup victory over the outstanding Leeds United side in 1973 marks Sunderland's only major honour in the postwar era. Formed in 1879, the club won four of its six Championships in an 11-year spell between 1892 and 1902. In 1898 Sunderland took up residence at Roker Park, which would be the club's home for nearly 100 years. Sunderland lifted the Championship again in 1912–13, and nearly completed a famous Double but went down 1–0 to Aston Villa in the FA Cup final. In 1935–36 Sunderland won the last of their Championships in style, scoring 109 goals and finishing 12 points clear of Derby. The following season the team came from behind to beat Preston 3–1 in the FA Cup final, with an outstanding performance from captain and legend Raich Carter.

Peter Reid brought a modicum of success back to the club in the late 1990s and with the superb Stadium of Light as their new home, expectations were high. Reid found it hard to build on that success, and was shown the door early in the 2002–03 season. Howard Wilkinson had a brief spell in charge before Mick McCarthy took the helm. He failed to stave off relegation, but after just one season out of the top flight, McCarthy led Sunderland back to the Premiership as Championship winners in 2005. It was a brief return, Sunderland notching just 15 points in 2005–06, breaking their own Premiership record for the fewest points scored in a season. McCarthy was sacked in March 2006, when relegation was all but inevitable.

Former hero Niall Quinn returned to take control of the club, and occupied the manager's chair briefly. Sunderland made a disastrous start to the 2006–07 campaign, but new boss Roy Keane steered the club from the relegation zone to division champions. The team survived its first season back in the Premiership, but Keane resigned after an indifferent start to the 2008-09 campaign.

Bobby Kerr is lifted by his teammates after Sunderland defeated Leeds United in the 1973 FA Cup final.

Torino Italy

Founded: 1894
Colours: Maroon; white; maroon
Honours: 7 League titles; 5 Italian Cups

Torino's last piece of silverware came with a Coppa Italia win in 1993. Three years later the club was relegated to Serie B. The lean recent years are a far cry from the late 1940s, when Torino boasted the cream of Italian football. The club won four successive championships between 1946 and 1949, and were well on course to make it five in a row when, in May 1949, the entire team was wiped out in a plane crash. Only one player, Carapellese, returned home, his susceptibility to air-sickness causing him to opt to travel by train instead. Italy's greatest ever club side also provided the majority of the national team, including captain Valentino Mazzola, father of 1960s star Sandro.

Torino have won just one Serie A title since, in 1976, and in the modern era have remained in the shadows of their Turin neighbours Juventus. The team did reach the UEFA Cup final in 1992. Having put out Real Madrid in the semis, Torino needed to beat Ajax to win their first European trophy. The clubs drew 2–2 in Turin and 0–0 in Amsterdam, Torino thus losing on away goals.

Dave Mackay (right) and Alan Mullery hold the FA Cup after beating Chelsea in the 1967 final.

Tottenham Hotspur England

Founded: 1882

Colours: White; blue; white

Honours: 2 League titles; 8 FA Cups; European Cup Winners' Cup 1963; UEFA Cup 1972, 1984

Despite a relative lack of success in recent years, Tottenham will always be remembered as the club who won the first Double of the 20th century. By 1960 the demands of the modern game led many to believe it impossible for any club to emulate the achievements of Preston and Aston Villa in the previous century. Bill Nicholson's brilliant side proved all the pundits wrong. A team that boasted Blanchflower, Mackay, Jones and White finished eight points ahead of nearest rivals Sheffield Wednesday in the League, scoring 115 goals in the process. Spurs went on to beat Leicester City 2–0 in the FA Cup final. Nicholson's side played scintillating football and a record 2.5 million people watched them during the course of the season.

Spurs' only other Championship success had come a decade earlier. Under Arthur Rowe the team played dazzling push-and-run football. It brought Spurs the Division Two title in 1949–50, and the Division One crown the following season. Although there have been only two League successes in Spurs' 120-year history, the club has always had a fine Cup pedigree. They have won the FA Cup eight times and League Cup on three occasions. They also became the first British

club to lift a European trophy when they routed Atletico Madrid 5–1 in the Cup Winners' Cup final of 1963. Nine years later Spurs beat Wolves 3–2 on aggregate to win the inaugural UEFA Cup. They won the same trophy in 1984, following a penalty shoot-out victory over Anderlecht.

The return of one of Spurs' favourite sons, Glenn Hoddle, as manager gave fans fresh hope that the club would soon be challenging for top honours again. However, in September 2003 his contract was terminated. Former France coach Jacques Santini came and went in quick succession, and in November 2004 his assistant Martin Jol was given the top job, the club's ninth manager in thirteen years. Over the following three years Jol moulded a side packed with talent, but in October 2007 paid the price for failing to break the stranglehold of the division's Big Four. Juande Ramos arrived at White Hart Lane with impressive credentials, having won the Uefa Cup twice with Sevilla. Within four months of Ramos's arrival, Spurs fans were celebrating a Carling Cup victory, the club's first trophy for nine years. The team's league form nosedived, however, and Ramos was dismissed in October 2008, replaced by Harry Redknapp, who had just led Portsmouth to FA Cup glory.

Kanoute playing for Spurs is challenged by Bernard of Newcastle.

Valencia Spain

Founded: 1919
Colours: White/red/yellow; white; white
Honours: 6 League titles; 7 Spanish Cups; Fairs Cup 1962, 1963; European Cup Winners' Cup 1980; European Super Cup 1981; UEFA Cup 2004

Valencia suffered successive defeats in the Champions League final in 2000 and 2001, losing to Real Madrid and Bayern Munich respectively. There was consolation in the form of Primera Liga success in 2001–02, Valencia's first championship for 31 years. Real Madrid regained the crown the following season but in 2003–04 Valencia won the Primera Liga for the sixth time. Valencia's resurgence in the 1990s began under Claudio Ranieri and was continued by Hector Cuper. It was Rafael Benitez who steered the club to the championship in 2002 and 2004, adding a UEFA Cup final victory over Marseille before departing to Anfield.

Before the club's recent run of good form, Valencia had enjoyed only intermittent success. There were three championships in the 1940s and an isolated league title in 1971. Valencia won the Fairs Cup in both 1962 and 1963, Barcelona 7–3 on aggregate to win their first European trophy and retaining it with a 4–1 win over Dinamo Zagreb.

The team made the final again in 1964 but were denied a famous hat-trick when they went down 2–1 to Real Zaragoza. Valencia's only other major honour came in 1980, when they beat Arsenal in the European Cup Winners' Cup final. The team included Argentina's World Cup hero Mario Kempes and German international Rainer Bonhof, but neither could spark the Spanish side and the game ended goalless. Valencia won the game 5–4 on penalties, the first major European competition to be decided in this way.

The Wanderers England

Founded: 1859
Colours: Purple/black/pink; white; white/black
Honours: 5 FA Cups

Although the Wanderers disbanded in 1881, their place in the history books was secured by winning the inaugural FA Cup competition in 1872, then lifting the trophy four more times

Arsenal's Willie Young is beaten to the ball by Valencia's goalkeeper, Pereira, during the 1980 European Cup Winners' Cup final.

during that decade. The club, whose players came from the cream of the public schools and universities, beat the favourites the Royal Engineers 1–0 in that famous first Cup final, staged at Kennington Oval. The competition comprised only fifteen clubs, however. Life was even easier for The Wanderers the following season, for as holders they qualified automatically for the final, in which they beat Oxford University 2–0.

Bobby Moore kisses the trophy after West Ham beat Preston North End in the 1964 FA Cup final.

West Ham United England

Founded: 1895
Colours: Claret/blue; white; claret
Honours: 3 FA Cups; European Cup Winners' Cup 1965

The mid-1960s was West Ham's most successful period. Not only did the club pick up two of the four trophies it has won to date but it also famously provided three players in England's World Cup-winning side of 1966. A Geoff Hurst hat-trick and a Martin Peters strike meant that all the goals in the final came from the West Ham academy, while Bobby Moore captained his country in imperious style.

A dramatic 3–2 victory over Preston in the 1964 FA Cup final gave West Ham entry into the following year's Cup Winners' Cup competition. The Hammers put out favourites Real Zaragoza en route to the final, where they met Munich 1860. A scintillating match at Wembley was decided by a brace from Alan Sealey within three minutes. The game epitomised the philosophy of manager Ron Greenwood, whose hallmark was stylish football played in a true sporting spirit. Bobby Moore collected his second trophy in as many years at Wembley, and in the following summer's World Cup he made it a hat-trick which confirmed his legendary status within the game.

West Ham won the FA Cup again in 1975, beating a Fulham side which included Moore. The Hammers won through to the final of the following year's Cup Winners' Cup but this time they suffered a 4–2 defeat at the hands of Anderlecht. The club's last major honour came in 1980, another Upton Park hero Trevor Brooking scoring the goal which beat Arsenal in the FA Cup final.

Under Harry Redknapp in the 1990s West Ham consolidated their Premiership place, and brought through some outstanding youngsters, including Rio Ferdinand, Joe Cole and Michael Carrick. Fortunes dipped after Redknapp was replaced by Glenn Roeder, culminating in relegation in 2002–03. Alan Pardew took the Hammers back to the top flight in 2005, the club finishing in the top half of the Premiership and coming within a whisker of beating Liverpool in the FA Cup final.

In 2006 an Icelandic consortium led by Eggert Magnusson took control. West Ham's fortunes dipped in 2006–07 and Alan Curbishley took over the managerial reins midway through the season. The Hammers looked relegation certainties but survived the drop thanks to seven wins in their last nine games. Curbishley departed early in the 2008–09 season following a disagreement over the sale of players, Chelsea legend Gianfranco Zola taking over in what was his first taste of club management.

The
Countries

Algeria

Founded: 1962
Colours: Green; white; red
World Cup Appearances: 2 **Best**: Ist round 1982, 1986
Honours: African Nations Cup winners 1990

The Algerian Football Association was formed in 1962, the year Algeria gained independence from France, with FIFA membership following a year later. Algeria has featured in two African Nations Cup finals, losing 3–0 to Nigeria in 1980 and beating the same country 1–0 a decade later. Algeria reached the World Cup finals in 1982 and 1986. A single point from a draw against New Zealand saw the team make an early exit in 1986. But in Spain four years earlier Algeria beat both West Germany and Chile to accumulate four points. Unfortunately, West Germany and Austria met after Algeria had completed its fixtures, knowing that a 1–0 win for the Germans would see both countries progress. This result was duly delivered in a match that left a very sour taste in the mouth. The stars of the Algerian side were Lakdar Belloumi and Rabah Madjer, who became the only players from Algeria to win the African Footballer of the Year award, the former in 1981 and the latter in 1987. Madjer went on to play for Porto, with whom he won a European Cup winners' medal in 1987. Madjer scored in the Portuguese club's 2–1 win over Bayern Munich in the final.

Benhamlat of Algeria and Foe of Cameroon in action in Ghana, 2000.

Argentina

Founded: 1893
Colours: Blue/white; black; white
World Cup Appearances: 14 **Best**: winners 1978, 1986
Honours: South American Championship/Copa America Winners: 1910, 1921, 1925, 1927, 1929, 1937, 1941, 1945, 1946, 1947, 1955, 1957, 1991, 1993; Confederations Cup winners 1993; Olympic winners 2004, 2008

After a shock first-round defeat at the 2002 World Cup, Argentina were many people's favourites to lift the trophy four years later in Germany. The team turned on the style in the group stage, notably in a 6–0 rout of Serbia and Montenegro, before going down to the hosts in the quarter-finals. Even so, Argentina remains a powerhouse in world football. Germany marked the country's 14th appearance in the finals, and Mexico 1970 is the only time since 1958 that the South Americans have failed to qualify. Argentina has also won the Copa America, the South American Championship, 14 times since its inception in 1910, although four of those victories were deemed unofficial tournaments. Even so, Argentina remains the most successful nation in the competition's history.

Football was introduced to Buenos Aires by the British in the 1860s. By the turn of the century the game had proliferated and the country's FA had been formed. Argentina's first international match took place in 1901 in Montevideo, a 3–2 win over Uruguay. The early years of Argentine football were bedevilled by splits and the formation of rival leagues. But after the country finished runner-up in both the 1928 Olympic Games and the inaugural World Cup two years later, a period of stability followed. An 18-strong professional league was established in 1931. This proved to be a double-edged sword as players were lured to Italy to ply their trade for greater reward. One of the highest profile moves involved Raimundo Orsi, who not only left Independiente to join Juventus but rubbed salt into the wound by turning out for Italy. The aggrieved Argentine FA responded to the exodus by sending a second-string side to Italy to contest the 1934 World Cup. The tournament was organized on a knockout basis and Argentina made the long trip for just one game, a 3–2 defeat by Sweden.

The Argentine team celebrate during the 1990 World Cup Semi-Final against Italy in Naples. The match ended in a 1-1 draw but Argentina won 4-3 on penalties

A players' strike in the late 1940s led to even more stars heading for Europe. In the 1950s Argentina boasted a star trio of forwards in Omar Sivori, Humberto Maschio and Antonio Angelillo. Having missed the 1950 and 1954 World Cups, Argentina were among the favourites for the 1958 tournament but the team's three stars all left to play in Italy and were dropped from the squad as a result. Argentina finished bottom of their group.

The 1966 World Cup side was one of the most talented ever to leave the country's shores: goalkeeper Roma was brilliantly acrobatic; Marzolini and Perfumo were among the world's best defenders; captain Antonio Rattin was an outstanding wing-half; Artime and Onega were clinical finishers. But against England in the quarter-final the Argentine team chose to show its cynical side instead. Rattin had one conversation too many with the German referee and the game was held up for several minutes when the captain refused to leave the field. England manager Alf Ramsey was left fuming, despite his team's 1–0 win.

Argentina made it to the second round in 1974 but it was as hosts four years later that the country was finally crowned world champions. Mario Kempes, Leopoldo Luque, Osvaldo Ardiles and Daniel Pasarella starred as Argentina beat a highly-rated Dutch side 3–1 in the final. A young Diego Maradona just missed out on a place in Cesar Menotti's squad that year, but in the following decade he became the world's top player. At Mexico '86 Maradona was in scintillating form, at times seemingly taking on the opposition single-handed. Against England in the quarter-final he scored one of the best goals ever seen, although he also punched the ball past Peter Shilton in the same match, the infamous 'Hand of God' helping Argentina to reach the last four. Argentina went on to beat West Germany in the final. It was a different story four years later in Italy, when the same two countries contested the final. Argentina had two players sent off in an ill-tempered match, won for the Germans by an Andy Brehme penalty.

At USA '94 Argentina squeezed through to the second round despite finishing third in their group. Maradona made a brief appearance before being sent home after failing a drugs test. Without their talismanic star Argentina were soon knocked out, beaten 3–2 by Romania in the second round. At France '98 Argentina and England clashed for the third time in a World Cup. David Beckham's red card for a petulant kick at Diego Simeone was the game's major talking point. A 10-man England team held out for a draw but Argentina went through on penalties. The South Americans were themselves eliminated in the quarter-final against Holland. Claudio Lopez equalized after Kluivert put the Dutch in front. After a sending-off on each side, Dennis Bergkamp ended Argentina's hopes with a virtuoso strike in the dying seconds.

Australia

Founded: 1961
Colours: Gold; green; white
World Cup Appearances: 2   **Best**: 2nd round 2006

Australia made an inauspicious World Cup debut in 1974, finishing bottom of their group with a single point gained from a draw against Chile. By the 1990s, Australian football had come on in leaps and bounds, with many of the country's star players plying their trade in England and Italy. The Socceroos were regular Oceania group winners, but play-off defeats against Argentina, Iran and Uruguay cost them a place at the 1994, 1998 and 2002 World Cup finals respectively. In February 2003 Australia stunned England with a 3–1 victory at Upton Park, and went on to enjoy their best ever run in reaching Germany 2006. Drilled by Guus Hiddink, the team gained its revenge over Uruguay in the play-offs, beating the South American side on penalties to reach the finals for the first time in 32 years. Nor were they there to make up the numbers, as Croatia found in the group decider. The Socceroos went down in the second round to eventual champions Italy, who looked mightily relieved as Francesco Totti converted a controversial late penalty to go through.

Football in Australia is still a relatively young sport. The Australian Soccer Federation wasn't formed until 1961, with FIFA membership following two years later. Competition from both rugby codes, cricket and Aussie Rules has impeded progress. But with stars such as Harry Kewell, Mark Viduka and Brett Emerton in the side, the prospects for success look bright.

Sol Campbell shields the ball from Australia's Harry Kewell.

Austria

Founded: 1904
Colours: White; black; white
World Cup Appearances: 7   **Best**: Quarter-final 1954

Austria was one of the world's top sides in the 1930s. Under legendary coach Hugo Meisl, Austria's prodigiously skilful side was dubbed the 'Wunderteam'. When Meisl brought his side to Stamford Bridge in December 1932 it was on the back of an 18-match unbeaten run. England brought it to an end with a 4–3 victory, but the Austrians had been very impressive. Two years later they were among the favourites to win the second World Cup. After an ill-tempered quarter-final victory over Hungary, the team went down 1–0 to Italy. Conditions were poor and the pitch was heavy, which didn't suit the artistry of Meisl's men.

Austria qualified for the 1938 World Cup, but before the tournament took place the country had been annexed by Germany and its best players were drafted into the German side. By the early 1950s Austria had another strong team and once again vied with England for the title of unofficial champions of Europe. The sides met on 25 May 1950, a game that will be forever associated with Nat Lofthouse. The Bolton centre-forward hit a dramatic winner in a 3–2 victory. Austria reached the quarter-finals of the 1954 World Cup and the group stage at Sweden '58. But thereafter the country went into a period of decline.

It was 20 years before Austria featured in another World Cup. In 1978 they topped a group including Brazil but finished bottom of the second-round mini-league. The team's star was centre-forward Hans Krankl, who won Europe's Golden Boot the same year. Spain '82 saw Austria qualify for the second round again, this time amid controversy. A tame 1–0 defeat by West Germany in the final group match was enough to see both teams through at the expense of Algeria. In the second-round mini-league France proved too strong. There were first-round exits at both Italia '90 and France '98. Austria's poor record in the European Championship continued as the team missed out on a place at Portugal 2004, finishing behind Holland and the Czech Republic. A joint bid with Switzerland to host Euro 2008 was successful, and the country scored its first championship point with a draw against Poland, though defeats against Germany and Croatia meant a first-round exit.

Belgium's star Enzo Scifo calls for the ball.

Belgium

Founded: 1895
Colours: Red; red; red
World Cup Appearances: 11 **Best**: 4th 1986
Honours: Olympic winners 1920

Apart from taking Olympic gold in 1920, Belgium has never won a major tournament. However, the country has been one of the most consistent performers in the modern era, having reached the World Cup finals on 11 occasions. 1978 is the last time Belgium failed to qualify, and four years earlier the country missed out on a place in the finals in Germany despite going through the qualifying series without conceding a goal. Holland went through instead.

A semi-final appearance at Mexico '86 represents the country's best World Cup showing, eventual winners Argentina – and in particular Maradona – proving to be the stumbling block after the team had accounted for Russia and Spain in the knockout stage. But Belgium's best tournament finish came in the European Championship in 1980. They topped a group including hosts Italy and England before going down to West Germany 2–1 in the final. Frankie Van der Elst, Jan Ceulemans and Enzo Scifo were the stars of this era. Belgium reached the knockout stages of the World Cup in 1990, 1994 and 2002. They surprised many by beating the Czech Republic in a play-off to reach Japan and Korea, and were far from disgraced by a 2–0 defeat to eventual winners Brazil in the second round.

Belgium's Football Association was formed in 1895 and nine years later the country became one of FIFA's founder members. The country didn't embrace professionalism until 1972, but within two decades both Anderlecht and Mechelen had won the European Cup Winners' Cup. Anderlecht also won the UEFA Cup in 1983, a result that was tainted a decade later by a bribery scandal. In the last 20 years Anderlecht and Club Brugge have dominated the domestic scene, winning 16 championships between them.

Bolivia

Founded: 1925
Colours: Green; white; green
World Cup Appearances: 3 **Best**: 1st round 1930, 1950, 1994
Honours: South American Championship/Copa America winners 1963

One of the lesser lights of South American football, Bolivia has had little success since the formation of the country's football federation in 1925. In the inaugural World Cup in 1930 Bolivia finished bottom of their group without a point. In the 1950 tournament the Bolivians found themselves in a group consisting of just two nations and involving a single match. Unfortunately they crashed 8–0 against Uruguay. The country's only other World Cup appearance to date came at USA '94. Having done well in the qualifiers, with results including a victory over Brazil, the team went out at the first hurdle again. The country's only success in an international tournament came in 1963, when they were crowned South American Champions. There was another appearance in the Copa America final in 1997, but this time they went down 3–1 to Brazil. On both of these occasions Bolivia enjoyed home advantage, which because of the altitude was a significant factor.

Brazil

Founded: 1914
Colours: Yellow; blue; white
World Cup Appearances: 18   **Best**: winners 1958, 1962, 1970, 1994, 2002
Honours: South American Championship/Copa America winners 1919, 1922, 1949, 1989, 1997, 1999, 2004, 2007; Conferations Cup 1997, 2005

Brazil has become synonymous with stylish, successful football. The only country to have competed in all 18 World Cups, Brazil has reached the final seven times and lifted the trophy on a record five occasions. Football was introduced to the country by British sailors and railway workers in the 1870s and 1880s. Clubs sprang up and league football took off, although the geography of the country meant that the game remained regionalized for some years. Brazil's football federation was not founded until 1914, and international fixtures date from that time. In 1916 Brazil entered its first South American Championship. Having scratched from the inaugural tournament in 1910, Brazil finished third in the 1916 competition. After another third place in 1917 Brazil won the tournament for the first time two years later. Arthur Friedrenreich, Brazil's first star, scored the goal that beat Uruguay in the final. Surprisingly, Brazil has only emulated that success on seven other occasions and its record in the tournament that would later become the Copa America is less impressive than that of Argentina and Uruguay. One reason is the fact that the tournament has had spells when it has fallen out of favour and Brazil on occasions has competed with understrength teams. The Copa America has recaptured the imagination in recent years and Brazil won the biennial event in both 1997 and 1999. There was a shock defeat against Honduras in the 2001 quarter-final but Brazil took the title again in 2004, and beat Argentina 3–0 in the 2007 final to make it four wins in the last five tournaments.

The World Cup has been a different matter. In the first two tournaments Brazil suffered early exits, but in 1938 things went much better. The team knocked out Poland 6–5, helped by four goals from Lenidas da Silva. The runners-up from 1934, Czechoslovakia, were beaten 2–1 in a replay, but Brazil then went down by the same score in the semi-final against Italy. Confident of victory, the Brazilians had rested Lenidas, a decision that rebounded badly.

Postwar Successes

It was in the postwar period that Brazil began to assert itself on the world stage. In 1950 on home soil the team went down 2–1 in the final against Uruguay. Ademir hit nine goals in six games to make him the tournament's top scorer, but he failed to get on the scoresheet in the final. Eight years later the country went one better. A team boasting the likes of Didi, Vava, Zagallo and Garrincha, together with 17-year-old Pele, won the Jules Rimet Trophy in style. Pele hit six of the 16 goals Brazil scored in their five matches, including a hat-trick against France in the semis and two against Sweden in the final.

Brazil retained the trophy in Chile four years later, despite losing Pele to injury early on. Amarildo filled his boots admirably and with the nucleus of the 1958 side still there Brazil swept all before them. The team averaged nearly three goals a match and they maintained that with a 3–1 win over Czechoslovakia in the final.

Pele came in for some rough treatment in 1966 and

Pele dribbles past his opponent in 1960.

played in just two matches. Brazil lost to both Hungary and Portugal and went out at the group stage. Mexico 1970 saw Brazil complete a hat-trick of World Cup wins playing champagne football that left the opposition reeling and fans everywhere purring. England provided the sternest test. Apart from a tight 1–0 victory over the holders, Brazil put at least three goals past every other team, and hit four against Italy in the final. Carlos Alberto captained a side including Gerson, Jairzinho, Tostao and Rivelino, as well as Pele, who was in majestic form despite nearing his 30th birthday. A third victory gave Brazil the Jules Rimet Trophy outright. Although Brazil reached the last four of the 1974 and 1978 World Cups that it was the 1982 side which looked most likely to win with the kind of panache that their 1970 counterparts had shown. A Paolo Rossi hat-trick ended the hopes of Socrates, Falcao and Co. in the second round, Brazil going down 3–2 to Italy.

Fourth World Cup Victory

Twelve years later, with arguably a less talented side, Brazil became world champions for the fourth time. The team boasted Bebeto and Romario up front, but with the workmanlike skipper Dunga in midfield Brazil had steel as well as flair. After a dull goalless final against Italy Roberto Baggio's penalty miss gave Brazil victory.

Dunga was still there at France '98 and with Cafu, Roberto Carlos, Rivaldo and new young star Ronaldo in the ranks, the Brazil side looked full of flair. After squeezing past Holland on penalties in the semis, Brazil faced hosts France in the final. There was a mystery surrounding Ronaldo's fitness but in the end he took the field. Unfortunately neither he nor the rest of the side performed on the day and Brazil were runners-up for the second time. Japan and Korea 2002 saw the Brazilians back on top of the pile. After a scratchy qualifying campaign the team got better and better as the tournament progressed. Ronaldo was back to his

irresistible best this time round. His two goals beat Germany in the final and put him on eight for the tournament. Ronaldo added three more at Germany 2006 to become the World Cup's record goalscorer, but the favourites misfired, going out to France in the quarter-final.

Brazil's captain, Cafu, holds the World Cup trophy in 2002.

Hristo Stoichkov of Bulgaria celebrates after scoring a penalty.

Bulgaria

Founded: 1923
Colours: White; green; red
World Cup Appearances: 7   **Best**: 4th 1994

Prior to 1994 Bulgaria had had little impact on the footballing world. The country's football federation was formed in 1923, with FIFA membership following a year later. The Communist takeover after World War Two saw Bulgaria follow a typical Eastern bloc pattern. An army side, CSKA Sofia, was formed, professional in all but name. The style was rigid and functional with flair at a premium. Bulgaria made its World Cup debut in 1962. The team went out at the group stage without recording a win, setting a precedent that would endure for four more tournaments over the next 24 years. Mexico '86 left the country still looking for a first World Cup win, although draws against Italy and South Korea did allow the country to squeeze into the second round, where they went down 2–0 to host country Mexico. Eight years later the Bulgarian side was the surprise package in the USA. Players such as Lechkov, Balakov, Ivanov, together with star performer Hristo Stoichkov, carried Bulgaria to the semi-finals. Along the way they took some notable scalps: Greece, Argentina, Mexico

and holders Germany. A brace from Roberto Baggio ended their run but the team won many admirers and its talismanic star Stoichkov was later named European Footballer of the Year. At France '98 most of the heroes of the previous World Cup were either missing or past their best and Bulgaria finished bottom of their group. A resurgent side qualified for the Euro 2004 finals, but lost all three games to finish bottom of their group.

Cameroon

Founded: 1960
Colours: Green; red; yellow
World Cup Appearances: 5   **Best**: Quarter-finals 1990
Honours: African Nations Cup winners 1984, 1988, 2000, 2002
Olympic winners 2000

Along with Nigeria, Cameroon has been at the forefront of the rise of African football in the past 20 years. It is a testimony to the growing strength of Cameroon football that an early exit in the 2002 World Cup was met with some surprise. The country's big breakthrough came in 1982, just 20 years after the country's football federation had been formed. At that year's World Cup in Spain, Cameroon were unbeaten, results including a 1–1 draw with Italy, who went on to lift the trophy. The Indomitable Lions missed out on a second-round place by the narrowest of margins. Italy went through by virtue of scoring one more goal, the countries tied on both points and goal difference. In 1984 Cameroon

Cameroon's Marc Vivien Foe who died while playing for his country in the 2003 Confederations Cup.

were crowned African Champions for the first time. They failed to retain the trophy two years later, beaten on penalties by hosts Egypt, but recaptured it in 1988 with a 1–0 victory over Nigeria. At the 1990 World Cup, Cameroon took on Argentina in the opening match and stunned the reigning champions with a 1–0 win. They also took the scalp of Romania to finish group winners and beat Colombia in the second round to set up a quarter-final clash with England. Thirty-eight-year-old Roger Milla, who had been African Footballer of the Year back in 1976, hit four goals and entertained the world with his famous corner flag dance celebration. In the last eight Cameroon went down to England, who converted two penalties to squeeze through 3–2 in extra-time. Cameroon disappointed in both the 1994 and 1998 World Cups, although in the USA 42-year-old Milla had the honour of becoming the oldest player to score a World Cup goal. In 2000 Cameroon beat Nigeria to win the African Nations Cup for the third time, and also took Olympic gold in Sydney. The blow of a disappointing 2002 World Cup was softened by another African Nations Cup victory in the same year, Cameroon beating Senegal on penalties. Marc Vivien Foe was a key member of that side and the country was shocked by his untimely death while playing for his country in a tournament in France in the summer of 2003.

Canada

Founded: 1912
Colours: Red; red; red
World Cup Appearances: 1 **Best**: 1st round 1986
Honours: Olympic winners 1904 (Galt FC); CONCACAF winners 2000

The history of Canadian football dates back a hundred years. Galt FC prevailed at the 1904 Olympics, albeit when football was still a demonstration sport and only a handful of representatives' sides competed. Over the years Canadian administrators have tried to relaunch the game but the twin problems of competition from the more established sports and the vast scale of the country have always militated against its growth. Canada made its first attempt to reach a World Cup in 1958 but it wasn't until Mexico '86 that the ambition was finally realized. The team failed to register a point or a goal but neither Hungary, France nor the Soviet Union put more than two past them. This remains Canada's only World Cup appearance to date. In 2000 the country recorded its first major tournament success, beating Colombia to win the CONCACAF Gold Cup.

Cameroon celebrate after scoring against Spain in the 2000 Olympics.

Chile

Founded: 1895
Colours: Red; blue; white
World Cup Appearances: 7   **Best**: 3rd 1962

Visiting British seamen introduced football to Chile in the late 19th century. The similarity with Brazil ends there. Even allowing for Chile's much smaller population, the achievements of the last century have been modest. Chile contested the inaugural World Cup in 1930, a 13-strong tournament, but defeat by Argentina cost the side a semi-final place. There have been six postwar appearances, most of which have been disappointing. The exception was 1962, when with home advantage Chile reached the last four. Defeat by favourites and the eventual winners Brazil was no disgrace. The same couldn't be said for the 2–0 victory over Italy at the group stage. In one of the most violent matches ever witnessed, Italy were reduced to nine men, though both teams were equally culpable. Leonel Sanchez, Chile's most capped player, hit four goals to finish joint top-scorer. In 1966, 1974 and 1982 Chile suffered first-round exits, failing to register a win in nine matches. The team that went to France '98 was more promising. With Marcelo Salas and Ivan Zamorano up front, Chile reached the second round for only the second time in its history. As in 1962, Brazil proved to be Chile's undoing, running out 4–1 winners. Chile has reached the final of the Copa America three times – four including the unofficial 1956 tournament – but has finished runner-up on each occasion.

China

Founded: 1924
Colours: Red; white; red
World Cup Appearances: 1   **Best**: 1st round 2002

A forerunner of football was played in China around 200 BC. The modern game was introduced to the country at the end of the 19th century by British expatriates in Shanghai and Hong Kong. League football arrived in the 1920s and FIFA membership came in 1931. FIFA's recognition of the Nationalist regime on Taiwan led China to withdraw from the world body in 1959, a rift that lasted 21 years. China's vast population and huge interest in football hasn't yet translated to success on the field. China were runners-up in the 1984 Asian Cup, and a decade later lost 4–2 to Uzbekistan in the final of the Asian Games. China had a degree of revenge in qualifying for the 2002 World Cup, in a group including Uzbekistan. Coach Bora Milutinovic

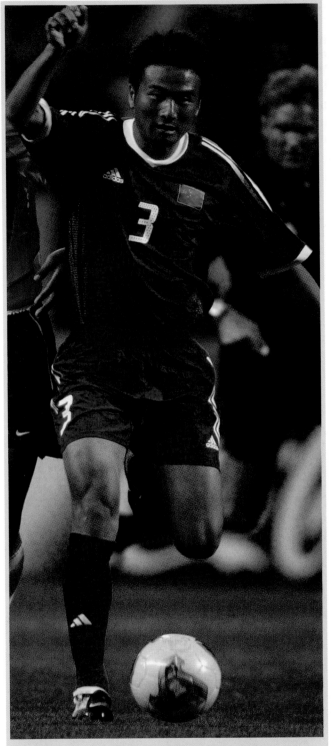

China's Pu Yang in the 2002 World Cup Finals.

led China to its first World Cup campaign, and although the team finished bottom of its group it did face eventual winners Brazil and semi-finalists Turkey. China hosted the 2004 Asian Cup, its team going down 3–1 to Japan in the final.

Colombia

Founded: 1924
Colours: Red; blue; red/white/blue
World Cup Appearances: 4 **Best**: 2nd round 1990
Honours: Copa America winners 2001

In 2001 Colombia finally lost its reputation as a talented also-ran by winning its first major tournament. It came in the Copa America, with Colombia taking full advantage of playing on home soil. A 1–0 win over Mexico in the final prompted wild celebrations in a country where passion has all too often spilled over into violence.

League football in the country took off in the 1920s with a national championship and FIFA membership following a decade later. The country operated outside FIFA's jurisdiction when a pirate league was formed between 1948 and 1953. During this time the teams attracted stars from all over the continent, including Alfredo di Stefano.

Colombia's World Cup debut came in 1962. There was no victory, and the team suffered a 5–0 hammering by Yugoslavia. However, a 4–4 draw with the Soviet Union earned the country its first World Cup point. Finishing runners-up to Peru in the revamped 1975 South American Championship was Colombia's best showing of the next 25 years. A second World Cup appearance came at Italia '90. Colombia not only gained its first victory, over the United Arab Emirates, but also drew 1–1 with West Germany, who went on to win the trophy. These results weren't enough to take Colombia to the knockout stage, though. Four years later Colombia made it to the USA with qualifying results including a 5–0 win over Argentina. Expectations were accordingly much higher, but the team crashed out, beaten by both Romania and the USA. Andreas Escobar, who had put the ball through his own net in the USA match, was shot dead shortly afterwards back home in Medellin. In 1998 the Colombians reached their third successive World Cup, but defeats against England and Romania meant yet another first-round exit.

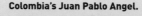

Colombia's Juan Pablo Angel.

Costa Rica

Founded: 1921
Colours: Red; blue; white
World Cup Appearances: 3   **Best**: 2nd round 1990
Honours: CONCACAF winners 1941, 1946, 1948, 1953, 1955, 1960, 1961, 1963, 1969, 1989

Costa Rica has won the championship for North and Central America ten times, more than any other country. However, these championships, which date back to 1941, have had a variety of formats and the number of participating teams has varied considerably. Since 1991, when the CONCACAF Championship was relaunched as the Gold Cup, it has been considerably more competitive. Costa Rica has featured in the final just once, losing to the USA in 2002.

Costa Rica made an impressive World Cup debut at Italia '90, beating both Sweden and Scotland before going out to Czechoslovakia in the second round. The Costa Ricans topped their 2002 World Cup qualifying group, which included Mexico and the USA. In Japan and Korea they lost out to Turkey on goal difference for a place in the second round. With Brazil also in its group, Costa Rica was unfortunate in meeting the countries that would go on to finish first and third. It was also the only country to score twice against Brazil, although it did go down 5–2 in its group encounter. 'Los Ticos' also made it to Germany 2006, but three straight defeats and nine goals conceded made it a tournament to forget.

Croatia

Founded: 1991
Colours: Red; white, blue
World Cup Appearances: 3   **Best**: 3rd 1998

Croatia has performed phenomenally well since 1991, when it became an independent nation once again. After 50 years of being part of Yugoslavia, Croatia wasted little time in making a mark on the footballing world. It formed its FA in 1991 – almost 80 years after it had done so first time round – and became affiliated to FIFA the following year. Croatia was fortunate in having a wealth of talent, with the likes of Robert Prosinecki, Alen Boksic and Zvonimir Boban. The country made its debut at Euro '96 and the quality of the side carried it to the quarter-final, where an indisciplined performance against Germany proved costly. Davor Suker scored a brilliant goal but Germany went through 2–1. Two years later, at France '98, Croatia avenged that defeat with a 3–0 win over Germany, also at the quarter-final stage. Suker was again on target in the semi-final against hosts France, and Croatia also had the dubious advantage of playing against 10 men, Slaven Bilic's histrionics having got Laurent Blanc sent off. Two Lilian Thuram goals turned the game around for France. Croatia went on to finish third, while Suker won the Golden Boot for his 6-goal tally.

By Euro 2000 the golden generation was ageing and Croatia didn't reach the finals in Holland and Belgium. A crop of poor results saw Croatia slip to 19th in the FIFA rankings. The team qualified for Japan and Korea, but defeats against both Mexico and Ecuador meant an early exit. The team's one victory, over Italy, was achieved with a liberal slice of luck. Coach Mirko Jozic paid the price shortly afterwards. His successor Otto Baric was soon under pressure as Croatia got off to a rocky start in the Euro 2004 qualifiers. The team recovered to reach Portugal via the play-offs but finished behind France and England in their group. Croatia crashed out of the 2006 World Cup after a dramatic 2–2 draw with Australia in their final group match, though the damage had been done earlier, when the team took only one point off Japan. Croatia had already qualified for Euro 2008 when the side came to Wembley for the final group match and, with the pressure off, broke England fans' hearts by running out 3–2 winners. Slaven Bilic's team reached the quarter-finals of the tournament, where they led Turkey with seconds to go before conceding an equaliser and going out on penalties.

Paulo Wanchope of Costa Rica competes with Turkey's Ozat.

Croatia's striker Alen Boksic is tackled by Augusto Porozo of Ecuador.

Czech Republic

Founded: 1994
Colours: Red; white; blue
World Cup Appearances: 1 (8 as Czechoslovakia) **Best**: Final 1934, 1962
Honours: European Championship winners 1976; Olympic winners 1980 (both
as Czechoslovakia)

A quarter-final defeat by West Germany at Italia '90 marked
the swansong appearance of Czechoslovakia in international
football. Three years later the country split into the Czech
Republic and Slovakia, with separate league and cup
competitions and with each independently affiliated
to FIFA and UEFA. Slovakia has struggled to make an
impact on the international stage. Not so the Czech
Republic, who made a dramatic tournament debut at
Euro '96, reaching the final in which they met
Germany. Pavel Nedved, Patrik Berger and Karel
Poborsky were among those who took the eye in the
tournament, and it was Berger who put the Czechs
ahead in the final. A brace from Oliver Bierhoff – the
second an extra-time golden goal – meant that they
had to settle for the runners-up spot.

The Czechs failed to reach the World Cup
finals in 1998, and in 2002 they lost a play-off against
Belgium. Euro 2000 saw the country eliminated at
the group stage. In Portugal, four years later, the
team impressed by reaching the semi-final where

they fell victim to surprise package and eventual
winners Greece. The Czech side that made its World
Cup debut at Germany 2006 was ranked third in
the world by Fifa, but after an impressive opening
win over USA, defeats against Italy and Ghana
signalled an early exit.

Football in what was Bohemia and Slovakia
dates back to the 19th century. Slavia Prague and
Sparta Prague, the oldest clubs, were founded in
1893. Czechoslovakia itself was created in 1918 in
the wake of the defeat of Austro-Hungary in World
War One. The fledgling country beat Yugoslavia 7–0
in its debut appearance in 1920. Slavia and Sparta
enjoyed considerable success in the late 1920s and
1930s in the Mitropa Cup, an early prototype of the
European Cup. The national side was also runner-up
to Italy in the 1934 World Cup final. Czechoslovakia
was occupied by the Germans in 1938 and in the
aftermath of World War Two fell under the
Communist sphere of influence. Dukla Prague
became the army and de facto state side, a situation
that was replicated in many Eastern bloc countries.
Czechoslovakia reached the World Cup finals in 1954, 1958
and 1962. At Chile '62 the team's star was wing-half Josef
Masopust, who would later be named European Footballer of
the Year. Masopust put Czechoslovakia ahead against Brazil in
the final but the holders came back to win 3–1. In 1976
Czechoslovakia went one better, beating West Germany on
penalties to become European Champions. The Czechs also
finished third four years later in Italy.

Hornak (right) and Kadlec (left) pursue Luis Figo during the
quarter-final of Euro '96 which the Czech Republic won 1–0.

Denmark

Founded: 1889
Colours: Red; white; red
World Cup Appearances: 3   **Best**: 2nd round 1986, 2002
Honours: Olympic winners 1906; European Championship winners 1992; Confederations Cup winners 1995/6

Denmark has produced a host of star players over the years, and came from nowhere to win the 1992 European Championship. Yet Japan and Korea 2002 was only the third time that the Danes had qualified for a World Cup. One of the impediments was the fact that Denmark embraced professionalism as recently as 1978.

A jubilant Michael Laudrup holds the European Nations trophy after Denmark defeated Germany by 2–0 in 1992.

Amateurism was no handicap in the early years of the 20th century, when the Danes were the main challengers to England's supremacy on the international stage. It is said that the first ball to arrive in the country came in a parcel delivered to an English schoolboy studying at one of Denmark's exclusive schools. The Danes took to the game quickly, playing skilful football underpinned by resilience and tactical awareness. In 1908, when football became an Olympic sport and in effect the world championship, the Danes reached the final. The team was coached by Charlie Williams, a former Spurs and Manchester City goalkeeper. One of the stars was centre-half Nils Middelboe, who would go on to play for Chelsea for almost a decade. Another was Harald Bohr, whose younger brother Nils was reserve 'keeper and future nuclear physicist of world renown. The team beat France's 'B' side 17–1 in the semis before losing to England 2–0 in the final. Many of the same players were at the 1912 Games in Stockholm, where the same two sides contested the final. This time England won 4–2.

Over the next 60 years Denmark's progress was hampered by the FA ruling that banned overseas professionals from playing for the national team. A semi-final appearance at the 1964 European Championship – where the team lost to the USSR – was the high point of the period. Even here the Danes were favoured by having to beat only Malta, Albania and Luxembourg.

The winds of change blew over the country in the 1970s, paying dividends in the following decade. An Allan Simonsen penalty at Wembley gave the Danes their first ever victory over England and helped the team reach Euro '84. Under Sepp Piontek the Danes reached the semi-final, going out to Spain on penalties. Two years later Denmark reached its first World Cup. Michael Laudrup starred in a team that had excellent wins over Uruguay and West Germany before losing again to Spain, this time 5–1.

The 1992 European Championship was pure fairytale. Having finished runners-up to Yugoslavia in qualifying, the Danes were given a dramatic late entry into the tournament after the Balkans conflict erupted. The squad had less than two weeks to prepare and started slowly. Needing a victory over France in the final group match, the Danes made it to the semis with a goal from substitute Lars Elstrup. Semi-final opponents Holland boasted the AC Milan stars Van Basten and Rijkaard, and the majestic Ruud Gullit. It went to a shoot-out, where Peter Schmeichel saved from Van Basten. The fairytale ending saw the Danes beat world champions Germany in the final, John Jensen and Kim Vilfort grabbing the goals. After a disappointing Euro '96, the Danes performed well at the 1998 World Cup, edged out by Brazil in a five-goal quarter-final thriller. Euro 2000 was another setback, the team conceding eight goals without reply in three defeats. The 2002 World Cup saw Denmark grouped with France for the third tournament running. It was a famous victory this time, and Denmark went on to be the surprise winners of its group before being soundly beaten by England in the second round. The Danes reached the last eight in Euro 2004, beaten 3–0 by the Czech Republic.

Ronaldinho Gaucho (right) of Brazil heads the ball to score against Ecuador in their World Cup qualifier in Manaus.

Ecuador

Founded: 1925
Colours: Yellow; blue; red
World Cup Appearances: 2 **Best**: 1st round

Ecuador made its World Cup debut in 2002 after qualifying in some style. The team finished second to Argentina in the powerful South American group, looking more secure and accomplished than Brazil. The path to the finals included a 1–0 victory over the country that had been crowned World Champions four times, although the team was undoubtedly helped by the rarefied atmosphere of Quito, high in the Andes. Ecuador registered its first World Cup points with a 1–0 victory over Croatia, who had finished third in the tournament four years earlier, this followed defeats by Italy and Mexico and Ecuadoreans were on their way home. The team went one better at Germany 2006, beating Poland and Costa Rica to reach the knockout stage, where their hopes were ended by England and a David Beckham free kick.

Ecuador has made little impression in the Copa America, the South American Championship, defeat in the third-place play-off on home soil in 1993 being the country's best effort to date. As far as club football is concerned, Barcelona of Guayaquil has twice reached the final of the Copa Libertadores, in 1990 and 1998, losing to Olimpia of Paraguay and Brazilian side Vasco da Gama respectively.

Egypt

Founded: 1921
Colours: Red; white; black
World Cup Appearances: 2 **Best**: 1st round 1934, 1990
Honours: Africa Nations Cup winners 1957, 1959, 1986, 1998, 2006

Egypt was the first African nation to make a mark on the world stage. In 1920 it became the first African country to enter a team in the Olympic football tournament. Three years later Egypt affiliated to FIFA, again a first for the continent. And in 1934 an Egyptian side competed in the World Cup. Their tournament lasted just one match for it was organized on a straight knockout basis. The team put up a good showing in a 4–2 defeat by Hungary. In 1957 Egypt became a founder member of the African Footballing Federation and won the inaugural tournament which marked the foundation of the new body. However, membership was limited to independent nations and only three teams competed. Egypt came out on top against the same opposition – Ethiopia and Sudan – in 1959, but an Ethiopian victory in 1962 prevented a hat-trick. Egypt's African Nations Cup victories in 1986, 1998, 2006 and 2008 were more impressive as competition was much more intense. The team that defended its title in Ghana in 2008 wasn't expected to do well, but triumphed after beating a highly rated Ivory Coast side 4–1 in the semis and Cameroon 1–0 in the final, the scoreline in the latter failing to reflect Egypt's superiority. A sixth tournament victory extended the Pharaohs' lead at the top of the all-time winners table. In 1990 Egypt made its second World Cup appearance. Draws against Holland and the Republic of Ireland, and only a 1–0 defeat by England, represented a highly creditable performance, though not good enough for the country to progress to the second round.

Corrales of El Salvador drives past Hejduk of the United States in the first round of Gold Cup soccer in 2003.

El Salvador

Founded: 1935
Colours: Blue; blue; blue
World Cup Appearances: 2 **Best**: 1st round 1970, 1982
Honours: CONCACAF winners 1943

El Salvador's Football Association was formed in 1935 and the country affiliated to FIFA three years later. The country's only success on the international stage came in 1943, with a victory involving CCCF countries (Confederacion Centroamericano y del Caribe de Futbol).

Twenty years later this organization would be reconstituted as part of the new and much stronger CONCACAF Federation, but in 1943 it was a relatively weak event. El Salvador's first World Cup appearance came in 1970, after an explosive qualifying campaign which included a play-off victory over neighbouring Honduras. Relations between the countries were tense and the situation eventually erupted into war. At the tournament itself El salvador lost all three of their games and failed to register a single goal. Things were much the same twelve years later in Spain, the country's only other World Cup appearance to date. That team did manage to score but it came in a 10–1 thrashing at the hands of Hungary. No other country has conceded double figures at a World Cup.

England

Founded: 1863
Colours: White; navy blue; white
World Cup Appearances: 12   **Best**: Winners 1966
Honours: Olympic gold 1908, 1912

It was the great public schools and universities that championed association football in the mid-19th century. Even before that term was coined, the men of Eton, Charterhouse, Cambridge and elsewhere were in dispute with the proponents of rugby football. The irrevocable split came in 1863, when the Football Association was founded. Ironically, handling remained within the laws for some years, in which a hybrid between the two footballing codes was played. The dribbling game enjoyed greater popularity and within a generation football had become the sport of the masses.

In 1871 FA Secretary Charles Alcock proposed the idea of a challenge cup. With league competition still a long way off, this captured the imagination of the affiliated clubs. Logistical problems meant that only 15 entered the inaugural competition, in which The Wanderers beat the Royal Engineers 1–0 at Kennington Oval.

The first decade was dominated by clubs made up of gentleman-amateurs. By the 1880s many clubs were professional in all but name. The FA initially tried to stem the tide but the clubs found all manner of means to reward their players covertly and in 1885 the governing body finally relented.

1872 saw England and Scotland contest the world's first international match. The teams played out a 0–0 draw at the West of Scotland Cricket Ground, Partick, Glasgow, watched by a 2000-strong crowd who had paid a shilling apiece. A photographer was in attendance but he refused to record the event as he was given no guarantee that he would be able to sell his prints.

League Formed

League football arrived in 1888, with Preston North End's 'Invincibles' setting the early pace. By the dawn of the 20th century an aggregate of seven million people was turning out to watch two 18-strong divisions do battle for league supremacy and FA Cup glory. Amateur sides, notably Corinthians, could still hold their own against the top professionals, and some amateur players even made the England side on a regular basis. That all came to an end in 1907, when the FA sought to bring all players under its jurisdiction. The amateurs baulked at the idea and formed their own association.

In 1908 England was finally able to test its national side against opposition other than the home countries, when football became an Olympic sport. England won that tournament and retained the title in 1912, beating Denmark on both occasions.

28 April 1923 saw Bolton beat West Ham 2–0 in the first FA Cup final to be staged at the new Wembley Stadium. With a 127,000 capacity – 70,000 more than had watched the previous year's final – the FA thought it would accommodate all the fans comfortably. But tens of thousands poured in by any available means and the game was held up for 45 minutes as hordes spilled onto the pitch. PC George Scorey and his white horse Billy helped to restore order and went down in the annals of the game.

West Ham and Bolton Wanderers players wait for the police to clear the pitch of spectators before the 1923 FA Cup final at the newly-completed Wembley Stadium.

England's Stanley Matthews (left), Duncan Edwards and captain Billy Wright (right) in a training session at Highbury Stadium before their match against Scotland at Wembley in 1957.

Hungary all dented England's claim to be the number one footballing nation. This was an era in which the backbone of the national side came from an Arsenal team that Herbert Chapman had forged into the dominant force in the land.

In 1947 England celebrated its return to the international fold with a 10–0 win over Portugal. Victories over Belgium, Sweden and Italy followed, but any suggestion that England was about to resume its position at the top of the footballing tree was about to be dashed. A 1–0 defeat by the USA in Belo Horizonte was the low point in a disappointing first World Cup campaign in 1950. The team also lost to Spain and didn't hang around to watch the remaining matches.

Any remaining doubts that England's long period in the international wilderness had had no adverse effect were dispelled in November 1953, when the brilliant Hungarians came to Wembley and gave England a footballing lesson. It was 6–3 that day, and an even more emphatic 7–1 in a return meeting in Budapest the following year.

At the 1954 World Cup in Switzerland, England went down 4–2 to holders Uruguay in the quarter-final. In Sweden four years later manager Walter Winterbottom was hampered by the loss of his Manchester United stars, including Duncan Edwards and Tommy Taylor, killed in the Munich air disaster four months earlier. England lost a group play-off match 1–0 to the USSR and had to watch as both Wales and Northern Ireland went further in the tournament.

The International Game

England had joined FIFA in 1905 but withdrew in the 1920s in a dispute over rejoining competitions with the countries it had fought against in World War One. That rift was healed in 1924 but another argument with the world governing body erupted over broken-time payments to amateurs, and in 1928 England withdrew from FIFA again. This time reconciliation would not be achieved until after the World War Two. England thus remained on the sidelines as the World Cup got under way. Even so, there were signs that its position of pre-eminence was already under threat. Scotland's 'Wembley Wizards' inflicted a stunning 5–1 victory on the Auld Enemy in 1928, and a year later England were beaten 4–3 by Spain in Madrid, the country's first defeat by foreign opposition. In the early 1930s defeats by France, Czechoslovakia and

Jack (left) and Bobby Charlton during an England training session at Stamford Bridge in 1965.

Bobby Moore holds the Jules Rimet Trophy as England celebrate their victory over West Germany in the 1966 World Cup.

World Cup Glory

The 1960s began promisingly. Players of the calibre of Bobby Charlton, Bobby Smith and Johnny Haynes – the country's first £100-a-week footballer after the abolition of the maximum wage – suggested that England could again compete with the best in the world. But the 1962 World Cup in Chile was another disappointment. The team did reach the last eight, but won just one match. Alf Ramsey, who had steered unfashionable Ipswich to the championship, took over from Winterbottom and was soon bullishly predicting an England World Cup victory on home soil in 1966. Ramsey had some top wingers in his squad, including Liverpool's Ian Callaghan and Manchester United's John Connelly. But he decided to dispense with wide players altogether. The superb Banks was in goal; Cohen, Wilson and Jackie Charlton were marshalled by skipper Bobby Moore; Nobby Stiles patrolled in front of the back four giving defensive strength; Bobby Charlton played as a deep-lying centre-forward, with Martin Peters and Alan Ball also tucked into the midfield. From the quarter-final Roger Hunt and Geoff Hurst formed the strike force, the latter replacing Jimmy Greaves. It was an inspired decision,

Hurst hitting the only goal of the game against Argentina in the quarters and a hat-trick in the 4–2 win over West Germany in the final.

England went down 1–0 to Yugoslavia in a bruising semi-final in the 1968 European Championship. Alan Mullery's retaliation to a late tackle led him to be the first England player to be sent off. By the end of the 1960s English clubs had won five European trophies, with Manchester United becoming the country's first team to win the European Cup. Success at club level would continue, but in the 1970s England sides struggled to reach the finals of the big tournaments, let alone look like winning them.

A Decade of Disappointments

Many thought the team Ramsey took to the 1970 World Cup was even stronger than the one that had won it four years earlier. They lost 1–0 to Brazil at the group stage and it was widely thought that these two joint-favourites would also contest the final. That hope disappeared in Leon, where quarter-final opponents West Germany came back from 2–0 down to win 3–2, Gerd Müller volleying the extra-time winner. Two years later, at the same stage of the European Championship, the West Germans came to Wembley and won 3–1. When England were held 1–1 at Wembley by Poland in

October 1973, a result that meant failure to
reach the World Cup finals for the first time in
seven attempts, the writing was on the wall for
Ramsey.

His successor, Don Revie, failed to
recreate the success he had enjoyed at club level
with Leeds United. England
did not make the latter stages of the 1976
European Championship, and with World Cup
qualification looking a distant prospect Revie
walked away. Ron Greenwood came in and built
a side around the team that was dominating
both domestic and European football —
Liverpool. In this era the Reds provided England
with players such as Ray Clemence, Phil Neal,
Phil Thompson, Ray Kennedy, Terry McDermott
Emlyn Hughes and Kevin Keegan.

False Starts

In 1980 England made it to the European
Championship finals but were out of contention
by the time they recorded a 2–1 win over Spain
in the final group match. After a scratchy
qualifying series, Greenwood's side reached
Spain '82. Bryan Robson led from the front,
making World Cup history by scoring after just
27 seconds against France. The team cruised
through to the second round, where goalless
draws against West Germany and Spain weren't
enough to secure a semi-final place. Bobby
Robson, who, like Ramsey a generation earlier,
had transformed Ipswich into one of the
strongest sides in the land, took over from
Greenwood. An Allan Simonsen penalty gave
Denmark an historic victory at Wembley and
helped the Danes to qualify for Euro '84 at
England's expense. In Mexico in 1986 a Gary
Lineker hat-trick against Poland in the final
group match helped England to squeeze through
to the second phase. A comprehensive win over
Paraguay set up a quarter-final clash with
Argentina. Maradona won the tie with a
mesmerizing solo goal, but only after he had
punched the ball past Shilton to open the
scoring. Lineker headed his 6th goal in the 2–1
defeat and ended the tournament as top scorer.

Euro '88 was a huge disappointment.
After qualifying for the tournament, staged in
West Germany, England went down to a Ray
Houghton goal for the Republic of Ireland in the

**Stuart Pearce celebrates after scoring in the penalty shoot-out
against Spain during Euro '96.**

Alan Shearer is jubilant after scoring for England in 1999.

opening fixture. Defeats against Holland and the USSR followed and England limped out as wooden spoonists.

Italia '90

Robson announced that he would be returning to club management before a ball was kicked at Italia '90. Paul Gascoigne lit up the tournament with his performances and with his display of emotion in the semi-final against Germany. His tears after incurring a booking that would have kept him out of the final proved to be unnecessary. Stuart Pearce and Chris Waddle both missed from the spot after the game ended 1–1.

Graham Taylor was appointed to the England job on the strength of his achievements at Watford and Aston Villa. At Euro '92 England needed to beat hosts Sweden in the final group match but went down 2–1. This was to be Gary Lineker's last game in an England shirt. The fact that the country's premier striker was substituted when England needed to score mystified many. On a personal level it meant that Lineker remained on 48 goals, one short of Bobby Charlton's record.

Taylor came in for even more vitriolic criticism after some abject performances in the qualifiers for USA '94. The low point came against San Marino, when England conceded in under 10 seconds. The team needed to win 7–0 and for Holland to lose if they were to make it to the World Cup. In the event neither part of the equation worked out and Taylor departed.

With home advantage at Euro '96 and the flamboyant and tactically astute Terry Venables in charge, there was a party atmosphere as the team marched on to the semis. Gascoigne had scored against Scotland with a sublime piece of skill and the team demolished a powerful Dutch side 4–1. Alan Shearer, who had taken Lineker's mantle as the country's top striker, put England ahead against the Germans. But almost inevitably it went to penalties and once again England came up short. Gareth Southgate, who had been outstanding at the back, missed the vital spot-kick this time.

Business interests and ongoing legal battles forced Venables to step down and the FA appointed the youngest-ever England coach, Glenn Hoddle. Many felt that the national side should have been built around Hoddle in the 1980s and that, under his guidance, flair and skill would be encouraged. At France '98 Hoddle initially left 17-year-old wonderkid Michael Owen on the bench when the fans were clamouring for his inclusion. Owen came off the bench to score against Romania in the group phase, and although the game ended in defeat England still set up a clash with Argentina in the last eight. Owen scored the goal of the tournament to put England 2–1 up. Argentina equalized, David Beckham was sent off for kicking out at Diego Simeone and when Sol Campbell's header in extra-time was ruled out it was yet another shoot-out. Paul Ince and David Batty missed and England were out. Arguments raged about penalty taking and the degree to which practising the art would help when it came to a shoot-out in a major tournament. In the end it was Hoddle's ill-judged comments outside his footballing remit which precipitated his downfall.

World Cup 2002

Howard Wilkinson took temporary charge but it was the fans' choice, Kevin Keegan, who was named as the long-term successor. England underperformed at Euro 2000, snatching defeat from the jaws of victory against both Portugal and Romania. Ironically, a 1–0 win over Germany was worthless on this occasion. With qualification for the 2002 World Cup in the balance Keegan resigned, questioning his ability at the highest level. The FA's decision to appoint Sven-Goran Eriksson was applauded by some, condemned by others. A stunning 5–1 win over Germany in Munich silenced the critics, and David Beckham sealed World Cup qualification with a scintillating free-kick in the 2–2 draw against Greece at Old Trafford. Beckham, vilified after France '98, was the hero as he slotted home the penalty that beat Argentina. Draws against Sweden and Nigeria got England out of the 'Group of Death', and Eriksson's men booked a quarter-final berth against Brazil with a comprehensive win

Despair for England following defeat in the England v Brazil, 2002 World Cup Quarter final. Brazil won the match 2–1.

over Denmark in the second round. Owen put England ahead, Ronaldinho's blistering run set up Rivaldo's equalizer. Ronaldinho's looping free-kick floated over Seaman's head and although he was later red-carded Brazil comfortably held out for victory.

England qualified for Euro 2004 unbeaten, and in their opening match against France were denied victory by two injury-time goals from Zidane. Wayne Rooney netted four times in the wins over Switzerland and Croatia and was hailed as the new wunderkind but limped off early in the quarter-final against hosts Portugal. Owen and Lampard scored in a game that finished 2–2 after extra-time. Beckham and Rui Costa both missed in the shoot-out and it went to sudden death. Portugal's keeper, Ricardo saved from Vassell and then beat James to make it another agonising defeat for England fans.

England qualified comfortably for Germany 2006, and with the likes of Terry, Lampard and Rooney added to the nucleus of the the 2002 squad, hopes were high that Eriksson's men might go all the way in the coach's swansong tournament. The team failed to convince in reaching the quarter-final, where Portugal again came out on top in a shoot-out. Rooney was red-carded – shades of Beckham in 1998 – but Eriksson conceded that reaching the last eight this time was an underachievement.

The new man in the hot seat was Sven's number two Steve McClaren, whose honeymoon period came to an abrupt end after a shaky start to the Euro 2008 qualifying campaign. A goalless home draw against Macedonia and a lacklustre display in a 2–0 defeat in Croatia left England trailing Croatia and Russia. The ship was steadied with a string of good results before a 2–1 defeat in Russia in the penultimate game put qualification out of England's hands. Israel did the team a favour by beating Russia, leaving England needing only a

David Beckham takes a free kick during England's match against Turkey in October 2003.

home draw against Croatia, a team that had already qualified. A 3–2 defeat meant that England failed to qualify for a major tournament for the first time since the 1994 World Cup. McClaren paid the price, and the FA again looked abroad for a replacement. Fabio Capello arrived with an impressive cv, having won nine championships with four different clubs in his 15 seasons in club management. The new regime got off to an impressive start, England taking maximum points from the first four qualifiers for South Africa 2010. They included a stunning 4–1 win in Croatia, Theo Walcott bagging a hat-trick against the side that had derailed England's European Championship hopes a year earlier.

Finland

Founded: 1907
Colours: White; blue; white
World Cup Appearances: 0

Jari Litmanen and Sami Hyypia have been Finland's top footballing exports in recent years. Litmanen was a member of the brilliant Ajax side that won the 1995 European Cup, becoming the first Finnish player to do so. Domestic football remains a part-time sport, even for the country's top clubs. In 2003 HJK Helsinki, the country's most successful club, secured its 21st championship.

Finland's Jari Litmanen (right) is chased by Zambrotta of Italy.

France

Founded: 1918
Colours: Blue; white; red
World Cup Appearances: 12   **Best**: winners 1998
Honours: European Championship winners 1984, 2000; Olympic winners 1984

France has been at the heart of just about all the major developments in football over the past century. It was first FIFA President Jules Rimet whose vision of a World Cup came to fruition in 1930. It was even a French sculptor who crafted the original trophy. A contemporary of Rimet's and head of the French FA, Henri Delaunay, came up with the idea of a European Championship in the 1920s. It was an idea ahead of its time then, but after UEFA was founded in 1954 the concept was revived. By the time the first tournament was staged in 1960, Delaunay had died but he had taken his place in the history books. The premier European club competition also owes a debt to a Frenchman. Gabriel Hanot, the editor of *L'Equipe*, came up with the idea of the Champions Cup after Wolves were unofficially declared Europe's best following their famous victories over Spartak Moscow and Honved in the early 1950s.

Even though France was a founder member of FIFA in 1904, football took a considerable time to become established. A united football association wasn't formed until 1918, a nationwide league didn't arrive until the late 1920s and professionalism wasn't fully embraced until 1932. France did compete in all three prewar World Cups, though, a quarter-final defeat by Italy in 1938 representing the country's best showing.

First European Cup Final

In the 1950s Stade de Reims was France's top club side, winning the championship five times in ten years. Reims contested the first European Cup final in 1956, losing 4–3 to Real Madrid. The same two sides met in 1959 too, Reims going down 2–0 this time. This era produced France's first superstar, Raymond Kopa. He played for Reims in the 1956 European Cup final against Real, and joined the Spanish giants shortly afterwards.

Michel Platini (left) of France with coach Michel Hidalgo after France's victory in the European Championship in 1984.

The 1958 World Cup produced another star – Just Fontaine. France scored 17 goals in a run that was ended by Brazil in the semi-final, Fontaine hitting 13 of them, which remains a World Cup record. After another semi-final defeat in the inaugural European Championship in 1960, the next two decades were fairly lean, at both club and international level. St Etienne dominated the domestic scene in the 1960s and 1970s but lost to Bayern Munich in the semi-final of the 1974–75 European Cup, and also went down to the same German side in the following year's final.

Increasing success

The early 1980s saw French football reach new heights without accumulating the silverware it deserved. The chief architect was Michel Hidalgo, who had played for Reims in the 1956 European Cup final. His sparkling side, including the brilliant midfield trio of Tigana, Giresse and Platini, was crowned European Champions on home soil in 1984. Platini, who went on to win the European Footballer of Year award three times, hit nine goals in five games.

At the 1982 and 1986 World Cups, France fell at the semi-final stage, both times to West Germany. Spain '82 will be remembered for Germany 'keeper Harald Schumacher's sickening challenge on Patrick Battiston. France let a 3–1 lead slip and lost on penalties. After that great side disintegrated, France had a fallow period, failing to reach the 1990 or 1994 World Cups. That era did produce France's first European Cup winners, however. Bernard Tapie took over as president of Marseille in 1985, pumping in money that would bring five championships in a row and, in 1993, a 1–0 victory over AC Milan in the European Cup final. Within days, news of a match-fixing scandal broke. Marseille was subsequently stripped of the 1993 championship but not the European Cup, Tapie was imprisoned and the club relegated.

Zinedine Zidane lifts the trophy after winning the 1998 World Cup final against Brazil.

Pires, Dacourt, Trezeguet and Henry celebrate a goal during a friendly match against Germany in 2003.

World Cup Victory

Five years later the French put that unsavoury episode behind them with a glorious World Cup triumph on home soil. With Barthez in goal, Thuram, Desailly, Blanc and Lizarazu in defence, and Deschamps, Petit and Zidane in midfield, Aime Jacquet's team boasted a formidable array of talent. Strikers were a little more thin on the ground, but with Thuram, Blanc, Zidane and Petit all getting on the scoresheet it didn't prove an encumbrance. A resounding 3–0 victory over Brazil

rounded off a superb tournament and ended a 68-year wait for the trophy to return home to the country that had spawned the idea.

Two years later France added the European Nations Cup, beating Italy in the final. The Golden Goal winner that day came from David Trezeguet, and with Thierry Henry and Sylvain Wiltord also establishing themselves as world-class strikers the team looked even stronger than the one which had won the World Cup. No one anticipated the script as France embarked on its bid to retain the world crown in Japan and Korea. The team was stunned by a 1–0 defeat at the

Germany

Founded: 1900
Colours: White; black; white
World Cup Appearances: 16   **Best**: winners 1954, 1974, 1990
Honours: European Championship winners 1972, 1980, 1996; Olympic winners 1976 (East Germany)

France's Zinedine Zidane in action.

The last five years has shown German football at its resilient best. After an indifferent showing at France '98 and Euro 2000, Germany was not fancied to do well at the 2002 World Cup. But the old adage 'Never write off Germany' was never more appropriate. The consummate tournament side recovered from a 5–1 home defeat to England during qualifying, beat Ukraine in a play-off, and got stronger as they progressed in Japan and Korea. Brazil were worthy winners in the final, but Germany had added to its impressive tournament record. Four years later, Jurgen Klinsmann took an equally unfancied side to the semis on home soil. It meant that in 16 of the 18 World Cups staged (they didn't take part in the inaugural tournament and were barred from the 1950 competition) Germany has chalked up three victories, finished runners-up four times and reached at least the last eight on seven other occasions.

Football was introduced to the country mainly through British students studying at Karlsruhe and Strassburg in the 1870s. In 1875 an Oxford University team visited Germany, thought to be the first touring side ever. An England team toured in 1899 and scored 30 goals in three games, conceding just four. When the Germans paid a return visit in 1901, the aggregate score over two games was 0–22.

These early reverses didn't deter the game's adherents. The German FA was formed in 1900 and four years later Germany became a FIFA member. Czechoslovakia halted Germany's progress in the 1934 World Cup, the Germans sorely missing their star centre-forward Richard Hoffman through injury. In 1938 several Austrian players were co-opted into the side after Germany's annexation of the country, but the team somewhat surprisingly went down 4–2 to Switzerland.

Germany Divides

1950 saw the country, now divided by the Iron Curtain, welcomed back into the footballing fold, ending a four-year expulsion. Coach Sepp Herberger, who had led the team at

hands of newcomers Senegal in the opening match. Things got even worse when Henry was red carded in the goalless draw with Uruguay. Zidane, struggling for fitness, was brought in for the crunch game against Denmark. Not even he could galvanize Les Bleus, who thus relinquished their crown at the first hurdle and without scoring a single goal.

France qualified for Euro 2004 with maximum points, the team looking back to its best. In Portugal France topped a group including England before losing to eventual winners Greece 1–0 in the quarter-final.

France went for experience at Germany 2006, the squad containing a number of players who had lifted the trophy eight years earlier. After an indifferent start the golden generation hit top gear, eliminating favourites Brazil en route to the final, where they went down on penalties to Italy.

Captain Franz Beckenbauer and the West German team with the trophy after winning the 1974 World Cup final 2–1 against Holland at the Olympiastadion in Munich.

France '38, took West Germany to the 1954 World Cup and masterminded a stunning victory over a Hungary side that hadn't lost for four years. Herberger fielded a weakened team when the two countries met at the group stage, realizing that defeat would still allow Germany to progress. Hungary won 8–3, but the Germans went on to the final via the easier half of the draw. Hungary took a 2–0 lead, despite a half-fit Puskas. But as the 'Galloping Major' faded, Germany got stronger. The Germans rode their luck and Rahn hit the winner five minutes from time. A team featuring six Kaiserslautern players had given Germany its first major honour.

Ill discipline cost the Germans dear in 1958. With the score 1–1 against hosts Sweden in the semis, Juskowiak was sent off for kicking Hamrin. The 10-man team lost 3–1.

West Germany didn't compete in the first two European Nations' Cup Championships in the 1960s, and in the 1962 World Cup lost to Yugoslavia, a team it had beaten in the previous two tournaments. In 1963 the Bundesliga was formed to replace the existing regional competitions; professionalism came at the same time. Three years later Helmut Schoen's side reached the World

Germany celebrated on the pitch after defeating Argentina 1–0 in the 1990 World Cup final.

Cup final after a violent encounter with Uruguay in the semis, a game in which two South Americans were sent off. England were the extra-time winners on that occasion, but four years later in Mexico West Germany had its revenge. The team recovered from 2–0 down to force extra-time, where Gerd Müller volleyed the winner. That put West Germany into the semis, where another 120 minutes against Italy proved too much. The score was 1–1 after 90 minutes, and with the players tiring in the heat five goals were scored in extra-time. Rivera got the winner as Germany went down 4–3. The 1970s West Germany side was outstanding, becoming European and World Champions in 1972 and 1974 respectively. Maier, Breitner, Müller and Beckenbauer were among the stars of an era in which Bayern Munich also won a hat-trick of European Cups. The 1974 World Cup saw West Germany lose to their Communist neighbours at the group stage. But in the final the team overcame the stars of Holland. Vogts shackled Cruyff and Müller hit the winner after both teams had scored from the spot. West Germany continued to show an extraordinary level of consistency. They were runners-up in the 1976 European Nations' Cup and winners for a second time four years later in Italy. In the mid-1980s Beckenbauer returned as coach. Despite having no experience of the job at club level, he guided West Germany to the World Cup final in 1986 and to victory at Italia '90. The wheel turned full circle in 1991 as the country became united once again. Matthias Sammer was the star of the former East Germany and he helped the reunited country to win Euro '96.

At Euro 2008 Germany added to their remarkable record of reaching major finals. A late Phillip Lahm goal put Turkey out in a five-goal semi-final thriller, and Germany were through to their sixth Euro championship final. They couldn't add to their tally of three wins against form side Spain, for whom Fernando Torres scored the only goal of the game.

Michael Ballack is jubilant after scoring the winning goal during the 2002 World Cup semi-final between Germany and South Korea.

Kader Abdel Coubadja of Togo pursues Ghana's Kuffour (right) in the African Nations Cup, 2000.

Ghana

Founded: 1957
Colours: Yellow; yellow; yellow
World Cup Appearances: 1
Honours: African Nations Cup winners: 1963, 1965, 1978, 1982

Ghana has won the African Nations Cup four times since the competition began in 1957. The Black Stars, as the team is known, first entered the tournament in 1963, winning it with a 3–2 victory over Tunisia. After retaining the trophy in 1965, it was hoped that Ghana would have secured a place at the 1966 World Cup, but FIFA refused the African Football Federation's request for an automatic place at the finals, and so no African side was allowed to participate in the qualifying round. Ghana also reached the African Nations Cup final in both 1968 and 1970, making it four in a row, but on these occasions the country finished runners-up. A 2–0 win over Uganda in 1978 brought Ghana its third African Nations Cup victory. The team beat Libya 7–6 on penalties in 1982, but lost out in 1992 11–10 on penalties to the Ivory Coast. The undoubted star of the modern era is Michael Essien, who was at the forefront of Ghana's drive to reach Germany

2006, the country's first appearance at the World Cup finals. The Black Stars impressed as they emerged from a tough group at the Czech Republic and USA's expense, while a 3–0 defeat against holders Brazil in the second round was a somewhat harsh result.

Greece

Founded: 1926
Colours: White; blue; white
World Cup Appearances: 1   **Best**: 1st round 1994
Honours: European Championship winners 2004

Greece secured a place at Euro 2004 coming top of their group qualifying for a major competition for only the third time in their history. However, few would have predicted that Greece, under new German coach Rehhagel, would knock out holders France in the quarter-final and then the much fancied team from the Czech Republic on their way to the final against the hosts Portugal. A well-drilled Greek defence managed to hold onto a 1-0 lead for most of the second half, preventing the Portuguese from scoring, and Greece won its first-ever trophy.

The big three Athens clubs – Panathinaikos, AEK and Olympiakos – have dominated the domestic championship and also proved difficult opposition for any visiting European teams. But Greek sides have rarely travelled well, and Panathinaikos's run in the 1971 European Cup remains the best achievement of a Greek club side in European competition. That was the runners-up spot, the team losing to an Ajax side that was about to embark on a hat-trick of victories.

The national side achieved little in its first 60 years. Greece's first international in 1920 was a 9–0 defeat by Sweden. Things got even worse in 1938 when Hungary beat the Greeks 11–1 in a World Cup qualifier. It wasn't until the

Greece's Trainos Dellas jumps in front of Sweden's Prica during a friendly international in 2003.

1980 European Championship that Greece made it to the finals. Professionalism had been introduced only a year earlier and the team went to Italy looking to launch the new era with a good performance. They found themselves in a difficult group including holders Czechoslovakia, Holland and West Germany. A goalless draw with the Germans was all Greece had to show for their efforts. USA '94 saw the Greeks qualify for their first and only World Cup to date. Three straight defeats meant a disappointing early exit. However, it was an improvement on 1974 when a 4–2 home defeat to Yugoslavia in a World Cup qualifier so incensed the Greek FA that the players were fined for their inept performance.

Guatemala

Founded: 1926
Colours: White/blue; blue; white
World Cup Appearances: 0
Honours: CONCACAF winners 1967

In the 1940s Guatemala was twice runner-up in the tournament to decide the champions of Central America and the Caribbean. When CONCACAF was formed in 1961, Guatemala became a founder member. The team won the CONCACAF Championship in 1967 and twice finished runners-up in that decade. Guatemala has struggled for success since then, though football is supported passionately. In October 1996 the febrile atmosphere before a World Cup qualifier against Costa Rica led to tragedy. The use of forged tickets was said to have filled Guatemala's stadium beyond capacity. A staircase collapsed and 81 fans were killed.

Haiti

Founded: 1904
Colours: Red; black; red
World Cup Appearances: 1 **Best**: 1st round 1974
Honours: CONCACAF winners 1957, 1973

Haiti's proudest moments in the game came in the early 1970s. Victory in the 1973 CONCACAF Championship earned the country entry to the following year's World Cup. They crashed out at the first hurdle in a powerful group, losing to Italy, Poland and Argentina. But in the opening fixture Emanuel Sanon briefly rocked Italy by scoring. Although the two-time world champions won the match 3–1, it was a result that proved costly as they went out to Argentina on goal difference.

Holland

Founded: 1889
Colours: Orange; white; orange
World Cup Appearances: 8 **Best**: Final 1974, 1978
Honours: European Nations' Cup winners 1988

For the number of outstanding players Holland has produced over the years the country has tended to fall short in terms of tournament success. The glorious exception came in 1988, when the likes of Gullit, Van Basten, Rijkaard and Koeman helped the Dutch to win the European Nations' Cup in style, beating the Soviet Union in the final. The man who masterminded that victory was returning hero Rinus Michels, the visionary coach who had introduced the concept of 'Total Football' at Ajax in the 1960s and to the national side thereafter. Under Michels Holland were outstanding in the 1974 World Cup, yet were beaten by West Germany in the final. By 1978 Michels and star player Johan Cruyff had gone but the Dutch were again in top form. However, they had to settle for runners-up spot once more as hosts Argentina ran out 3–1 winners in the final. Semi-final appearances at the 1976 European Naitons' Cup and the 1998 World Cup are Holland's best other finishes in a major tournament. As so often with Dutch sides, the one that played at France '98 won many plaudits for its quality and style yet lost, on that occasion on penalties to Brazil. Internal wrangling has also played its part. Edgar Davids was sent home during Euro '96, following a bust-up with coach Guus Hiddink. And in 2003 Ruud van Nistelrooy was dropped by Dick Advocaat after a spat following defeat by the Czech Republic in a European Championship qualifier. Holland needed a play-off victory to reach Euro 2004. The team was tipped to go all the way by many but fell to the hosts Portugal in the semis. The same opposition proved to be the stumbling block at Germany 2006, this time in an incendiary second-round encounter which saw the referee brandish four red cards and 16 yellows.

Holland established a national championship in 1898 and was one of FIFA's founder members in 1904. The country didn't embrace professionalism until the mid-1950s, though. Feyenoord won the

1992: (left–right) Marco Van Basten, Ruud Gullit, Frank Rijkaard, Dennis Bergkamp and Rob Witschge form a wall for a free kick.

Giovanni van Bronckhorst and Edgar Davids (left) of Holland battle with Darren Fletcher of Scotland during the qualifiers for Euro 2004.

country's first European trophy, the Champions Cup in 1970. Ajax succeeded them with a hat-trick of wins in the same competion, and PSV Eindhoven have also been crowned European champions. Between them these clubs have dominated the domestic scene for nearly 40 years. AZ 67 Alkmaar's title success in 1981 is the only time since 1964 that the championship hasn't gone to one of the big three.

Honduras

Founded: 1935
Colours: Blue; blue; blue
World Cup Appearances: 1 **Best**: 1st round 1982

Football was introduced to Honduras by the British and Spanish in the late 19th century. In the postwar era the country has hit the headlines only sporadically, and not always for the right reasons. Relations with neighbouring El Salvador were not good when the two sides met in a World Cup qualifier in 1969. Hostilities erupted into all-out war as El Salvador won the play-off, which eventually led to a place in the finals the following year. Honduras had to wait until 1982 for its debut on the biggest stage. There were worthy draws against Spain and Northern Ireland, but a 1–0 defeat by Yugoslavia meant an exit with honour. In 1991 Honduras finished runners-up to the USA in the inaugural CONCACAF Gold Cup. But probably the country's greatest moment came in the 2001 Copa America. The team showed great form in beating Bolivia and Uruguay at the group stage, setting up a quarter-final clash with Brazil. The four-time World Champions were out of sorts, but that couldn't detract from the Hondurans' superb 2–0 victory. In the semis the team went down by the same score to Colombia, who went on to win the trophy.

Hungary

Founded: 1901
Colours: Red; white; green
World Cup Appearances: 9   **Best**: Final 1938, 1954
Honours: Olympic winners 1952, 1964, 1968

Hungary's poor recent record in international football is a far cry from the time when it was one of the most powerful nations in the game. Three of its most famous clubs – MTK, Ferencvaros and Ujpest – were formed by the beginning of the 20th century. The country's FA was established in 1901, with Ferencvaros dominating the early years, when football was an amateur sport. In June 1908 England came to Budapest and gave the national team a 7–0 mauling, showing the superiority of the country that had helped to introduce the game to Hungary. Professionalism came in 1927, and in 1934 Hungary took part in its first World Cup. A quarter-final defeat against Hugo Meisl's Austrian 'Wunderteam' was a bad-tempered affair. Four years later Hungary qualified for the World Cup by beating Greece 11–1, a record margin. They romped into the final with a 5–1 win over Sweden. The star was centre-forward Gyorgy Sarosi, and he got on the scoresheet in the final against holders Italy. But Vittorio Pozzo's team ran out worthy 4–2 winners.

It was in the postwar era, under Communist rule, that Hungary enjoyed its greatest successes. All the talents and resources were allocated to Honved, a club that had had a modest record under its former name, Kispest. Having the star players together at club level reaped impressive rewards. Honved were Hungarian champions four times between 1950 and 1955. The performance of the national side was even more astonishing. The Mighty Magyars were beaten just once between 1950 and 1956. The team was led by Ferenc Puskas, but there were other outstanding players: Zoltan Czibor, Nandor Hidegkuti and Sandor Kocsis. Hungary won the 1952 Olympic title, and in November the following year came to Wembley and beat England 6–3. It was the first time England had lost to Continental opposition on home soil, and sweet revenge for 1908. A return fixture in Budapest in May 1954 was even more comprehensive, a 7–1 win for Hungary. The team went on to that summer's World Cup as hot favourites and marched all the way to the final, where they faced West Germany, a team they had beaten 8–3 at the group stage. The Hungarians went 2–0 up in the final, despite the fact that Puskas was carrying an injury. The Germans hit back to win 3–2. The end was nigh for this great side. Honved was on tour in Spain in 1956 when the uprising against Communist rule took place, and several of the team's stars, including Puskas, decided not to go home.

Hungary won the Olympic title twice in the 1960s, and the side that competed in the 1966 World Cup impressed on the way to a quarter-final defeat by the USSR.

1953 England v Hungary: Captains Ferenc Puskas (left) and Billy Wright lead out the teams at Wembley. England lost 6–3, their first home defeat by a Continental team. In the return match in Budapest Hungary won again, 7–1.

But since then Hungary has made just three cameo World Cup appearances, won only two of the nine games played and gone out in the first round each time.

Iran

Founded: 1920
Colours: Green; white; red
World Cup Appearances: 3   **Best**: 1st round 1978, 1998
Honours: Asian Cup winners 1968, 1972, 1976

Iran is one the strongest footballing countries in Asia. After winning a hat-trick of Asian Cups between 1968 and 1976, Iran made its first World Cup appearance in 1978. The team finished bottom of its group but stunned Scottish fans by taking a point off their side, a result that effectively cost the Scots a place in the second round. In 1998 Iran beat Oceania Champions Australia for a place at that year's World Cup in France. Once again it was an early exit but there was a victory over the USA, one with political overtones. Iran also reached the play-offs for the 2002 World Cup, but this time lost out to the Republic of Ireland. There was consolation in the form of a 2–1 win over Japan in the final of the Asian Games, Iran's third win in four tournaments. The team also qualified for Germany 2006, where defeats against Mexico and Portugal meant they were eliminated by the time they shared the points with Angola in the final group game.

Israel

Founded: 1928
Colours: White; blue; white
World Cup Appearances: 1   **Best**: 1st round 1970
Honours: Asian Championship winners 1964

Football in Israel has been dogged by political interference. The country finished runners-up in the inaugural Asian Cup in 1956. The result was skewed by the fact that the competition was organized on a league basis and both Pakistan and Afghanistan refused to play the Israelis. The country was also runner-up in 1960 and 1968, and won the trophy in 1964. These successes were also overshadowed by the political situation. Israel made its only World Cup appearance to date in 1970. Draws against Italy and Sweden meant an early exit but certainly no disgrace. After yet more withdrawals at the 1974 Asian Games, which again helped Israel to reach the final, matters came to a head. The Asian Football Federation expelled Israel, and for some time the country became affiliated to the Oceania countries. In 1992 Israel was admitted to UEFA and has since competed in Europe. Avi Cohen, Ronnie Rosenthal and Eyal Berkovic are among those who have made their mark on the top flight of English football, while the current squad includes Chelsea's Tal Ben Haim and Liverpool midfielder Yossi Benayoun.

Roy Keane of the Republic of Ireland in action against Iran during the World Cup qualifying play-off in 2001.

Italy

Founded: 1898
Colours: Blue; white; blue
World Cup Appearances: 16   **Best**: Winners 1934, 1938, 1982, 2006
Honours: European Championship winners 1968; Olympic winners 1936

Italy has competed in 15 of the 17 World Cups, reaching the final on five occasions and winning the tournament three times. Only Brazil has a better record, Italy vying with Germany for the second most successful country in the history of world football. The Italians' list of credits also includes two appearances in the European Championship final, with one victory, in 1968. At club level the three major European trophies have gone to Italian sides on 26 occasions.

Association football arrived in Italy in the late 19th century, although a forerunner of the modern game was already ingrained in the culture. Harpastum – in which two teams competed on a rectangle of land, each trying to kick or carry a ball over the opponent's line – was a game dating back to Ancient Rome. The Italian FA was established in 1898, and an early countrywide championship was organized in the same year. Regional football was stronger at this time, however, and it would take a generation for the national competition to take hold.

The championship was revamped in 1930, and a top division was established. With it came professionalism. The passion was already there, from big business as well as ordinary fans. The link between some of the giant corporations and football dates from this time and continues to the present.

Italy's first crack at the World Cup came in 1934 on home soil. The Azzurri, as the national side is known, won the Jules Rimet Trophy with a 2–1 win over Czechoslovakia in the final, although the key match was the 1–0 victory over Austria's 'Wunderteam' in the semis. The man who masterminded the victory was coach Vittorio Pozzo, and with a rebuilt side he led Italy to victory four years later in France too.

The outbreak of war meant that Italy had to wait 12 years to defend its title. At the 1950 tournament the country was still reeling from the loss of a number of its star players. All but one of the Torino first-team squad – the outstanding side of the era – had been

killed in a plane crash the year before. A 3–2 defeat to Sweden in only a three-team pool meant early elimination.

Fierce domestic competition led the top club sides to pay big money for overseas stars. Brazil's Jose Altafini and Argentina's Omar Sivori were among the first to be lured to the glamour and wealth of the Italian top division, a trend that is still much in evidence. Both Altafini and Sivori also played international football for their adopted country, although Italy enjoyed much greater success at club level for most of the 1950s and 1960s. The team lost to Switzerland in a group play-off in 1954, and a 2–1 defeat against Northern Ireland in January 1958 meant that Italy missed out on that year's World Cup tournament, the last time that the country has failed to reach the finals.

Chile 1962 saw the Italians eliminated after a 2–0 defeat by the hosts in what was one of the most disgraceful international matches ever seen, littered with acts of violence. Four years later Italy suffered the ignominy of a first-round exit after a 1–0 defeat by the minnows of North Korea, for which the team was pelted with rotten fruit on its return home.

By now Italian sides had developed and perfected the 'catenaccio' or 'bolted gate' defensive system. Italian football boasted some star midfielders and forwards, including

Altobelli of Italy (right) beats Germany's Karl–Heinz Forster to the ball in the 1982 World Cup final.

Italian captain Fabio Cannavaro holds the World Cup trophy amid his teammates after the 2006 World Cup final.

Mazzola, Riva and Rivera. But it was defenders such as Facchetti who seemed to epitomize the country's footballing style. It brought success, however. Italy was crowned European Champions in 1968 and finished runners-up to Brazil in the World Cup two years later. In the 1970s success proved harder to come by, both at club and country level. The Azzurri reached the semi-final at the 1978 World Cup, while Juventus and AC Milan won the 1977 UEFA Cup and 1973 Cup Winners' Cup respectively.

The glory days returned in 1982, when Enzo Bearzot's side, spearheaded by Paolo Rossi, brought the World Cup back to Italy for a third time. The Italians looked strong contenders for a fourth victory on home soil in 1990 but went out on penalties to holders Argentina in the semis. In 1994 the team suffered further shoot-out agony, this time against Brazil in the final. Roberto Baggio, the team's star player and one of the best in the world, was the man who missed the vital spot-kick.

At both France '98 and Euro 2000 Italy went down to the eventual winners France. It was another shoot-out defeat in 1998, while in 2000 Italy were seconds away from being crowned European Champions for a second time. A late Sylvain Wiltord goal took the game into extra time, when David Trezeguet's golden goal won the trophy for France. Trapattoni's side crashed out of the 2002 World Cup to another golden goal, this time from South Korea's Jung Hwan Ahn. It was no consolation that he, like Trezeguet, was plying his trade at club level in Italy. At Euro 2004 Italy bemoaned the 2–2 draw between Sweden and Denmark, a result which saw both sides go through the to knockout stage at Italy's expense.

More than half of the Azzurri squad that went to Germany 2006 played for clubs embroiled in a corruption scandal, yet under Marcello Lippi the team put aside domestic concerns to win the World Cup for a fourth time, beating France on penalties in the final.

Ivory Coast

Founded: 1960
Colours: Orange White Green
World Cup Appearances: 1 **Best**: 1st round 2006
Honours: Africa Cup of Nations winners 1992

With a side boasting an array of Premiership stars, Ivory Coast has enjoyed a rapid rise up the Fifa rankings in recent years, breaking into the top twenty in 2006. That was the year the 'Elephants' took their World Cup bow, their line-up including Didier Zokora, Salomon Kalou, Emmanuel Eboue and Kolo Toure, as well as all-time leading scorer Didier Drogba. The team impressed in the tournament's 'Group of Death', losing by the odd goal to Argentina and Holland before overturning a 2–0 deficit against Serbia and Montenegro to chalk up a maiden victory on the biggest stage. Ivory Coast claimed its sole piece of silverware with an Africa Cup of Nations victory in 1992, a success noteworthy for providing the highest scoring penalty shoot-out of any major final in international competition. The team beat Ghana 11–10 after neither side managed a goal in regulation time.

Japan

Founded: 1921
Colours: Blue; white; blue
World Cup Appearances: 3 **Best**: 2nd round 2002
Honours: Asian Cup winners 1992, 2000, 2004

Although the Japanese FA was founded in 1921, it is in the last decade that the greatest strides have been made on the field. A 1–0 victory over holders Saudi Arabia in the final of the Asian Cup in 1992 marked Japan's first tournament success. The J-League was established the following year. Although the domestic game boasted many high-profile imports, including Zico and Gary Lineker, the fans soon had their own stars to cheer. Japan just missed out on a place at USA '94 and finally made their first World Cup appearance in France four years later. Defeats against Argentina and Croatia were hardly surprising, but less predictable was the defeat by the Jamaicans,

who were also making their debut in the tournament. In 2004 Japan beat China in the Asian Cup Final, the country's third win in four tournaments. As joint hosts of the 2002 World Cup the team, now led by experienced coach Philippe Troussier, didn't need to qualify. Japan surprised many by topping a group including Belgium and Russia before losing to Turkey 1–0 in the second round. Hidetoshi Nakata confirmed his reputation as a world-class midfielder, while Juanichi Inamoto, who had been kicking his heels at Arsenal, showed what he could do given the chance. His form on the biggest stage earned him a move to Fulham shortly afterwards. Troussier stepped down after the World Cup and when his successor, Zico, guided the team to Asian Cup glory in 2004, hopes were high for the World Cup in Germany. However, Japan propped up a group including Brazil, with just a point gained from a draw with Croatia.

Hidetoshi Nakata (right) of Japan tackles Hakan Unsal of Turkey during the 2002 World Cup finals.

Korea

Founded: 1928
Colours: Red; red; red
World Cup Appearances: 7 **Best**: 4th 2002
Honours: Asian Cup winners 1956, 1960

A Korean Football Association was established in 1928, but the game had little time to flourish in a united country. Since the division of the land in 1948 South Korea has enjoyed much greater success. Winners of the Asian Cup in 1956 and 1960 and finalists on three other occasions, South Korea has also featured in six World Cups. In the first three of those – 1954, 1986 and 1990, the team finished as group wooden spoonists. USA '94 was much more encouraging. The team drew with both Spain and Bolivia and only went down to reigning champions Germany 3–2. France '98 also ended in early disappointment, although the South Koreans did find themselves in a strong group. It was as co-hosts of the 2002 tournament that the country made a significant leap forward.

Under Guus Hiddink the team played a high-tempo pressing game and topped a group including Portugal and Poland. Pin-up boy Jung Hwan Ahn then provided the country with its greatest ever footballing moment, a golden goal header that accounted for Italy in the second round. The team enjoyed the rub of the green in beating Spain on penalties in the quarter-final, after the game had ended goalless. The glorious run was ended by Germany at the semi-final stage, but South Korea had already made history by becoming the first Asian country to get to the last four in a World Cup.

North Korea briefly eclipsed its southern neighbours in 1966 with an heroic effort at that year's World Cup. Pak Doo Ik scored to give the country a famous 1–0 win over Italy. Having already drawn with Chile, North Korea went through to the quarter-final. At Goodison Park the North Koreans rocked Portugal, one of the tournament favourites, by taking a three-goal lead. But with Eusebio in inspired form, the Portuguese hit back to win 5–3.

Players from Turkey and South Korea embrace each other after the 2002 World Cup third place play-off match that was won by Turkey 3–2.

George Weah of Liberia.

Latvia

Founded: 1921
Colours: Red; white; red
World Cup Appearances: 0

Latvia regained its independence in 1991, ending a 50-year period under the Soviet sphere of influence. Since then domestic football has been dominated by Skonto Riga, who have been champions every year. Internationally the Latvian side has started to impress. The team qualified for Euro 2004, its first major championship, after finishing runner-up to Sweden in the qualifying series. Latvia finished ahead of Poland and Hungary, countries with much bigger footballing reputations. The team then scored an impressive 3-2 aggregate victory over World Cup semi-finalists Turkey in the play-offs and were far from disgraced in Portugal.

Liberia

Founded: 1936
Colours: Blue/white; white; blue/white
World Cup Appearances: 0

Liberian football is synonymous with one name: that of George Weah. Weah became the country's greatest footballing export, winning the World, European and African Footballer of the Year awards. Weah never forgot his roots, however, and in recent years he has often used his personal wealth to help fund Liberia's preparations for some of the big tournaments. As a player, Weah signed off after Liberia's exit at the group stage in the 2002 African Nations Cup.

Macedonia

Founded: 1992
Colours: Red; red; red
World Cup Appearances: 0

Macedonia emerged from the fragmentation of Yugoslavia in 1991. Its Football Association was formed the following year and both UEFA and FIFA membership was granted in 1994. Since its first international match in 1993 – a 4–1 win over another fledgling state, Slovenia – Macedonia has failed to make an impact on the international stage. The country finished a long way off the pace behind England and Turkey in the Euro 2004 qualifiers. However, there were some optimistic signs. In October 2002 the team went down narrowly to Turkey 2–1, and a few days later took a 2–1 lead against England at St Mary's Stadium, Southampton. Steven Gerrard hit an equalizer, but an away draw against the 2002 World Cup quarter-finalists represented one of the country's best results to date.

Mexico

Founded: 1927
Colours: Green; white; green
World Cup Appearances: 13 **Best**: Quarter-finals 1970, 1986
Honours: CONCACAF winners 1965, 1971, 1977, 1993, 1996, 1998, 2003; Confederations Cup winners 1999

One of the powerhouses of CONCACAF, Mexico has produced teams that have done well on the world stage. Germany 2006 was Mexico's 13th appearance in the World Cup finals, which the country has hosted twice. And it was on home soil in 1970 and 1986 that Mexico enjoyed its best moments. In 1970 the team dropped just one point at the group stage and reached the last eight, losing 4–1 to eventual runners-up Italy. Sixteen years later Mexico again notched five points out of six in the opening phase, and then beat Bulgaria in the second round. The team's star was Real Madrid striker Hugo Sanchez. Germany provided the quarter-final opposition this time and they squeezed through on penalties. Mexico's 1990 World Cup ended before it began, the team barred for fielding ineligible players in a youth tournament. At USA '94 Mexico topped an extraordinary group in which all four teams had the same number of points and the same goal difference. It was another agonizing shoot-out defeat in the second round, this time against Bulgaria. Germany again proved to be too strong at France '98, where Cuauhtemoc Blanco emerged as a new star.

At Japan and Korea 2002 some scintillating play suggested that Mexico might finally reach the quarter-finals for the first time on foreign soil. They were up against the USA, arch-rivals in CONCACAF, with whom they had shared the honours in the qualifying series. It was a bruising encounter, won 2–0 by the Americans.

The CONCACAF championship was revamped in 1991 and renamed the Gold Cup. Mexico enjoyed a hat-trick of wins in the biennial tournament, including victory over Brazil in the 1996 final. In 1993 Mexico, along with the USA, was invited to compete in the Copa America. The Mexican side reached the final at the first attempt, but a brace from Gabriel Batistuta won the match for Argentina. After semi-final appearances in 1997 and 1999, Mexico reached the final again in 2001, this time going down 1–0 to Colombia. In 2003 Mexico again beat Brazil in the CONCACAF Gold Cup final, although Brazil had entered its under-23 squad.

Coach Javier Aguirre resigned after the 2002 World Cup and was replaced by former Argentina international 'keeper Ricardo Lavolpe, who was brought in to lead the country through to Germany 2006. Lavolpe found himself up against his native country in a titanic second-round clash, where Mexico's skipper, Barcelona star Rafael Marquez, opened the scoring before Argentina snatched victory in extra-time. Lavolpe stepped down, replaced by Hugo Sanchez, the most illustrious name in Mexican football. He lasted barely a year, and his replacement, Sven-Goran Eriksson, was sacked after one season in charge.

Cannavaro of Italy wins the header against Blanco of Mexico during the 2002 World Cup finals.

Morocco

Founded: 1955
Colours: Red; green; red
World Cup Appearances: 4
Best: 2nd round 1986
Honours: African Nations Cup winners 1976

In 1970 Morocco became the first African side to reach a World Cup. A draw against Bulgaria and a narrow 2–1 defeat by West Germany represented a fine showing, although it wasn't enough to lift the team off the bottom of the table. Six years later Morocco won its only African Nations Cup. In an experimental one-off league format, Morocco faced title rivals Guinea in the final match. Guinea took the lead but a Morocco equalizer four minutes from time allowed the North African side to win the trophy by a single point. Morocco were African Nations Cup semi-finalists three times in the 1980s and lost 2–1 to Tunisia in the 2004

Zi'ed Jaziri of Tunisia and Talal El Karkouri of Morocco (right) during the 2004 African Nations Cup final.

final, but the country's best moment came in 1986 when it went to Mexico for its second World Cup appearance. The African side topped a strong group including England, Portugal and Poland. Runners-up England went on to face Paraguay in the second round, while Morocco were somewhat unfortunate in having to face West Germany in Monterrey. A Lothar Matthaus free-kick two minutes from time decided the match. USA '94 was less memorable, Morocco losing all three of their games. But the appointment of former France and Cameroon coach Henri Michel the following year revived the country's fortunes. Michel's team was unbeaten in qualifying for France '98 and acquitted itself well in the finals. Mustapha Hadji was one of the tournament's stars. His exhilarating performances won him the African Player of the Year award and made him the country's best-known player since Just Fontaine in the 1950s. The highlight for Morocco was a 3–0 win over Scotland, although it wasn't enough to prevent Norway from edging the African side for the runners-up spot behind Brazil.

New Zealand

Founded: 1938
Colours: White; black; green
World Cup Appearances: 1   **Best**: 1st round 1982

Competitive football in New Zealand dates back to the 1920s, although in the face of competition from the likes of rugby and cricket it has remained a second-string sport. New Zealand has won the Oceania Cup three times. It has contested the last three finals, all against Australia. The Kiwi team has had the edge, winning in both 1998 and 2002. Success in this competition has not led to automatic World Cup qualification. Under current rules a play-off against either a South American or European side has been necessary, a system that has militated against representation from Oceania in recent years. New Zealand has made just one World Cup appearance, Spain '82. It proved to be a difficult baptism, the team losing all three games and conceding 12 goals.

Nigeria

Founded: 1945
Colours: Green; white; green
World Cup Appearances: 3　**Best**: 2nd round 1994, 1998
Honours: African Nations Cup winners 1980, 1994; Olympic winners 1996

Nigeria's first success came as recently as 1980, when the country won its first African Nations Cup. Since then Nigerian football has made enormous strides and the Super Eagles have not only become one of Africa's strongest teams but have also made their mark on the world stage. Nigeria were African Nations Cup runners-up in 1984 and 1988. Between 1985 and 1993 the country reached the final of the World Under-17 Championship four times, winning the tournament twice. The 1993 side included Nwankwo Kanu and Celestine Babayaro, who would go on to make an impact on the Premiership.

In 1994 Super Eagles completed a memorable double: a second African Nations Cup victory and a first appearance at the World Cup. Nigeria topped a strong group including Argentina before going down to Italy in extra-time in the second round. Security concerns led Nigeria to withdraw from the 1996 African Nations Cup, which was belatedly switched to South Africa. However, an Under-23 side captained by Kanu won that year's Olympic title in Atlanta. In the final Nigeria overcame an Argentine team that included Claudio Lopez and Hernan Crespo.

At France '98 Nigeria were a known quantity, no longer able to catch teams cold. Even so, the Super Eagles again topped a strong group, including Spain, Paraguay and Bulgaria. The team was well beaten in the second round though, Denmark running out 4–1 winners.

In 2000 Nigeria were back in the African Nations Cup final, beaten by Cameroon on penalties. The team went into the 2002 World Cup after a semi-final defeat in the same competition by Senegal, a game in which they had two players red carded. Japan and Korea proved to be an anti-climax, Nigeria finishing bottom of the 'Group of Death'.

Juan Veron of Argentina tackles Nigeria's Jay Jay Okocha during the group stages of the 2002 World Cup Finals.

Northern Ireland

Founded: 1880

Colours: Green; white; green

World Cup Appearances: 3   **Best**: Quarter-finals 1958

Northern Ireland has the third oldest league and cup competitions in the world and has been playing international football since 1883. That was when the country was united, of course. Partition in the 1920s left the six counties with a relatively small pool to choose from. However, selection remained a grey area for decades. Irish players were still allowed to turn out for both Northern Ireland and the Republic, Manchester United's Johnny Carey being among the most famous of the players to do just that in the early postwar years. In 1954 FIFA finally closed this loophole. It was in this decade that Northern Ireland enjoyed some notable successes. There were a number of excellent results in the Home International Championship and an historic first victory over England. That came in November 1957, the Irish running out 3–2 winners at Wembley. A superb victory over Italy in the World Cup qualifiers helped a Northern Ireland side including Danny Blanchflower and

Billy Bingham and coached by Peter Doherty reached the quarter-finals. Ravaged by injuries, the Irish finally capitulated to France 4–0.

By the time Northern Ireland made it to another World Cup in 1982 the country's greatest ever player, and one of the best of all time, had begun and ended his career. George Best lit up British football in the 1960s but the international side achieved little either in that decade or the next. It was only when former player Billy Bingham took over as manager that the glory days returned. In 1980 Northern Ireland won the Home International championship outright for only the second time in history. At Spain '82 Gerry Armstrong's goal against Spain in the final group match took the country into the second round. Unfortunately, France was again the stumbling block, the all-star line-up of Les Bleus proving too strong in the second-phase round-robin. Had an early Martin O'Neill goal not been ruled out – a seemingly harsh decision – things might have been even better. Even so, the team had acquitted itself superbly, and in Norman Whiteside – just 17 years 42 days – the country now boasted the youngest ever World Cup player, a record previously held by Pele. It was a player at the other end of the age scale that made the news at Mexico '86.

Northern Ireland's footballing brothers Jackie (left) and Danny Blanchflower during a training session in 1957.

Norway

Norman Whiteside in action for Northern Ireland in 1985.

Founded: 1902

Colours: Red; white; blue/white

World Cup Appearances: 3   **Best**: 2nd round 1998

A football league was established in Norway as early as 1902, but for much of the past century the country has been a poor relation in Scandinavia as regards success on the pitch. Norway's first international match, in 1908, was an 11–3 thrashing by Sweden. The Norwegians' first taste of success came in the mid-1930s. The team upset Adolf Hitler by beating Germany in the 1936 Olympic Games, only to lose to Italy in the semi-final. Norway beat Poland to take the bronze medal. There was no professionalism in the country, so it was much the same group of amateurs who went to the 1938 World Cup in France. Norway, who qualified by beating the Republic of Ireland, found themselves up against holders Italy in what was a straight knockout tournament. The Italians went ahead, but Norway hit back, having previously struck the woodwork three times. The game went into extra-time and Italy were grateful to star striker Silvio Piola for the winner.

It wasn't until the 1990s that Norway made another significant impact on the international scene. The improvement in fortunes coincided with the appointment of Egil Olsen. Olsen's team employed simple but effective tactics: a high-tempo pressing game when defending and getting the ball forward quickly after winning possession. Norway qualified for USA '94 after topping a group

Pat Jennings played his 119th and final game for Northern Ireland on his 41st birthday. It came in the country's final group match, a 3–0 defeat by Brazil.

Since then Northern Ireland has had a thin time on the international stage. From the 1950s to the 1980s the team invariably boasted one or two world-class players. A lack of such talent in recent years was reflected in the qualifying series for Euro 2004. Northern Ireland finished bottom of their group, behind Spain, Greece, Ukraine and Armenia. The team had failed to find the net once during the campaign and coach Sammy McIlroy resigned shortly afterwards. Under new boss Lawrie Sanchez Northern Ireland immediately ended the goal drought, albeit in a defeat by Norway. However, just three draws from six games left Sanchez's men well off the pace in the World Cup 2006 qualifiers.

David Healy scored a record 13 goals in the Euro 2008 qualifiers, beating the mark set by Davor Suker. A 3–2 home win over Spain was the highlight – Healy grabbing a hat-trick – but at the business end of the qualifiers the team was edged into third place behind Spain and Sweden.

Norway's Tore-Andre Flo.

including England, Holland and Poland. The team finished bottom of their group, but Olsen's men were unlucky. They had an identical record and goal difference to the other three teams and only lost out on goals scored. Four years later at France '98 Norway enjoyed a famous 2–1 win over Brazil, although the South Americans had already qualified. Norway made it through to the knockout phase, where Italy again halted their progress. Christian Vieri hit his fifth goal of the tournament and Norway were out.

Olsen stepped down but it didn't halt the country's progress. In 2000 Norway qualified for the finals of the European Championship for the first time. There was a good win over Spain, but the team failed to reach the second round on goal difference.

Norway has also had success at club level. Perennial champions Rosenborg have been regulars in the Champions League, and in 1996–97 qualified for the quarter-final at the expense of AC Milan. A 3–1 defeat by holders Juventus represented a remarkable achievement. Like all Norwegian clubs, Rosenborg faced the ongoing problem of seeing its best players lured away to stronger and richer leagues. Many Norwegians have played in the Premiership, including Ole-Gunnar Solskjaer, Tore Andre Flo, Henning Berg and Oyvind Leonhardsen.

Ole Gunnar Solskjaer scores a penalty for Norway.

Paraguay

Founded: 1906
Colours: Red/white; blue; blue
World Cup Appearances: 7   **Best**: 2nd round 1953, 1979, 2002
Honours: South American Championship winners 1953, 1979

For a small impoverished country with a tiny population, Paraguay has performed well in international competition. It won the South American Championship for the first time in 1953, beating Brazil 3–2 in the final. A second title came in 1979 with a play-off victory over Chile. The country has also qualified for the World Cup competition six times. In 1986 Paraguay went down 3–0 to England in the second round. They also made it to the knockout stage at France '98 and Japan and Korea 2002. On each occasion they were inspired by their talismanic goalkeeper Jose Luis Chilavert, the the man who fancies himself as a dead ball specialist as well as a shot stopper. In 1998 the team drew with Bulgaria and Spain, then beat Nigeria 3–1, although the African side had already qualified. It took a Laurent Blanc golden goal to end their interest in the second round. Paraguay qualified ahead of Brazil for the 2002 tournament. The team emerged from their group after a dramatic victory over Slovenia in their final match. It put the South Americans through ahead of South Africa by virtue of having scored one more goal, the two sides having identical records. The second round match against Germany was a dour affair, won by an Oliver Neuville goal in the dying minutes.

Paraguay's inspirational goalkeeper Jose Luis Chilavert.

Peru

Founded: 1922
Colours: White/red; white; white
World Cup Appearances: 4   **Best**: Quarter-finals 1970
Honours: South American Championship winners 1939, 1975

As was the case with so many South American countries, football was introduced into Peru by the British in the 19th century. The country was well off the pace compared to the continent's big three: Brazil, Argentina and Uruguay. It was Uruguay who provided Peru's first opposition in 1927. That ended in a 4–0 defeat, but Peru was still offered a place at the inaugural World Cup three years later. The Peruvians lost both their matches, to Uruguay and Romania. The game went professional in 1931, and in 1939 Peru became South American Champions. With the benefit of home advantage, Peru met Uruguay in the deciding match, the two sides level on points. Uruguay successfully managed to shackle star striker Teodoro Fernandez but still lost 2–1. It was the 16th championship and the first time that a country outside the big three had won.

Peruvian football experienced a drought for the next 30 years. It was when former Brazilian star Didi took over that the country embarked on its greatest period of success. The team made it to the quarter-final of the 1970 World Cup, losing 4–2 to Brazil. In 1975 Peru beat Colombia to claim its second South American Championship, renamed the Copa America that year. This success was somewhat undermined by the the dismissive attitude of the leading lights of South American football as far as this competition was concerned. The stars of the era were Teofilio Cubillas and Hector Chumpitaz, Peru's most prolific goalscorer and most capped player respectively. At the 1978 World Cup Peru reached the second round, but in the mini-league things went badly. After

Paraguay lined up against England again at Germany 2006, a game settled by a Carlos Gamarra own goal from a Beckham free kick. Another 1–0 defeat, against Sweden, rendered the 2–0 win over Trinidad and Tobago academic. Many of the team's veterans – including Chilavert – retired after the tournament, though star striker Roque Santa Cruz should be around for some time. He impressed in his debut season in the Premiership with Blackburn, following a move from Bayern Munich in summer 2007.

defeats by Brazil and Poland, Peru were playing merely for pride against an Argentine side that needed a four-goal win to reach the final. The hosts won 6–0, equalling Peru's worst-ever defeat. It was a result that left a sour taste in the mouths of Brazilian fans and many regarded it with suspicion. By 1982, Peru's fourth and last World Cup appearance thus far, the team's stars of the previous decade had gone and it fell at the first hurdle, finishing bottom of a group including Poland, Italy and Cameroon.

Poland

Founded: 1919
Colours: White; red; white/red
World Cup Appearances: 6   **Best**: 3rd 1974, 1982
Honours: Olympic winners 1972

Football was played in Poland long before the birth of the country. KS Cracovia, Poland's oldest club, was formed in 1906, 12 years before the Polish state emerged from the ashes of World War One. The country's FA was formed the following year and a national league was established in 1921. After World War Two Poland fell under the Soviet sphere of influence and football followed a pattern familiar to many Soviet satellite states. In 1970 Gornik came close to bringing Poland its first piece of silverware in European competition. Gornik put out Roma in the semi-final of the Cup Winners' Cup, although they needed the toss of a coin to do so, the

Jerzy Dudek in action for Poland.

teams locked at 3–3 after a play-off. The Gornik side, including the giant blond defender Jerzy Gorgon and striker Wlodek Lubanski, went down to Manchester City 2–1 in the final, the closest any Polish team has come to winning a major European trophy.

The national side went on to take Olympic gold in 1972, ushering in the most successful period in the country's history. In 1973 the Poles broke the hearts of England fans by qualifying for the following year's World Cup tournament in West Germany. But a side including Lato, Szarmach and Deyna, as well as Gorgon and Lubanski, lit up the 1974 competition with some sparkling performances. There were victories over Italy and Argentina at the group stage and only a Gerd Müller goal for West Germany prevented the Poles from making it to the final.

Poland topped their group in Argentina in 1978 but in the second round came up against a strong group including Brazil and the hosts. At Spain '82 the Poles opened their account with a goalless draw against Italy. Five games later the two teams met again in the semi-final, a brace from Paolo Rossi proving decisive. Poland were unfortunate in having their star, Zbigniew Boniek, suspended for the encounter. Even so, it meant that the country finished third in two out of three World Cups.

Since then Poland has struggled to repeat the successes of those heady days. Jerzy Engel's side made it to the 2002 World Cup but was hugely disappointing. Liverpool 'keeper Jerzy Dudek was just one of several players out of form as the team was eliminated at the group stage, beaten by both South Korea and Portugal. Engel was replaced by former star Boniek, but he failed to get the Poles through the qualifying group for Euro 2004. The team made it to the World Cup in Germany two years later, but lost out to Ecuador for the group runners-up spot behind the hosts.

Portugal

Founded: 1914
Colours: Red; white; red
World Cup Appearances: 4   **Best**: 3rd 1966

Portugal may have been dubbed the Brazil of Europe, but while its tradition for flair and skill is out of the South American mould, the Portuguese have largely failed to translate this style into success on the pitch.

It was Lisbon's English residents who brought the game to the country in the 1870s. Boavista, Porto, Sporting Lisbon and Benfica were all formed in the early years of the 20th century. A national FA was set up in 1914, and Portugal

Luis Figo for Portugal is chased by Paul Scholes during an international friendly against England in 2004.

played its first international in 1921, losing 3–1 to Spain in Madrid. At the 1928 Olympics Portugal lost to Egypt, and in May 1947 England came to Lisbon and handed the team a 10–0 thrashing, the country's worst-ever defeat.

It was in the 1960s that Portugal finally enjoyed some success. Benfica took over Real Madrid's mantle as Europe's top club, reaching the European Cup final five times and winning the trophy twice. Sporting Lisbon won the Cup Winners' Cup in 1964, adding to the country's roll of honour. The big three clubs provided a powerful squad that went to England in 1966 for Portugal's World Cup debut. Having eased through their group, beating both Hungary and Brazil, the team looked like falling victim to one of the greatest shocks ever. Portugal went three behind against North Korea in the quarter-final at Goodison Park. Star player Eusebio almost single-handedly led the fightback,

scoring four in a 5–3 victory. It was a new individual scoring record for a World Cup game. The semi-final against England was a very sporting affair. Eusebio scored from the spot, but this time it wasn't enough, Bobby Charlton having already twice found the back of the net. Portugal beat the USSR in the third-place play-off, and Eusebio had the consolation of being the tournament's hotshot, with nine goals in five games.

The 1970s was a lean time for Portuguese football. The next highlight came in 1984, when Portugal reached its second major semi-final. A Michel Platini goal in the last minute of extra time won the game for France. Two years later Portugal made it to their second World Cup. It started well, Carlos Manuel scoring the only goal of the game against England. But defeats by Poland and Morocco followed and Portugal were out. A year later Porto provided a much-needed fillip by winning the European Cup, and at the end of the decade, Carlos Queiroz assembled a youth team which twice won the World Championship for that age group. Rui Costa, Joao Pinto and Luis Figo were among the stars of that outstanding side. In the 1990s, as these talented young players matured, Portugal was regularly tipped to do well in the big tournaments. A quarter-final place at Euro '96 and the semis at Euro 2000 was the best it could manage. The 2002 World Cup was seen as a chance for many of the stars of the era to win a major trophy. They were on top form in the qualifiers, but in Korea the Portuguese went behind to both the USA and South Korea, and this time there was no 1966-like comeback. However, as hosts of Euro 2004, Portugal reached the final, losing 1-0 to Greece. At Germany 2006 Portugal breezed through to the knockout stage, where they were involved in some controversial encounters. Deco and Costinha were among the four players ordered off in a tempestuous second-round clash with Holland, which was won by a Maniche strike. Portugal then saw off England in a shoot-out, a game in which Wayne Rooney was red carded for a stamping incident involving Ricardo Carvalho. The team's luck ran out against France in the semis, where Zidane's penalty separated the sides. Ricardo, Carvalho, Maniche and Figo all made it into the select 'All Star Squad', while Portugal were voted the tournament's most entertaining team.

Robbie Keane celebrates the Republic of Ireland's equalizer against Germany in the 2002 World Cup finals.

Portugal's Pedro Miguel Pauleta.

Republic of Ireland

Founded: 1921
Colours: Green; white; green
World Cup Appearances: 3   **Best**: Quarter-finals 1990

From the partition of Ireland in 1921 until the 1970s football in the Republic of Ireland suffered from the preferential treatment given to the traditional games of hurling and Gaelic football, an institutionalized bias that went right up to government level. Even so, the Republic had been willing competitors. A 1–0 win over Bulgaria in May 1924 marked the Republic's debut on the international scene. In 1931 the team lost 5–0 in Dublin to a Spanish side that had itself been thrashed 7–1 by England a few days earlier. Undeterred, the

Republic was soon on the World Cup trail, and has qualified three times since 1934. The country's first major success came with a 2–0 win over England at Goodison Park in September 1949. This victory came four years before Hungary's famous 6–3 win at Wembley and so technically it was the Republic, not Puskas and Co., who became the first foreign team to win on English soil.

The relaxation of the eligibility rules in the 1970s made a huge difference to the Republic's footballing fortunes. Michael Robinson, who played for Brighton and Liverpool, was able to don the green shirt by dint of his great-grandmother's Irish roots. Andy Townsend, John Aldridge and Ray Houghton were other top English League players who achieved international status by such tenuous but perfectly legitimate means. The arch-exponent of the loose eligibility rules was Jack Charlton, who was appointed coach in 1986. Two years later the Republic reached the finals of the European Championship. Although they went out at the group stage, there was the satisfaction of finishing ahead of England, whom they had beaten with a rare Ray Houghton header.

Two World Cup adventures followed. At Italia '90 Charlton's men enjoyed a superb run which ended in a 1–0 defeat against the hosts in the quarter-final. Four years later the Republic qualified ahead of Italy but went down to Holland in the second round. Charlton stood down after the team failed to reach Euro '96, his place in the record books and Irish fans' affections secure. Under former captain Mick McCarthy the team made it to the 2002 World Cup, coming through a group at Holland's expense. After play-off victory over Iran, McCarthy's men went to Japan and Korea for their third World Cup campaign. It started disastrously as Roy Keane walked out over a spat with his manager over facilities and organization. The team recovered from the blow of losing its one world-class player to finish group runners-up. Three missed penalties in a second-round shoot-out against Spain ended another creditable performance. McCarthy stood down soon afterwards. His successor, Brian Kerr, failed to get the Republic to Euro 2004, and although the team lost just one Germany 2006 qualifier, a spate of draws in a tight group wasn't enough to make the finals. Kerr was replaced with the country's most capped player, Steve Staunton, in January 2006. A 1–0 defeat in Germany in his first competitive game was no disgrace, but dropping five points against Cyprus proved disastrous in a group that also included the Czech Republic. Staunton made way for seasoned campaigner Giovanni Trapattoni as the FAI looked beyond its shores for a coach with the Midas touch.

Roy Keane is tackled by Portugal's Rui Costa during the World Cup qualifier at Lansdowne Road in June 2001.

Romania

Founded: 1908
Colours: Yellow; blue; red
World Cup Appearances: 7　**Best**: Quarter-finals 1994

Romania was in the vanguard of the Eastern European countries when it came to absorbing football into its cultural fabric. The fact that Prince Carol, the heir to the throne, was so keen on the game helped it to become established in the early years of the 20th century. In 1930 the same man, now King Carol, was instrumental in enabling Romania to compete in the inaugural World Cup, one of only four European teams to do so. He made sure the players suffered no financial loss from their journey to Uruguay and was rewarded when his countrymen beat Peru 3–1. A 4–0 defeat against the hosts and eventual winners ended their involvement. Romania also competed in 1934 and 1938, losing to Czechoslovakia and Cuba respectively. Success in the postwar period proved elusive for a long time. Romania qualified for Mexico 1970 but found themselves in a strong group including holders England and favourites Brazil. They lost to both. In 1984 Romania made it to the finals of the European Championship for the first time but finished bottom of a group including Spain, Portugal and West Germany. A more significant event occurred two years later, when Steaua Bucharest became the first Eastern bloc side to win the European Cup. Romania's army team finished runners-up three years later too, and it was its success which sparked the national side's strong showing in the 1990s. Former Steaua boss Emerich Jenei took over as Romania's coach and led the country to the knockout stage at Italia '90. A penalty shoot-out defeat against the Republic of Ireland ended their run. Marius Lacatus was the star, and Gheorghe Hagi also made a name for himself. Four years later the Romanians were impressive again, beating Argentina in the second round before going out on penalties, this time to Sweden, in the quarter-final. Ilie Dumitrescu and Gica Popescu, who both went on to play for Spurs, were on top form, while Hagi confirmed his reputation as the 'Maradona of the Carpathians'. Romania slumped at Euro '96, although they were somewhat unlucky to have a goal disallowed against France, a game they lost 1–0. At France '98 Romania reached the second round for the third successive time, having topped a group including England. A Davor Suker penalty for Croatia ended their hopes. At Euro 2000 Romania again beat England in a major tournament, but goals from Totti and Inzaghi in the last eight meant that Italy went on to the semis. By now the golden period seemed to be drawing to a close as many of Romania's gifted stars were approaching veteran status. Even so, it was something of a surprise when the team lost a play-off to Slovenia for a place at the 2002 World Cup. Romania also missed out on Euro 2004 after finishing behind Denmark and Norway in the qualifiers. The team was unable to upset the form book when drawn with Holland and the Czech Republic in the qualifiers for Germany 2006, but made it through to Euro 2008, only the fourth time the country had reached the finals.

Ilie Dumitrescu of Romania (front) in action against Philippe Albert of Belgium in 1993.

Russia

Founded: 1922
Colours: White; blue; white
World Cup Appearances: 5　**Best**: semi-final 1966
Honours: European Championship winners 1960; Olympic winners 1956, 1988 (all as Soviet Union)

The footballing heritage of Russia is inextricably linked with the political history of the country. Two Lancastrian brothers, Clement and Harry Charnock, are credited with establishing Russia's first club, Morozovotsky. They managed a textile factory near Moscow but were so fanatical about the game

Andrei Kanchelskis of Russia is chased by Maldini of Italy during their Euro '96 game at Anfield.

that when advertising at home for tradesmen they asked for men who had footballing as well as engineering skills. The Czarist regime had its suspicions but tentatively welcomed the game as a means of diverting the Proletariat away from a dissolute lifestyle and subversive activity.

A Moscow league was formed in 1901 and in 1912 Russia made an inauspicious international debut at the Olympic Games, beaten 16–0 by Germany. After the 1917 Revolution Russians found themselves playing alongside men from Georgia, Ukraine and other states in the new USSR. International contact was frowned upon, while Morozovotsky found itself absorbed into the Soviet Electrical Trades Union, renamed Moscow Dynamo. In 1945 Western clubs and fans got to see the quality of Russian football when Moscow Dynamo toured Britain and Scandinavia. The team put on some dazzling displays, includung a 4–3 win over Arsenal.

The USSR competed in the 1952 Olympics, its first international outing since the 1920s. Yugoslavia ended their run, but four years later in Melbourne the Soviet Union took Olympic gold. Sweden 1958 marked the country's World Cup debut, and the country reached the quarter-final after beating England in a group play-off. In the last eight they went down 2–0 to hosts Sweden.

In 1960 the USSR won the inaugural European Championship, its only major title to date. However, there was no British representation and neither Italy nor West Germany took part. Also, when the USSR was drawn against Spain in the second round, the latter withdrew. The 1960s side, with the great Lev Yashin in goal, enjoyed some notable successes: quarter-finalists in the 1962 World Cup, runners-up in the 1964 European Championship and semi-finalists in the 1966 World Cup. England '66 marks the Russians' best World Cup performance, although the 2–1 defeat by West Germany would have been heavier had it not been for Yashin.

In the 1970s and 80s Russian sides became known for their technical quality. Dynamo Kiev led the way, twice winning the European Cup Winners' Cup, while Dynamo Tbilisi also won the same trophy. Kiev's Oleg Blokhin was the star performer of the era, becoming only the second Russian to win the European Footballer of the Year award. In 1988 Russia finished runners-up to Holland in the European Championship, the last major competition it participated in before the collapse of the old Communist order. Russia briefly emerged as the CIS – Commonwealth of Independent States – and competed under that name at Euro '92, finishing bottom of their group. By 1994, when the team qualified for the World Cup, it took the field as Russia. It was a disappointing first-round exit there, as it was two years later at Euro '96. After missing out on France '98 and Euro 2000, coach Oleg Romantsev got his side to Japan and Korea. Things went badly as Russia became Japan's first-ever World Cup scalp. The team also lost to Belgium and crashed out at the first hurdle. Romantsev resigned shortly afterwards. Russia won a play-off against Wales to reach Euro 2004. The team finished bottom of their qualifiying group, though had the consolation of beating eventual winners Greece. The poor run continued as Russia finished behind Portugal and Slovakia in the 2006 World Cup qualifiers, but things took a turn for the better under Guus Hiddink's stewardship. The team not only reached the finals of Euro 2008 at England's expense, but proved to be one of the surprise packages of the tournament in reaching the semis, where they went down to eventual winners Spain. Andrei Arshavin and Roman Pavlyuchenko were among the players who took the eye, and it wasn't long before both were parading their skills in the Premiership, for Arsenal and Spurs respectively.

Saudi Arabia

Founded: 1959
Colours: White; green; white
World Cup Appearances: 4   **Best**: 2nd round 1994
Honours: Asian Cup winners: 1984, 1988, 1996

Saudi Arabia is a young footballing nation, its Football Federation having been founded as recently as 1959, with FIFA membership granted the same year. The country's wealth meant that it was able to invest heavily in facilities and coaching and the dividends have been reaped over the past 20 years. Saudi Arabia has reached five successive Asian Cup finals (1984-2000), winning the tournament in 1984, 1988 and 1996. In both 1992 and 2000 the Saudis went down 1–0 to Japan. The country has enjoyed four World Cup campaigns. Victories over Morocco and Belgium at USA '94 put the Saudis into the knockout phase, where they lost 3–1 to Sweden. It was the first time an Asian team had got beyond the group stage since North Korea's exploits in 1966. Four years later at France '98 the Saudis themselves limped out at the first hurdle, notching just one point from a draw with South Africa. In Japan and Korea the Saudis didn't even manage that. After an 8–0 mauling by Germany the team lost to Cameroon and the Republic of Ireland, conceding another four goals in those games without managing to reply. There was another first-round exit at Germany 2006, and the team missed out on a fourth Asian Cup victory when it went down 1-0 to Iraq in the final of the 2007 tournament.

Scotland's Billy Bremner (front) and Francis Munroe (right) wait for a cross with England's Martin Chivers at Wembley in 1971.

Scotland

Founded: 1873
Colours: Dark blue; white; red
World Cup Appearances: 8   **Best**: 1st round (all)

Scotland contested the world's first international match, drawing 0–0 with England at the West of Scotland Cricket Ground, Partick, on 30 November, 1872. The Scottish side featured nine Queen's Park players, plus two who used to play for the club before relocating to London. Queens Park was the dominant force in Scottish football in the amateur era, and also played in two FA Cup finals south of the border.

After professionalism arrived in the country in 1893 Queen's Park's determination to preserve its amateur status saw its star wane and the emergence of two giants from the city of Glasgow: Celtic and Rangers. Since the formation of the Scottish League in 1891 Rangers and Celtic have won the championship 89 times between them. Their rivalry goes beyond the tribal. Brother Walfrid, of the Catholic order of Marist Brothers, founded Celtic in 1887. Although Rangers had no particular affinity to Protestantism in its roots, the religious divide between the clubs became established and added another dimension to one of the most intense rivalries in the game.

In the late 19th century it was Scottish teams which were credited with developing a passing game. While their English counterparts tended to rely on individual virtuosity, the Scots quickly recognized that football was a team game. This had an unfortunate consequence in that a steady flow of the country's top players migrated south, to clubs who could offer more lucrative terms.

On the international front Scotland has dazzled

occasionally but too often flattered to deceive. One of the first great moments in Scottish footballing history came in 1928, when a team including Alex James, Alex Jackson and Hughie Gallacher went to Wembley and routed England 5–1. That same year saw the Scots withdraw from FIFA for the second time, due to a protracted dispute over broken-time payments to amateurs. After rejoining the international fold in 1946, Scotland should have made their World Cup debut in Brazil four years later. The team qualified by dint of finishing runners-up to England in the Home International Championship. But the Scottish Football Association had stubbornly insisted they would not go unless it was as champions. Switzerland 1954 thus marked the Scots' World Cup baptism. Defeats in both matches, including a 7–0 thrashing by Uruguay, rendered it a tournament to forget. Four years later in Sweden, Scotland finished bottom again, a performance made all the worse by the fact that Wales and Northern Ireland both reached the last eight.

The 1960s saw the emergence of some of the greatest players in the country's history, including Law, Mackay, Bremner and Baxter, yet the national side failed to qualify for any major tournament. The highlight of this era was a 3–2 victory over England in 1967, a result which confirmed Scotland as unofficial world champions, at least according to their passionate fans. Celtic's win over Inter Milan in that year's European Cup final – the country's only success in the competition to date – capped a memorable year for Scottish football.

Since 1974 the pattern has been all too familiar: solid qualifying campaigns, high expectations and disappointment. Of the seven World Cups between 1974 and 1998 the Scots reached the finals on six occasions. Each time the team has failed at the first hurdle, and all too often the stumbling block has been one of the supposed lesser teams rather than the big guns. Failing to score more than two goals against Zaire proved costly in 1974, as did a draw against Iran four years later. In Argentina the Scots pulled off a remarkable 3–2 win against an outstanding Dutch side, Archie Gemmill scoring one of the greatest ever World Cup goals. This made the dropped point against Iran even more galling for Scottish fans. Spain '82 saw the Scots go out on goal difference yet again, two goals conceded against New Zealand returning to haunt Jock Stein's team. Costa Rica's 1–0 victory over the Scots at Italia '90 and Morocco's 3–0 win at France '98 continued the theme, although the latter results proved to be academic.

The European Championship has hardly proved to be a happier hunting ground. Scotland first qualified in 1992, but missed out on a semi-final appearance after defeats by Holland and Germany. The Scots met the Dutch again at Euro '96 and this time got a creditable point. They went down 2–0 to the Auld Enemy (England) with Gary McAllister missing a penalty and Paul Gascoigne scoring with a breathtaking piece of skill. A 1–0 win over Switzerland, courtesy of an Ally McCoist goal, wasn't enough to prevent Scotland from going out on goal difference in a major tournament yet again.

In 2002, following the end of Craig Brown's reign as Scotland coach, the SFA appointed Berti Vogts, who had led Germany to victory at Euro '96.

Kenny Dalglish in action in 1985.

Ally McCoist is challenged by Holland's van Tiggelen during their Euro '92 game.

Senegal

Founded: 1960
Colours: White/green; white/green; white/green
World Cup Appearances: 1　**Best**: Quarter-finals 2002

One of the World Cup new boys in 2002, Senegal went into the tournament as the weakest of the 32 nations according to FIFA rankings. The African side quickly reminded everyone that the game is played on the pitch, not on paper. A 1–0 win over holders France in the curtain-raiser made the world sit up and take notice. Nor was it a fluke. Draws against Denmark and Uruguay followed, and after a golden goal from Henri Camara beat Sweden in the second round, Bruno Metsu's side found themselves in the last eight. The dream ended with another golden goal, this time scored by Ilhan Mansiz for Turkey, but Senegal had covered themselves in glory.

Earlier in the year the team had reached the final of the African Nations Cup for the first time, and although it ended in defeat on penalties against Cameroon, 2002 remained the year that Senegal made its big breakthrough. One of the stars of the side was striker El Hadji Diouf. He put the seal on a big-money move to Liverpool shortly after the World Cup and was also named African Player of the Year, a title he retained in 2002–03. The skilful but controversial player failed to make an impact on Anfield, and 2004–05 saw him move to Bolton.

Slovenia

Founded: 1992
Colours: White; white; white
World Cup Appearances: 1　**Best**: 1st round 2002

Slovenia emerged from the break-up of Yugoslavia in 1991, becoming a FIFA member as an independent nation the following year. Slovenian football has shown steady rather than spectacular improvement since. After failing to reach the finals of Euro '96 or France '98, Slovenia finally made its tournament debut at Euro 2000. The team finished bottom of their group but went home with some credit. They threw away a three-goal lead against Yugoslavia and in the end had to struggle for a draw. A narrow defeat against Spain followed and a goalless draw against Norway rounded off their first tournament. Slovenia surprised many by beating Romania in a play-off to reach the 2002 World Cup. A 12-match unbeaten run to reach Japan and Korea came to an end in dramatic style once they got there. The team slumped to three group defeats, their cause not helped by internal wrangling, notably between coach Srecko Katanec and star player Zlatko Zahovic. Slovenia finished runners-up to France in their Euro 2004 qualifying group to book a place in the play-offs against neighbours Croatia, but lost out 2–1 on aggregate.

Early results were poor but the team recovered to finish runners-up to Germany in the Euro 2004 qualifiers. After a fine 1–0 victory over Holland in the first leg of the play-off, the Scots crashed 6–0 in the return and thus missed out on a third appearance in the finals. Vogts resigned after a poor start to the 2006 World Cup qualifying campaign. His replacement was former Rangers and Everton boss Walter Smith, who was appointed in December 2004. A rejuvenated Scotland made the early running in the Euro 2008 qualifiers, ahead of Germany 2006 finalists Italy and France. Gary Caldwell scored the only goal in an historic win over France at Hampden, Les Bleus' first defeat in a qualifier for seven years. Smith quit in January 2007 to return to Ibrox, and in an ironic twist, the SFA appointed Alex McLeish, who had parted company with Rangers a year earlier following a poor run of results.

McLeish inherited a side heading its Euro 2008 qualification group, and built on the foundation laid by Smith with victories over Georgia, the Faroe Islands, Lithuania, France and Ukraine. Defeats against Georgia and Italy proved crucial, however, and in the wake of heroic failure, McLeish ended his brief tenure. In January 2008 the SFA turned to Southampton boss George Burley to take the national team forward.

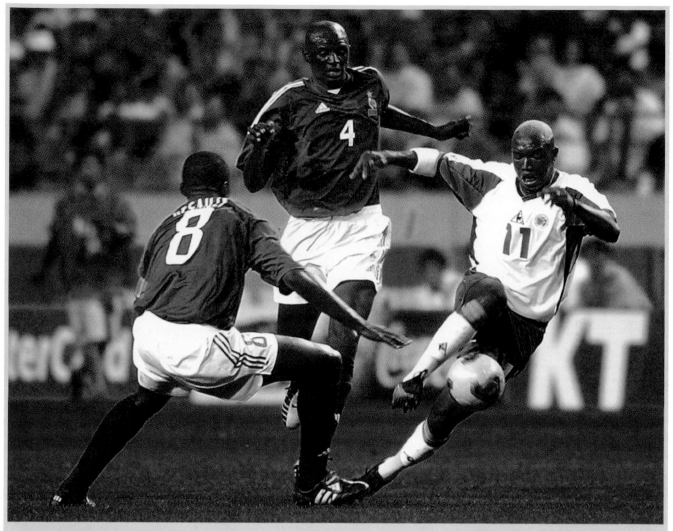

El Hadji Diouf (right) of Senegal takes the ball round Desailly (left) and Vieira in the opening match of the 2002 World Cup finals.

South Africa

Founded: 1892
Colours: Gold; black; white
World Cup Appearances: 2   **Best**: 1st round 1998, 2002
Honours: African Nations Cup winners 1996

South Africa wasted little time after returning to the international footballing community in 1992. That was the year the country was readmitted to FIFA after 28 years in the wilderness during the apartheid era. Bafana Bafana, as the national side is known, won the African Nations Cup on home soil in 1996, then made its debut appearance at a World Cup two years later. Elimination came at the first hurdle, but the team was not disgraced. Hosts and eventual champions France beat South Africa 3–0, but then came creditable draws against Denmark and Saudi Arabia. The

South Africans made it to the African Nations Cup final the same year, but Egypt prevented Bafana Bafana from retaining the title. At the 2002 World Cup South Africa came within a whisker of qualifying for the knockout stage. In the final round of matches they went down 3–2 to group winners Spain, while Paraguay beat Slovenia 3–1. As the goals went in the balance swung back and forth between South Africa and Paraguay, but at the final whistle the South American side snatched the runners-up spot.

The fact that players such as Lucas Radebe, Shaun Bartlett, Quinton Fortune, Benni McCarthy, Aaron Mokoena and Steven Pienaar have all plied their trade in the Premiership has helped South Africa become one of the continent's strongest footballing nations in the past 15 years. Home advantage at the 2010 World Cup will boost the team's chances still further.

Spain

Founded: 1913
Colours: Red; dark blue; black
World Cup Appearances: 12   **Best**: 4th 1950
Honours: European Championship winners 1964, 2008; Olympic winners 1992

Spain are the perennial underachievers in world football. The wealth and talent of the Primera Liga has rarely translated to the international stage. Japan and Korea 2002 was Spain's 11th World Cup appearance, showing that qualification hasn't been the problem. Fourth place in 1950 was the country's best performance and many felt that a team including Raul, Morientes, Casillas and Mendieta might do even better in 2002. The team was impressive in the group stage, winning all three games. A second-round penalty shoot-out victory over the Republic of Ireland was less convincing. Two disallowed goals in the quarter-final clash with South Korea proved costly and the Spaniards lost on penalties after the game ended goalless. Germany 2006 was a similar story, a team boasting the likes of Fabregas, Alonso, Villa and Torres strolling through the group stage with maximum points before crashing out to France in the last 16.

Many of the country's top clubs were formed in the late 19th and early 20th century, including Barcelona and the two Madrid sides, Real and Atletico. The royal family gave its official seal to a number of clubs, allowing them to use the 'Real' prefix. These included Betis, Zaragoza and Sociedad, as well as Madrid.

A national league and professionalism arrived together in 1929, and in May of that year the Spanish team became the first overseas opposition to beat England, winning 4–3 in Madrid. Spain's coach was Fred Pentland, a former Middlesbrough and England winger. But the star was Ricardo Zamora, the world's top 'keeper.

Spain's first World Cup campaign was in 1934. After a violent second-round match against Italy, which ended 1–1, Spain had to make seven changes. Italy won the replay. Civil war forced Spain's withdrawal from the 1938 tournament, and in 1950 the team had no answer to Brazil's artistry in the

second group, losing 6–1. Fourth in the final pool that year still represents Spain's best World Cup finish. Despite the success of Spanish clubs in European competition, Spain continued to disappoint on the biggest stages. The one exception was the 1964 European Championship, which they won, beating the USSR in the final. Even Spain's cavalier attitude to eligibility didn't help. Coach Helenio Herrera managed to get several overseas stars into a Spanish shirt, including Puskas.

Euro '84 was the only other time Spain has come close to winning a major trophy. The team reached the final but Platini's France won 2–0. A late Roberto Baggio goal won Italy the quarter-final clash with Spain at USA '94. At Euro '96 Seaman was England's hero and Spain's villain in the penalty shoot-out, also in the last eight. There was a first-round exit at France '98 while at Euro 2000 France was once again the stumbling block in the quarter-final. Euro 2004 was another typical showing. Widely tipped to go all the way, Spain failed at the group stage, finishing behind Portugal and Greece. Four years later, it all came right in Austria and

Spain's Gaizka Mendieta chases Zuma of South Africa (right) during their World Cup group match in 2002.

Switzerland as Spain swept all before them playing champagne football. The scalps of holders Greece and world champions Italy were taken along the way, and a brilliant Torres strike was enough to beat Germany in the final.

Sweden

Founded: 1904
Colours: Yellow; blue; yellow/blue
World Cup Appearances: 11   **Best**: Final 1958
Honours: Olympic winners 1948

With a population of less than 10 million and domestic football organized on a part-time basis, Sweden has performed remarkably on the European and world stage, both at club and country level. Malmo reached the European Cup final in 1979, and IFK Gothenburg won the UEFA Cup twice in the following decade. The Swedes have featured in 10 World Cups, reaching the semi-finals in 1938, 1950 and 1994, and finishing runners-up to Brazil in 1958. The 1958 tournament on home soil was a watershed for Swedish football, as professionalism was finally introduced to the national side. Since the formation of the country's football association in 1904, the representative side had been strictly amateur. Sweden were Olympic champions in 1948 under this regime, but some of the top players were being lured abroad. Most famous of these were Nils Liedholm, Gunnar Gren and Gunnar Nordahl, who all moved to AC Milan. With the lifting of the ban these strikers were available for the 1958 tournament. Their inclusion helped Sweden to reach the final but the team had little answer to an irresistible Brazil side.

Freddie Ljungberg of Sweden makes a break.

Sweden's best performances since then came in the early 1990s, under coach Tommy Svensson. The Swedes made their first appearance at the European Championship in 1992 as hosts and made it to the semis. Tomas Brolin hit three goals in four games, including the one that ended England's hopes, but the team went down 3–2 to Germany. It was the semis again two years later USA '94, when Brazil again proved too strong. At the 2002 World Cup the Swedes were the unlikely winners of the 'Group of Death', finishing ahead of England, Argentina and Nigeria before going out to a Senegal golden goal in the second round. The team topped a difficult group at Euro 2004 on goal difference before going down to Holland on penalties in the quarter-final. At Germany 2006 Lars Lagerback's men again qualified for the knockout stage along with England, but again their progress was halted in the second round, this time by a 2–0 defeat by the hosts.

Switzerland

Founded: 1895
Colours: Red; white; red
World Cup Appearances: 8 **Best**: Quarter-finals 1934, 1938, 1954

Switzerland has enjoyed a revival in fortune in recent years. Under Roy Hodgson the Swiss qualified for USA '94, reaching the second round before going down to Spain 3–0. The team topped a qualifying group including Russia and the Republic of Ireland in reaching Euro 2004, and headed France in the group stage at Germany 2006. In the latter tournament, a second-round shoot-out defeat by Ukraine prevented the Swiss from reaching a World Cup quarter-final for the first time in over 50 years. The team didn't concede in open play in any of their four games, though they crumbled against Shevchenko and Co. in the penalty competition, failing to register a single goal.

In contrast with these recent sporadic successes, Switzerland was a consistently strong force in the first half of the 20th century. A side coached by Jimmy Hogan, the Englishman who had such an influence on Austrian and Hungarian football, reached the 1924 Olympic final. Czechoslovakia, Italy and Sweden were all beaten on the way to the final, where Uruguay proved too strong and won 3–0.

In the 1934 World Cup the Swiss gave eventual runners-up Czechoslovakia a scare, taking the lead in their second-round match before going down 3–2. Four years later Switzerland went to France buoyed by a recent 2–1 win over England. At the World Cup they stunned Germany, one of the favourites, in the first round by drawing 1–1. The Germans looked to be in control in the replay, taking a two-goal lead. Switzerland then hit four without reply, but that extra match didn't help their chances in the last eight, where they lost 2–0 to Hungary. There was a first-round exit in 1950, but with home advantage in 1954 the Swiss reached the quarter-final. They faced Austria in what was probably the most extraordinary World Cup match ever seen. The Swiss went 3–0 up, but within barely 10 minutes they found themselves 5–3 behind. The Austrians eventually prevailed 7–5.

Trinidad and Tobago

Founded: 1908
Colours: Red; black; red
World Cup Appearances: 1 **Best**: 1st round 2006

Trinidad and Tobago's Football Association dates from 1908 and it has one of the stronger Caribbean leagues. This hasn't translated to much international success, however. One of the country's proudest moments came in 1971, when it hosted the CONCACAF Championship. Despite home advantage the country finished fifth in the six-strong tournament. In terms of achievement, the high watermark thus far was reaching the 2006 World Cup finals, where the island minnows performed heroically and even managed to hold Sweden to a goalless draw.

Trinidad and Tobago's most famous footballing sons are Dwight Yorke and Shaka Hislop. Yorke was snapped up by Aston Villa boss Graham Taylor in 1989 during the club's pre-

Trinidad and Tobago's Dwight Yorke strikes the ball.

season tour of the Caribbean. Yorke continued to play for Trinidad and Tobago, while Hislop chose England for any representative honours that came his way.

Tunisia

Founded: 1956
Colours: Red; white; red
World Cup Appearances: 4   **Best**: 1st round
Honours: African Nations Cup winners 2004

Tunisia first entered the African Nations Cup in 1962, just six years after the country's FA had been formed and two since it had joined FIFA. A 4–2 defeat against eventual winners Ethiopia represented a creditable debut. Three years later Tunisia hosted the tournament and came agonizingly close to winning it. 2–1 up against holders Ghana with minutes to go, the Tunisians conceded a late equalizer and lost 3–2 in extra-time.

Tunisia made its World Cup debut in 1978. Although it ended in a first-round exit, the country did beat Mexico 3–1 to become the first African side to win a World Cup match.

There was also an impressive goalless draw with West Germany, who only finished a point ahead of the African side in the final group table. It was the mid-1990s before Tunisia enjoyed further success. In 1996 the country was runner-up in the African Nations Cup for the second time, losing to South Africa in the final. At France '98 the Tunisians lost their opening fixture to England and also went down to Colombia before notching a point in the last match against Romania. A third World Cup appearance in 2002 seemed to offer Tunisia its best chance to date of reaching the second round. The team found itself in the so-called 'Group of Life' with Japan the seeds and no obvious outstanding side. A draw against Belgium sandwiched between defeats by Russia and Japan left the team ranked 28 in the world propping up the table. However, in 2004 Tunisia, again hosts of the African Nations tournament, defeated their Moroccan neighbours by 2 goals to 1 and captured their first major honour. The country made it three World Cups in a row by qualifying for Germany 2006 - the best record of any African nation - though a single point gained from a draw with Saudi Arabia ended their interest at the group stage.

Tunisia's forward Silva Dos Santos is jubilant after scoring against Morocco in the 2004 African Nations Cup Final.

Turkey

Founded: 1923
Colours: White; white; white/red
World Cup Appearances: 2 **Best**: 3rd 2002

Turkey was the surprise package of the 2002 World Cup, beating South Korea 3–2 in the third-place play-off. The team played winners Brazil twice in the tournament. At the group stage they lost only 2–1, and also had Hakan Unsal sent off after a blatant piece of simulation by Rivaldo. A Ronaldo strike was the difference between the sides when they met again in the semi-final. Ironically, the country's most famous player and talisman, Hakan Sukur, had had a poor tournament and it was some of the lesser known names who shone, including Hakan Sas, Ilhan Mansiz and goalkeeper Rustu. Alpay was also in top form in the centre of the defence.

2002 was yet another staging post in a decade which has seen Turkish football firmly on the up. When Turkey made it to Euro '96 it ended a 42-year run in which the country had failed to reach the finals of any major tournament. Although the Turks made a swift exit, with neither a point nor a goal to their name, it was a step in the right direction. Four years later in Holland and Belgium, Turkey finished above Belgium and Sweden to qualify for the second round, where they went down to Portugal. In the same year Galatasaray made the breakthrough at club level, beating Arsenal in the final of the UEFA Cup. Six years later, at Euro 2008, Turkey once again showed their footballing credentials on a big stage. After emerging from a group that included Portugal and the Czech Republic, the team knocked out Croatia before going down to Germany in a five-goal semi-final thriller.

Galatasaray is one of the country's big three Istanbul clubs, monopolizing the domestic scene along with Besiktas and Fenerbahce. Between 1959, when the country's league was created, and 2005, these three between them won 41 of the 47 championships contested. In 2002–03 the momentum swung Besiktas's way. Having reached the quarter-final of the UEFA Cup, the team romped to the championship and then made an excellent start to the 2003–04 Champions League campaign by beating Chelsea's all-stars at Stamford Bridge.

The impressive strides of recent years are a far cry from the early days of Turkish football. The game was banned in the early years of the 20th century, the rulers of the Ottoman Empire suspicious of any perceived Western influences. The game flourished in secret, however, and by 1910 the big three clubs had all been formed. Professionalism didn't arrive until 1951, and three years later Turkey had its only other noteworthy success. The country enjoyed some good fortune in making it to the 1954 World Cup in Switzerland. After a play-off against Spain ended all-square, lots had to be drawn and Turkey came out of the hat. They made it to a group play-off against West Germany for a place in the quarter-finals but crashed 7–2 against the team that would go on to lift the trophy.

Hakan Sukur (right) of Turkey plays against South Korea in the 2002 World Cup.

Ukrainian Andriy Shevchenko (right) fights for the ball with Macedonian Goce Sedloski.

Ukraine

Founded: 1991
Colours: Yellow/blue; yellow/blue; yellow/blue
World Cup Appearances: 1 **Best:** 2nd round

The Football Federation of Ukraine was born in 1991, following the break-up of the Soviet Union. Unsurprisingly, the most successful Soviet side in history, Dynamo Kiev, established its supremacy in the new league. Kiev enjoyed a clean sweep of titles between 1993 and 2001. Shakhtar Donetsk knocked Kiev off their perch in 2001–02, a season in which Kiev was rocked by the death of legendary coach Valery Lobanovski. Lobanovski, who also had several spells in charge of the national side, had begun his coaching career at Kiev in the early 1970s. Former player Alexei Mikhailichenko took over the reins and under his guidance Kiev were back on top in 2002–03. Play-off defeats against Slovenia and Germany cost Ukraine a place at Euro 2000 and the 2002 World Cup. The team also failed to reach Euro 2004, but under legendary former player Oleg Blokhin, Ukraine qualified for its first major tournament, Germany 2006. Andriy Shevchenko was the team's sole major star, but Ukraine surprised many in reaching the quarter-finals, where it went down 3–0 to eventual champions Italy.

United States of America

Founded: 1913
Colours: White; blue; red
World Cup Appearances: 8 **Best**: Semi-finals 1930
Honours: CONCACAF winners 1991, 2002, 2005, 2007

There has been a revival in the fortunes of American football in recent years. The Americans have made five successive World Cup appearances since 1990, the highlight of which was an outstanding run to reach the quarter-finals in Japan and Korea 2002. The history of the game in the United States goes back much further, however. Football was played there in the 19th century, and in 1913 the country became affiliated to FIFA. After fielding sides at both the 1924 and 1928 Olympic Games, the USA entered the first World Cup in 1930. The team scored victories over Belgium and Paraguay to reach the semi-final, where they crashed 6–1 to Argentina. The 1934 tournament ended after just one match. A 7–1 thrashing by Italy sent the USA home as that year's competition was organized on a straight knockout basis.

Brad Friedel of the USA during the 2002 World Cup finals.

At the 1950 World Cup in Brazil the USA finished bottom of their group on goal difference, but did have the consolation of an historic 1–0 win over a much-vaunted England side. A Larry Gaetjens header was enough to beat a team including Mortensen, Finney and Mannion, and Belo Horizonte 1950 went down in the annals as one of English football's blackest days.

The North American Soccer League was formed in the late 1960s but despite the razzmatazz and introduction of such luminaries as Pele, Beckenbauer and Best, football struggled to compete with the more established American sports. The league folded in 1984. Six years later the USA ended a 40-year World Cup drought by reaching the finals in Italy. The team went home without a point, but it was a different story four years later. With home advantage and experienced Yugoslav coach Bora Milutinovic in charge, the USA drew with Switzerland and beat the much-fancied Colombia to reach the knockout stage. There they lost to eventual winners Brazil by only a single goal. France '98 was another disappointment but under Bruce Arena the team performed superbly in Japan and Korea. A 3–2 victory over seeded side Portugal got the team off to a flying start, and after qualifying behind South Korea they faced arch-rivals Mexico in the second round. These two had had a victory apiece in the qualifiers but this time it was the USA that prevailed. In the last eight against Germany the Americans were unlucky to lose to a Michael Ballack goal.

The USA has won the CONCACAF Gold Cup four times, including three of the past four tournaments. The 2007 final resulted in a 2–1 win over Mexico, the country that had beaten them in the showpiece twice in the 1990s. The USA has

also been invited to compete in the Copa America, and the country's best result to date came in 1993 when it reached the semi-final, beating Argentina 3–0 along the way.

1996 saw the latest attempt to launch league football in America. Major League Soccer has enjoyed considerable success, but despite the country's commendable efforts at the 2002 World Cup, two teams have folded – Tampa Bay Mutiny and Miami Fusion.

Claudio Reyna of the USA pursues Miroslav Klose of Germany during the 2002 World Cup quarter-final.

Uruguay

Founded: 1900
Colours: Light blue; black; black
World Cup Appearances: 9   **Best**: Winners 1930, 1950
Honours: South American Championship winners 1916, 1917, 1929, 1923, 1924, 1926, 1935, 1942, 1956, 1959, 1967, 1983, 1987, 1995; Olympic winners 1924, 1928

In the first half of the 20th century Uruguay could lay claim to be the number one footballing country in the world. The South Americans mesmerized the opposition in the 1924 Olympic Games in Paris. Four years later in Amsterdam, arch-rivals Argentina also competed and the two sides met in the final. Uruguay retained their title with a 2–1 victory after a replay, and was given the honour of hosting the inaugural World Cup two years later. Uruguay was celebrating its centenary as an independent country and built the Centenario Stadium in Montevideo to mark the occasion. The team topped its group and then put six goals past Yugoslavia to set up a final clash with Argentina. Uruguay came back from 2–1 down to win 4–2, and Jose Nasazzi became the first man to lift the Jules Rimet Trophy.

Angered by the number of countries that had refused to compete in 1930, Uruguay refused to defend its crown in 1934, and didn't feature in the 1938 tournament either. The country continued to contest the South American Championship, which had been instituted in 1910. Uruguay claimed seven titles in the prewar period, although two of these were in unofficial tournaments.

The early postwar era was a golden one, and produced the country's greatest ever player, Juan Schiaffino. Uruguay's passage at the 1950 World Cup in Brazil was eased by a number of late withdrawals which meant that its route consisted of just one fixture: an emphatic 8–0 win over Bolivia. The round-robin games which made up the second phase pitted Uruguay and Brazil in the last match, and this became the de facto final, Brazil needing only a draw to win the trophy. Brazil scored first, Schiaffino equalized and Ghiggia hit the winner ten minutes from time. It was a result that stunned the home fans in the new Maracana Stadium, and it meant that Uruguay remained unbeaten in World Cup competition. That record came to an end in the semi-final of the 1954 tournament. Uruguay lost to the Magic Magyars of Hungary in a match that was acclaimed for its quality.

Uruguay's national team pictured at the first World Cup finals in 1930.

The 4–2 extra-time defeat was Uruguay's first reverse in 12 World Cup encounters.

Uruguay has continued to feature regularly in World Cups but has yet to scale the same heights. 1970 saw the team grind out another semi-final appearance. In five games the Uruguayans scored just four goals, eventually going down 3–1 to Brazil in the semis. This game is best remembered for Pele's outrageous dummy which left Uruguayan 'keeper Mazurkiewicz bamboozled. Pele put the shot just wide of the post but it hardly mattered.

In the last 20 years Uruguay's successes have been confined to the South American championship. In both 1983 and 1995 Uruguay beat Brazil in the Copa America final, and 1987 saw the team beat Chile 1–0 in the same competition. In 2002 Uruguay made its first World Cup appearance since Italia '90. The team recovered from 3–0 down to snatch a dramatic draw against the tournament's surprise package, Senegal, in their final group match. A point wasn't enough, however, and the South Americans were on their way home. Even so, Uruguay remains one of only seven countries to be crowned world champions and one of only five to have won the World Cup on more than one occasion.

Uruguay's Diego Forlan (right) talks with teammates Sebastian Abreu (left) and Alvaro Recoba.

Yugoslavia (Serbia)

Founded: 1919
Colours: Blue; white; red
World Cup Appearances: 6 **Best**: Semi-final 1962
Honours: Olympic winners 1960

Yugoslavia qualified for Euro '92 with a star-studded squad and was tipped as one of the favourites to win the tournament. The country never got the chance to lift its first major trophy. The Balkans erupted into conflict and Denmark not only replaced Yugoslavia in Sweden but won the championship. The ensuing fragmentation of the country saw Macedonia, Slovenia, Croatia and Bosnia-Herzegovina establish themselves as independent states, leaving Serbia and Montenegro as the political and sporting entity for the new Yugoslavia. The reconstituted country qualified for both France '98 and Euro 2000. In the former tournament the team went down to a last-minute goal by Holland in the second round after Pedrag Mijatovic had missed a penalty. At Euro 2000 a dramatic 4–3 defeat by Spain in the final group match looked to have put them out, but the Norway–Slovenia result went in their favour and put them into the last eight. Holland was again their downfall, and with a 6–1 scoreline there was no ill-luck to blame this time. During the qualifying series for Euro 2004 the Yugoslavian FA officially became the FA of Serbia and Montenegro. It didn't help their fortunes on the pitch as they finished behind Italy and Wales. An iron defence was the key to a successful qualifying campaign for Germany 2006, the team shipping just one goal in 10 games. It was a different story at the tournament itself, Serbia and Montenegro conceding 10 times in defeats against Holland, Argentina and Ivory Coast.

The 1990s was not the only period of turmoil for the peoples of this region. Yugoslavia came into existence in 1918, from territories that had been part of the Austro–Hungarian Empire. A 7–0 defeat by Czechoslovakia in 1920 marked the country's international debut. But ten years later Yugoslavia was one of just four European teams to travel to Uruguay for the inaugural World Cup. There was a fine victory over Brazil en route to the semis, where the hosts handed out a 6–1 thrashing. There was more political upheaval in 1945 when Tito declared a People's Republic and Yugoslavia fell behind the Iron Curtain. The country was somewhat unfortunate to go out at the quarter-final stage of the 1954 and 1958 World Cups, losing both times to West Germany. The team got its revenge in 1962, beating West Germany on the way to the semis, which remains the country's best performance. In the 1960s Yugoslavia also twice finished runners-up in the European championship. Dragan Dzajic was the star of the side which lost to Italy in 1968 after a replay and is regarded as one of the greatest players in Yugoslavia's history.

At club level Dinamo Zagreb and the Belgrade clubs Partizan and Red Star represented formidable opposition. The players were technically amateurs but in practice part-time professionals, albeit poorly paid. Within weeks of Partizan's European Cup final appearance in 1966, virtually the whole team had left the country. The exodus became a torrent and eventually the authorities caved in and embraced professionalism. Yugoslavia reached the World Cup finals in 1974 and 1982. In 1991 Red Star Belgrade won the European Cup, only the second Eastern European side to do so. In 1992 Red Star also reached the quarter-finals of the competition, despite being homeless due to the conflict. In 2006 Serbia and Montenegro went their separate ways after the former declared independence. Fifa recognizes the Serbia team as the direct descendant of Yugoslavia and the short-lived state of Serbia & Montenegro.

Serbia and Montenegro's Djordjevic (left) vies with Tacchinadi of Italy in their Euro 2004 qualifying match.

Wales

Founded: 1876
Colours: Red; red; red
World Cup Appearances: 1 **Best**: Quarter-final 1958

In the autumn of 2002 Wales sat on top of their Euro 2004 qualifying group. A 2–0 win in Finland was impressive but nothing compared to the historic 2–1 victory over the giants of Italy at the Millennium Stadium. A year later Welsh fans had returned to earth with a slight jolt. The team was comprehensively beaten in Italy but still secured the runners-up spot, ahead of both Serbia & Montenegro and Finland. After a play-off defeat against Russia it emerged that Igor Titov had taken a banned substance. UEFA refused to overturn the result and Mark Hughes's men missed out on a second appearance in a major championship. Even so, the performance of the team had put Welsh football in the spotlight and captured the imagination of the fans at a time when the country's rugby team was hardly setting the world alight.

If football has supplanted rugby in Wales – even temporarily – it has taken a long time to do so. The country's FA was founded in 1876, and its first international that same year brought a 4–0 reverse at the hands of Scotland. After seven games the Wales side had scored four and conceded 28, losing every match. A 1–0 win over England in February 1881 was the country's first taste of success, but in the next century these high points were to be a few and far between.

Mark Hughes (left) and Ian Rush of Wales.

The first came at club level, with Cardiff City's 1–0 win over mighty Arsenal in the 1927 FA Cup final, the only time the trophy has gone out of England. That ushered in a first sustained period of success for the national side. Wales won the Home International championship three times in the 1930s and was undefeated from 1932 to 1934. But the country's proudest moment came in the 1958 World Cup. The Welsh needed a slice of good fortune to make it to Sweden, beating Israel in a lucky losers play-off. But once there a team boasting the likes of Ivor Allchurch and John Charles performed heroically. Wales had to face Hungary, the runners-up of 1954, in a group play-off match. The game ended 2–1, Spurs' winger Terry Medwin hitting the goal which put Wales through to the quarter-final against Brazil. A late goal from 17-year-old Pele ended Welsh hopes, the team hampered by the loss of Charles through injury.

Wales just missed out on a semi-final place in the 1976 European Championship, losing to Yugoslavia 3–1 on aggregate in an ill-tempered tie. The Welsh felt that they were denied a stonewall penalty on that occasion, and two years later it was another penalty incident that cost the team a place at the World Cup finals in Argentina. Playing Scotland at Anfield, the Welsh were on top when they were penalized for

Ryan Giggs of Wales.

a handball in the box. The hand in question belonged to Scotland's Joe Jordan, and the Scots capitalized on their stroke of luck.

In the 1980s Wales produced several world-class players, including Kevin Ratcliffe, Neville Southall, Ian Rush and Mark Hughes. Lack of depth meant that the national team invariably included players from the lower leagues too, which hindered its chances at the highest level. In the 1990s Ryan Giggs emerged as the jewel in the crown of Welsh football. Players such as John Hartson, Craig Bellamy, Gary Speed and Simon Davies also came through, and a strong Premiership contingent helped to make Wales a formidable side, as demonstrated in the Euro 2004 qualifiers. John Toshack was appointed Wales coach in November 2004, his second spell in charge of the national team. By the following spring Wales had garnered just two points from six Germany 2006 qualifiers and Welsh fans' hopes of a second World Cup adventure had evaporated.

With a defeat in the Czech Republic followed by a 5–1 mauling in Cardiff at the hands of Slovakia, Wales made a disastrous start to their Euro 2008 campaign. The team took points off Germany and the Czech Republic, but inconsistency left Wales fifth in the seven-strong group. The only bright note in the latter game was a first international goal from Southampton wunderkind Gareth Bale, who at 17 became the youngest player to score in a senior international for his country.

Zambia

Founded: 1929
Colours: Green; white; black
World Cup Appearances: 0

Zambia finished runners-up to Zaire in the 1974 African Nations Cup and it was the latter country which thus had the honour of being Africa's first representative at a World Cup. A shock 4–0 win over Italy at the Seoul Olympics in 1988 was the next highlight in Zambia's footballing history. Five years later, in April 1993, tragedy struck when the country's entire 18-man squad was wiped out when the plane carrying the team to an African Nations Cup qualifier against Senegal crashed into the sea. Five European-based players who were not on board formed the core of the side that won through to the final of the competition the following year. However, Zambia had to settle for the runners-up spot again, Nigeria winning the match 2–1.

Major
Competitions

The World Cup

1930

The first World Cup took place 26 years after FIFA was founded. A global tournament had been a long-cherished objective of Jules Rimet, who became FIFA president in 1920. It was already embodied in the organisation's constitution and merely required the administrators to set the ball rolling. They did so at a meeting in 1929, and a year later the great festival of football got under way.

Uruguay, the 1928 Olympic champions, was selected as the host country. Although only 13 countries took part in the first tournament it quickly took over from the Olympics as the game's world championship.

France, Yugoslavia, Romania and Belgium accepted the Uruguayan authorities' offer to pay their expenses and represented Europe. None of the home countries participated. A rift over a broken-time payments to amateurs had led to all four UK Football Associations withdrawing from FIFA, a row that rumbled on until after the Second World War.

South Americans

Argentina and Uruguay, who had met in the Olympic final two years earlier, were the strongest sides and both progressed through the tournament comfortably. They were joined in the semi-finals by Yugoslavia and the USA, all four teams emerging with a hundred percent record. Yugoslavia was by no means among the strongest sides in Europe, however, and was on the receiving end of a 6–1 thrashing by Uruguay in the last four. Argentina overcame the USA by the same score in the other semi. The American side was strengthened by six British professionals and had trained hard. Their athleticism was such that the French dubbed them 'the shot-putters'. Against Argentina they lost one player early on with a broken leg and had a couple of others carrying injuries. These were the days before substitutes and it was no surprise that Argentina hit five second-half goals.

The two great South American rivals met at Montevideo's new Centenario Stadium on 30 July. Argentina took a 2–1 half-time lead, despite the fact that inside-forward Pancho Varallo had a broken bone in his foot. Uruguay scored three times without reply in the second half and the team's captain Jose Nasazzi became the first man to raise the Jules Rimet trophy aloft. Uruguayans enjoyed a public holiday while the country's embassy in Buenos Aires was attacked by disaffected Argentine supporters. The World Cup was up and running.

Uruguay celebrates winning the first world cup in Montevideo.

1934

FIFA deliberated long and hard before awarding Italy the honour of hosting the second World Cup. Many European countries were in straitened economic circumstances, but Italy under Mussolini was keen to showcase its facilities and organisational ability. There was a strong entry and qualification matches were needed – even Italy had to beat Greece in order to take part. The holders didn't defend their crown, though. Uruguay was still piqued by what they saw as a snub by many countries four years earlier and stayed away. Brazil and Argentina represented South America. The Argentine side was lacking some of its top players, the country's FA fearing that they might be poached. The loss of Raimundo Orsi – who was now turning out for Juventus and Italy – still rankled. The weakness of the team was reflected

on the pitch, and defeat by Sweden ended Argentina's interest, the tournament being organized on a straight knockout basis. The USA, Brazil and Egypt all lost, leaving eight European teams to battle it out.

Eight European Sides in Quarter-finals

Italy and Austria were the favourites, two outstanding sides led respectively by Vittorio Pozzo and Hugo Meisl, who were among the outstanding coaches of the era. Italy needed a replay to beat Spain in what was a violent tie. Giuseppe Meazza's header was the difference between the two sides. Just two days later Italy had to face Austria in the semis. Somewhat surprisingly it was Meisl's side that looked leg-weary on a heavy pitch. Guaita, another of Italy's naturalised Argentinians, scored the game's only goal.

In the final Italy met Czechoslovakia, whom Meisl himself had tipped to do well. The Czechs came from behind to beat both Romania and Switzerland, inside-forward Nejedly scoring the winner on each occasion. He hit two more in the 3–1 win over Germany in the semis. In the final Nejedly's strike partner Antonin Puc put the Czechs in front with 20 minutes left. Orsi equalized with a bizarre swerving, dipping shot which looped over Planicka in the Czechoslovakia goal. Italy were stronger in extra-time, perhaps galvanized by the watching Mussolini, who had demanded nothing less than victory. Schiavio scored the winner seven minutes into the extra period. It wasn't the most sporting tournament, and football had been cynically used for propaganda purposes, but Italy were duly crowned world champions.

Members of the victorious Italian team carry their manager Vittorio Pozzo.

1938

The 1938 tournament took place in France with Spain engaged in a civil war and the rest of Europe on the brink. Germany had annexed Austria and incorporated the country's best players into its own squad. Neither Uruguay nor Argentina made the trip. Brazil and Cuba were the only representatives of the Americas, each enjoying a free ride in qualifying after other countries withdrew and both made it to the second round. The 'Greater Germany' side didn't, losing to Switzerland in a replay despite going 2–0 up and playing much of the match with a man advantage. The Cubans came down to earth in the last eight, thrashed 8–0 by Sweden. Brazil put out Czechoslovakia in an ugly tie which had more sendings off and players hospitalised than goals. Brazil won a replay 2–1 after the first match ended one apiece. That result cheered Italy, for Czechoslovakia was the only country to have beaten the holders in the past four years. Pozzo's side was unrecognizable from the one that had won in 1934. Only Meazza and Ferrari remained, but a new generation of stars had emerged, notably striker Silvio Piola. Even so the Italians had wobbled against the amateurs of Norway in the first round. France was dispatched more convincingly, setting up a semi-final clash with Brazil. The Brazilians blundered by resting centre-forward Leonidas, who had hit four against Poland in the first round. The man who is said to have invented the bicycle kick could only watch as his team went down 2–1. Hungary and Sweden contested the other semi, both having had a comfortable passage. Indeed the Swedes had been given a bye in the first round and had only the 8–0 demolition of Cuba to warm up for the semi-final. Sweden scored in the first minute through winger Nyberg, but thereafter the Hungarian defence was largely untroubled. Zsengeller hit a hat-trick as Hungary ran out 5–1 winners. Hungary's star player was Georges Sarosi, a noted academic and lawyer who also represented his country at tennis, swimming and fencing. Although he scored against Italy in the final he was not at his best, unsettled by some of the robust challenges by the uncompromising Italian defenders. Piola and Colaussi hit a brace each and Italy retained the World Cup quite comfortably.

1950

Brazil was chosen to host the first postwar World Cup. The country was unscathed by war and as the previous two tournaments had been staged in Europe it was a sensible decision. There was the usual crop of withdrawals, however. These included Argentina, France and Turkey. Germany was excluded. The home countries were given two places based on the international championship. England came top and made its World Cup debut, but runners-up Scotland refused to take its place. The Scots apparently suffered an attack of hubris, refusing to go to Brazil as anything other than champions. England was seeded along with Brazil,

Alfredo Foni of Italy tries in vain to reach a cross during the 1938 World Cup Final against Hungary. Italy won the match and trophy 4-2.

England goalkeeper Bert Williams who played in the match that England lost to the USA in the 1950 World Cup.

Uruguay and Italy. They were expected to emerge as the four group winners, who would then play a round-robin series of matches for the title. Uruguay and Brazil made it to the final pool, although in Uruguay's case that meant playing just one match. The spate of late withdrawals left Uruguay only having to beat Bolivia, which they duly did with ease. Brazil dropped a point against Switzerland and had to beat Yugoslavia in the final match to get through. Jair had already taken the eye with his ferocious shooting, and Ademir and Zizinho were drafted into the side to play alongside him. This devastating inside-forward trio helped secure a 2–0 win over Yugoslavia.

England and Italy, the other seeds, fell by the wayside. England laboured to victory over Chile, then lost to the USA in Belo Horizonte. America's Haitian-born centre forward Larry Gaetjens headed in after 37 minutes and the team rode its luck to cause one of the shocks of all time. It also signalled that making England one of the favourites perhaps owed more to the past than the present. England could still force a play-off by beating Spain in their final match. Matthews returned but to no avail. Zarra scored the only goal and Spain went through with maximum points.

Holders Italy struggled to come to terms with the loss of ten internationals killed in an air crash which wiped out the all-conquering Torino side a year earlier. They were also without Vittorio Pozzo, who had quit as national team boss. A 3–2 defeat by Sweden was the key fixture, the Swedes going through to the second phase.

Brazil Favourites

Brazil were in sparkling form in the first two final pool matches, beating Sweden and Spain 7–1 and 6–1 respectively. Their main rivals Uruguay could only draw with Spain and came from behind against the Swedes to sneak a 3–2 win. The last match saw the two big guns do battle. This was the de facto final, much to the relief of the organizers who had not included a showpiece conclusion to the competition in the schedule. Brazil only needed a draw to be crowned world champions, and looked odds-on when they took the lead through Friaca. But in Schiaffino and Ghiggia Uruguay had forwards who were the equal of Brazil's stars. The pair combined for Schiaffino to equalize, and eleven minutes from time Ghiggia squeezed the ball between Brazilian 'keeper Barbosa and the post. Most of the 200,000-strong crowd at the Maracana Stadium had come to see Brazil crowned but it was Uruguay who came away with the Jules Rimet trophy.

Morlock of West Germany scores against Hungary in 1954.

1954

Switzerland '54 was the first televised World Cup, giving millions the chance to see the top players in action. Gemany was back in the fold, though now divided by the Iron Curtain. The West Germany side was led by Sepp Herberger, who had taken charge of the team that had competed in 1938. One of his first tasks was to find a way of beating Hungary, the red-hot favourites who hadn't lost for four years. Herberger's answer was barely to try. He fielded an understrength side against Puskas and Co at the group stage, and although his team lost 8–3, Herberger knew that West Germany could still progress. They did so by hammering Turkey in a play-off.

Each of the four groups contained two seeded sides who did not play each other at that stage. Apart from Hungary, Uruguay and Austria were the only other sides to reach the quarter-finals unbeaten. England topped their group despite letting a 3–1 lead slip against Belgium, the game ending 4–4. Scotland's debut wasn't memorable, beaten by Austria and thrashed 7–0 by holders Uruguay. Brazil and Yugoslavia drew 1–1 after gaining a victory apiece and also went through.

It was unfortunate that the draw pitted Hungary against Brazil in the quarter-finals, a match that would have graced the final, or would have done had it not descended into a brawl that started on the pitch and continued in the dressing rooms. Three players were sent off, Hungary's Bozsik and Santos and Tozzi of Brazil. Even without Puskas, injured in the group match against West Germany, Hungary proved too strong and won the match 4–2.

Uruguay's First Defeat

The canny Herberger, meanwhile, had avoided Brazil by finishing behind Hungary at the group stage. Instead the Germans eased into the semis by beating Yugoslavia. England were no match for holders Uruguay, but the tie of the round was Austria's 7–5 win over Switzerland. At one point the Austrians were 3–0 down. The porousness of Austria's defence was also in evidence against West Germany in the semis, but this time their attack couldn't get them out of trouble. The Hungary–Uruguay encounter was a much closer affair. Hohberg scored twice for Uruguay in the last fifteen minutes to make the score 2–2 and forced extra time. Sandor Kocsis, renowned for his aerial power, put away two headers to seal a 4–2 victory. It was Uruguay's first ever World Cup defeat but there was consolation in having taken part in one of the greatest exhibitions of football ever seen.

A half-fit Puskas returned for the final. He opened the scoring and Hungary were 2–0 up inside ten minutes. But as the Galloping Major faded the Germans got stronger. Morlock and Rahn levelled the score, and after Hungary squandered numerous chances to put the game beyond doubt they fell to a sucker-punch. Rahn hit a late winner, beating Grosics from 15 yards, and 81-year-old Jules Rimet presented West Germany's Fritz Walter with the coveted trophy.

1958

By 1958 the Hungarian uprising had taken place, many of the country's top players had fled the country and Hungary lost the chance to make amends for the shock defeat in the 1954 final. This time the flair and style would come from Vincente Feola's Brazil. In the final group match against the USSR Feola settled on an irresistible blend. In came centre-forward Vava and 17-year-old Pele returned to the side. But the star was Garrincha, whose deformed left leg didn't stop him from terrorising defences. The Russians did well to keep the score to 2–0.

England went into a play-off with Russia having drawn all three matches. Against Brazil Billy Wright marshalled the defence superbly and the game ended 0–0. But without the Manchester United stars killed four months earlier in the Munich disaster England were rather lacklustre and lost the play-off 1–0.

Home Nations Teams in Finals

Scotland, Northern Ireland and Wales also made it to the finals. The Scots again disappointed but Wales and Northern Ireland marched on to the quarter-finals after play-off victories over Hungary and Czechoslovakia respectively. A Pele goal was the difference between Brazil and Wales when the two sides met in the last eight. It was a fine performance by the Welsh, who were missing John Charles through injury. At the same stage Northern Ireland found France too strong. Real Madrid's Raymond Kopa was the star turn, while Just

1958: Wales' Ivor Allchurch jumps for the ball against Bellini and Nilton De Sordi of Brazil.

Fontaine added two more goals to a tally that would eventually make him the tournament's record marksman.

The Brazil–France semi-final was a classic. Vava put Brazil ahead after two minutes, Kopa and Fontaine combined to give a swift reply. Fontaine's goal was the first time that Brazil's defence had been breached. An injury to centre-half Jonquet before half time was a turning point and Pele capitalised with a hat-trick after the break.

In the other semi-final hosts Sweden took on West Germany. The Germans had made steady if unspectacular progress. They topped their group despite drawing two of their three games, and then put out Yugoslavia in the quarter-final with a goal from the hero of the 1954 final Helmut Rahn. Sweden, coached by Englishman George Raynor, had only just allowed professionals to play for the national side. This decision allowed Raynor to call on services of some of the country's top players who were plying their trade in Italy, including Skoglund, Liedholm and Hamrin. West Germany took the lead through Schaefer, another survivor from 1954. Skoglund equalised and with the game in the balance Germany's Ernst Juskowiak was sent off for a retaliatory kick at Kurt Hamrin. The depleted Germans couldn't hold out and Hamrin himself scored a fabulous solo goal to make the final score 3–1.

Raynor pinned his hopes on scoring first in the final and the Swedes did just that through Liedholm. Brazil's response to going behind for the first time was to go through the gears rather than panic. Garrincha gave full-back Axbom a roasting and set up two goals for Vava. Brazil's third came from a Pele party piece, the 17-year old taking the ball on his chest and flicking it over Gustavsson's head before volleying past Svensson. Zagallo made it four and although Sweden pulled one back Pele rounded off the scoring with a neat header. Brazil were world champions for the first time and the first country to win the trophy outside their own continent.

1962

Pele lasted just two games in Chile. After helping Brazil begin the defence of their crown by scoring against Mexico he then tore a muscle in the goalless draw against Czechoslovakia. There was one question on every Brazilian supporters' lips: could the team win without him? The final group match against Spain was a nervy affair, with Spain ahead for a long spell before Amarildo scored twice to retrieve the situation. The young Brazilian went on to star as Pele's replacement, while Garrincha was at his mesmerizing best.

England benefited from the new rule which introduced goal difference to separate teams, eliminating the need for play-offs. Having lost to Hungary in their opener England won well against Argentina and a dull goalless draw against Bulgaria saw them through. Argentina, who also finished on three points, went out on goal difference.

Meanwhile the tournament was already being besmirched by cynical gamesmanship and violence. One of the worst examples of the unseemly side of football came in the Chile–Italy encounter. Italian journalists had attacked Chile's organization of the

Pele and the Swedish goalkeeper Kalle Svensson jump for the ball in 1958.

The Brazilian team photographed before the final against Czechoslovakia.

issue. Chile showed their footballing rather than fighting skills in beating the USSR, for whom Lev Yashin had an uncharacteristic off day in goal.

Garrincha was again the star in Brazil's 4–2 win over Chile in the semi-final. He scored two before being sent off for retaliation, although the provocation had been extreme. FIFA took this into consideration and sensibly allowed him to take the field in the final. There Brazil faced the surprise package Czechoslovakia. The Czechs had eliminated Hungary and the highly fancied Yugoslavia in the quarter- and semi-finals. The team which had needed to beat Scotland in a play-off just to reach Chile now had the holder's in their sights. They started well, Josef Masopust putting them ahead after 15 minutes. Czech goalkeeper Schroiff, who had been in excellent form throughout the tournament, then made a string of blunders which contributed to his side's downfall. Amarildo, Zito and Vava all found the net and Brazil retained the trophy.

tournament and the bad blood spilled over onto the pitch. Referee Ken Aston sent off two Italians but the tally could have been much higher. Chile won 2–0 and went through with West Germany. Italy's victory over Switzerland in their final match was to no avail and they went home under a cloud. Officials gathered all the participating team managers together to lay down the law over foul play but to little effect. 1962 would not be remembered for its sportsmanship.

The USSR and Yugoslavia, finalists at the inaugural European Championship two years earlier, came through at the expense of Uruguay. It was the South Americans' first real taste of failure in a tournament they had entered.

In the quarter-finals England held Brazil at 1–1 for a while but two explosive goals from Garrincha settled the

Zito of Brazil jumps for joy after scoring in the 1962 final.

1966

Shortly after taking over the England manager's job from Walter Winterbottom in 1963 Alf Ramsey had boldly claimed that his team would win the World Cup three years later. Ramsey's first game in charge was a 5–2 defeat against an ordinary France side, but the former Ipswich boss remained resolute about 1966.

The drama began even before a ball was kicked as the trophy was stolen from a London exhibition. Pickles the dog came to the rescue and the trophy was ready to be fought for when the competition got under way on 11 July. England topped their group without hitting top gear. After a goalless draw against Uruguay a Bobby Charlton thunderbolt helped the team to a 2–0 win over Mexico. A Roger Hunt brace then accounted for France. West Germany looked strong in winning Group 2, putting five goals past Switzerland and beating Spain. They played out a 0–0 draw with Argentina and both sides progressed to the last eight.

England manager Alf Ramsey prevents George Cohen from swapping shirts with an Argentinian player after the 1966 quarter final.

Brazil and Italy Knocked Out

The shocks came in the other two groups. Holders and favourites Brazil crashed at the first hurdle, as did Italy. The Brazilian squad was nowhere near as strong as 1958 or 1962 and needed their star Pele to inspire them. But he came in for some rough treatment in the opening match, a victory over Bulgaria. Without him Brazil went down 3–1 to Hungary. A half-fit Pele returned against Portugal, whose defenders also treated him to some rudimentary tackling. Portugal won 3–1 and went through with the Hungarians. Brazil's elimination paled against Italy's. They went to Ayresome Park to face the minnows of North Korea needing a win to be sure of progressing. The Asian side was fast and skilful, Pak Doo Ik scored just before half time and the shell-shocked Italians never recovered. The team was welcomed home with a bombardment of rotten fruit.

Greaves out of Form

The North Koreans looked like causing another seismic shock when they went 3–0 up against Portugal in the quarter-final. But with four goals from Eusebio the Portuguese turned the game around and won 5–3. The USSR and West Germany eased into the semis with victories over Hungary and Uruguay respectively. The England–

England's controversial third goal against West Germany in the final.

Argentina clash was explosive. Argentine captain Antonio Rattin spoke out of turn once too often for the liking of the German referee and chaos ensued for several minutes as Rattin refused to walk. The game was settled by a glancing header from Geoff Hurst, who was making his first appearance in the tournament. The country's premier goalscorer, Jimmy Greaves, was out of form and injured. His World Cup was over.

Ramsey finally settled on his best team and tactics. Earlier he had tried out wingers John Connelly, Ian Callaghan and Terry Paine but now the England boss decided to dispense with wide players altogether. With Nobby Stiles a defensive anchor in front of the back four and Martin Peters and Alan Ball in midfield, it left Bobby Charlton as a deep-lying centre-forward behind Hurst and Hunt.

Two Bobby Charlton specials were enough to beat Portugal in the semis in a sporting match full of free-flowing football. Eusebio scored from the spot to make it 2–1 and had the consolation of finishing as the tournament's top scorer. In the other semi-final West Germany beat the USSR, who were reduced to ten men when Chislenko was sent off.

Ramsey Fulfills his Dream

The Germans struck first in the final, Haller capitalising on a mistake from Ray Wilson. Bobby Moore picked out his West Ham teammate Hurst with a free-kick and the latter heading in a goal. The third member of the Upton Park contingent, Martin Peters, volleyed in from close range with less than 15 minutes left, but in the dying seconds England conceded a free kick and Weber equalized after the ball went through a sea of players in the box. In the first period of extra-time Hurst pivoted on an Alan Ball cross and thudded his shot against the underside of the bar. It was cleared after bouncing down but had it crossed the line? Russian linesman Bakhramov gave the referee the nod. In the dying seconds Hurst latched onto a long clearance from Moore and lashed the ball past Tilkowski. He had become the only man to score a hat-trick in a World Cup final, while Ramsey had fulfilled his dream and promise. England became the fifth country to win football's greatest prize.

England on their lap of honour carrying the Jules Rimet trophy.

Jairzinho of Brazil scores in the 1970 competition.

1970

Pele had been so disenchanted with the experience of 1966 that he had intimated he wouldn't play in Mexico four years later. In the end he had a change of heart and this time he had an array of talent alongside him that was reminiscent of 1958 and 1962. Carlos Alberto was commanding at the back; Gerson was a supreme midfield general; Jairzinho was the new Garrincha; Rivelino had a shot like a thunderbolt; and Tostao was a fox of a player, both a maker and taker of chances. Goalkeeper Felix might not have been the greatest but could any opponents score more than they conceded against this star line-up?

Brazil and England were co-favourites and drawn in the same group. Pele set up Jairzinho for the only goal of the match after seeing his powerful downward header miraculously saved by Banks. Both teams won their other two matches and many thought they had seen a rehearsal of the final.

Brazil and West Germany Impress

West Germany had been impressive in qualifying and like Brazil reached the quarter-finals with three victories. Morocco, who only lost 2–1 to the Germans and picked up a point against Bulgaria, celebrated becoming Africa's first representative at a World Cup. Italy made sure they avoided the mistakes of '66 but hardly inspired with a 1–0 win over Sweden followed by goalless draws against Uruguay and Israel. The famous catenaccio system took them into the last eight without putting the millions watching on colour television for the first time, on the edge of their seat.

England took a two goal lead against West Germany in their quarter-final clash in Leon. Goals from Mullery and

Peters temporarily wiped out concerns over the absence of Gordon Banks, who had fallen victim to a stomach bug. His deputy Peter Bonetti should have done better with Beckenbauer's shot which squeezed under his body. With the score at 2–1 Ramsey – now Sir Alf – replaced Bobby Charlton with Colin Bell and the tide turned. A looping back-header from Seeler floated over Bonetti's head to tie the score, and in extra-time Gerd Müller – 'Der Bomber' – volleyed the winner.

Brazil and Italy won their quarter-finals comfortably, and Uruguay edged out the USSR to reach the last four.

Italy came out on top in the European battle to reach the final. After taking the lead against West Germany through Boninsegna early on, the Italians went into their shell and tried to hold out. This time they came unstuck, conceding a last-minute equaliser. Five goals flew in during extra-time, the advantage passing back and forth. Rivera had the final say, Italy winning 4–3. In the other semi Uruguay scored first but never really looked like holding Brazil, who replied with goals from Clodoaldo, Rivelino and Jairzinho, who thus kept up his record of scoring in every match.

Brazil Awarded the Jules Rimet Trophy

The final lived up to its billing, and the exuberant flair of the Brazilians prevailed over the cautious and methodical Italians. Pele headed Brazil into the lead but Boninsegna latched onto a loose pass to equalize. In the second half Brazil cut loose. Gerson's shot from outside the box restored their lead and Pele set up goals for Jairzinho and Carlos Alberto, the latter a marvellous flowing move started deep in defence. As three-time winners Brazil kept the Jules Rimet trophy outright; they also left the fans with memories of some of the most breathtaking football ever seen.

Hoeness brings down Cruyff in the first minute of the 1974 final.

1974

The 1974 World Cup, like the preceding tournament, is probably best remembered for a team which played exhibition football, although on this occasion it didn't end in victory. Rinus Michels' Holland side included many of the Ajax stars he had nurtured in the 1960s, players who had won a hat-trick of European Cups. 'Total Football' entered the vocabulary and it seemed that Michels was about to unleash it onto the world stage.

England couldn't stop them. A draw against Poland at Wembley in the qualifiers meant that Ramsey's men missed out on a place in the finals. Peru, who had entertained on their way to the last eight in Mexico, also missed out this time round, as did Portugal, Spain and Hungary. Brazil made it but with just three survivors from 1970 they were a shadow of the team that had lifted the cup in Mexico. The holders qualified behind Yugoslavia and only edged out Scotland on goal difference.

Germany Tipped to Win

West Germany looked strong despite finishing behind neighbours the GDR in Group 1. Beckenbauer, Breitner, Overath and Müller had helped West Germany win the 1972 European Championship, and with home advantage Helmut Schoen's side was strongly tipped. As runners-up in their group the West Germans also avoided the Dutch in the second-round group phase. Under this new format the top eight sides from the first round were split into two new groups with the winners meeting in the final. One team which failed to reach the second round was Italy. They were beaten by an outstanding Poland side, who finished with maximum points and provided a crumb of comfort for England supporters. The Italians drew with Argentina, effectively leaving the runners-up spot to whichever of them could score more goals against newcomers Haiti. Italy's defence, unbeaten in over 16 hours of international football, was pierced by the Haitians, and although they recovered to win 3–1 it wasn't to be enough. Argentina's 4–1 win meant that the finalists of 1970 were out.

In Group B Poland and West Germany beat Sweden and Yugoslavia and met in what was effectively a semi-final showdown. In the torrential conditions Gerd Müller scored the only goal of the match. Poland went on to finish third and had entertained royally. The pattern in Group A was much the same. Holland and Brazil met after each side had recorded victories over East Germany and Argentina. The Dutch were irresistible, scoring through Neeskens and Cruyff. The Brazilians turned to increasingly desperate measures to stop them, and Luis Perreira's sending off was

Germany's Gerd Müller holds the trophy as his teammate Overath waves in 1974.

indicative of the country's decline over the past four years.

Holland took a dramatic first-minute lead in the final, Neeskens scoring from the spot after Cruyff's surging run into the box was halted unfairly by Hoeness. If the Dutch unconsciously thought this was going to be a routine victory they were to be disappointed. Breitner equalized from a more marginal penalty, and just before the break the deadly Müller spun and shot the Germans ahead before the Dutch defence could react. Holland pressed in the second half but couldn't turn territorial advantage into goals. West Germany won 2–1 and the Dutch masters left the Olympic Stadium highly acclaimed but clutching the runners-up medals.

1978

The world's best player of the time, Johan Cruyff decided not to go to Argentina in 1978. Even so the Dutch squad included many of the stars that had come so close to winning in 1974 and they were among the favourites this time round. England failed to reach the finals yet again. Under Don Revie England shared the points in the two matches against Italy, but failure to score enough goals against Luxembourg and Finland proved critical. Scotland again flew the flag for the home countries. Ally MacLeod had some outstanding players, including Dalglish, Buchan, Gemmill, Jordan and Macari. The team also had the fervent backing of 'Ally's Army'. But the wheels came off early as the Scots were beaten 3–1 by Peru. Things got even worse when winger Willie Johnston failed a drug test and was sent home. A feeble 1–1 draw against Iran followed. The Scots saved the best till last, beating Holland 3–2. It wasn't enough to stop them going out yet again on goal difference, but Archie Gemmill scored one of the best World Cup goals ever and the team at least salvaged some pride.

Italy and hosts Argentina had already made sure of qualifying for the second round when they met in Group 1. A Roberto Bettega goal won it for Italy but as had happened with West Germany in 1974, the runners-up spot turned out to be a blessing as Argentina went into the easier of the second round groups.

Poland showed that 1974 was no fluke by topping a group including West Germany. The Germans could only manage a 0–0 draw with Tunisia in their final match, enough to secure second spot ahead of the impressive African side. As in 1974 Brazil made it to the second round without looking convincing. After two draws they scraped a 1–0 win over an Austrian side that had already qualified.

In the second round Argentina and Brazil both beat Poland and drew their match 0–0. When Argentina met Peru in the final match, Brazil had already completed its fixtures. The hosts knew that a 4–1 scoreline or better would see them through to the final. Peru capitulated, conceding six goals without reply. Both the scheduling and the Peruvian defence were highly unsatisfactory. In the other group Italy and West Germany opted for caution while Holland stepped up a gear up and comfortably came out on top.

Argentina v Holland

In the final Argentina's two big advantages over the Dutch were the passionate home support and the strike partnership of Leopoldo Luque and Mario Kempes. Kempes, who would be named Player of the Tournament, put Argentina 1–0 up. The Dutch were wasteful with their chances until nine minutes from time, when substitute Nanninga headed an equalizer. Kempes, the Valencia striker who was the only Europe-based player in Cesar Menotti's squad, broke through the Dutch defence to score his second in the first period of extra time. He then set up Bertoni to score the goal which sealed Argentina's victory.

1982

FIFA responded to the burgeoning World Cup entry by expanding the finals to accommodate 24 countries instead of 16. The growth in Asian and African football was finally acknowledged with the award of two places for each. Kuwait and New Zealand failed to make much of an impression but

Mario Kempes celebrates scoring for Argentina in the 1978 Final against Holland.

Cameroon and Algeria fared much better. Algeria beat West Germany in their opening match and also overcame Chile. The African side was then the subject of a disgraceful piece of manipulation. In the final group fixture West Germany and Austria contrived a 1–0 win for the former, a result which put both through at Algeria's expense. Cameroon also went out on goal difference. They were unbeaten but were pipped for second place by Italy, who also drew all three of their matches.

In Group 3 Hungary notched a record 10–1 win over El Salvador but still went out. Belgium, European Championship runners-up two years earlier, topped the group, beating holders Argentina along the way.

England and Northern Ireland rejoined the party, while for Scotland it was a familiar tale: qualification followed by an early exit on goal difference. In their final match the Scots needed to beat the USSR, who had a better goal difference. A 2–2 draw wasn't enough. That group was won at a canter by Brazil who, after two disappointing tournaments, once again had the personnel who could both win and entertain. Northern Ireland had their best result since 1958. A Gerry Armstrong goal beat Spain in their final match and put them into the second phase as group winners, relegating the hosts to the runners-up spot.

England got off to a flier, Bryan Robson scoring against France after just 27 seconds, the fastest ever World Cup goal. Wins over Czechoslovakia and Kuwait followed and Ron Greenwood's men joined Brazil as the only sides to go through with a 100 percent record.

In the second round goalless draws against West Germany and Spain meant England went out with something of a whimper. They needed a two-goal victory over Spain to go through but wasted their chances. The Germans' 2–1 win over Spain was the only positive result and they booked their place in the semis. Northern Ireland's bubble burst when they lost 4–1 to France, but Billy Bingham's men had performed admirably and in 17-year-old Norman Whiteside they had a player who was younger than Pele had been when the latter burst onto the World Cup scene in 1958.

Poland's class of '82 was not as strong as the team which finished third in 1974 but still managed to edge out the USSR on goal difference, thanks to a 3–0 win over Belgium. Group C saw Italy, Brazil and Argentina do battle for the last semi-final place. Italy and Brazil met in a winner-take-all match after both teams had beaten Argentina. Italy, so close to elimination in their group, got stronger as the tournament went on and in Paolo Rossi had the ace with which to beat the favourites. A Rossi hat-trick gave Italy a superb 3–2 victory.

Scirea and Dino Zoff of Italy hold the trophy aloft after the 1982 World Cup final.

Italy Equals Brazil's Record

The France–West Germany semi-final was marred by Germany 'keeper Harald Schumacher's sickening flying challenge on Patrick Battiston. France's midfield engine of Platini, Tigana and Giresse was purring and in extra time they took a 3–1 lead. Two late goals from Rummenigge and Fischer gave the tournament its first penalty shoot-out and the stylish French were eliminated. In the other semi a brace from Rossi was enough to beat Poland. The final wasn't a classic. Cabrini's penalty miss summed up a poor first half. Rossi broke the deadlock with his sixth goal, enough to make him the tournament's top scorer. Tardelli and Altobelli made it 3–0 before Breitner got a late consolation for West Germany. Italy thus joined Brazil as the only countries to win the trophy on three occasions.

1986

The unwieldy format of a second group phase was finally dispensed with in favour of a straight knockout competition after round one. The downside was that to make a 16-team second round it was necessary for the four best third-placed teams to join the winners and runners-up from the six groups. Put another way, the group phase, consisting of 36 matches, eliminated just eight teams.

Portugal, Northern Ireland and Scotland were among the early casualties, although in the Scots' case at least their elimination was more clear-cut this time. Their preparation had been disrupted by the untimely death of Jock Stein, and Alex Ferguson had stepped into the breach.

England's tournament took off when they met Poland, a game Bobby Robson's men needed to win to ensure progress. After a defeat by Portugal and a draw against Morocco, Robson had to ring the changes. An injured

shoulder ended Bryan Robson's World Cup, while Ray Wilkins was sent off against Morocco. Waddle and Hateley were dropped. In came Trevor Steven, Steve Hodge, Peter Reid and Peter Beardsley. Lineker grabbed the headlines with a hat-trick against the Poles but the whole team looked much more impressive.

Denmark and Brazil went through with three victories. France started slowly but had the nucleus of the side that had won the European Championship two years earlier. The USSR emerged from the same group, edging France into second place on goal difference. Italy, Argentina, Spain and West Germany all progressed, so some big guns had to go out in the second round. Denmark and Italy were two of them. The Danes crashed 5–1 to Spain, Emilio Butragueno – 'The Vulture' – emulating Eusebio's 1966 feat by scoring four goals in one match. France hit their stride in the 2–0 win over holders Italy. Brazil confirmed their position as favourites with a comfortable 4–0 win over Poland. Lineker added two more goals to his tally in the 3–0 win over Paraguay, but the tie of the round was Belgium's 4–3 victory over the USSR. Belgium had qualified for the tournament with a play-off victory over Holland, and they now started to show their best form.

The Hand of God

Brazil and France were unlucky to meet in the last eight. It was a superb match that would have graced the final. The only pity was that it had to be decided on penalties, as would three of the four matches at this stage. France won the shoot-out, leaving Zico to regret a spot-kick missed during normal time. West Germany also needed penalties to put out hosts Mexico and thus reached the last four without really impressing. Belgium's run continued with a shoot-out victory over Spain. The only match to be decided in 90 minutes was Argentina's 2–1 win over England. Diego Maradona provided the two lasting images of the tournament. In the 51st minute he punched the ball past Peter Shilton, none of the officials spotting the offence. Four minutes later Maradona left half the England team trailing in his wake to score one of the greatest solo goals of all time. Lineker got one back but Argentina marched into the last four.

Maradona ended Belgium's fine run in the semis. He scored both goals in the 2–0 win and at times seemed to be playing the Belgians on his own. France again fell to West Germany, although the French could have no complaints about the 2–0 defeat. Maradona didn't score in the final but

England's striker Gary Lineker.

he was instrumental in Argentina's victory as the West German players concentrated a lot of effort in trying to subdue him. The South Americans went 2–0 up, the Germans fought back to level the score and extra time loomed. Maradona's delightful pass set up Burruchaga to hit the winner. Notwithstanding the infamous 'Hand of God' goal Maradona had confirmed himself as the world's best player.

1990

Luciano Pavarotti's sonorous voice whetted the appetite for Italia '90 but this was no feast of football. Referees brandished a record number of cards, which didn't help, but even so the 14th World Cup was not one that would live long in the memory.

Cameroon stunned holders Argentina with a 1–0 win in the opening match, and followed it up with a 2–1 victory over Romania to top Group B. 38-year-old Roger Milla celebrated his brace with a corner-flag samba. Argentina sneaked through as one of the best third-place teams. Bobby Robson had already announced his decision to take over at PSV after the finals. His England side was drawn with Jack Charlton's Republic of Ireland - making their World Cup debut - and European champions Holland. Five of the six group matches were drawn, England's 1–0 win over Egypt enough to see them through as winners.

Scotland's seventh World Cup adventure pitted them against Brazil again, but with Costa Rica and Sweden in the group, the Tartan Army must have fancied their chances of progressing. A 1–0 defeat by Costa Rica put paid to that, and with Brazil winning all three games and Sweden losing all theirs it proved to be crucial.

Italy also progressed with three wins. Juventus striker Salvatore 'Toto' Schillaci, who went into the tournament as a fringe player, became one of its stars. He came off the bench to score the winner against Austria, and was a fixture in the team thereafter. Czechoslovakia joined Italy in Round Two as Group A runners-up.

Franz Beckenbauer saw his team rack up 10 goals in topping Group D, while a late Uruguay goal against South Korea in Group F put the South Americans through behind Spain and Belgium.

Holland and the Republic had finished with identical records, and lots were drawn to decide their Second Round opponents. Charlton's men got the better deal, Romania, and David O'Leary's penalty in the shoot-out put the Irish into the last eight. Holland met Germany in the tie of the round.

A confrontation between Frank Rijkaard and Rudi Voller saw both dismissed, and goals from Klinsmann and Brehme settled the issue.

Maradona showed in flashes that he was still the world's best player. A few of those came in Argentina's 1–0 win over Brazil. England made it to the quarters at the expense of Belgium, thanks to a David Platt volley deep into extra-time. Paul Gascoigne's free kick set up the chance and the Spurs midfielder was emerging as one of the stars of the tournament.

Yugoslavia and Cameroon also needed 120 minutes to get past Spain and Colombia respectively, while Czechoslovakia's 4–1 win over Costa Rica was less emphatic than it sounded. Favourites Italy marched on with a victory over Uruguay, and a Schillaci goal against the Republic booked their place in the semis. Argentina again failed to impress in their shoot-out victory over Yugoslavia, while a Lothar Matthaus penalty beat Czechoslovakia and put West Germany into the semis for the 9th time in 12 attempts.

The England-Cameroon match provided the greatest drama in the last eight. Leading 2–1, the African side naively conceded two reckless penalties, both converted by Lineker. Cameroon departed with the consolation of becoming Africa's first World Cup quarter-finalist.

In the semis West Germany took the lead against England with a deflected Andy Brehme free kick beating Shilton. Lineker equalized ten minutes from time, and it remained 1–1 after 120 minutes. Tears flowed as Gascoigne's mistimed tackle on Berthold earned him a yellow card which would have kept him out of the final. Penalty misses by Pearce and Waddle made that academic.

Maradona kisses the cup after Argentina's victory in 1986.

In the other Argentina's Claudio Carniggia cancelled out Schillaci's sixth goal of the tournament, and Goycochea saved twice in the shoot-out. In reaching the final Argentina had won two, drawn three and lost one in open play.

The final, a repeat of 1986, was a poor spectacle. Argentina were at their cynical worst, encapsulated by the red cards shown to Monzon and Dezotti, the first players to be sent off in a World Cup final. West Germany were deserving winners, although the foul which led to Brehme's decisive penalty was marginal. Franz Beckenbauer thus became the first man to both captain and manage a World Cup-winning team.

1994

At USA '94 FIFA introduced several new measures aimed at improving the World Cup as a spectacle. Tackles from behind would earn the perpetrator an automatic red card; the offside law wouldn't apply if players weren't deemed to be interfering with the action; and three points would be awarded for a win at the group stage. All these contributed to what was an exciting festival of football.

England Fails to Qualify

There was no British representation. England's qualification series under Graham Taylor had been disastrous. There were defeats against Norway and Holland – who both went through – and even the ignominy of going 1–0 down to San Marino in under ten seconds. Jack Charlton's Republic of Ireland made it again, and qualified for the second round again too. Their group, which included Mexico, Italy and Norway, was incredibly tight, each team recording a win, a draw and a defeat. Norway could consider themselves unlucky to miss out on a place in the knockout stage having notched four points.

The hosts made it past the group stage for the first time in their history. A draw against Switzerland and victory over Colombia – who many regarded as dark horses to go a long way in the tournament – saw the USA through as one of the best third-place sides. The 2–1 win over Colombia precipitated a tragedy which would overshadow matters on the pitch. Andres Escobar, who had put through his own net in that match, was shot dead in Medellin shortly afterwards.

Romania topped the USA's group and they, along with

The victorious Brazil team in 1994.

Branco of Brazil holds off a challenge from Italy's Donadoni in 1994.

Bulgaria Reaches the Semis

The Dutch weren't on their best form but in the second round were good enough to beat the Republic of Ireland, who contributed to their downfall with defensive errors. There were few surprises at this stage. Italy came from 1–0 down with seconds remaining to beat Nigeria. Baggio equalised and then scored the winner from the spot in extra time. The hosts went out to Brazil, Spain and Sweden came through comfortably against Switzerland and Saudi Arabia. Romania marched on with a 3–2 win over Argentina, the South Americans still reeling from the loss of their talisman. Bulgaria put out Mexico in the only shoot-out of the round and then made everyone sit up and take notice with a 2–1 win over Germany in the quarter-finals. Late goals from Stoichkov and Lechkov put the Bulgarians into the semis having achieved nothing in their five previous World Cup campaigns. They were jubilant, but for Germany it marked their worst performance in the tournament since 1978.

Romania nearly made it two East European sides in the last four but they went down on penalties to Sweden after the game ended 2–2. Baggio again proved himself to be the jewel in Italy's crown in their 2–1 win over Spain. Holland finally showed some form against Brazil but with the score at 2–2 a rocket from full-back Branco won the game for the favourites. Brazil reached the final by beating Sweden more comfortably than the 1–0 scoreline suggested. Bulgaria's bubble was finally pricked by Italy, Baggio scoring both goals in their 2–1 victory. Having only scraped through their group in third-place and enjoyed their fair share of luck in reaching the final, the Italians went into their shell against Brazil.

Bulgaria, were two of the most impressive sides on show. Hagi and Stoichkov respectively were the stars of these East European teams but both had an array of talented individuals.

Bulgaria, Nigeria and Argentina qualified with two victories each, Greece being the group's whipping boys. Argentina had recalled Maradona after a scratchy qualifying series which included an uninspiring play-off victory over Australia. He helped the team to a convincing win over Greece but failed a drug test following the victory over Nigeria. He had played his last World Cup game for his country.

While Cameroon failed to scale the heights of 1990, Nigeria showed that African football was getting stronger by the year. Despite a 2–1 defeat against Argentina, Nigeria beat Bulgaria and Greece to top the group on goal difference.

Brazil hadn't set the world on fire in reaching the USA but eased into the second round comfortably and were most people's favourites to lift the trophy. Romario and Bebeto was just about the best strike pairing in the competition. Germany and Holland topped their groups to ensure that the knockout phase included a mixture of big guns and unheralded teams.

David Beckham congratulates Michael Owen who scored against Romania in their Group G match in 1998.

Defences were on top in a dull game that was still goalless after 120 minutes. In the first penalty shoot-out to decide a World Cup Baggio had to score the last of Italy's five penalties to keep his country alive. The man who had done so much to help his team reach the final failed to score and Brazil were world champions for the fourth time.

1998

France had failed to reach USA '94. Defeat against Bulgaria, in which David Ginola's wayward pass had led to the winning goal, was still painfully fresh in the memory of Les Bleus fans. Four years later, under Aime Jacquet, the French put that disaster behind them in style. They warmed up with maximum points in their group, taking full advantage of having South Africa and Saudi Arabia as their first two opponents. Brazil lost their final group fixture against Norway but had already done enough to get through. Scotland crashed 3–0 to Morocco but Norway's win over the holders made that result irrelevant.

    Group D was the 'Group of Death' this time round. The extended 32-nation tournament meant that only the top two from each of the eight groups would go forward.

Holland's de Boer brings down Ronaldo.

Nigeria and Paraguay progressed from Group D, leaving a dangerous Spain side and Bulgaria — semi-finalists four years earlier — on their way home. The Paraguayans, led by their stocky extrovert 'keeper Jose Luis Chilavert, had the luxury

French captain Deschamps and teammate Boghossian show their delight after France win the 1998 World Cup Final.

Owen celebrates after scoring against Denmark in June 2002.

of playing a Nigeria side that had already qualified in their final group match. The South Americans took full advantage, rendering Spain's 6–1 thrashing of Bulgaria academic.

Dan Petrescu's goal gave Romania a 2–1 win over England but both sides went through comfortably. Michael Owen came off the bench to score in the Romania game, leaving fans wondering if coach Glenn Hoddle would give the Liverpool prodigy a place in the starting line-up in the second round.

Argentina was the only team other than France to emerge from the group stage with three wins. Gabriel Batistuta scored an eleven-minute hat-trick in the 5–0 win over Jamaica. The 'Reggae Boyz' signed off with a victory, 2–1 over Japan, but it was Croatia who went through with the South Americans.

Group F had an even more intriguing battle for the

wooden spoon. Iran's 2–1 win over the USA was overlaid with political as as well as sporting significance, although as expected both were beaten by the group's big two, Germany and Yugoslavia. With 64 matches to play in barely a month the second round got under way without a pause for breath. A Christian Vieri goal was enough to beat Norway and put Italy into the last eight. Brazil and Denmark hit four goals each against Chile and Nigeria respectively. Ronaldo scored twice for Brazil and everyone – coach Mario Zagallo included – wondered whether the star striker would go on to take the tournament by the scruff of the neck. All the other games were decided by the odd goal, while the England-Argentina clash went to a shoot-out. This was the most dramatic tie of the round. With the score at 1–1, both sides having converted penalties, Michael Owen ran half the length of the field and rifled the ball into the top corner for the goal of the tournament. Argentina equalised from a clever free kick on the stroke of half time and just after the break David Beckham was red carded for a petulant kick on the Diego Simeone, which the latter milked for all it was worth. England gamely held out and thought they'd won it when Sol Campbell powered in a header in extra time. That was ruled out for an infringement and England went on to lose yet another shoot-out. Paul Ince and David Batty joined Waddle, Pearce and Southgate in one of the least prestigious clubs in English football.

France's Laurent Blanc scored the extra-time winner against Paraguay, the first ever golden goal in a World Cup match. The Romanian players all dyed their hair blond for the match against Croatia but to little avail; a Davor Suker penalty saw Croatia through to the last eight at their first World Cup. Germany came from behind to beat Mexico, while the Dutch hit a last-minute winner against Yugoslavia.

France's quarter-final victory over Italy on penalties after a goalless 120 minutes confirmed that their weakness was up front. Croatia's 3–0 win over Germany was the most emphatic result of the round. The Germans had Christian Worms sent off but still couldn't complain about their worst World Cup result for over 40 years. Dennis Bergkamp's sublime finish in the dying seconds against Argentina was a worthy winner, the score at 1–1 and a red card apiece at the time. Denmark gave Brazil a stern test, scoring after just two minutes against the holders. Brazil came through 3–2 to set up a semi-final clash with Holland. Patrick Kluivert scored a late equalizer and the match went to

penalties. Taffarel saved from Cocu and Ronald de Boer and Brazil were in the final again. Lillian Thuram was the star of the other semi. The full-back scored both goals in the 2–1 win over Croatia. The only blot was Blanc's dismissal after a cynical piece of play-acting by Slaven Bilic. Suker's sixth goal of the tournament gave him the consolation of being the tournament's hotshot.

The drama of the final began before a ball was kicked. Rumours over Ronaldo's fitness abounded, Brazil's star striker supposedly having suffered a seizure. After initially being left out of the team Ronaldo added to the confusion by taking the field. Neither he nor his teammates performed on the day, however. Zidane headed two goals and Emanuel Petit sealed a comprehensive victory when he stroked the ball past Taffarel in the last minute. The World Cup had been the dream of a Frenchman 70 years earlier; the 16th tournament saw France finally get its hands on the trophy.

Zinedine Zidane of France fends off Italian player Gianluca Pessotto in the match between France and Italy in the 1998 World Cup.

David Beckham celebrates after scoring the opening goal in England's match against Argentina.

2002

2002 saw the world's greatest footballing jamboree staged in Asia for the first time. The final was contested by the two most successful countries in the tournament's history, and yet it will be remembered as a competition of shocks that turned footballing orthodoxy on its head.

The first of those came in the curtain-raiser, in which it was widely thought that debutants Senegal would give holders France little more than a gentle workout. The African Nations Cup runners-up had other ideas. El Hadji Diouf terrorised France's defence and Senegal ran out 1–0 winners. Things got even worse for France against Uruguay when they had Thierry Henry sent off for a rash tackle. Zidane was struggling for fitness but in desperation he was brought back to face Denmark in the crunch final match. The gamble didn't pay off and the reigning champions went out with neither a victory nor a goal to their name.

England Defeat Argentina

Of all the permutations in Group F, this year's 'Group of Death', Argentina being eliminated wasn't one that had many takers. Argentina had romped through the qualifiers and looked far more impressive than Brazil. After a win over Nigeria, Argentina faced England, who had been held 1–1 by Sweden in their opener. Michael Owen won a penalty and David Beckham exorcised the memory of 1998 by firing home from the spot. A point from the final match against Sweden wasn't enough for the South Americans. Sweden topped the group from England on goal difference.

South Korea and the USA came through from Group D, ending Portugal and Poland's interest at the first hurdle. Portugal was the seeded side and tipped by many to go a long way. The USA rocked Figo and Co with three early goals in the opening match, and although the Portuguese recovered to hammer a disappointing Poland, a 1–0 defeat by Guus Hiddink's South Korea signalled the end of the road. Portugal had two players sent off as they became increasingly desperate and ill-disciplined.

Groups B and C took a similar pattern. Spain and Brazil won all their games, Slovenia and China lost all theirs. The race for second place was won by Paraguay and Turkey respectively, who went through by edging out South Africa and Costa Rica on goal difference. Turkey's progress was helped by the fact that they lost only 2–1 to Brazil, a game which saw one of the worst examples of 'simulation' – FIFA's new buzz word for cheating. Hakan Unsal was sent off after firing the ball at Rivaldo. It hit the Brazilian on the thigh but he went down holding his face, a display of histrionics the tournament could well have done without. He was subsequently fined, but it amounted to a mere slap on the wrist.

Germany put eight past Saudi Arabia on their way to topping Group E. Having lost 5–1 to England in the qualifiers, the Germans had needed a play-off victory over Ukraine to reach the finals. They scored eleven goals and conceded just one in the first phase, yet this was not regarded as one of the country's better sides in recent years. Mick McCarthy's Ireland gained a crucial point against Germany to go through as runners-up, leaving African Nations Cup winners Cameroon as another surprise early casualty.

Mexico played some superb football in winning Group G. Italy went through in second place. Trapattoni's side would be on the receiving end of a number of controversial decisions throughout the tournaments and would go down as the unluckiest side. Co-hosts Japan were seeded in Group H, which was dubbed the 'Group of Life' as it seemed so open. Japan were as good as their billing, victories over Russia and Tunisia marking their first ever in World Cup competition. As the Japanese fans went wild there were ugly scenes in Russia as their team crashed out.

Cafu smiles as he holds aloft the World Cup trophy in 2002.

Ireland–Spain encounter went to penalties after the game ended 1–1. Ireland failed twice from the spot and Gaizka Mendieta scored the goal which put Spain through. The USA put out arch-rivals Mexico 2–0 in an ill-tempered match. Brazil beat Belgium by the same score, although this was a close match. The Belgians were unlucky to have a Marc Wilmots header ruled out and only conceded a second goal late in the game when they were throwing men forward. Japan's fine run was ended by Turkey, who scored early on through Umit Davala and never really looked threatened.

In the quarter-finals Michael Owen put England in front against Brazil with a neat finish. Ronaldinho set up Rivaldo to equalize, then floated a 35-yard free kick over Seaman's head for the winner. He rounded off a memorable match by being red carded. A Michael Ballack goal gave Germany victory over the USA, who were unlucky not to be awarded a penalty for a handling incident on the goal line. Spain had two goals disallowed against South Korea and went out on penalties feeling mightily aggrieved. The Turkey–Senegal game also went to extra time, but it was just four minutes old when Ilhan Mansiz broke the deadlock with a golden goal winner. Turkey had not reached a World Cup since 1954; now they were in the semis. Turkey met Brazil for the second time and again went down narrowly. A piece of Ronaldo magic was needed to beat Turkey's excellent 'keeper Rustu. South Korea ran out of steam against Germany. Michael Ballack again scored the only goal of the match, and picked up a booking that would keep him out of the final.

Brazil's Fifth Victory

A second-half brace from Ronaldo gave Brazil their fifth World Cup victory. It put him on eight for the tournament, easily enough to make him the top marksman. After the disappointment of 1998, Ronaldo and Brazil showed that they were, both personally and collectively, back on top of the world.

Ireland Goes Out on Penalties

The second round got off to an uninspiring start. A late Oliver Neuville goal put Germany into the quarter-final at the expense of Paraguay in a drab encounter. England's three first-half goals against Denmark settled that match, the most emphatic result of the round. Senegal and South Korea both enjoyed golden goal victories to book their places in the last eight. Henri Camara's strike put out Sweden while Ahn Jung-hwan headed a late winner against Italy. The fact that he was playing for Perugia didn't endear the golden boy of Korean football to Azzurri fans. The

2006

Fourth crown for the Azzurri

In 1982 Italy claimed their third World Cup victory in the wake of a bribery scandal. Twenty-four years on, the Azzurri went to Germany with domestic football in virtual meltdown following corruption allegations involving four Serie A sides, yet under Marcello Lippi they found strength in adversity and were worthy winners of the eighteenth tournament.

Four teams recorded maximum points in the group stage. A flowing Germany hit eight goals in topping Group A, and the home fans, who had been writing off their side's chances and calling for Jurgen Klinsmann's head, suddenly began to believe that the hosts might go all the way. Portugal and Spain impressed in winning Group D and H respectively, albeit against somewhat modest opposition. Favourites Brazil clinched top spot in Group F with a 4–1 victory over Japan, though the 'golden quartet' of Ronaldo, Ronaldinho, Adriano and Kaka was hardly firing on all cylinders. The clash between Croatia and Australia to decide who would go through with the five-time winners was one of the most dramatic matches of the tournament. Seven of the Socceroos squad had Croatian roots, while three Croatia players were born and bred in Oz, giving the encounter an added edge. Australia twice came from behind to take the point they needed, and it wasn't just the Croatians who were packing their bags: referee Graham Poll yellow-carded Simunic three times before sending him off, showing that it wasn't only players who suffered occasional rushes of blood to the head.

Contender for best goal ever

England failed to set the pulse racing but still qualified from Group B with a game to spare, something they hadn't managed since Spain '82, and a 2–2 draw with Sweden in the game to decide top spot meant that Eriksson's men avoided Germany in the last 16. Group C had been given the 'Group of Death' tag, but in the event it was clear-cut. The big guns of Argentina and Holland overcame debutants Ivory Coast and Serbia and Montenegro, then played out a goalless draw in a match to decide the final placings. Those bald statistics hid the fact that Ivory Coast gave an excellent account of themselves and would probably have progressed in a less demanding group. Argentina's 6–0 demolition of Serbia and Montenegro produced a contender for best World Cup goal ever, a sublime 24-pass move finished off by Esteban Cambiasso. Having routed a team whose miserly defence had shipped just one goal in the qualifiers, Argentina became most people's favourites to lift the trophy.

Black Stars reach knockout stage

Group E produced the first major shock, Ghana advancing as runners-up to Italy. The Black Stars beat the Czech Republic – ranked second in the world when the draw was made – and the USA, who had reached the quarter-finals in Japan and Korea. On paper Group G looked to be one of the weaker sections of the draw, but 1998 world champions France left it late to secure their place in the knockout stage. Having managed only to share the points with Switzerland and South Korea, Les Bleus kick-started their campaign with

a 2–0 win over Togo. It was only good enough for second spot, Switzerland becoming the unlikeliest of the eight group winners.

Last Sixteen

A first-half brace from Lukas Podolski gave Germany a comfortable 2–0 victory over Sweden, who must have known it wasn't to be their day when Teddy Lucic was sent off and Henrik Larsson blazed over from the spot. Argentina and Mexico turned on the style in a match full of champagne moments. 1–1 inside 10 minutes, the game was decided by Maxi Rodriguez's stunning volley in extra-time. David Beckham answered his many critics with a trademark free kick that was enough to beat Ecuador, becoming the first English player to get on the scoresheet in three World Cups. Portugal midfielder Maniche had scored the winner against Holland in the semi-final of Euro 2004, and his goal separated the sides again in what was an incendiary affair. There were 16 yellow cards and the game finished nine versus nine, a new World Cup record.

Guus Hiddink had masterminded the downfall of Italy as coach of South Korea in 2002, and he came close to repeating the trick with Australia this time round. Italy were down to 10 men with extra-time looming when Fabio Grosso surged into the box and tumbled over Lucas Neill, who had invitingly gone to ground. Totti made no mistake from the spot. Ukraine beat Switzerland on penalties after a drab 120 minutes. The Swiss went out despite having kept a clean sheet in all four games — no other team managed that — yet their lack of endeavour won them few friends. Brazil's 3–0 victory over Ghana was highly flattering. One of the goals was clearly offside, and Ghana squandered some golden opportunities. The Black Stars had become only the fifth African team to reach the second round, and it could so easily have been an even bigger story. Ronaldo still looked a sluggish shadow of his former self, yet he followed up his brace against Japan with the opener against Ghana, his fifteenth World Cup goal putting him ahead of Gerd Muller in the all-time list. Spain had been far more impressive than France in the group stage, and looked a good bet to end their drought against Les Bleus in competitive fixtures. David Villa put Luis Aragones' men 1–0 up from the spot, but the veteran French side was improving all the time and hit back with goals from Ribery, Vieira and Zidane.

South American giants crash in quarters

Argentina and Brazil both crashed out in the last eight. Jose Pekerman carried the can for Argentina's defeat by Germany, resigning shortly after the hosts had won their quarter-final on penalties. Ayala headed in from Riquelme's corner early in the second half, and Pekerman's decision to withdraw his ace playmaker and shut up shop backfired when Klose scored a late equaliser. It was the German striker's fifth goal, a haul which would bring him the Golden Shoe. Extra-time produced no goals and Jens Lehmann became the local hero with two fine saves.

A dreamlike visitation had prompted Zinedine Zidane to come out of international retirement during France's qualifying campaign, and against Brazil he showed a return to the kind of form that had brought him the World Footballer of the Year award on three occasions. Zizou pulled the strings, and it was his fifty-seventh-minute free kick which picked out Thierry Henry, who volleyed home for the only goal of the game.

More shoot-out agony for England

Italy brushed Ukraine aside as expected, and Portugal joined an all-European semi-final line-up at England's expense. For the third tournament running Luis Felipe Scolari went head-to-head with Sven-Goran Eriksson at the quarter-final stage. 'Big Phil' orchestrated Brazil's 2–1 victory in Japan and Korea, and led Portugal to a shoot-out success at Euro 2004. It came down to penalties again this time, neither side managing to conjure a goal in 120 minutes. England played for almost an hour with 10 men, Wayne Rooney having been red-carded for a stamping incident involving Ricardo Carvalho, yet the team's heroics went unrewarded. Portugal missed twice in the shoot-out, but penalty specialist Ricardo saved from Lampard, Gerrard and Carragher to put his side into the last four for the first time since 1966.

New-style Italy eliminate hosts

The Germany-Italy semi-final, a repeat of the 1982 final, was a terrific game. Italy had conceded just once thus far in the tournament – and that a Christian Zaccardo own-goal against USA – suggesting a dour application of the famous catenaccio system. But while Italy's defence, marshalled by the superb Fabio Cannavaro, was as resilient as ever, they were also fluid and expansive going forward. Lippi played four attackers in extra-time, and it paid off handsomely. Grosso curled a beauty past Lehmann with 90 seconds to go, and del Piero finished off an incisive counter-attack to put the icing on the cake.

The France-Portugal semi was a tight affair with few chances. Zidane's first-half penalty, awarded for Carvalho's challenge on Henry, was the difference between the sides.

Germany beat Portugal 3–1 in the third-place play-off, the enthusiastic reception Klinsmann's team received from the home fans reflecting the widespread view that they had performed beyond expectations. It was the 11th time

Italian defender Fabio Cannavaro waves the trophy after the 2006 World Cup final.

Germany had reached at least the semis; not even Brazil could match that.

And so to the final, a dramatic affair in which Azzurri defender Marco Materazzi was the key figure in all the turning points. It was his seventh-minute challenge on Florent Malouda that led to the opening goal, Zidane deftly chipping his penalty in via the underside of the bar. It was a magical piece of impudence, particularly as he was facing Gianluigi Buffon, the man who would pick up the Lev Yashin award for the tournament's outstanding goalkeeper. Zidane became only the fourth player to score in two World Cup finals, following in the footsteps of Brazil's Vava and Pele, and Paul Breitner of West Germany.

Sad end to a glorious career

Materazzi levelled for Italy with a towering header from a Pirlo corner on 19 minutes. At half-time Zidane was named as the Golden Ball winner, ahead of two of his opponents, Fabio Cannavaro and Andrea Pirlo. Whether he would have been voted player of the tournament had the poll been taken two hours later is a moot point. For in extra-time with the teams locked at 1–1, Zidane was sent off for head-butting Materazzi after the pair were involved in a verbal spat. It was an inglorious end to a glittering career, for Zidane had already announced his retirement from the game.

The Italians could hardly have relished the prospect of the second penalty shoot-out to decide a World Cup final. They had been on the sharp end of the first, losing to Brazil in '94, and on two other occasions Italy had gone out of the competition on spot-kicks. But it all came right this time. Materazzi was one of the scorers in a perfect set of five, rubbing further salt into France's wounds. David Trezeguet's golden goal had broken Italian hearts in the Euro 2000 final, but this time it was his miss against his Juventus teammate Buffon which left Fabio Grosso to set the seal on Italy's

fourth World Cup victory. Fabio Cannavaro, winning his one hudredth cap, lifted the coveted trophy, Italy becoming the most successful European country in the tournament's history. It also meant that Europe had drawn level with South America on nine World Cup wins apiece.

The consensus was that it had been a good tournament rather than a great one. Simulation, Fifa's buzzword for cheating in 2002, was an even greater blight this time round. And the 64-match marathon didn't produce a truly outstanding team. Many thought that the young tyros such as Messi, Rooney, Kaka and Torres would take the tournament by the scruff of the neck. But while they played cameo roles, the stars were the old guard, the likes of Ayala, Figo, Lehmann, Cannavaro, Thuram, Vieira. And, of course, the incomparable Zidane.

THE WORLD CUP

1930	Final	MONTEVIDEO	**Uruguay** v Argentina	**4–2** (1–2)	Centenario
1934	Final	ROME	**Italy** v Czechoslovakia	**2–1** a.e.t 1–1 (0–0)	Nazionale PNF
	3rd/4th	NAPLES	**Germany** v Austria	**3–2** (3–1)	Giorgio Ascarelli
1938	Final	COLOMBES-PARIS	**Italy** v Hungary	**4–2** (3–1)	Olympique
	3rd/4th	BORDEAUX	**Brazil** v Sweden	**4–2** (1–2)	Parc Lescure
1950	Final	RIO DE JANEIRO	**Uruguay** v Brazil	**2–1** (0–0)	Maracana
1954	Final	BERNE	**West Germany** v Hungary	**3–2** (2–2)	Wankdorf
	3rd/4th	ZURICH	**Austria** v Uruguay	**3–1** (1–1)	Hardturm
1958	Final	STOCKHOLM	**Brazil** v Sweden	**5–2** (2–1)	Rasunda
	3rd/4th	GOTHENBURG	**France** v West Germany	**6–3** (3–1)	Nya Ullevi
1962	Final	SANTIAGO DE CHILE	**Brazil** v Czechoslovakia	**3–1** (1–1)	Nacional
	3rd/4th	SANTIAGO DE CHILE	**Chile** v Yugoslavia	**1–0** (0–0)	Nacional
1966	Final	LONDON	**England** v West Germany	**4–2** a.e.t 2–2 (1–1)	Wembley
	3rd/4th	LONDON	**Portugal** v Soviet Union	**2–1** (1–1)	Wembley
1970	Final	MEXICO CITY	**Brazil** v Italy	**4–1** (1–1) .	Azteca
	3rd/4th	MEXICO CITY	**West Germany** v Uruguay	**1–0** (1–0)	Azteca
1974	Final	MUNICH	Netherlands v **West Germany**	**1–2** (1–2)	Olympiastadion
	3rd/4th	MUNICH	Brazil v **Poland**	**0–1** (0–0)	Olympiastadion
1978	Final	BUENOS AIRES	**Argentina** v Netherlands	**3–1** a.e.t 1–1 (1–0)	River Plate
	3rd/4th	BUENOS AIRES	**Brazil** v Italy	**2–1** (0–1)	River Plate
1982	Final	MADRID	**Italy** v West Germany	**3–1** (0–0)	Santiago Bernabeu
	3rd/4th	ALICANTE	**Poland** v France	**3–2** (2–1)	Jose Rico Perez
1986	Final	MEXICO CITY	**Argentina** v West Germany	**3–2** (1–0)	Azteca
	3rd/4th	PUEBLA	**France** v Belgium	**4–2** a.e.t 2–2 (2–1)	Cuauhtemoc
1990	Final	ROME	**West Germany** v Argentina	**1–0** (0–0)	Olimpico
	3rd/4th	BARI	**Italy** v England	**2–1** (0–0)	Sant Nicola
1994	Final	LOS ANGELES	**Brazil** v Italy	**0–0** a.e.t 3–2 on pens	Rose Bowl
	3rd/4th	LOS ANGELES	**Sweden** v Bulgaria	**4–0** (4–0)	Rose Bowl
1998	Final	SAINT-DENIS	Brazil v **France**	**0–3** (0–2)	Stade de France
	3rd/4th	PARIS	Netherlands v **Croatia**	**1–2** (1–2)	Parc des Princes
2002	Final	YOKOHAMA	West Germany v **Brazil**	**0–2** (0–0)	Yokohama
	3rd/4th	DAEGU	Korea Republic v **Turkey**	**2–3** (1–3)	Daegu Stadium
2006	Final	BERLIN	**Italy** v France	**1–1** a.e.t 5–3 on pens	Olympiastadion
	3rd/4th	STUTTGART	**Germany** v Portugal	**3–1** (1–0)	Gottlied-Daimler-Stadion

The European Championship

A European championship was first mooted in the 1920s by Henri Delaunay, secretary of the French Football Federation. When the World Cup took off the idea remained on the back burner until 1954, when UEFA was founded. Once Europe had its administrative body, Delaunay's idea was revived. It would take three years for the competition to win the approval of the UEFA member nations, and it was by no means unanimous. Among the sceptics were the UK football associations. The home countries dragged their feet, feeling that a new tournament in the calendar would undermine their annual domestic championship.

The draw for the first competition was made in August 1958, timed so as not to clash with the World Cup. Seventeen countries entered, and they would be whittled down to four on a knockout basis, with games being played over two legs. The semi-finalists would then do battle for the trophy at a single venue. France was named as the host country for the inaugural finals. The trophy was named after Delaunay, who died in 1955, a fitting tribute to the man who had done so much to bring the dream to fruition.

1960

A 17-strong entry meant that a qualifying match was necessary. Czechoslovakia beat the Republic of Ireland 4–2 and 16 teams proceeded to the knockout stage. Politics reared their head in the quarter-finals when Spain's fascist dictator General Franco refused to sanction his country's meeting with the Soviet Union. The latter thus reached the finals by default. The USSR comfortably beat Czechoslovakia in their semi-final but the other was full of drama. The French went 4–2 up against Yugoslavia and appeared to be coasting to victory, despite missing the two big stars of the 1958 World Cup, Raymond Kopa and Just Fontaine. It all went wrong as the French conceded three late goals and went down 5–4. Yugoslavia took a first-half lead in the final but this time they were on the receiving end of a comeback. Metrevelli equalized for the Soviet Union early in the second half and the game went into extra time. Yugoslavia couldn't find a way past the outstanding Lev Yashin and Viktor Ponedelnik hit the winner for the Soviet Union in the first period of extra time.

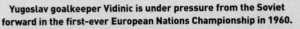

Yugoslav goalkeeper Vidinic is under pressure from the Soviet forward in the first-ever European Nations Championship in 1960.

1964

England deigned to enter the tournament in 1964 but after a 5–2 defeat in France – Alf Ramsey's first game in charge – their interest was soon over. Twenty-six countries contested the first round, with holders the USSR, Austria and Luxembourg all given byes. Hosts Spain started impressively, as did Italy, who were also making their first appearance. The big shock was the elimination of Czechoslovakia, who had finished third in the inaugural tournament and runners-up to Brazil in the 1962 World Cup. The Czechs went down 3–2 on aggregate to the GDR. Second-round casualties included Yugoslavia and Holland, beaten by Sweden and Luxembourg respectively. The Soviet Union halted Italy's progress, a Yashin penalty save in Rome helping the holders to protect a 2–0 advantage gained at home. Spain thrashed the Republic of Ireland in the last eight and were joined in the finals by the Soviet Union, Denmark and Hungary. The draw kept apart Spain and the Soviet Union, who had been involved in a political row four years earlier. Both went through to the final, too. The Russians comfortably beat Denmark, while Spain got through thanks to an extra-time winner from Amancio. A 100,000-strong crowd at the Bernebeu Stadium saw Spain win its first major tournament. After a goal from either side inside the first ten minutes the game remained in the balance until Marcelino hit the winner for Spain six minutes from time.

Spain v USSR in the 1964 European Championship final.

1968

World Cup runners-up West Germany made their debut in 1968 as the entry increased yet again. Only Iceland and Malta declined to participate in the third championship. Qualification for the finals, to be staged in Italy, was on a league rather than knockout basis. Each of the eight groups had a seeded team and these were expected to form the quarter-final line-up. There were two upsets, however. West Germany, needing a win in Albania in their final match, could only draw, allowing Yugoslavia to top the group. Meanwhile Portugal, World Cup semi-finalists two years earlier, surprisingly went out following a crucial away defeat against Bulgaria, who thus made it to the last eight.

England took on Spain – the world champions against the European champions. England took a 1–0 lead to Madrid for the second leg. Amancio levelled the tie early in the second half but goals from Peters and Hunter put England through. Ramsey's men booked their place in Italy and in their semi-final faced Yugoslavia, who had beaten France 6–2 on aggregate in the quarters. It was a nasty encounter, one in which Alan Mullery's retaliatory kick on an opponent made him the first England player to be sent off. Yugoslavia's brilliant left winger Dragan Dzajic volleyed the only goal of the game. In the final Yugoslavia faced hosts Italy, who won their semi against the USSR on the toss of a coin after the game ended goalless. Dzajic was again on target but Domenghini equalized from a free kick ten minutes from

time. The game ended 1–1 and a replay was required. This time Italy scored early through Luigi Riva and ran out comfortable winners, the final score 2–0.

1972

The European Nations Cup was rechristened the European Championship as 32 of the 33 UEFA-affiliated countries fought to make it to the finals in Belgium. Only Iceland remained on the sidelines. West Germany was the outstanding team. Helmut Schoen had revamped the side which had reached the semi-final of the 1970 World Cup into a dauntingly impressive unit. Müller and Beckenbauer were still there but other stars were emerging: Sepp Maier in goal, full-back Paul Breitner, Uli Hoeness in midfield and Jupp Heynckes up front. But the man who pulled the strings was Borussia Moenchengladbach's Gunter Netzer. This was the nucleus of the team that would go on to lift the 1974 World Cup, yet by common consent it reached its zenith in 1972. England was on the receiving end in the quarter-finals. The Germans outclassed Ramsey's side at Wembley in a 3–1 victory. England salvaged some pride with a goalless draw in the second leg but the damage had been done. In the semi-final West Germany faced hosts Belgium, who had put out reigning champions Italy in the last eight. A brace from Gerd Müller put Schoen's side into

England captain Bobby Moore (left) chats with West German captain Franz Beckenbauer in 1972.

the final, where they faced the Soviet Union, who had beaten Hungary 1–0 in the other semi. Müller grabbed two more to make it eleven in all for the tournament. Herbert Wimmer also got on the scoresheet in a match which West Germany won at a canter.

1976

The 1976 European Championship was the most exciting so far and remains one of the most dramatic international tournaments of all time. When Czechoslovakia came to Wembley and lost 3–0 in their opening match of the qualifiers, few would have bet that the beaten team would go on to qualify, let alone win the trophy. The Czechs booked their place in the last eight with a 2–1 home victory over England, a result which put them top of the group by one point. In the 4–2 aggregate win over arch-rivals the Soviet Union, the Czechs showed that they were a formidable team with a crop of gifted players. Captain Anton Ondrus was outstanding in midfield, while up front Marian Masny had trickery and flair in abundance. Holland and West Germany, the World Cup finalists of 1974, also made it to the finals, along with hosts Yugoslavia. The Yugoslavians had put out Wales in the quarters in an ill-tempered encounter, the Welsh feeling they were denied a clear penalty by the German referee.

The four games of the finals produced 19 goals in open play, plus eight more in a dramatic penalty shoot-out. West Germany came from two behind against Yugoslavia to win 4–2 in extra time, largely thanks to a hat-trick from Dieter Müller. The other semi also required an extra 30 minutes. Czechoslovakia beat a Holland side that was reduced to nine men by the end, 3–1 the final score.

It was another famous fightback in the third-place match, Yugoslavia coming from behind to beat the Dutch 3–2, another game which required extra time. In the final West Germany found themselves 2–0 down for the second match running. Beckenbauer was still there, winning his 100th cap, but Gerd Müller had retired from international football, and Breitner and Heynckes were also missing. Even so the Germans hit back with a Dieter Müller volley and pressed for an equalizer. It came in the last minute, Holzenbein heading in at the near post. There was no score in extra time and the match went to penalties, the first major tournament to be decided on a shoot-out. After seven successful spot-kicks Uli Hoeness blazed over. Antonin Panenka coolly beat Maier with the next and Czechoslovakia were champions.

Wimmer of West Germany scores his second goal against the Soviet Union in 1972.

1980

In 1980 the European Championship returned to Italy for the second time, but with a revised format. Eight teams instead of four would contest the finals. These were split into two groups who would play a round-robin series, the winners going through to the final. For the first time the hosts were given automatic qualification, leaving the rest of Europe vying for seven places.

England dropped just one point, away to the Republic of Ireland, and booked their place with plenty to spare. 1976 runners-up West Germany also qualified comfortably. Holders Czechoslovakia made it at the expense of France, and World Cup finalists Holland also topped their group. 1976 semi-finalists Yugoslavia missed out, though, finishing behind Spain.

The tournament promised much but generally failed to deliver. After the exciting goal-fest last time around the group matches were something of a yawn. The six Group 2 games produced just nine goals. England began with a goalless draw against Belgium, a match in which riot police had to be deployed to deal with hooligans. A Marco Tardelli goal was enough to beat Ron Greenwood's men in their second match and England were eliminated. Victory over Spain in the final game simply meant avoiding the wooden spoon. Italy needed to beat Belgium to finish top of the group. It was yet another goalless draw and the Belgians reached their first major final by virtue of having scored more goals.

In Group 1 West Germany opened with a 1–0 win over Czechoslovakia. A Karl-Heinz Rummenigge goal gave the Germans revenge for defeat in the 1976 final. Klaus Allofs hit a hat-trick against Holland, who replied with two late goals in the highest-scoring match of the competition. West Germany got the point they needed against Greece to reach the final for the third tournament in a row.

The Germans took the lead after ten minutes through the giant blond Hamburg striker Horst Hrubesch. Van der Eycken equalized from a penalty with 20 minutes left. The

The West German team pose before the final against Belgium in 1980.

German defenders complained that Stielike brought down Van der Elst outside the box, but the player was clean through and justice was served. With extra time looming, Hrubesch headed in from a corner and Germany became the first country to win the trophy twice.

1984

France's outstanding side of the early 1980s got its reward at Euro '84. Denied by West Germany in the semis at both the 1982 and 1986 World Cups, Michel Hidalgo's team won in style on home soil in 1984. England missed out on a place in the finals, a 1–0 home defeat by Denmark being the crucial result. Northern Ireland also missed out, but only on goal difference, to West Germany. A Norman Whiteside goal gave Billy Bingham's side an historic 1–0 win in Germany, but although the Irish completed a double over West Germany the group favourites only had to beat Albania in their final game to reach the finals. Northern Ireland put up a far better showing than world champions Italy, whose only victory in their eight matches was at home to Cyprus. The story of the qualifiers was Spain's 12–1 win over Malta. The Spanish went

into their final match knowing they needed an eleven-goal margin of victory to pip Holland. They did just that, and even missed a penalty.

Denmark and France were the outstanding teams in Group 1 and met in the opening match. Platini scored the only goal of the game, while the Danes lost Simonsen with a broken leg. Both teams went on to beat Belgium and Yugoslavia. Platini hit hat-tricks in each of France's games, putting him on seven after the group stage. Denmark also progressed as UEFA dispensed with the third-place play-off in favour of semi-finals. Spain and Portugal emerged from Group 2, which meant a rare first-round exit in a major tournament for West Germany. The Germans' lacklustre showing meant that Jupp Derwall's days were numbered; he was soon replaced by Franz Beckenbauer.

Spain and Portugal each won just one of their three group matches and scored only five goals between them in reaching the semis. France and Denmark were the form sides and looked likely to meet again in the final. France made it, although they needed a goal in the last minute of extra time to beat Portugal. But Denmark missed out, Spain winning a shoot-out after the game ended 1–1.

European Championship in Germany. Jack Charlton's Republic of Ireland reached the finals of a major tournament for the first time, and the two were drawn in the same group. The Republic boasted the First Division's top scorer in John Aldridge but it was another Liverpool player who made the telling contribution when the two sides opened their campaign in Stuttgart. Ray Houghton headed the Republic into a sixth-minute lead, his first goal for his country in 16 appearances. Bonner was outstanding in goal for Ireland, who held out for a famous victory.

A Marco Van Basten hat-trick ended England's hopes, and after another 3–1 defeat against the USSR England were anchored to the bottom of the group.

Charlton's men earned a creditable draw against an excellent Soviet Union side which included Mikhailichenko, Rats, and former European Footballer of the Year Igor Belanov. But a 1–0 defeat against the Dutch meant that the Republic of Ireland also missed out on a place in the semis.

West Germany and Italy drew their opening match, then both beat Denmark and Spain to finish on five points. The Germans scored one more goal to top the group, which meant a semi-final clash with Holland. After a penalty apiece, Van Basten scored the winner two minutes from time. The Soviet Union beat Italy in the other semi to set up a second meeting with Holland, this time for the title.

The final took place at the Olympic Stadium, Munich, where Holland had lost in the 1974 World Cup final. Now, as then, Rinus Michels was in charge of the Dutch side. This time it ended in victory. A Ruud Gullit header put Holland 1–0 up, and a stunning Van Basten volley doubled their lead eight minutes after the break. Hans Van Breukelen made up for conceding a penalty by saving Igor Belanov's spot-kick, and with that the Soviet Union's chance of staging a comeback disappeared. Van Basten, who had arrived in Germany as a fringe player, left to universal acclaim as the player of the tournament.

French captain Michel Platini holds aloft the cup in 1984.

In the final, staged at the Parc des Princes, Platini opened the scoring when Arconada failed to hold his free kick. It was his ninth goal in five games. The final was not a great spectacle, but France sealed victory with a last-minute goal from Bruno Bellone.

1988

After missing out on Euro '84 and falling victim to the best and worst of Maradona at the 1986 World Cup, Bobby Robson's England side qualified comfortably for the 1988

1992

England scraped into Euro '92 with a late Gary Lineker goal which gave Graham Taylor's team the draw they needed in Poland. Lineker's volley 13 minutes from time, meant that the Republic of Ireland missed out on qualifying for a second successive European Championship. Scotland, making its first appearance in the finals, gave Britain two representatives when the action got under way in Sweden.

As in 1988, England failed to register a win and finished bottom of the group. The team opened with a goalless draw against Denmark, who had been given a

Rijkaard of Holland and Dave McPherson of Scotland jump for the ball in their 1992 match in Sweden.

The reunification of Germany meant that the country was competing as one nation in a major tournament for the first time since World War Two. Most of the squad hailed from the former West Germany, although Matthias Sammer quickly established himself in the side. Germany lost to Holland but went through to the semis as runners-up.

Henrik Larsen twice put Denmark ahead against Holland, who pulled level through Bergkamp and, five minutes from time, through Rijkaard. Having used all their substitutes, Denmark had to carry an injured John Sivebaek through extra time. They did so, and when Peter Schmeichel saved from Van Basten it left Kim Christofte to score with his spot-kick to put Denmark into the final.

Germany beat Sweden in the other semi, Karl-Heinz Riedle grabbing a brace. Germany were favourites to win the trophy but John Jensen shot Denmark into an 18th-minute lead. That remained the score until twelve minutes from time, when Kim Vilfort added the killer second. Denmark had come from nowhere to beat the reigning world champions and register their first tournament victory.

1996

On the 30th anniversary of its World Cup success, England staged its second major championship. 'Football's coming home' rang round the stadiums and there was a party atmosphere as the expanded 16-nation tournament got down to business. England and Scotland were the only home countries' representatives and found themselves in the same group. Both had notched up one point when they met in the second match. David Seaman saved a Garry McAllister penalty and a piece of Gascoigne magic sealed a 2–0 victory. Terry Venables' side saved the best until last, thumping Holland 4–1. Holland's consolation goal from Patrick Kluivert was vital as it meant they edged out Scotland for the group's runners-up spot.

Bulgaria and Romania, who had done so well at the 1994 World Cup, both went out at the first hurdle. Spain and France went through to the last eight unbeaten. Berti Vogts' Germany comfortably topped Group C, with international newcomers the Czech Republic edging out a highly rated Italy for second place. The Czech side was expected to be the whipping boy of a powerful group, which also included Russia, and that seemed a fair assumption when they went down 2–0 to Germany in their opening match. After a victory over Italy the Czechs faced a Russian side that was already out of contention. Vladimir Smicer's last-minute equaliser put the Czech side through at Italy's expense.

dramatic late entry into the tournament as replacement for Yugoslavia. Denmark had finished runners-up to Yugoslavia in the qualifiers, and when the Balkans erupted into civil war UEFA called up the Danes at less than two weeks' notice. England then played out another 0–0 draw against France, while Denmark went down to Sweden to confirm the general view that they were rank outsiders. Needing to beat Sweden to progress, England scored early through Platt. Eriksson equalised early in the second half and Taylor then substituted Lineker, a decision which mystified fans and pundits alike. It was to be his last game in an international shirt and he remained on 48 goals, one short of Bobby Charlton's record. Tomas Brolin's winner, with eight minutes to go, only served to turn up the heat on the England coach. Denmark went from bottom of the group to runners-up with a 2–1 win over France.

Favourites Holland topped Group B, dropping just one point by drawing against the Commonwealth of Independent States. This would be the only tournament that would feature the CIS. By the time the 1994 World Cup came around, the former Soviet states would be competing as separate entities.

David Seaman was the penalty shoot-out hero against Spain after a goalless draw. There were no goals in the France–Holland match either. Clarence Seedorf's miss in the shoot-out put the French through. The Germany–Croatia clash provided three of the four goals scored at the quarter-final stage, but this was no classic. Sammer scored the winner on the hour in a game which was littered with fouls.

Alan Shearer headed England in front just two minutes into their semi-final against Germany. Stefan Kuntz levelled and it was yet another shoot-out. Gareth Southgate had been outstanding at the back but it was his miss that left Andy Moller to shoot Germany into the final. The Czech Republic's great run continued against France, a game which also went to penalties after a goalless 120 minutes. The Czechs enjoyed the support of most neutrals when they faced Germany in the final and took the lead through a Patrik Berger penalty after Poborsky was brought down. Substitute Oliver Bierhoff headed Germany level with just under 20 minutes to go and the same player won the trophy by scoring the golden goal winner four minutes into extra time.

England's Paul Gascoigne is jubilant after scoring against Scotland in 1996.

Gareth Southgate is consoled after missing a penalty in the semi-final against Germany in 1996.

Another country making its debut on the international scene emerged from Group D. Croatia had a crop of star individuals, including Boban, Prosinecki, Suker and Boksic. A 3–0 win over holders Denmark in their second match made sure of a place in the last eight whatever happened in the final game. That was a 3–0 defeat against the Portuguese, who topped the group.

The Portuguese team was built around the players who had won the World Youth championship in 1991, including Figo, Rui Costa and Joao Pinto. This outstanding side was surprisingly halted in the quarter-finals by the Czech Republic and would struggle to shake off the underachievers tag.

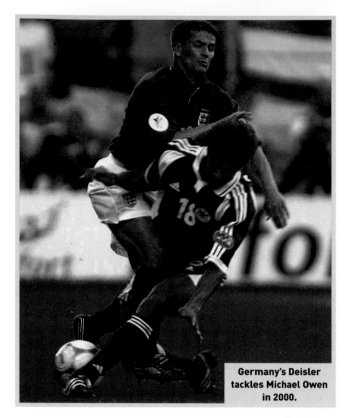

Germany's Deisler tackles Michael Owen in 2000.

2000

There was yet another England–Germany clash at Euro 2000, and after the disappointments of 1990 and 1996 England finally came out on top. Alan Shearer headed the only goal of the match, but in the end it turned out to be a battle for last place. England threw away a two-goal lead in the opener against Portugal, and Keegan's men were also in front against Romania in the final group match. With the score 2–2, Phil Neville gave away a last-minute penalty which Ganea converted.

Portugal took maximum points from Group A, results including a 3–0 win over Germany courtesy of a Sergio Conceicao hat-trick. Romania finished runners-up.

Italy and Holland also progressed to the last eight with three victories each. In Group B Belgium looked favourites to finish second to Italy. But the co-host's defeat against Turkey, together with an understrength Italy's 2–1 win over Sweden, meant that Turkey were through.

In Group D Holland met France in the final group match, both sides having won their first two games. In a match of fluctuating fortunes, Zenden scored the winner in a five-goal thriller to secure top spot for the Dutch. It meant early elimination for Denmark and the Czech Republic, winners and runners-up in 1992 and 1996 respectively.

Group C saw Slovenia make its debut in international tournament football. Two draws and a narrow 2–1 defeat against Spain was creditable, but it could have been better had they not let a three-goal lead slip against Yugoslavia in the opening match. The Slovenians even had the advantage of playing the latter stages against ten men after Sinisa Mihajlovic was red-carded.

That drama was superseded as the final group matches were played out. With time virtually up, Yugoslavia led Spain 3–2, a result which would have put them top, with Norway through in second place and Spain out. Spain then hit two goals in injury time. The Spanish were now top, with Yugoslavia relegated to second; Norway had had qualification snatched away.

There were no surprises in the quarter-finals. Kluivert hit a hat-trick and Overmars a brace as Holland thrashed Yugoslavia 6–1. Portugal and Italy had relatively comfortable wins over Turkey and Romania. The Spain–France encounter was closer. France took a 2–1 first-half lead and the second 45 minutes provided no further goals. It did produce a penalty however, but Raul fluffed his lines.

Both semis went to extra time. Holland paid the price for missing five penalties against Italy, two in normal time and three in the shoot-out after the game ended 0–0. The Portugal–France match was three minutes away from penalties when Abel Xavier handled in the box and Zidane scored from the spot.

Italy had kept the Dutch at bay for almost 90 minutes with ten men in the semis. In the final they only needed to keep France out for a few seconds to win the trophy. But with time just about up Sylvain Wiltord equalised Marco Delvecchio's 56th-minute goal. David Trezeguet then struck the hammer blow as he hit the golden goal winner in the first period of extra time. France had come back from the brink of defeat to add the European Championship to their world crown.

2004

England, once again the only home country representative in the finals, opened with a defeat against holders and favourites France. A Lampard header put England ahead but a Zidane double in injury time - a stunning free kick and a penalty - turned the game on its head. A brace from Wayne Rooney helped England to a 3–0 win over Switzerland. Rooney became the youngest scorer in the championship's history, and although that record quickly fell to Switzerland's Johan Vonlanthen, it was the Everton striker's name that was on everyone's lips. Rooney hit two more in the 4–2 victory over Croatia, a result which sealed England's place in the last eight as runners-up to France.

Portugal recovered from a defeat against Greece to win Group A. Greece proved to be the surprise package of the tournament. Otto Rehhagel's men lost to Russia in their final match, but Spain's 1–0 defeat by Portugal saw them through. Spain went home as underachievers.

Italy was the big early casualty from Group C. As Trapattoni's side went into their final game against Bulgaria, the mathematicians were working overtime. If Denmark and Sweden drew 2–2, they would both progress, irrespective of Italy's result. The Italians snatched a late winner, but joy turned to despair as news of Mattias Jonson's last-minute strike for Sweden came through, giving the result Azzurri fans dreaded. Italy, unbeaten and with five points, was out.

Group D yielded the only 100 per cent record. The Czech Republic came from behind to win all three matches in style. The Czechs fielded virtually a reserve team against Germany in the final match but still emerged with a 2–1 victory. Holland clinched the runners-up spot with a 3–0 win over Latvia, while the Baltic nation's greatest moment came in a goalless draw against Germany.

Michael Owen fired England into a third-minute lead over Portugal in their quarter-final. Rooney limped off with a foot injury and Portugal gained the ascendancy. Postiga equalised on 83 minutes, and when Campbell's header was ruled out in the dying seconds the game went to extra-time. Rui Costa put Portugal ahead but Lampard scored his third goal of the tournament to take the game to penalties. Beckham looked ruefully at a pudding of a penalty spot as he blasted over. Rui Costa did likewise and it went to sudden death. Darius Vassell's effort was saved by Ricardo, who then scored to put Portugal through.

80–1 outsiders Greece, not content with making the knockout stage of a major championship for the first time, put out France. It was a tactical triumph for Rehhagel whose team reduced Les Bleus to very few chances and scored with a bullet header from Charisteas in the 65th minute.

Holland and Sweden couldn't manufacture a goal between them in 120 minutes, although both sides hit the woodwork. Aston Villa's Olof Mellberg had his penalty saved by Van der Sar and 20-year-old Arjen Robben scored the goal which put the Dutch through.

The Czech Republic again impressed in the 3–0 win over Denmark, the most decisive result of the round. Jan Koller headed the Czechs in front early in the second half, and as the Danes pushed forward Milan Baros scored twice, making his tally five goals in four games.

Portugal and Holland, the beaten semi-finalists at Euro

France celebrate victory in 2000.

2000, met at the same stage this time round. The hosts, inspired by Figo, ran out worthy winners. Ronaldo headed Portugal in front, and Maniche's stunning angled drive flew into the top corner to make it 2–0. A Jorge Andrade own goal gave Holland hope but Portugal's margin of victory could and should have been much greater.

Having put out the pre-tournament favourites, Greece caused another upset by eliminating form team the Czech Republic in the other semi. The Czechs lost playmaker Nedved early on but still created several good chances. The game was settled by a silver goal in the first period of extra-time. Defender Traianos Dellas, once of Sheffield United, headed in from a corner and there was no time for the Czechs to respond. For the first time in the championship's history the final was thus a repeat of the tournament's opening fixture.

The Final completed the biggest-ever upset in international competition as a second half Charisteas header brought heartbreak for the hosts and the championship to Greece. In a game of few chances the Portugal coach spoke of 'nerves' affecting his players who failed to break down a strong Greece defence.

Greece had never won a match in any previous competition. In a tournament in which many of the top stars failed to deliver, the final words came from the Greece coach: 'Bigger football nations are getting smaller'.

2008

If 2004 had been a victory for defensive football, the 2008 tournament, staged in Austria and Switzerland, was full of open, attacking play, which kept home nations' fans glued to their TV screens, even though they had no partisan interest in the outcome.

Group A favourites Portugal became the first team through to the second phase with wins over Turkey and Czech Republic. Ronaldo opened his account in the 3–1 win over Karel Bruckner's side, and had a hand in both of the other goals. Co-hosts Switzerland packed their bags after losing a thriller against Turkey, a game played in a downpour. It looked set for a draw – a result which suited neither side after opening-round defeats – when Arda's deflected shot looped over the Swiss 'keeper in injury-time. It left a winnertake-all encounter between Turkey and Czech Republic for a place in the last eight, and the latter side seemed to be cruising to victory when they took a two-goal lead. A Petr Cech howler allowed Nihat to level with three minutes to go, and the same player curled a stunning winner into the top corner in the 89th minute in one of the most dramatic finales ever seen in tournament football.

Germany hadn't won a game at the Euro finals since their 1996 triumph, but were still favourites to lift the trophy this time round. Lukas Podolski gave Joachim Low's men a flying start in Group B, hitting both goals in the 2–0 win over Poland, though the Bayern Munich striker's celebrations were muted as he dented the qualification hopes of his native country. Croatia went into the tournament with just two defeats in four years in competitive matches, and continued their fine run with a maximum haul in the group phase, including a 2–1 win over Germany. Goals from Srna and Olic gave Croatia only their second victory over their opponents, following the historic win at France '98. Coach Slaven Bilic had been a member of that side, and his touchline joy was unrestrained as the tournament's smallest nation – population less than five million – came out on top against one of the footballing giants. A Michael Ballack rocket free-kick saw off Austria in the final round of matches, but Germany couldn't overhaul Croatia, whose second-string side was still good enough to beat Poland. For Ivan Klasnic, scorer of the game's only goal, victory was simply being on the pitch, for he had undergone two kidney transplants in the previous 18 months.

Holland set Group C – and the tournament – alight with a stunning 3–0 win over Italy in their opening fixture. The world champions must have been shell-shocked as two of the goals came seconds after the Azzurri had threatened Edwin van der Sar's goal. It was Holland's first win over Italy since the 1978 World Cup, and the latter country's worst defeat for 25 years. The Dutch followed it up with an equally impressive 4–1 trouncing of France, making it a seven-goal blitz against the teams that had contested the 2006 World Cup final. Gianluigi Buffon kept Italy's hopes of surviving the 'Group of Death' alive with a late penalty save from Romania's Mutu, rescuing a vital point. Marco van Basten's B-team was still good enough to beat Romania, leaving Italy and France to battle for the runners-up spot. Nothing went right for Les Bleus. They lost Franck Ribery early on, and were reduced to ten men following Eric Abidal's crude tackle on Luca Toni, Andrea Pirlo converting from the spot. When De Rossi's free kick flicked off Thierry Henry's boot, wrong-footing France 'keeper Gregory Coupet, the result was never in doubt.

Many tipped this to be the year that Spain finally shook off their underachievers tag. They came into the tournament on the back of a 16-game unbeaten run, and stretched that with a 4–1 demolition of Russia in their Group D opener. David Villa bagged a hat-trick, while Cesc Fabregas weighed in with his first international goal. Villa also hit a late winner against Sweden to confirm Spain as group winners, no doubt upping Valencia's asking price for a player said to be on the shopping list of some of Europe's top clubs. Reigning champions Greece boasted seven players from their 2004 triumph, but the lustre of 'King Otto' Rehhagel's crown was tarnished as his team crashed out following defeats by Sweden and Russia. Sweden needed only a draw against Russia to go through as runners-up, but couldn't cope with Guus Hiddink's fast-improving side. Skipper Andrei Arshavin, suspended for the first two games, scored the killer second goal and was at the heart of an attacking display that was both potent and stylish.

Portugal's flair was nullified by Germany in a thrilling quarter-final encounter, which the favourites won 3–2. Bastian Schweinsteiger finished off a scintillating left-flank move to open the scoring, and Germany scored two headers from free kicks, exposing a weakness in the heart of the Portuguese defence. Nuno Gomes reduced the arrears to 2–1 – becoming only the third player to score in three Euro tournaments – and substitute Helder Postiga headed home in the 88th minute to make it a nervy last few minutes for German fans. But the favourites were well worth their victory against a below-par Portugal, and the defeated coach, Luiz Felipe Scolari, had the consolation that the inspirational Michael Ballack, scorer of the third goal, was soon to be playing for rather than against him when he took over at Stamford Bridge.

'Never write off Turkey' became part of the footballing lexicon after that country's remarkable victory over Croatia. It looked all over for the Turks when veteran 'keeper Rustu went walkabout and Ivan Klasnic put the ball into a vacant net with almost two hours on the clock. There was just time for one hopeful punt forward, and Semih latched onto the knockdown and crashed the ball into the top corner to force a shoot-out. Modric and Rakitic both missed the target, and when Rustu saved from Petric, Turkey were through to the last four with two spot-kicks in hand.

Guus Hiddink masterminded the downfall of his homeland in a sparkling Russia–Netherlands match. Ruud van Nistelrooy's 86th-minute header cancelled out Pavlyuchenko's goal and took the game into extra-time, where star man Andrei Arshavin again made the telling contribution. The Zenit St Petersburg striker set up Torbinsky to score, then beat van der Sar at the near post to put the result beyond doubt. Van Basten had no complaints as his side was outplayed in all facets of the game by the tournament's youngest team.

The Spain–Italy clash was a cagey affair, with few chances and defences on top. It looked destined for a shoot-out long before the 120 minutes were up. Iker Casillas saved two of the first four penalties he faced, Buffon one. Cesc Fabregas then drilled home the first spot-kick of his professional career to give Spain their first tournament win over Italy since the 1920 Olympic Games.

Few gave a Turkey squad shorn of nine players through injury and suspension a hope against Germany in the semis, yet Fatih Terim's patched-up side outplayed the favourites for much of the game. The Turks took a deserved lead through Ugur, and it was against the run of play when Schweinsteiger

timed his near-post run perfectly to clip Podolski's cross past Rustu for the equaliser. Miroslav Klose reached a high ball ahead of Rustu and headed into a gaping net with 11 minutes left, and it seemed that Germany had steadied the ship. But the late goal specialists did it again, Semih guiding the ball past Lehmann in the 86th minute after terrific work by Sabri on the right flank. With extra-time looming, Lahm surged forward, playing a delightful one-two with Hitzlsperger before crashing the winner into the roof of the net and taking Germany into their sixth Euro final.

Spain booked a place in their first final for 24 years by sweeping aside a Russian team that failed to deliver after playing some champagne football en route to the semis. The three-goal margin was a repeat of the teams' group meeting, with Fabregas giving a midfield masterclass after coming on for the injured Villa, who was ruled out of the Vienna showpiece.

In the 44 years since Spain's sole tournament triumph – the 1964 European Championship – Germany had been crowned champions of the continent on a record three occasions, and twice held the World Cup aloft. But on a sultry night in Vienna the 2008 favourites were outplayed by a Spanish side that had looked irresistible since their opening-day demolition of Russia. Fernando Torres scored the game's only goal, seizing on Xavi's pass and clipping the ball over Lehmann after outpacing Lahm. The gulf was much wider than the 1–0 scoreline suggested, and the tournament's best team prevailed, ending 44 years of hurt in scintillating style.

EUROPEAN CHAMPIONSHIP

1960 France
Final
USSR 2–1 Yugoslavia
3rd/4th
Czechoslovakia 2–0 France

1964 Spain
Final
Spain 2–1 USSR
3rd/4th
Hungary 3–1 Denmark

1968 Italy
Final
Italy 2–0 Yugoslavia
(after replay first game 1–1)
3rd/4th
England 2–0 USSR

1972 Belgium
Final
Germany 3–0 USSR
3rd/4th
Belgium 2–1 Hungary

1976 Yugoslavia
Final
Czechoslovakia 2–2 Germany
(Czechoslovakia win 5–3 on penalties)
3rd/4th
Netherlands 3–2 Yugoslavia

1980 Italy
Final
Germany 2–1 Belgium
3rd/4th
Czechoslovakia 1–1 Italy
(Czechoslovakia win 9–8 on penalties)

1984 France
Final
France 2–0 Spain

1988 Germany
Final
Netherlands 2–0 USSR

1992 Sweden
Final
Denmark 2–0 Germany

1996 England
Final
Germany 2–1 Czech Republic

2000 Belgium/Netherlands
Final
France 2–1 Italy

2004 Portugal
Final
Greece 1–0 Portugal

2008 Austria/Switzerland
Final
Spain 1–0 Germany

Olympic Games

Until the founding of the World Cup in 1930 the Olympic Games was the only major international football tournament. It was included as a demonstration sport in the first Games of the modern era, in 1896, and became an official Olympic event in 1908. Many of the strongest footballing nations had yet to embrace professionalism and so there was no conflict with the amateur ethos of the Olympic movement. Even in England, which had fought the battle over paying its players in the 1880s, the issue was not critical. Indeed, in the early years of the 20th century the top amateurs, such as those who turned out for the famous Corinthians, could hold their own against the professionals.

The 1908 Games, staged in London, was effectively the first world championship, although the entry was modest. The FA chose a team of amateurs to represent Great Britain, including the Spurs and England inside-forward Vivian Woodward. France sent two sides, while Denmark,

Holland and Sweden completed the six-strong entry. England beat Denmark 2–0 in the final. The same two teams contested the 1912 final in Stockholm. England prevailed again, 4–2 this time. Fourteen countries had entered, and even with three late withdrawals it represented a healthy increase on the previous tournament.

In 1924 Uruguay competed for the first time and dazzled their opponents as they took the title. The country retained its crown in 1928, beating debutants Argentina. Between 1929 and 1935 Brazil, Argentina, Uruguay, Italy, Spain and France were among those to embrace professional football, the World Cup was also taking off and the importance of the Olympic title naturally diminished. In 1932 the Los Angeles Games didn't include football at all.

The Scandinavian countries continued to maintain their amateur status and they, along with the state-sponsored East European countries, began to dominate. In 1948 Sweden beat Yugoslavia 3–1 at Wembley. In 1952 it was hardly surprising that world-beaters Hungary, including Puskas, Kocsis and Czibor, took the gold medal, Yugoslavia again the beaten finalists. Between 1952 and 1980 Eastern European

Capucho of Portugal and Ze Elias of Brazil chase the ball during the 1996 Olympic Games.

countries contested every Olympic final with the exception of Rome 1960, when Denmark lost 3–1 to Yugoslavia.

In 1980 FIFA barred any European or South American player who had played in a World Cup match from competing at the Olympics. The virtual monopoly of the Eastern European sides was broken at a stroke. Ironically, even under the new ruling, the Soviet Union managed to take gold at Seoul in 1988. Before the next Games in Barcelona FIFA had decreed that the Olympics would be an Under-23 competition open to all players. Spain took gold, beating Poland 3–2 in the final. The rules were tweaked yet again for Atlanta '96 with teams allowed to field three over-age players. Nwankwo Kanu captained a Nigeria side which beat Argentina to take the gold medal. Daniel Amokachi and

Celestine Babayaro were also on the winning side, while the Argentina line-up included Claudio Lopez and Hernan Crespo.

The dispensation to allow teams to include some star players was a compromise aimed at raising the profile of the competition, that continued in Sydney 2000 as Cameroon became the second African country to win Olympic gold, beating Spain on penalties in the final.

Argentina scored their first win in Athens in 2004, and retained the title in Beijing four years later. A side including Riquelme, Messi and Mascherano faced Nigeria in the final, Benfica striker Angel Di Maria scoring the gold medal-winning goal that avenged their 1996 defeat.

OLYMPIC WINNERS

1908	1936	1968	1992
Great Britain	Italy	Hungary	Spain
1912	1948	1972	1996
Great Britain	Sweden	Poland	Nigeria
1920	1952	1976	2000
Belgium	Hungary	East Germany	Cameroon
1924	1956	1980	2004
Uruguay	USSR	Czechoslovakia	Argentina
1928	1960	1984	2008
Uruguay	Yugoslavia	France	Argentina
1932	1964	1988	
No tournament	Hungary	USSR	

Cameroon celebrate winning gold in 2000.

Copa America

Some 50 years before the European Nations Cup got under way, South America launched its own competition for that continent's championship. International matches between Uruguay and Argentina took place in the early years of the 20th century, first for the Lipton Cup and then the Newton Cup. In 1910 Argentina's FA decided to widen the competition to include other neighbouring countries. Three agreed to participate in the first tournament, staged in Argentina that year. Brazil withdrew, leaving Uruguay, Chile and the hosts to battle it out. Argentina and Uruguay both comfortably beat Chile and met in the decider of the round-robin series. Some fans set fire to Buenos Aires' Gimnasia Stadium before the match and it was abandoned without a ball being kicked. The rescheduled game took place at Racing Club's ground the following day. Argentina won 4–1 to become the inaugural champions. However, as the South American Football Confederation was not formed until 1916, the 1910 tournament is generally accorded unofficial status in the record books.

Argentina and Uruguay dominated the early years. In the fifteen tournaments that were staged between 1910 and 1937 only one country made inroads into the duopoly. Brazil beat Uruguay in a play-off in 1919, star centre-forward Arthur Friedenreich scoring the only goal of the game. The Brazilians' only other pre-war success came in 1922. In 1939 Peru became the fourth country to win the championship, taking full advantage of playing at home. There had been a six-year hiatus between 1929 and 1935 as the championship fell victim to the newly instituted World Cup and was also hit by protracted wrangling over the introduction of professionalism.

In the late 1940s the competition was again disrupted, this time by a players' strike in Argentina. In 1949 Argentina would have been hot favorites to record a fourth successive victory. As the strike took hold, some of the country's top stars – including the young Alfredo di Stefano – went to play in a pirate league in Colombia. Argentina was also missing in 1953 when another new name was added to the list of winners. Paraguay, who had been thrashed 7–0 by Brazil in a play-off in 1949, reversed that result four years later; the score was 3–2.

Only two tournaments took place in the 1960s as the new club championship, the Copa Libertadores, was launched. Bolivia's victory in 1963 was at least in part attributable to the fact that both interest in and commitment to the championship was waning. Brazil, the best side in the

Cafu of Brazil lifts the trophy after victory over Uruguay in the Copa America Final at the Estadio Defensores del Chaco in Asuncion, Paraguay. Brazil won 3–0.

Argentinian soccer player Hernan Crespo (left), jumps for the ball with Venezuelan Wilfredo Alvarado

world during this era, regularly fielded understrength teams in South American Championship matches.

The 1970s again saw just two tournaments played. Second victories for Peru in 1975 and Paraguay four years later suggested that the trend of decline was continuing. In 1975 the championship was renamed the Copa America and the mini-league format, which had stood since 1910, was amended so that the competition at last had a showpiece final. It was also the first time that all ten CONMEBOL countries competed.

Since 1987 the competition has enjoyed much greater stability and prestige. From that year on, the biennial tournament has been hosted by a single country in Europe's close season, alleviating the thorny problem of player withdrawal which had dogged the competition previously. Not only did the CONMEBOL nations regard victory in the Copa America as a great prize but countries beyond South America were also invited to participate. Mexico and the USA were the first to join the party, in 1993. Mexico made it to the final, too, going down 2–1 to Argentina. The move to include countries from further afield had two major advantages. It was a shrewd commercial decision to extend the interest to such populous countries. Also, having wrestled with many ideas for structuring a ten-country competition over the years, the organisers now had more flexibility in

their choice of format. A group stage followed by knockout matches from the quarter-finals on is now the norm. In 2001 Argentina withdrew and Mexico, Honduras and Costa Rica took part in a twelve-strong tournament. The eight best sides from the group stage progressed to the quarter-finals. Honduras did magnificently in reaching the semis, while Mexico made it to the final for a the second time. It was the runners-up spot again, though, as hosts Colombia became the seventh country to add its name to the roll of honour.

Brazil took the title in 2004 and 2007 to make it four wins in five tournaments. They made a hesitant start in Peru in 2004, losing to Paraguay in the opening round, and needing a shoot-out to claim victory over Uruguay and Argentina, in the semi-final and final respectively. Adriano was in top form, cracking in seven goals to pick up the Golden Shoe award. Three years later, in Venezuela, Dunga came in for some criticism for fielding a team shorn of the talents of Kaka and Ronaldinho. There was another group-phase defeat, this time to Mexico, and another shoot-out victory over Uruguay in the semis. The final again pitted Brazil against arch-rivals Argentina, who fielded their A-team and were hot favourites to take the title, having scored 16 goals in five games en route to the showpiece. But it all turned sour for Alfio Basile's side as Julio Baptiste and Daniel Alves netted for Brazil, with a Roberto Ayala own goal sandwiched in between. It gave Brazil their eighth South American championship, though they still trail well behind Argentina and Uruguay, who have 14 wins apiece.

COPA AMERICA WINNERS	
1910 **Argentina***	1953 **Paraguay**
1916 **Uruguay***	1955 **Argentina**
1917 **Uruguay**	1956 **Uruguay***
1919 **Brazil**	1957 **Argentina**
1920 **Uruguay**	1959 **Argentina**
1921 **Argentina**	1959 **Uruguay***
1922 **Brazil**	1963 **Bolivia**
1923 **Uruguay**	1967 **Uruguay**
1924 **Uruguay**	1975 **Peru**
1925 **Argentina**	1979 **Paraguay**
1926 **Uruguay**	1983 **Uruguay**
1927 **Argentina**	1987 **Uruguay**
1929 **Argentina**	1989 **Brazil**
1935 **Uruguay***	1991 **Argentina**
1937 **Argentina**	1993 **Argentina**
1939 **Peru**	1995 **Uruguay**
1941 **Argentina***	1997 **Brazil**
1942 **Uruguay**	1999 **Brazil**
1945 **Argentina***	2001 **Colombia**
1946 **Argentina***	2004 **Brazil**
1947 **Argentina**	2007 **Brazil**
1949 **Brazil**	*Unofficial tournaments

Africa Cup of Nations

The first African Nations Cup was held in 1957, the year the Confédération de Football Africain was founded. Just four teams participated in the inaugural tournament, staged in Sudan. That was reduced to three after South Africa's refusal to send a mixed-race side, something that CAF had insisted on. Egypt, the continent's most powerful footballing country, had little difficulty in beating the hosts and then Ethiopia, for whom South Africa's withdrawal meant a bye to the final.

Two years later Egypt hosted and won the second tournament, in which the same three countries competed, this time playing on a round-robin basis.

In the 1960s the African Nations Cup slowly gained momentum, a trend which went hand-in-hand with the decolonisation that swept across Africa during that decade. By 1965 CAF felt that the strength of African football warranted an automatic World Cup place. When this was refused, CAF forbade its members countries from participating in the qualifying matches for the 1966 World Cup. As a result the African Nations Cup competitions of 1965 and 1968 assumed even greater importance.

Ghana took over the mantle as the strongest side of this era, reaching four successive finals and winning the tournament twice. By 1968 the entry was large enough to require a qualifying round. CAF also decided that the tournament would now be held biennially.

Between 1965 and 1982 countries were allowed to field only two overseas-based players. By the early 1980s African countries had made their mark on the World Cup and many players were plying their trade in Europe. Pragmatism prevailed and CAF rescinded this rule.

Nigeria and Cameroon have been the most successful countries in recent

2002 Africa Cup of Nations Final, Cameroon v Senegal, (3–2 on penalties). Cameroon celebrate with trophy.

years. Since 1980 Nigeria has reached the final on six occasions, winning the tournament twice. Cameroon's first victory didn't come until 1984 but it has won the trophy three more times since, including successive victories in 2000 and 2002. South Africa was readmitted to both CAF and FIFA in 1992 and wasted little time in making its mark on the continent's most prestigious tournament. South Africa beat Tunisia 2–0 in the 1996 final and was runner-up to Egypt two years later. In 1994 Zambia reached the final despite having almost its entire squad wiped out in a plane crash the previous year. The final hurdle proved too great and the Zambian side went down 2–1 to Nigeria.

Since 1996 the finals of the tournament have featured 16 teams. These are split into four groups with the top two from each going through to the knockout stages. The finals are played in January to coincide with the winter break many European countries have, thus alleviating the problem of clubs releasing players from important domestic fixtures.

Several countries were banned from participating in the 1998 tournament, a sanction imposed for withdrawals two years earlier. The biggest casualty was Nigeria, who had refused to go to South Africa '96 for security reasons.

Tunisian Hatem Trabelsi (R) with Moroccan Youssef Mokhtari (L) during the final of the 2004 Africa Cup of Nations.

Egypt met holders South Africa in the final, despite the fact that neither won its group. Egypt won its fourth title with a 2–0 victory. Cameroon won the next two tournaments. At the 2000 jamboree, co-hosted by Ghana and Nigeria, Cameroon topped its group on goal difference after all four sides won, drew and lost a match. After eliminating Algeria and Tunisia in the knockout stage, Cameroon beat Nigeria on penalties in the final.

It was another shoot-out victory for Cameroon in 2002, this time over a Senegal team which would go on to impress at that summer's World Cup. Neither Tunisia nor Morocco made it out of their group that year, both sides underperforming. They made up for it two years later by reaching the final. Tunisia, enjoying home advantage and guided by former France coach Roger Lemerre, won 2–1 to record their first success in the tournament. It was another home win in 2006, Egypt claiming a fifth victory as the tournament was staged for the twenty-fifth time. The hosts beat Ivory Coast in the group stage, and the two sides met again in the final. Ivory Coast had come through an extraordinary 24-shot penalty shoot-out against Cameroon in the quarters, Barcelona's Samuel Eto'o missing the crucial spot-kick. The Ivorians' luck ran out in the final, though, Egypt winning that shoot-out 4–2 after a goalless 120 minutes.

The Pharaohs retained their title against all expectations at the Ghana 2008 tournament. They once again put out a highly rated Ivory Coast side in the semis – 4–1 this time – and richly deserved their victory over Cameroon in the final, the 1–0 scoreline failing to reflect the holders' superiority. Abo Terika capitalised on a mistake by veteran Indomitable Lions defender Rigobert Song to hit the only goal of the game. Terika's 76th-minute strike was the 99th goal of the competition, a new record, while Egypt's sixth victory extended their lead at the top of the all-time list.

AFRICA CUP OF NATIONS WINNERS

1957 **Egypt**	1984 **Cameroon**
1959 **Egypt**	1986 **Egypt**
1960 **Ethiopia**	1988 **Cameroon**
1963 **Ghana**	1990 **Algeria**
1965 **Ghana**	1992 **Ivory Coast**
1968 **Congo-Kinshasa**	1994 **Nigeria**
1970 **Sudan**	1996 **South Africa**
1972 **Congo**	1998 **Egypt**
1974 **Zaire**	2000 **Cameroon**
1976 **Morocco**	2002 **Cameroon**
1978 **Ghana**	2004 **Tunisia**
1980 **Nigeria**	2006 **Egypt**
1982 **Ghana**	2008 **Egypt**

Club World Cup

In the late 1950s UEFA's General Secretary Henri Delaunay came up with the idea of the European club champions and their South American counterparts meeting for the unofficial title of best club side in the world. The European Cup had already been established, and when the Copa Libertadores got under way in 1960, Delaunay's idea came to fruition. Penarol, the inaugural winners of South America's club championship, took on Real Madrid, who had just won the European Cup for the fifth time. The teams drew 0–0 in Montevideo's Centenario Stadium, then Real overran their Uruguayan opponents at the Bernebeu two months later. Puskas, di Stefano and Gento all found the net in the Spanish side's 5–1 win.

By the end of the decade the competition was under threat. Several finals had been marred by violence, notably the three successive matches featuring Estudiantes. Manchester United bore the brunt of some cynical foul play in 1968, and AC Milan and Feyenoord got more of the same in the following two years.

In 1971 matters came to a head when Ajax refused to play the match against Nacional Montevideo. European Cup runners-up Panathinaikos stepped into the breach, losing 3–2 on aggregate. This was the first of five withdrawals by the European champions, while in 1975 and 1978 the match didn't take place at all.

In 1980 the World Club Cup received a much-needed shot in the arm. It would now be played as a one-off match rather than over two legs. Tokyo would be the venue and Toyota provided welcome sponsorship. There were no more withdrawals and the competition regained its credibility.

In 2000 the competition seemed to be under threat again when FIFA launched the World Club Champion-ship. As well as the South American and European champions, this mini-tournament featured the champions of Asia, Africa, CONCACAF and Oceania. It took place in January 2000, Manchester United's participation forcing the club to withdraw from that season's FA Cup. In the event United went out early and the final was contested between the Vasco da Gama, winners of the Copa Libertadores, and Corinthians Sao Paulo, who were invited to take part as champions of host country Brazil. Corinthians won a shoot-out after a 0–0 draw and the overall verdict on the new tournament was one of disappointment. The World Club Cup took place at the end of the year as usual, Boca Juniors beating Real Madrid. In the following two years victories for Bayern Munich and Real Madrid helped to maintain the upper hand the European champions have enjoyed in recent years. In December 2005 the World Club Championship was relaunched as a six-club tournament, with each of the regional football confederations represented in Japan. Seeded sides Liverpool and Sao Paulo met in the final, making it a Europe-South America clash in the tradition of the World Club Cup. Liverpool dominated the game and had three goals ruled out, but went down 1–0.

2006 saw another win for the Copa Libertadores winners over the Champions League victors, Internacional

Boca Juniors' captain Diego Cagna (right) with the World Club Cup after their win over AC Milan in 2003.

taking the honours with a 1–0 win over Barcelona. The following year, the format was amended to allow host country Japan to be represented. A play-off between the J-League winners and their Oceania counterparts was scheduled, the winners going through to the quarter-final stage. But as Japanese side Urawa Red Diamonds were already in the draw by right as winners of the Asian Champions League, the Oceania representative Waitekere instead faced Iranian side Sepahan FC, who had lost to Urawa in the final. It mattered little as the big guns of Europe and

South America again battled for the silverware, AC Milan picking up the trophy with a 4–2 victory over Boca Juniors. Pippo Inzaghi grabbed a brace, while Kaka won the Golden Ball award for the tournament's best player.

The 2008 final pitted Manchester United against LDU de Quito, the first Ecuadorian side to win the Copa Libertadores. United dominated despite having Vidic red carded, and Wayne Rooney's third goal of the tournament was enough to see them crowned world champions.

CLUB WORLD CUP WINNERS

1960
Penarol 0–0 Real Madrid
Real Madrid 5–1 Penarol
Winners: **Real Madrid**

1961
Benfica 1–0 Penarol
Penarol 5–0 Benfica
Play-off
Penarol 2–1 Benfica
Winners: **Penarol***

1962
Santos 3–2 Benfica
Benfica 2–5 Santos
Winners: **Santos**

1963
AC Milan 4–2 Santos
Santos 4–2 AC Milan
Play-off
Santos 1–0 AC Milan
Winners: **Santos***

1964
Independiente 1–0 Inter Milan
Inter Milan 2–0 Independiente
Play-off
Inter Milan 1–0 Independiente
Winners: **Inter Milan***

1965
Inter Milan 3–0 Independiente
Independiente 0–0 Inter Milan
Winners: **Inter Milan**

1966
Penarol 2–0 Real Madrid
Real Madrid 0–2 Penarol
Winners: **Penarol**

1967
Celtic 1–0 Racing Club
Racing Club 2–1 Celtic
Play-off
Racing Club 1–0 Celtic
Winners: **Racing Club***

1968
Estudiantes 1–0 Manchester United
Manchester United 1–1 Estudiantes
Winners: **Estudiantes**

1969
AC Milan 3–0 Estudiantes
Estudiantes 2–1 AC Milan
Winners: **AC Milan**

1970
Estudiantes 2–2 Feyenoord
Feyenoord 1–0 Estudiantes
Winners: **Estudiantes**

1971**
Panathinaikos 1–1 Nacional Montevideo
Nacional Montevideo 2–1 Panathinaikos
Winners: **Nacional Montevideo**

1972
Independiente 1–1 Ajax
Ajax 3–0 Independiente
Winners: **Ajax**

1973**
Independiente 1–0 Juventus

1974**
Independiente 1–0 Atletico Madrid
Atletico Madrid 2–0 Independiente
Winners: **Atletico Madrid**

1975
Not contested

1976
Bayern Munich 2–0 Cruzeiro
Cruzeiro 0–0 Bayern Munich
Winners: **Bayern Munich**

1977**
Boca Juniors 2–2 Borussia Moenchengladbach
Borussia Moenchengladbach 0–3 Boca Juniors
Winners: **Boca Juniors**

1978
Not contested

1979**
Malmo 0–1 Olimpia
Olimpia 2–1 Malmo
Winners: **Olimpia**

1980
Nacional 1–0 Nottingham Forest

1981
Flamengo 3–0 Liverpool

1982
Penarol 2–0 Aston Villa

1983
Gremio 2–1 SV Hamburg

1984
Independiente 1–0 Liverpool

1985
Juventus 2–2 Argentinos Juniors
(Juventus won 4–2 on penalties)

1986
River Plate 1–0 Steaua Bucharest

1987
Porto 2–1 Penarol

1988
Nacional 2–2 PSV Eindhoven
(Nacional won 7–6 on penalties)

1989
AC Milan 1–0 Atletico Nacional

1990
AC Milan 3–0 Olimpia

1991
Red Star Belgrade 3–0 Colo Colo

1992
Sao Paulo 2–1 Barcelona

1993
Sao Paulo 3–2 AC Milan

1994
Velez Sarsfield 2–0 AC Milan

1995
Ajax 0–0 Gremio
(Ajax won 4–3 on penalties)

1996
Juventus 1–0 River Plate

1997
Borussia Dortmund 2–0 Cruzeiro

1998
Real Madrid 2–1 Vasco da Gama

1999
Manchester United 1–0 Palmeiras

2000
Boca Juniors 2–1 Real Madrid

2001
Bayern Munich 1–0 Boca Juniors

2002
Real Madrid 2–0 Olimpia

2003
Boca Juniors 1–1 AC Milan
(Boca Juniors won 3–2 on penalties)

2004
Porto 0–0 Once Caldas
(Porto won 8–7 on penalties)

2005
Sao Paulo 1–0 Liverpool

2006
Internacional 1—0 Barcelona

2007
AC Milan 4–2 Boca Juniors

2008
Manchester United 1—0 LDU Quito

*Up to 1968 aggregate score was not used to decide matches; if teams won one match each there was a play-off

**European Cup runners-up participated after winners withdrew

European Cup

Almost as soon as the World Cup was established, ideas for a pan-European club competition were floated. In 1934 Gabriel Hanot, a sports journalist and former French international, presented a blueprint for a European league. His revolutionary plan was rejected as impractical, but the administrators did consider a cup competition involving nominated clubs from Europe's top footballing countries. The stumbling block was that a knockout competition for clubs from Central European countries already existed. Teams from Italy, Austria, Hungary and Czechoslovakia – some of the continent's finest at the time – had contested the Mitropa Cup since 1927. This was hugely popular in the pre-war period, but as the political map was redrawn post-1945 the Mitropa Cup went into decline. The time was ripe for Hanot, now editor of L'Equipe, to revive his plan. He outlined his idea for a European cup but both FIFA and the newly-formed UEFA vacillated. Hanot threatened to bypass these bodies and deal with the clubs direct, and in April 1955 he attracted representatives from 18 clubs, including Real Madrid and AC Milan, to discuss his proposals. FIFA belatedly came on board and gave its approval, inviting the fledgling UEFA to oversee the new competition, which would be launched the following season.

Not every country warmly embraced the new Champions Cup. Chelsea, England's Division One winners in 1954–55, withdrew after the Football League expressed concerns over fixture congestion. Even so, the European Cup got off to a dream start as a dream team dominated for the first five years. Real Madrid, boasting the attacking talents of Alfredo Di Stefano, Francisco Gento and Hector Rial, beat Reims 4–3 to become the inaugural European Cup winners. Real added Reims' star Raymond Kopa to their ranks and after the Hungarian Revolution Ferenc Puskas made the Spanish giants even more formidable.

Real Madrid Dominate

AC Milan ran Real close in 1958, taking the game to extra time, where Gento hit the winner. The 1960 final, in which Real beat Eintracht Frankfurt 7–3, marked the zenith for this marvellous side and is still widely regarded as the greatest club match ever staged.

Benfica took over Real's mantle and became the team of the 1960s. The Portuguese side looked to its African colonies for talent and found it in abundance, notably in Mario Coluna and Eusebio, who was dubbed Europe's Pele. After beating Barcelona in the 1961 final, Benfica defended their crown against Real Madrid the following year. Benfica won the battle of the giants, Eusebio scoring twice in a 5–3

Benfica's Eusebio running past the AC Milan player, Giovanni Trapattoni, during the European Cup final at Wembley.

victory. The unlucky Puskas scored a hat-trick but ended the game with a losers' medal.

AC Milan provided an upset in 1963 and prevented Benfica from recording a hat-trick of victories. Milan's neighbours Internazionale won in 1964 and 1965, relying heavily on a new defensive system which was the brainchild of coach Helenio Herrera. In the 1965 final Inter beat Benfica, who had won the trophy twice and finished runners-up twice in five seasons.

Manchester United Tipped for Victory

In 1965–6 the Portuguese side crashed 5–1 to Manchester United in the last eight and Matt Busby's side were favourites to become England's first European champions. United surprisingly went down in the semis to Partizan Belgrade, who became the first East European side to reach the final. They in turn were beaten by a new-look Real Madrid. It was Real's sixth victory but it would be 32 years before they would lift the trophy again.

First British Winners

Glasgow Celtic became the first British winners in 1967. Jock Stein's side beat Inter in the Stadium of Light to go down in history as the Lisbon Lions. Remarkably, the entire team came from the Glasgow area.

European Cup victory had been Matt Busby's goal since the competition began and in 1968, ten years on from the Munich disaster, he finally got his hands on the trophy. Two goals from Bobby Charlton helped United to a 4–1 win over Benfica at Wembley. Milan won for the second time in 1969, but although they thrashed Ajax 4–1 in the final, it was the revolutionary new style of Dutch football which was about to take the footballing world by storm. The enterprise and flair of Feyenoord and Ajax was a breath of fresh air compared with the defensive sterility of many Italian sides. Feyenoord lifted the trophy in 1970 and Ajax then became only the second club to record a hat-trick of victories. Johan Cruyff was the linchpin of an Ajax side whose technical ability and fluid movement was encapsulated in a new term: total football.

Bayern's Hat-trick

In the mid-1970s Bayern Munich took over as Europe's outstanding club side. With the nucleus of the West Germany team, which became European and world champions in 1972 and 1974, Bayern also notched a hat-trick of European Cups. The German side came within seconds of defeat against Atletico Madrid in 1974 but, after a last-gasp equaliser from defender Georg Schwarzenbeck, they romped to a 4–0 victory in the replay. Franz Roth scored one of the goals in the 2–0 victory over Leeds United in 1975 and joined an exclusive club when he also hit the goal which beat St Etienne a year later.

A period of dominance by English clubs was ushered in in 1977. Liverpool won their fifth championship in 14 years, and the most consistent side in England finally translated dominance of the domestic game to success in Europe's premier competition. Veteran defender Tommy Smith headed the winner against Borussia Moenchengladbach in 1977, a game which marked Kevin Keegan's swansong for the club. A year later it was the Reds' new No. 7 hero, Kenny Dalglish, who scored the goal which beat FC Bruges at Wembley.

Liverpool were unlucky to draw Nottingham Forest in the first round in 1978–9. Brian Clough's side won 2–0 on aggregate and marched all the way to the final, where they faced Sweden's Malmo. Clough's recent signing, Trevor Francis, Britain's first million-pound player, began repaying his fee by heading the only goal of the game. A year later Forest faced a Hamburg side which now included Keegan, the European Footballer of the Year. Again one goal decided the game and it was scored by Forest's Scotland international winger John Robertson.

Villa's Victory

The 1981 final was a cagey affair between Liverpool and Real Madrid, settled by the unlikely boot of Reds' full-back Alan

Billy McNeill of Glasgow Celtic receives the European Cup after their 2-1 victory over Inter Milan in 1967.

Kennedy. In 1982 Aston Villa brought the European Cup to England for the sixth successive year. The odds were against Villa. Manager Ron Saunders had recently departed, leaving assistant Tony Barton in charge. Injury to 'keeper Jimmy Rimmer meant that Nigel Spink, with only one senior appearance to his name, had to face the might of three-time winners Bayern Munich. Peter Withe scored from close range midway through the second half and the superb Spink kept a clean sheet.

1983 saw the sixth final in a row settled by a solitary goal. On this occasion it was a Felix Magath strike which gave Hamburg a surprise victory over a star-studded Juventus side.

Liverpool recorded their fourth victory in the competition in 1984. Roma provided the opposition, and, as the venue was the Olympic Stadium, the Italians enjoyed home advantage. With the score 1–1 after 120 minutes it went to a penalty shoot-out. Reds 'keeper Bruce Grobbelaar pretended his knees had gone to jelly but it was Conti and Graziani who lost their nerve, both players blazing over. For the second time Alan Kennedy scored the goal which took the European Cup to Anfield.

Two years after finishing runners-up, Juventus were back in the final in 1985, staged at Brussels' Heysel Stadium. Liverpool were there again, making their fifth appearance. A Michel Platini penalty won the match, but events on the pitch were rendered irrelevant following appalling scenes of hooliganism and a collapsed wall which left 39 Italian fans dead. English clubs were subsequently banned from European competition for five years.

First Eastern European Winner

In 1986 Steaua Bucharest became the first East European side to lift the Champions Cup, beating Terry Venables' Barcelona on penalties after a goalless 120 minutes. Porto became only the second Portuguese club to win the trophy in 1987, and the following year yet another new name was added to the roll of honour when PSV Eindhoven beat Benfica on penalties. PSV had overtaken former winners Ajax and Feyenoord as Holland's top club side and also provided several players who won the European Championship that year. The Dutch superstar trio of Gullit, Van Basten and Rijkaard influenced the destination of the European Cup in

the following seasons as AC Milan, bankrolled by Silvio Berlusconi, became Europe's outstanding side. Gullit and Van Basten both hit two in the 4–0 demolition of Steaua Bucharest in 1989, while Rijkaard scored the goal which beat Benfica and kept the trophy in Milan the following year.

Red Star Belgrade became only the second East European side to win the trophy in 1991, although the shoot-out victory over Marseille after a dull goalless match was hardly memorable.

A Change of Format

A league system was introduced in 1991–92. The format would be amended several times in the following years, including eventually admitting clubs who had not won their domestic league. Barcelona were the first winners under the new system, a Ronald Koeman extra-time free-kick beating Sampdoria. The experiment was so successful that the European Cup was formally rechristened the Champions League.

Marseille beat Milan in 1993 but were then embroiled in a match-fixing scandal. It cost Marseille their domestic title

Liverpool celebrate their victory in the 1984 European Cup final against Roma.

although the European Cup victory was allowed to stand. Milan reached the next two finals, thrashing Barcelona 4–0 in 1994, then losing to a Patrick Kluivert goal for Ajax the following year. It meant that Milan had reached five finals in seven years, winning the trophy on three occasions.

Louis van Gaal's brilliant young Ajax side looked capable of becoming a major force for years to come, but after reaching the final again in 1996 – when they lost on penalties to Juventus – the team was broken up. Juventus joined a select band of clubs to have won all three major trophies, and in 1997 the Turin side was looking to make it back-to-back victories in the premier competition. Having beaten Ajax in the semis, a repeat of the previous year's showpiece, they were hot favourites to beat Borussia Dortmund in the final. A brace from Karlheinz Riedle helped Dortmund to a shock 3–1 victory and the Champions Cup went to Germany for the first time since 1983.

Real Madrid Back at the Top

In 1997–98 an expanded 24-team competition included runners-up from the top eight countries, but it was the champions of Spain and Italy who won through to the final. Juventus' all-star team against a resurgent Real Madrid side which had been expensively assembled by Fabio Capello was a mouthwatering prospect. The former Milan boss had gone by the time the teams met in Amsterdam, and Juve were again favourites. But a Pedrag Mijatovic goal put Real back on top of the European pile for the first time since 1966.

In 1999 another club scaled the heights for the first time in over 30 years. Manchester United were 1–0 behind against Bayern Munich with seconds to go and it looked highly unlikely that they would repeat their 1968 achievement. Two goals in a minute, from Sheringham and Solskjaer, turned the tie on its head.

Valencia were runners-up to Real Madrid in 2000, then went down on penalties to Bayern Munich in the 2001 final. A Zidane volley helped Real Madrid to a 2–1 win over Bayer Leverkusen in 2002. AC Milan notched their sixth success with a shoot-out victory over Juventus in 2003. Porto and Monaco flew the flag for the lesser leagues in 2004, Jose Mourinho's side adding the top trophy to their UEFA Cup victory a year earlier.

Liverpool put their erratic league form behind them

Teddy Sheringham holds the Cup in 1999, the year Manchester United won the Treble.

to reach the 2004–05 final, knocking out Juventus and Chelsea to set up a clash with Milan. It looked a formality when the Italian giants took a 3–0 half-time lead, but a Steven Gerrard-inspired comeback took the game to penalties, which Liverpool won to record their fifth success, earning them the trophy outright.

Arsenal looked like emulating Liverpool in 2005–06. Beaten 11 times in the Premiership, the Gunners went on a

The AC Milan team celebrate after penalty shoot-out against Juventus

record-breaking run in the Champions League, going ten games without conceding. Arsenal had never been beyond the quarters before, but victories over Real Madrid, Juventus and Villareal in the knockout stage set up a showdown with favourites Barcelona in the Paris final. The match turned on the 18th-minute red card shown to Jens Lehmann for bringing down Samuel Eto'o, the German becoming the first player to be sent off in a Champions League showpiece. Sol Campbell headed the Gunners into the lead, but Eto'o equalised in the 76th minute and substitute Juliano Belletti hit the winner four minutes later, both goals created by Henrik Larsson. In 2007 three English sides reached the semi finals of the competition. The final in Athens was a repeat of the line-up of the 2005 final but this time Inzaghi's two goals for AC Milan were enough to see Liverpool off. Kuyt pulled one back in the final minutes of the game but this time there was no miraculous comeback from Liverpool.

Premiership clubs dominated the competition in 2007–08, the Big Four reaching the quarter-finals for the first time in history. Manchester United eased past Roma to set up an enticing semi-final clash with Barcelona. Chelsea overturned a 2–1 away defeat against outsiders Fenerbahce, but the tie of the round was Liverpool's 5–3 win over Arsenal.

Chelsea made it third time lucky in Champions League semi-finals against Liverpool. A Riise own-goal at Anfield left it all square going into the second leg, and Drogba's brace in a 3–2 win at the Bridge avenged two defeats at the same stage during the Mourinho era. Paul Scholes's 25-yarder at Old Trafford was enough to beat Barcelona, and Sir Alex Ferguson announced that the first name on the teamsheet for the final in Moscow would be the 33-year-old midfield magician, who had missed the 1999 victory through suspension.

The final was a pulsating clash between Premiership titans. Ronaldo capped a blistering start by United with a soaring header, his 42nd goal of the season. Lampard pounced on a loose ball to level on the stroke of half-time, and Chelsea continued in the ascendancy after the break. It remained 1–1 after extra-time, though by then Chelsea were down to ten men following Drogba's dismissal for his part in a fracas. When Ronaldo failed from 12 yards in the shoot-out, it left John Terry with the chance to convert for Blue glory. His miss meant sudden death, and when van der Sar parried Anelka's drive, United were crowned kings of Europe for the third time, forty years on from their first success and fifty years after the Munich disaster.

The Premiership's Big Four reached the quarter-finals again in 2008–09. Chelsea came out on top in a thriller against Liverpool, 7–5 on aggregate, to secure their fifth semi-final place in six years. Their opponents were Barcelona, who brushed aside a Bayern Munich team that had put 12 past Sporting Lisbon in the previous round. Manchester United reached the semis after becoming the first English side to win at Porto, setting up a clash with Arsenal, conquerors of Villareal.

Chelsea left the Nou Camp with a goalless draw, the first visitors of the season to keep a clean sheet. A thunderous Essien volley put Chelsea ahead at the Bridge, a lead they comfortably maintained until injury time, when Iniesta found the top corner from the edge of the box. Manchester United ran out comfortable winners against a below-par Arsenal, winning both matches. The only blight in a comprehensive victory was Fletcher's red card, which sidelined him for the final in Rome.

Many people's dream showdown failed to live up to its billing. Barcelona, shorn of three first-choice defenders, dominated after weathering an early United salvo. Xavi and Iniesta pulled the strings, while Eto'o and Messi struck in each half to consign United to their first defeat in a major European final.

EUROPEAN CHAMPIONS

1956
Real Madrid 4–3 Reims

1957
Real Madrid 2–0 Fiorentina

1958
Real Madrid 3–2 Milan

1959
Real Madrid 2–0 Reims

1960
Real Madrid 7–3 Eintracht Frankfurt

1961
Benfica 3–2 Barcelona

1962
Benfica 5–3 Real Madrid

1963
AC Milan 2–1 Benfica

1964
Internazionale 3–1 Real Madrid

1965
Internazionale 1–0 Benfica

1966
Real Madrid 2–1 Partizan Belgrade

1967
Celtic 2–1 Internazionale

1968
Manchester United 4–1 Benfica

1969
AC Milan 4–1 Ajax

1970
Feyenoord 2–1 Celtic

1971
Ajax 2–0 Panathinaikos

1972
Ajax 2–0 Internazionale

1973
Ajax 1–0 Juventus

1974
Bayern Munich 4–0 Atlético Madrid
(after replay first game finished 1–1)

1975
Bayern Munich 2–0 Leeds

1976
Bayern Munich 1–0 St Etienne

1977
Liverpool 3–1 BorussiaMoenchengladbach

1978
Liverpool 1–0 FC Bruges

1979
Nottingham Forest 1–0 Malmö

1980
Nottingham Forest 1–0 Hamburg

1981
Liverpool 1–0 Real Madrid

1982
Aston Villa 1–0 Bayern Munich

1983
Hamburg 1–0 Juventus

1984
Liverpool 1–1 Roma (4–2 on penalties)

1985
Juventus 1–0 Liverpool

1986
Steaua Bucharest 0–0 Barcelona
(2–0 on penalties)

1987
FC Porto 2–1 Bayern Munich

1988
PSV Eindhoven 0–0 Benfica (6–5 on penalties)

1989
AC Milan 4–0 Steaua Bucharest

1990
AC Milan 1–0 Benfica

1991
Red Star Belgrade 0–0 Marseille
(5–3 on penalties)

1992
Barcelona 1–0 Sampdoria

1993
Marseille 1–0 AC Milan

1994
AC Milan 4–0 Barcelona

1995
Ajax 1–0 AC Milan

1996
Juventus 1–1 Ajax (4–2 on penalties)

1997
Borussia Dortmund 3–1 Juventus

1998
Real Madrid 1–0 Juventus

1999
Manchester United 2–1 Bayern Munich

2000
Real Madrid 3–0 Valencia

2001
Bayern Munich 1–1 Valencia (5–4 on penalties)

2002
Real Madrid 2–1 Bayer Leverkusen

2003
AC Milan 0–0 Juventus (3–2 on penalties)

2004
FC Porto 3–0 Monaco

2005
Liverpool 3–3 AC Milan (3–2 on penalties)

2006
Barcelona 2–1 Arsenal

2007
AC Milan 2–1 Liverpool

2008
Manchester United 1–1 Chelsea (6–5 on penalties)

2009
Barcelona 2–0 Manchester United

European Fairs Cup

The Inter-Cities Fairs Cup, launched in 1955, was conceived as a competition between clubs representing cities which staged trade fairs. While the European Cup quickly captured the imagination of both clubs and fans, the Fairs Cup had a faltering start. The fact that matches were supposed to coincide with the staging of the fairs meant that it took five years to complete the first two competitions.

Another early anomaly was that it was the cities themselves that were represented and it was thus possible to field a team selected from several clubs. The London side which reached the first final, against Barcelona in the spring of 1958, included Fulham's Johnny Haynes and Tottenham's Danny Blanchflower as well as players from Chelsea, Charlton and Arsenal. London could only draw 2–2 at home and Barcelona became the inaugural winners with a 6–0 rout at the Nou Camp.

Competition to Span a Single Season

Barca retained the trophy with a 4–1 aggregate victory over Birmingham City in 1960. The organizers had tried to reduce the unwieldy timescale of the first competition, yet it still took two years to find a winner from the 16-strong entry. For 1960–61 the Fairs Cup was compressed further so as to be concluded within a single season. The holders went out in the last eight but reached the final of the Champions Cup, UEFA not yet having introduced the ruling that clubs could enter only one competition. Birmingham City put out Inter Milan in the semis to reach their second successive final but then went down 4–2 on aggregate to another Italian club, Roma.

Twenty-eight teams entered in 1961–2, an indication of the growing interest in the competition. Barcelona reached their third final, where they met Valencia. The Catalan side included the veteran Hungarian striker Sandor Kocsis, and although he netted all three of Barca's goals over the two legs, Valencia ran out 7–3 aggregate winners. The Spanish side successfully defended the trophy in 1963, beating Dinamo Zagreb, who became the first Eastern European club to reach a major final. It was an all-Spanish affair again in 1964. Holders Valencia were favourites but lost 2–1 to Real Zaragoza. This was a single-leg final as Spain was playing host to the European Championships.

Ferencvaros needed a play-off to beat Manchester United in the semis of the 1964–65 competition, then overcame Juventus in Turin in another one-off showpiece final. In going one better than Dinamo Zagreb two years earlier the Hungarian side became the first from Eastern Europe to lift a major trophy.

English Success

Two English clubs, Chelsea and Leeds, made it to the last four in 1965–66 but both fell to Spanish opposition. This was the year prior to the introduction of the away goals rule and both ties went to a play-off. Barcelona hammered Chelsea 5–0 in their decider, while Real Zaragoza won 3–1 at Elland Road. It was a return to two legs for the final. Zaragoza came away from the Nou Camp with a 1–0 victory and also went two up at home before Barca stormed back to level the tie on aggregate. Barcelona's Pujol struck the goal which won the cup deep into extra-time to record a famous victory for the Catalan club.

English teams now began a run of success in the competition. Leeds reached the final in 1967, 68 and 71, winning the trophy on the latter two occasions. In 1969 and 1970 the cup also stayed in England as Newcastle and Arsenal respectively prevailed. Newcastle had finished only tenth in Division One in 1968 but qualified for the Fairs Cup because of the rule which excluded more than one club per city. Skipper Bobby Moncur was the hero in the final, where Ujpest Dozsa provided the opposition. The defender scored twice in the 3–0 home win, his first goals for seven years. Ujpest threatened a famous comeback by taking a 2–0 lead in Budapest, when Moncur again got on the scoresheet. Newcastle scored twice more for a 6–2 aggregate victory.

A year later Arsenal beat Ajax in the semis to set up a final against Anderlecht. The Belgian side took a 3–1 lead to Highbury for the second leg but goals from Kelly, Radford and Sammels won the cup for the Gunners, their first major honour for 17 years.

UEFA Cup

The original idea of linking a cup competition to trade fairs had long since fallen by the wayside, and for the 1971–72 season it was reborn as the UEFA Cup. Barcelona beat Leeds in a specially arranged match for the old trophy, but English clubs continued their domination of the new one. Spurs and Wolves contested the first UEFA Cup final. A Martin Chivers brace gave Spurs a 2–1 win at Molineux. Wolves fought out a 1–1 draw at White Hart Lane but it was Spurs who lifted the trophy. Having won the Cup Winners' Cup in 1963, Tottenham became the first English club to win two of Europe's three major prizes.

Liverpool's victory over Borussia Moenchengladbach in 1973 meant a sixth successive victory for English clubs. The Reds squeezed past holders Spurs in the semis thanks to a Steve Heighway away goal. In the first leg of the final Liverpool won 3–0, and although they lost the return 2–0 their efforts at Anfield were the key to the outcome.

Spurs were back in the final in 1974, where Dutch champions Feyenoord provided the opposition. After a 2–2 draw at White Hart Lane Feyenoord won the cup with a 2–0 win in Rotterdam. It was the first time Spurs had lost in a cup final. 1975 saw the rare sight of no English representation in the showpiece event. Borussia Moenchengladbach, who provided several players in West Germany's 1974 World Cup-winning squad, hammered Twente Enschede 5–1 in the second leg in Holland after the Dutch side had earned a creditable goalless draw in Dusseldorf.

Second Success for Liverpool

Liverpool got their name on the trophy again in 1976, despite falling 2–0 behind to FC Bruges in the first leg of the final at home. Goals from Kennedy, Case and Keegan turned the game around. Both teams had just secured their domestic championships when they met for the second leg. Keegan levelled after an early goal for the Belgian side and Liverpool held out for a 4–3 aggregate victory.

In 1977 Juventus prevailed in the final against Atletico Bilbao. A Marco Tardelli goal gave Juventus a 1–0 win in Turin, and a Roberto Bettega strike put the Italians 2–0 up on aggregate early in the return. Bilbao scored twice but Juve took the cup on away goals.

In 1978 PSV Eindhoven reached their first major final, where they faced one of Europe's lesser lights, Bastia of France. The PSV side included the Dutch international twins Rene and Willy Van der Kerkhof, while Bastia had their own Dutch star in Johnny Rep. After a 0–0 draw in France PSV romped to a 3–0 victory at home. Borussia Moenchengladbach reached the next two finals, beating Red Star Belgrade in 1979 but going down to Eintracht Frankfurt on away goals the following season. Bobby Robson's Ipswich Town brought the cup back to England in 1981. After a 3–0 win over AZ 67 Alkmaar at Portman Road, Ipswich went ahead early in the return through Frans Thijssen. It left the new Dutch champions with an impossible

Alan Mullery holds the UEFA Cup trophy in 1972.

task, and although they eventually won 4–2 it wasn't enough. John Wark hit 14 goals in Ipswich's glorious run, equalling the European record.

Surprise Winners IFK Gothenburg

Another unheralded side, Sweden's IFK Gothenburg, took the honours in 1982. Coach Sven-Goran Eriksson masterminded the victory over Kaiserslautern in the semis, and over another Bundesliga side, Hamburg, in the final. The German team included internationals Kaltz, Magath and Hrubesch and looked likely to overturn IFK's narrow 1–0 lead gained in Sweden. Instead of trying to hold their advantage, Eriksson's men scored three times without reply in Hamburg.

Eriksson was back in the final the following year, this time with Benfica. His team lost 1–0 to Anderlecht at Heysel Stadium and Lozano's equalizer for the Belgians in the return gave them a 2–1 aggregate victory. Anderlecht looked like retaining the trophy when they took the lead against Spurs at White Hart Lane in 1984, the teams having drawn 1–1 in the first leg in Belgium. A late Graham Roberts goal levelled the match, which then went to penalties. Two saves from the young Spurs 'keeper Tony Parks gave the London club a dramatic victory.

Real Madrid Resurgent

Real Madrid, who had not won a major honour since the 1960s, scored back-to-back UEFA Cup successes in 1985 and 1986. In the 1985 final they lost 1–0 at the Bernebeu to Videoton of Hungary and had a 3–0 away win in the first leg to thank for their victory. In 1986 it was the opposite story against Cologne. A resounding 5–1 win in Spain rendered Real's 2–0 defeat in the second leg academic.

INTER CITIES FAIRS AND UEFA CUP FINALS

57/58 IC Fairs
London XI v FC Barcelona 2-2 0-6

59/60 IC Fairs
Birmingham City v FC Barcelona 0-0 1-4

60/61 IC Fairs
Birmingham City v Roma 2-2 0-2

61/62 IC Fairs
Valencia v FC Barcelona 6-2 1-1

62/63 IC Fairs
NK Dinamo (Zagreb) v Valencia 1-2 0-2

63/64 IC Fairs
Real Zaragoza v Valencia 2-1

64/65 IC Fairs
Ferencvarosi v Juventus 1-0

65/66 IC Fairs
FC Barcelona v Real Zaragoza 0-1 4-2

66/67 IC Fairs
NK Dinamo (Zagreb) v Leeds United 2-0 0-0

67/68 IC Fairs
Leeds United v Ferencvarosi 1-0 0-0

68/69 IC Fairs
Newcastle United v Ujpesti Dozsa 3-0 3-2

69/70 IC Fairs
RSC Anderlecht v Arsenal 3-1 0-3

70/71 IC Fairs
Juventus v Leeds United 2-2 1-1

71/72 UEFA
Wolverhampton W v Tottenham Hotspur 1-2 1-1

72/73 UEFA
Liverpool v Borussia M'gladbach 3-0 0-2

73/74 UEFA
Tottenham Hotspur v Feyenoord Ned 2-2 0-2

74/75 UEFA
Borussia M'gladbach v FC Twente 0-0 5-1

75/76 UEFA
Liverpool v Club Brugge 3-2 1-1

76/77 UEFA
Juventus v Athletic Bilbao 1-0 1-2

77/78 UEFA
SEC Bastia v PSV Eindhoven 0-0 0-3

78/79 UEFA
Crvena Zvezda v Borussia M'gladbach 1-1 0-1

79/80 UEFA
Borussia M'gladbach v E Frankfurt 3-2 0-1

80/81 UEFA
Ipswich Town v AZ '67 (Alkmaar) 3-0 2-4

81/82 UEFA
IFK Göteborg v Hamburger SV 1-0 3-0

82/83 UEFA
RSC Anderlecht v SL Benfica 1-0 1-1

83/84 UEFA
Tottenham Hotspur v Anderlecht 1-1 1-1 4-3p

84/85 UEFA
Videoton v Real Madrid 0-3 1-0

85/86 UEFA
Real Madrid v 1.FC Köln 5-1 0-2

86/87 UEFA
IFK Gothenburg v Dundee United 1-0 1-1

87/88 UEFA
RCD Vanol v Bayer Leverkusen 3-0 0-3 2-3p

88/89 UEFA
SSC Napoli v VfB Stuttgart 2-1 3-3

89/90 UEFA
Juventus v AC Fiorentina 3-1 0-0

90/91 UEFA
Internazionale v AS Roma 2-0 0-1

91/92 UEFA
Torino v Ajax 2-2 0-0

92/93 UEFA
Borussia Dortmund v Juventus 1-3 0-3

93/94 UEFA
SV Casino Salzburg v Internazionale 0-1 0-1

94/95 UEFA
Parma v Juventus 1-0 1-1

95/96 UEFA
Bayern München v Girondins Bordeaux 2-0 3-1

96/97 UEFA
FC Schalke 04 v Internazionale 1-0 0-1 1-4p

97/98 UEFA
Internazionale v Lazio 3-0

98/99 UEFA
Parma v Olympique Marseille 3-0

99/00 UEFA
Galatasaray v Arsenal 0-0 4-1p

00/01 UEFA
Liverpool v CD Alavés (Vitoria) 5-4

01/02 UEFA
Feyenoord v Borussia Dortmund 3-2

02/03 UEFA
FC Porto v Celtic 3-2

03/04 UEFA
Valencia v Marseille 2-0

04/05 UEFA
CSKA Moscow v Sporting Lisbon 3–1

05/06 UEFA
Sevilla v Middlesbrough 4–0

06/07 UEFA
Sevilla v Espanyol 2–2 (3-1 p)

07/08 UEFA
Zenit St Petersburg v Rangers 2–0

08/09 UEFA
Shakhtar Donetsk v Werder Bremen 2–1

IFK Gothenburg were back in the final in 1987 and as their opponents were Dundee United it was the Swedes who had the pedigree of European success. Dundee had overcome Moenchengladbach in the semis but could not repeat the achievement against IFK. Dundee only trailed 1–0 when the teams took the field for the second leg at Tannadice. IFK scored first and the home side could do no better than a draw.

Bayer Leverkusen and Espanyol won through to the 1988 final. The Spanish side won the first leg of the final 3–0. That remained the aggregate score with half an hour to go in Germany, when Espanyol themselves conceded three goals. Leverkusen won the shoot-out for a remarkable debut victory in a major showpiece final.

The UEFA Cup then became almost exclusively Italian property, clubs from that country winning in six of the next seven years. Napoli, led by Maradona, narrowly beat Stuttgart in 1989, 5–4 on aggregate. The next two finals were all-Italian affairs. In 1990 Juventus beat a Fiorentina team including Brazil's Dunga and Roberto Baggio, a 3–1 win in Turin proving decisive. A year later Inter edged out Roma 2–1 on aggregate. The Milan side boasted three of Germany's World Cup winners in Brehme, Klinsmann and Matthaus, who also scored one of the goals in the 2–0 first-leg victory at home.

Ajax Breaks Italy's Hold

Ajax broke Italy's run in 1992, although even then the Dutch side had to overcome Serie A opposition. Ajax grabbed a 2–2 draw against Torino in Turin, and a 0–0 score line in the second leg gave them victory on away goals. Juventus had bought Roberto Baggio shortly after the 1990 final and he played a key role in the Turin club's victory over Borussia Dortmund three years later. Baggio scored twice in a 3–1 away win, and his namesake Dino did the same at the Delle Alpi Stadium. Juve won 6–1 on aggregate.

Nicola Berti had scored for Inter in the 1991 final and he was also on the mark in the away leg against Austria Salzburg in 1994. After two victories in five years Juve were on the receiving end in 1995, going down 2–1 on aggregate to Parma in yet another all-Italian final. By now the UEFA Cup was been contested by over 100 clubs. The entry was swelled by UEFA's decision to grant places based on the Fair Play awards and via the Intertoto Cup.

In 1996 Bordeaux underperformed in a 5–1 aggregate defeat against Bayern Munich. Schalke retained the cup for Germany in 1997, Marc Wilmots gave Schalke a 1–0 win over Inter at home, Ivan Zamorano levelled the tie in Italy, then the German side comfortably won the penalty shoot-out. Inter bounced back to lift the trophy in 1998, when the final reverted to a single leg format. Zamorano was again on

target, and Ronaldo also got on the scoresheet in the 3–0 win over Lazio. Parma's victory over Marseille by the same score in 1999 meant that Italian clubs had won 8 of the past 11 competitions. The UEFA Cup entry now included early Champions League casualties and with the demise of the Cup Winners' Cup in 1999 the victors in the domestic cup competitions were also usually granted automatic entry.

First Turkish Side To Win

In 2000 Galatasaray became the first Turkish side to win a major final, beating Arsenal on penalties after a goalless 120 minutes. The Liverpool–Alaves final in 2001 was a nine-goal thriller. Robbie Fowler put Liverpool 4–3 up with less than 20 minutes to go but Jordi Cruyff equalized in the dying seconds and an own goal gave the Reds their first European trophy since 1984.

Feyenoord's 3–2 win over Borussia Dortmund in 2002 marked the end of an even longer drought. Jon Dahl Tomasson's winner gave the Dutch club their first European trophy for 28 years. 2003 saw another high-scoring finale to the competition. Porto were appearing in their first final since their European Cup victory in 1987. Celtic hadn't reached a European showpiece occasion since their Champions Cup defeat in 1970. Porto twice took the lead only for Henrik Larsson to head Celtic level. Derlei hit the winner five minutes from the end of extra-time.

Middlesbrough staged four-goal comebacks against FC Basel and Steaua Bucharest to reach the 2005–06 final, but crashed to a classy Sevilla side 4–0 in the final. In 2006–07 Sevilla became the first team to retain the cup since Real Madrid in the mid 1980s, beating Espanyol 3–1 on penalites when the game ended 2–2 after extra time.

2007–08 saw a new name on a European trophy. Zenit St Petersburg, backed by Russia's largest company, Gazprom, met Rangers in the final. Zenit coach Dick Advocaat came out on top against the club he managed 1998–2002, his classy side taking a 1–0 lead through Denisov and adding a second in injury-time when Rangers were chasing the game.

2008–09 was the 38th and final staging of the Uefa Cup before it was rebranded as the Europa League. Manchester City carried the Premiership's hopes of becoming the last-ever winners, the division's sole representative in the quarter-finals. A 4–3 aggregate defeat at the hands of Martin Jol's Hamburg meant that City fans' wait for silverware would extend to a 34th year.

Hamburg's semi-final opponents were Werder Bremen, conquerors of favourites AC Milan. The other semi was an all-Ukrainian affair, Dynamo Kyiv taking on arch-rivals Shakhtar Donetsk. Kyiv and Hamburg were well ahead of their opponents in their domestic leagues, but home form went out of the window in the Uefa Cup ties. Ilsinho scored a late winner for Shakhtar when the tie seemed headed for extra-time. Hamburg, 1–0 winners in Bremen, extended their advantage through Olic, but the visitors struck back brilliantly with goals from Diego, Pizarro and Baumann before Olic headed a late consolation. Bremen were through on away goals, though a yellow card for Brazilian playmaker Diego ruled him out of the Istanbul final.

Luiz Adriano gave Shakhtar the lead on 25 minutes, deftly chipping Bremen 'keeper Tim Wiese. The Bundesliga side equalised through a Naldo free kick, which Andriy Pyatov could only parry into the net. It was another goalkeeping error that decided the outcome in extra-time. Jadson connected tamely with a right-wing cross but saw his effort squirt through Wiese's hands to bring Shakhtar their first European trophy.

European Cup Winners' Cup

In February 1960, five years after the European Cup had been successfully established, a committee met in Vienna to discuss the introduction of a competition between the continent's domestic cup winners. The European Cup Winners' Cup made its debut the following season.

Not all associations ran a cup competition at the time and just ten clubs vied to become the inaugural winners, with Rangers and Fiorentina reaching the final. Rangers had just signed Jim Baxter, whose flair greatly improved a team that had been thrashed by Eintracht Frankfurt in the previous year's European Cup semi-final. However, the first British club to reach a major final lost both legs against Fiorentina, 2–0 at Ibrox and 2–1 in Florence.

UEFA formally adopted the new competition for 1961-62 and the entry more than doubled. The final saw Fiorentina defend their title against Atletico Madrid. A

UEFA CUP WINNERS' CUP FINALS

1960/61
AC Fiorentina 2-1 Rangers FC
Rangers FC 0-2 **AC Fiorentina**

1961/62
Club Atlético de Madrid 3-0 AC Fiorentina
Club Atlético de Madrid 1-1 AC Fiorentina

1962/63
Club Atlético de Madrid 1-5 **Tottenham Hotspur**

1963/64
MTK Budapest 0-1 Sporting Clube de Portugal
MTK Budapest 3-3* **Sporting Clube de Portugal**

1964/65
West Ham United FC 2-0 TSV 1860 München

1965/66
Borussia Dortmund 2-1* Liverpool FC

1966/67
FC Bayern München 1-0* Rangers FC

1967/68
Hamburger SV 0-2 **AC Milan**

1968/69
Barcelona CF 2-3 **SK Slovan Bratislava**

1969/70
Manchester City FC 2-1 KS Górnik Zabrze

1970/71
Real Madrid CF 1-2 Chelsea FC
Real Madrid CF 1-1* **Chelsea FC**

1971/72
Rangers FC 3-2 Dinamo Moscow

1972/73
AC Milan 1-0 Leeds United AFC

1973/74
AC Milan 0-2 **FC Magdeburg**

1974/75
Ferencvárosi TC 0-3 **Dinamo Kiev**

1975/76
RSC Anderlechtois 4-2 West Ham United FC

1976/77
Hamburger SV 2-0 RSC Anderlechtois

1977/78
FK Austria Wien 0-4 **RSC Anderlechtois**

1978/79
Fortuna Düsseldorf 3-4* **FC Barcelona**

1979/80
Valencia CF 0-0** Arsenal FC

1980/81
FC Dinamo Tbilisi 2-1 FC Carl Zeiss Jena

1981/82
FC Barcelona 2-1 R. Standard de Liège

1982/83
Aberdeen FC 2-1* Real Madrid CF

1983/84
Juventus FC 2-1 FC Porto

1984/85
Everton FC 3-1 SK Rapid Wien

1985/86
Club Atlético de Madrid 0-3 **Dinamo Kiev**

1986/87
AFC Ajax 1-0 FC Lokomotive Leipzig

1987/88
KV Mechelen 1-0 AFC Ajax

1988/89
FC Barcelona 2-0 Sampdoria UC

1989/90
Sampdoria UC 2-0* RSC Anderlecht

1990/91
Manchester United FC 2-1 FC Barcelona

1991/92
AS Monaco 0-2 **SV Werder Bremen**

1992/93
R. Antwerp FC 1-3 **Parma AC**

1993/94
Arsenal FC 1-0 Parma AC

1994/95
Arsenal FC 1-2* **Real Zaragoza**

1995/96
Paris Saint-Germain FC 1-0 SK Rapid Wien

1996/97
FC Barcelona 1-0 Paris Saint-Germain FC

1997/98
Chelsea FC 1-0 VfB Stuttgart

1998/99
Real Mallorca 1-2 **S.S. Lazio**

* After extra-time
** After extra-time and penalty shoot-out

one-off final at Hampden Park ended 1–1, and as it was World Cup year the replay wasn't accommodated until September. Atletico cruised to a 3–0 victory.

Britain's First Winners

By winning the FA Cup in 1962 Tottenham thus had their first crack at the Cup Winners' Cup and became Britain's first winners of a European trophy. In the final Spurs brushed aside the holders in a 5–1 victory.

The following season Spurs fell to Manchester United in the second round. However, United then crashed to Sporting Lisbon, unable to defend a 4–1 lead in Portugal. Sporting went on to lift the Cup, beating MTK Budapest in another final that required a replay.

In the 1965 final West Ham took on Munich 1860 with the advantage of playing at Wembley, where they had beaten Preston in the previous year's FA Cup final. Two goals in as many minutes from second-string striker Alan Sealey won the match. In 1966, at Hampden Park, Liverpool met Borussia Dortmund, whose scalps included holders West Ham. Peter Thompson equalized Siggy Held's strike, with Reinhard Libuda hitting the extra-time winner.

Rangers suffered their second defeat in the 1967 final. A 1–0 extra-time defeat against Bayern Munich was made even worse for Rangers fans as Celtic beat Inter Milan to lift the European Cup. AC Milan knocked Bayern out at the semi-final stage in 1967–68 and a brace from their Swedish star Kurt Hamrin accounted for another German side, Hamburg, in the final. Barcelona were the strong favourites in 1969 but the trophy went to Czechoslovakia as Bratislava triumphed 3–2.

The Cup Winners' Cup returned to Britain for the next three years. Manchester City were worthy winners over Gornik in 1970 with a 2–1 victory. A year later Chelsea took on Real Madrid, who were making their ninth appearance in a European final. A Peter Osgood goal gave Chelsea the lead in Athens but Zoco scored a late equalizer to force extra- time. It was Chelsea who were hanging on in the extra period but there were no more goals. Dempsey and Osgood put Chelsea two up in the replay, Real scoring a consolation goal 15 minutes from the end.

Penalty Shoot-outs

In the 1972 final Rangers raced into a 3–0 lead against Moscow Dynamo with one goal from Stein and two from Johnston. Dynamo scored twice to make it a nervy last few minutes for Rangers' fans, who spoiled the occasion with a number of pitch invasions. 1971–72 was also notable for the introduction of penalty shoot-outs to settle matches if the away goals couldn't.

Leeds United should have made it four in a row for British clubs in 1973. Having gone 1–0 down to AC Milan early in the final, staged in Salonika, Leeds outplayed the Italian side but some dubious refereeing decisions helped Milan preserve their narrowed lead. Milan reached the final again in 1974 but this time had to settle for the runners-up spot as FC Magdeburg recorded an historic 2–0 victory.

The European Footballer of the Year, Dynamo Kiev's Oleg Blokhin, rounded off a superb display against Ferencvaros in the 1975 final by scoring Kiev's third goal, Vladimir Onischenko having put the team two up in the first half.

Anderlecht reached the next three finals. In 1976 they took full advantage of playing West Ham on home territory at Heysel Stadium. Pat Holland put the Hammers ahead but Frankie Van Der Elst and Dutch star Rob Rensenbrink both struck twice. Anderlecht missed out on becoming the first club to retain the trophy when they underperformed against Hamburg in the 1977 final, the German side winning 2–0. The Belgian side was back to its fluid best against FK Austria in 1978, Rensenbrink again netting twice in a comprehensive 4–0 victory.

In 1978–9 Barcelona overcame Fortuna Dusseldorf 4–3 in extra-time. Austria's premier striker Hans Krankl scored the decisive goal for the Catalan club. The 1980 final was dramatic, if not a goal-fest. The Arsenal-Valencia final ended 0–0 and the Spanish side won the first European trophy to be decided on penalties. Argentina's World Cup star Mario Kempes fluffed his lines in the shoot-out but Brady and Rix both failed from the spot to give Valencia victory. The 1981 final was an Eastern bloc affair, Soviet side Dynamo Tbilisi meeting East Germany's Carl Zeiss Jena. The East Germans scored first but Tbilisi, the better technical side, replied with two goals, their winner coming four minutes from time.

Standard Liege knocked the holders out in the semis the following year and then had to face Barcelona at the Nou Camp. Liege took an early lead but Danish striker Allan Simonsen equalized on the stroke of half-time and Quini hit the second-half winner.

Alex Ferguson's Aberdeen

Real Madrid were not the imperious side of the 1950s and 1960s yet few thought Alex Ferguson's Aberdeen could overcome a club making its 11th appearance in a major European final. After 90 minutes the 1983 final was locked at 1–1. Substitute John Hewitt sent Dons fans into raptures with an extra-time header which won the cup. Aberdeen lost to Porto in the 1984 semi-final, while Manchester United fell to Juventus in the other side of the draw. Giovanni Trapattoni's Juve side included Gentile, Scirea, Cabrini, Tardelli and Rossi, as well as overseas stars Boniek and Platini. Boniek put Juve 2–1 up just before the break and that was the end of the scoring.

Everton ended England's 14-year drought in the competition by beating Rapid Vienna in the 1985 final with second-half goals from Gray, Steven and Sheedy sealing victory. In 1986 Oleg Blokhin netted in Dynamo Kiev's 3–0 defeat of Atletico Madrid, 11 years after scoring in the victory over Ferencvaros.

Johan Cruyff's Ajax was the outstanding team in 1986–87. Rijkaard, Woters, Winter, Van Basten and a teenage Dennis Bergkamp were all part of a talented young squad. In the final Van Basten scored the goal that beat Lokomotive Leipzig. The Dutch ace had departed to AC Milan by the following summer, when Ajax faced Mechelen in the final. The Dutch side was still expected to win, but Mechelen upset the odds with the help of a Dutchman, Pieter Den Boer, who scored the game's only goal.

The Dutch theme continued in 1989 when Barcelona, now coached by Cruyff, beat Sampdoria 2–0 in the final. The Italian side returned a year later to face Anderlecht, and an extra-time brace from Gianluca Vialli made this a happier experience. Manchester United's entry into the 1990–91 competition was part of the process of rehabilitation of English clubs following the events at Heysel Stadium in 1985. Alex Ferguson's side wasted no time in bringing European cup glory back to the country and reprising his own success in the competition with Aberdeen eight years earlier. In the final against Barcelona, a Steve Bruce header opened the scoring for United and Hughes added a superb second from an acute angle.

A new UEFA directive not only limited the number of overseas players who could turn out in European competition but also classed the home countries as separate entities for these purposes. In particular this was a blow to top English clubs with a Scottish, Irish and Welsh contingent. Such players now had to be classified as foreigners when it came to selecting a team for European fixtures.

Seaman Beaten by Nayim Strike

In 1992 Monaco lost 2–0 to Werder Bremen, the German side's only European success to date. Three sides now tried to break the jinx of the cup holders. Parma beat Antwerp 3–1 at Wembley in 1993 but a year later lost to an Alan Smith goal for Arsenal. The Gunners in their turn made it to the 1995 final, where ex-Spurs midfielder Nayim scored a bizarre winner for an unheralded Real Zaragoza side. With the score 1–1 and seconds of extra-time remaining, Nayim's lob from 40 yards looped over Seaman into the net.

Paris St. Germain now tried to become the first side to retain the trophy. Victory over Rapid Vienna in the 1996 final wasn't as close as the 1–0 scoreline suggested. A year later PSG lost by the same score to Bobby Robson's Barcelona. Ronaldo scored the goal which gave Barca their fourth victory in the competition, the best record of any club.

UEFA's decision to expand the Champions League, allowing the runners-up of Europe's top eight footballing countries to enter the premier competition represented the first nail in the coffin for the Cup Winners' Cup. In 1997–98 holders Barcelona chose to enter the Champions League rather than attempt to retain the trophy. With the constituency of the entry debased, its days were numbered.

In the 1998 final Gianfranco Zola came off Chelsea's bench and scored within seconds against Stuttgart, the only goal of the game. In 1998–9 Lazio became the 39th and final winners of the trophy. The Rome side included an array of stars including Nesta, Vieri, Salas and Nedved. Few of the teams in that year's entry could match Lazio for talent and goals from Vieri and Nedved beat Real Mallorca in the final. From 1999 the winners of Europe's domestic cup competitions competed in an expanded UEFA Cup, which itself was regarded as a second prize for clubs failing to qualify for the Champions League.

European Super Cup

The European Super Cup, launched in 1972, was conceived as a showpiece challenge match between the European Cup winners and the holders of the Cup Winners' Cup. Ajax was the first team to win the trophy, beating Glasgow Rangers 6–3 on aggregate over two legs. Since 1998 the European Super Cup has been a one-off match played at a neutral venue. In 1999 Lazio became the last winners of the Cup Winners' Cup, which was then scrapped. The Rome club went on to beat Manchester United in the European Super Cup. Since 2000 the UEFA Cup winners have met the Champions League winners for the trophy. AC Milan retained the trophy after scoring their fifth victory in 2007, while Zenit St Petersburg became the first Russian side to lift the Super Cup after their 2–1 win over Manchester United in 2008.

Liverpool celebrate winning the 2001 European Super Cup after defeating Bayern Munich.

EUROPEAN SUPER CUP WINNERS

1972
Ajax 6–3 Rangers*

1973
Ajax 6–1 AC Milan*

1974
Not contested

1975
Dynamo Kiev 3–0 Bayern Munich*

1976
Andelecht 5–3 Bayern Munich*

1977
Liverpool 7–1 SV Hamburg*

1978
Anderlecht 4–3 Liverpool*

1979
Nottingham Forest 2–1 Barcelona*

1980
Nottingham Forest 2–2 Valencia*
(Forest won on away goals)

1981
Not contested

1982
Aston Villa 3–1 Barcelona*

1983
Aberdeen 2–0 SV Hamburg*

1984
Juventus 2–0 Liverpool

1985
Not contested

1986
Steaua Bucharest 1–0 Dynamo Kiev

1987
FC Porto 2–0 Ajax*

1988
Mechelen 3–1 PSV Eindhoven*

1989
AC Milan 2–1 Barcelona*

1990
AC Milan 3–1 Sampdoria*

1991
Manchester United 1–0 Red Star Belgrade

1992
Barcelona 3–2 Werder Bremen*

1993
Parma 2–1 AC Milan*

1994
AC Milan 2–0 Arsenal*

1995
Ajax 5–1 Real Zaragoza*

1996
Juventus 9–2 Paris St-Germain*

1997
Barcelona 3–1 Borussia Dortmund*

1998
Chelsea 1–0 Real Madrid

1999
Lazio 1–0 Manchester United

2000
Galatasaray 2–1 Real Madrid

2001
Liverpool 3–2 Bayern Munich

2002
Real Madrid 3–1 Feyenoord

2003
AC Milan 1–0 FC Porto

2004
Valencia 2–1 FC Porto

2005
Liverpool 3–1 CSKA Moscow aet

2006
Sevilla 3–0 Barcelona

2007
AC Milan 3–1 Sevilla

2008
Zenit St Petersburg 2–1 Manchester
United

*aggregate score over two legs

Copa Libertadores

South America experimented with an international club competition in 1948, eight years before the European Cup was launched. Brazil's Vasco da Gama came out on top but it was a commercial disaster and the idea was shelved. A decade later, following the success of the Champions Cup in Europe, the idea was revived. With the additional incentive of a prestigious and lucrative two-legged match between the champions of Europe and South America, the Copa Libertadores got under way. The champions of seven of the ten CONMEBOL countries took part in the inaugural competition, which was won by Penarol of Uruguay. It quickly captured the imagination of both fans and clubs, to the extent that the Copa America, CONMEBOL'S international championship, looked in danger of extinction.

In 1962, with Penarol looking for a hat-trick of wins, the volatility of the fans turned the final into a marathon. Santos had won the first leg in Montevideo but Penarol took a 3–2 lead in the return in Brazil. The game was then halted when the Chilean referee was knocked unconscious by a missile. It descended into confusion and farce as Santos thought they had levelled the score to win the trophy. That goal was eventually disregarded and the 3–2 result stood after the referee told CONMEBOL officials that he had been pressurised into restarting the match. A victory apiece meant a play-off – aggregate scores were not used at this time – where a brace by Pele helped Santos to a 3–0 victory.

Competition Extended

In 1966 the competition was extended to include runners-up from each of the CONMEBOL countries' championships as well as the winners. Brazil and Argentina, countries which had very competitive domestic leagues, were against a move which would increase the number of games. They were outvoted by those countries with weaker leagues who perceived regular entry into the Copa Libertadores as important both for the top-class competition it provided and for financial reasons. Brazil's response was to boycott the competition, and in 1969 Argentina also withdrew. CONMEBOL's answer was to amend the format so that there were fewer games.

The format of the Copa Libertadores has undergone many changes. Up to 1987 victory for each side in the two-legged final meant a play-off, regardless of the score. Aggregate scores and penalty shoot-outs were then introduced. Currently, 32 teams contest the group stage, with the top two from each of the eight groups going forward to the second round. It is similar to the World Cup, except that all matches from the last 16 on are played over two legs.

In 1998 Mexico was invited to compete for the first time. Cruz Azul, one of Mexico City's clubs, reached the final in 2001 but lost on penalties to Boca Juniors. Boca's 5–0 aggregate victory over Gremio in the 2007 final gave the club its fourth win in eight years. Juan Roman Riquelme, on loan from Villareal, played a major part in Boca's success, scoring eight goals and picking up the competition's Most Valuable Player award.

In 2008 Fluminense put out holders Boca Juniors in the semis, then faced LDU Quito in the final, a side they had taken four points from in the group stage. The teams were locked at 5–5 after the two legs, LDU Quito winning the shoot-out to become the first Ecuadorian side to lift the trophy.

Jorge Wagner (l), of Corinthians de Brasil and Fernando Cavenaghi, of River Plate de Argentinain. River Plate won 2–1.

COPA LIBERTADORES WINNERS

1960
Penarol 1–0 Olimpia
Olimpia 1–1 Penarol
Winners: **Penarol**

1961
Penarol 1–0 Palmeiras
Palmeiras 1–1 Penarol
Winners: **Penarol**

1962
Penarol 1–2 Santos
Santos 2–3 Penarol
Play-off
Santos 3–0 Penarol

1963
Santos 3–2 Boca Juniors
Boca Juniors 1–2 Santos
Winners: **Santos**

1964
Nacional 0–0 Independiente
Independiente 1–0 Nacional
Winners: **Independiente**

1965
Independiente 1–0 Penarol
Penarol 3–1 Independiente
Play-off
Independiente 4–1 Penarol

1966
Penarol 2–0 River Plate
River Plate 3–2 Penarol
Play-off
Penarol 4–2 River Plate

1967
Racing Club 0–0 Nacional
Nacional 0–0 Racing Club
Play-off
Racing Club 2–1 Nacional

1968
Estudiantes 2–1 Palmeiras
Palmeiras 3–1 Estudiantes
Play-off
Estudiantes 2–0 Palmeiras

1969
Nacional 0–1 Estudiantes
Estudiantes 2–0 Nacional
Winners: **Estudiantes**

1970
Estudiantes 1–0 Penarol
Penarol 0–0 Estudiantes
Winners: **Estudiantes**

1971
Estudiantes 1–0 Nacional
Nacional 1–0 Estudiantes
Play-off
Nacional 2–0 Estudiantes

1972
Universitario de Deportes 0–0
Independiente
Independiente 2–1 Universitario de
Deportes
Winners: **Independiente**

1973
Independiente 1–1 Colo Colo
Colo Colo 0–0 Independiente
Play-off
Independiente 2–1 Colo Colo

1974
Sao Paulo 2–1 Independiente
Independiente 2–0 Sao Paulo
Play-off
Independiente 1–0 sao Paulo

1975
Union Espanola 1–0 Independiente
Independiente 3–1 Union Espanola
Play-off
Independiente 2–0 Union Espanola

1976
Cruzeiro 4–1 River Plate
River Plate 2–1 Cruzeiro
Play-off
Cruzeiro 3–2 River Plate

1977
Boca Juniors 1–0 Cruzeiro
Cruzeiro 1–0 Boca Juniors
Play-off
Cruzeiro 0–0 Boca Juniors
(**Boca Juniors** won 5–4 on penalties)

1978
Deportivo Cali 0–0 Boca Juniors
Boca Juniors 4–0 Deportivo Cali
Winners: **Boca Juniors**

1979
Olimpia 2–0 Boca Juniors
Boca Juniors 0–0 Olimpia
Winners: **Olimpia**

1980
Internacional 0–0 Nacional
Nacional 1–0 Internacional
Winners: **Nacional**

1981
Flamengo 2–1 Cobreloa
Cobreloa 1–0 Flamengo
Play-off
Flamengo 2–0 Cobreloa

1982
Penarol 0–0 Cobreloa
Cobreloa 0–1 Penarol
Winners: **Penarol**

1983
Penarol 1–1 Gremio
Gremio 2–1 Penarol
Winners: **Gremio**

1984
Gremio 0–1 Independiente
Independiente 0–0 Gremio
Winners: **Independiente**

1985
Argentinos Juniors 1–0 America de Cali
America de Cali 1–0 Argentinos Juniors
Play-off
Argentinos Juniors 1–1 America de Cali
(**Argentinos Juniors** won 5–4 on
penalties)

1986
America de Cali 1–2 River Plate
River Plate 1–0 America de Cali
Winners: **River Plate**

1987
America de Cali 2–0 Penarol
Penarol 2–1 America de Cali
Play-off
Penarol 1–0 America de Cali

1988
Newell's Old Boys 1–0 Nacional
Nacional 3–1 Newell's Old Boys
Winners: **Nacional**

1989
Olimpia 2–0 Atletico Nacional
Atletico Nacional 2–0 Olimpia
(**Atletico Nacional** won 5–4 on
penalties)

1990
Olimpia 2–0 Barcelona
Barcelona 1–1 Olimpia
Winners: **Olimpia**

1991
Olimpia 0–0 Colo Colo
Colo Colo 3–0 Olimpia
Winners: **Colo Colo**

1992
Newell's Old Boys 1–0 Sao Paulo
Sao Paulo 1–0 Newell's Old Boys
(**Sao Paulo** won 3–2 on penalties)

1993
Sao Paulo 5–1 Universidad Catolica
Universidad Catolitca 2–0 Sao Paulo
Winners: **Sao Paulo**

1994
Velez Sarsfield 1–0 Sao Paulo
Sao Paulo 1–0 Velez Sarsfield
(**Velez Sarsfield** won 5–3 on penalties)

1995
Gremio 3–1 Atletico Nacional
Atletico Nacional 1–1 Gremio
Winners: **Gremio**

1996
America de Cali 1–0 River Plate
River Plate 2–0 America de Cali
Winners: **River Plate**

1997
Sporting Cristal 0–0 Cruzeiro
Cruzeiro 1–0 Sporting Cristal
Winners: **Cruzeiro**

1998
Vasco da Gama 2–0 Barcelona
Barcelona 1–2 Vasco da Gama
Winners: **Vasco da Gama**

1999
Deportivo Cali 1–0 Palmeiras
Palmeiras 2–1 Deportivo Cali
(**Palmeiras** won 4–3 on penalties)

2000
Boca Juniors 2–2 Palmeiras
Palmeiras 0–0 Boca Juniors
(**Boca Juniors** won 4–2 on penalties)

2001
Cruz Azul 0–1 Boca Juniors
Boca Juniors 0–1 Cruz Azul
(**Boca Juniors** won 3–1 on penalties)

2002
Olimpia 0–1 Sao Caetano
Sae Caetano 1–2 Olimpia
(**Olimpia** won 4–2 on penalties)

2003
Boca Juniors 2–0 Santos
Santos 1–3 Boca Juniors
Winners: **Boca Juniors**

2004
Boca Juniors 0–0 Once Caldas
Once Caldas 1–0 Boca Juniors
(**Once Caldas** won on penalties 2–0)

2005
Atletico Paranaense 1–1 Sao Paulo
Sao Paulo 4–0 Atletico Paranaense
Winners: **Sao Paulo**

2006
Internacional 2–1 Sao Paulo
Sao Paulo 2–2 Internacional
Winners: **Internacional**

2007
Gremio 0–3 Boca Juniors
Boca Juniors 2–0 Gremio
Winners: **Boca Juniors**

2008
LDU Quito 4–2 Fluminense
Fluminense 3–1 LDU Quito
(**LDU Quito** won on penalties 3–1)

CONCACAF Champions Cup

This was first contested in 1962, the year after CONCACAF was formed. Unlike the European Cup and Copa Libertadores, on which it was based, this competition has had a chequered history. Scheduling has been a problem and travel costs have proved prohibitively expensive on occasion. Unsurprisingly, Mexican clubs dominated the competition, and this continued to be the case despite the fact that since 1998 the top sides from that country have been allowed entry into the much more competitive and prestigious South American club championship. 2005 winners Deportivo Saprissa qualified for FIFA's revamped World Club Championship, where they went down to Liverpool in the semis but beat Al-Ittihad in the third place play-off. UNAM Pumas, runners-up to Deportivo, qualified for the Copa Sudamericana, the most prestigious

international club competition in the continent after the Copa Libertadores. CONCACAF introduced a Cup Winners' Cup competition in 1992 but this was abandoned in 1998. When Mexican side Pachuca retained the Champions Cup with a victory over Deportivo Saprissa in the 2008 final, it brought the curtain down on the 47-year-old competition, which was replaced by the expanded CONCACAF Champions League for 2008–09.

Other South American International Club Competitions

Since the late 1980s the CONMEBOL countries have sought to extend international club competition beyond the hugely successful Copa Libertadores. The Super Copa, which was launched in 1988, featured all previous winners of the Copa Libertadores. Naturally this found favour with clubs who had notched a victory in the premier competition as it guaranteed them entry to this new tournament and welcome revenue. In the inaugural Super Copa final, Racing Club of Argentina beat Cruzeiro 3–2 on aggregate.

Once the Super Copa was up and running, almost inevitably a play-off between the winners of that trophy and the reigning Copa Libertadores champions followed. The Recopa, as it was called, was first played in 1988 when Copa Libertadores winners Nacional of Uruguay beat Super Copa winners Racing Club 1–0 on aggregate.

In 1990 Olimpia of Paraguay won both the Copa Libertadores and the Super Copa and thus automatically claimed the Recopa. In 1991 the Recopa was relocated to Japan for commercial reasons.

In 1993 South America introduced the Copa CONMEBOL, its own version of the UEFA Cup. This was contested by the two teams from each of the national leagues who missed out on qualification for the Copa Libertadores.

1998 saw the introduction of two new international club competitions, the Mercosur and the Merconorte. Both were short lived, each lasting just four years. In 2002 both were replaced by a single new tournament, the Copa Sudamericana. San Lorenzo of Argentina beat Atletico Nacional of Colombia 4–0 in the inaugural final.

Another competition which has suffered in recent years is the Copa Interamericana. Launched in 1968, this trophy was contested by the champions of CONMEBOL and CONCACAF. It never really took off and on several occasions didn't take place at all. At other times the Copa Libertadores winners declined to play the match and the runners-up participated instead. Its future was further threatened after Mexican club sides were granted entry to the Copa Libertadores in 1998.

CONCACAF CHAMPIONS CUP WINNERS

1962 **Guadalajara** (Mexico)	1987 **America** (Mexico)
1963 **Racing Club** (Haiti)*	1988 **Olimpia** (Honduras)
1964–66 Not completed	1989 **UNAM** (Mexico)
1967 **Alianza** (El Salvador)	1990 **America** (Mexico)
1968 **Toluca** (Mexico)*	1991 **Puebla** (Mexico)
1969 **Cruz Azul** (Mexico)	1992 **America** (Mexico)
1970 **Cruz Azul** (Mexico)*	1993 **Deportivo Saprissa** (Costa Rica)
1971 **Cruz Azul** (Mexico)	1994 **CS Cartagines** (Costa Rica)
1972 **Olimpia** (Honduras)	1995 **Deportivo Saprissa** (Costa Rica)
1973 **Transvaal** (Surinam)*	1996 Not completed
1974 **Municipal** (Guatemala)	1997 **Cruz Azul** (Mexico)
1975 **Atletico Espanol** (Mexico)	1998 **DC United** ((USA)
1976 **Aguila** (El Salvador)*	1999 **Necaxa** (Mexico)
1977 **America** (Mexico)	2000–01 **Los Angeles Galaxy** (USA)
1978 **UAG Guadalajara** (Mexico)	2002 **Pachuca** (Mexico)
1979 **Deportivo FAS** (El Salvador)	2003 **Toluca** (Mexico)
1980 **UNAM** (Mexico)	2004 **LD Alajuelense** (Costa Rica)
1981 **Transvaal** (Surinam)	2005 **Deportivo Saprissa** (Costa Rica)
1982 **UNAM** (Mexico)	2006 **America** (Mexico)
1983 **Atlante** (Mexico)	2007 **Pachuca** (Mexico)
1984 **Violette** (Haiti)*	2008 **Pachuca** (Mexico)
1985 **Defence Force** (Trinidad)	*walkover in final
1986 **Liga Deportiva Alajuelense** (Costa Rica)	

African Cups

The Confédération Africaine de Football (CAF) has taken Europe as the model for its international club competitions. The Champions Cup came first, in 1964. Fourteen clubs entered the inaugural competition, the finals of which were staged in Accra. Cameroonian side Oryx Douala beat Stade Malien of Mali in the final to win the Kwame Nkrumah trophy, named after Ghana's serving president. The tournament was not a great success in terms of attendances, however, and no competition was held in 1965. It returned the following year with a revised format, ties being played on a knockout basis over two legs. In 1997 it was revamped along European lines as a Champions League. Eight quarter-

finalists are split into two mini-leagues with the winners meeting in the final. Zamelek's 1–0 aggregate win over Raja Casablanca in 2002 was a record fifth victory in the competition for the Egyptian club.

A Cup Winners' Cup was introduced in 1975, and since 1992 the winners of this trophy have met the victorious Champions Cup side in the Super Cup. The CAF Cup was introduced in the same year. The runners-up in the national league competitions participate in this tournament, which broadly mirrors the UEFA Cup.

2004 saw the launch of the new CAF Confederation Cup, which replaced the Cup Winners' Cup and the CAF Cup. The inaugural champions were Heart of Oak from Ghana.

CHAMPIONS CUP WINNERS

1964 **Oryx Douala** (Cameroon)	**1975** **Hafia Conakry** (Guinea)	**1987** **Al Ahly** (Egypt)	**1998** **ASEC Abidjan** (Ivory Coast)
1965 No competition	**1976** **Mouloudia d'Algiers** (Algeria)	**1988** **Entente Setif** (Algeria)	**1999** **Raja Casablanca** (Morocco)
1966 **Stade Abidjan** (Ivory Coast)	**1977** **Hafia Conakry** (Guinea)	**1989** **Raja Casablanca** (Morocco)	**2000** **Hearts of Oak** (Ghana)
1967 **TP Engelbert** (Zaire)	**1978** **Canon Yaounde** (Cameroon)	**1990** **JS Kabylie** (Algeria)	**2001** **Al Ahly** (Egypt)
1968 **TP Engelbert** (Zaire)	**1979** **Union Douala** (Cameroon)	**1991** **Club Africain** (Tunisia)	**2002** **Zamalek** (Egypt)
1969 **Al Ismaily** (Egypt)	**1980** **Canon Yaounde** (Cameroon)	**1992** **WAC Casablanca** (Morocco)	**2003** **Enyimba** (Nigeria)
1970 **Asante Kotoko** (Ghana)	**1981** **JE Tizi-Ouzou** (Algeria)	**1993** **Zamalek** (Egypt)	**2004** **Enyimba** (Nigeria)
1971 **Canon Yaounde** (Cameroon)	**1982** **Al Ahly** (Egypt)	**1994** **Esperance Sportive** (Tunisia)	**2005** **Al Ahly** (Egypt)
1972 **Hafia Conakry** (Guinea)	**1983** **Asante Kotoko** (Ghana)	**1995** **Orlando Pirates** (South Africa)	**2006** **Al Ahly** (Egypt)
1973 **AS Vita Club** (Zaire)	**1984** **Zamalek** (Egypt)	**1996** **Zamalek** (Egypt)	**2007** **Etoile du Sahel** (Tunisia)
1974 **CARA Brazzaville** (Congo)	**1985** **FAR Rabat** (Morocco)	**1997** **Raja Casablanca** (Morocco)	**2008** **Al Ahly** (Egypt)
	1986 **Zamalek** (Egypt)		

CUP WINNERS' CUP WINNERS

1975 **Tonnerre Yaounde** (Cameroon)	**1983** **Al Mokaoulom** (Egypt)	**1991** **Power Dynamos** (Zambia)	**1999** **Africa Sports** (Ivory Coast)
1976 **Shooting Stars** (Nigeria)	**1984** **Al Ahly** (Egypt)	**1992** **Africa Sports** (Ivory Coast)	**2000** **Zamalek** (Egypt)
1977 **Enugu Rangers** (Nigeria)	**1985** **Al Ahly** (Egypt)	**1993** **Al Ahly** (Egypt)	**2001** **Kaizer Chiefs** (South Africa)
1978 **Horoya AC** (Guinea)	**1986** **Al Ahly** (Egypt)	**1994** **DC Motema Pembe** (Zaire)	**2002** **WAC Casablanca** (Morocco)
1979 **Canon Yaounde** (Cameroon)	**1987** **Gor Mahia** (Kenya)	**1995** **JS Kabylie** (Algeria)	**2003** **Etoile du Sahel** (Tunisia)
1980 **TP Mazembe** (Zaire)	**1988** **CA Bizerte** (Tunisia)	**1996** **Arab Contractors** (Egypt)	
1981 **Union Douala** (Cameroon)	**1989** **Al Merreikh** (Sudan)	**1997** **Etoile du Sahel** (Tunisia)	
1982 **Al Mokaoulom** (Egypt)	**1990** **BCC Lions** (Nigeria)	**1998** **Esperance Sportive** (Tunisia)	

CAF CUP WINNERS

1992
Shooting Stars (Nigeria)
1993
Stella Club (Ivory Coast)
1994
Bendel Insurance (Nigeria)
1995
Etoile du Sahel (Tunisia)

1996
KAC Marrakech (Morocco)
1997
Esperance Sportive (Tunisia)
1998
CS Sfax (Tunisia)
1999
Etoile du Sahel (Tunisia)

2000
JS Kabylie (Algeria)
2001
JS Kabylie (Algeria)
2002
JS Kabylie (Algeria)
2003
Raja Casablanca (Morocco)

CAF CONFEDERATION CUP

2004
Hearts of Oak (Ghana)
2005
FAR Rabat (Morocco)
2006
Etoile du Sahel (Tunisia)
2007
CS Sfaxien (Tunisia)
2008
CS Sfaxien (Tunisia)

SUPER CUP WINNERS

1993
Africa Sports (Ivory Coast)
1994
Zamalek (Egypt)
1995
Esperance Sportive (Tunisia)
1996
Orlando Pirates (South Africa)
1997
Zamalek (Egypt)

1998
Etoile du Sahel (Tunisia)
1999
ASEC Mimosas (Ivory Coast)
2000
Raja Casablanca (Morocco)
2001
Hearts of Oak (Ghana)
2002
Al Ahly (Egypt)

2003
Zamalek (Egypt)
2004
Enyimba (Nigeria)
2005
Enyimba (Nigeria)
2006
Al Ahly (Egypt)
2007
Al Ahly (Egypt)

2008
Etoile du Sahel (Tunisia)
2009
Al Ahly (Egypt)

Etienne Kibong (right) of Cameroonian team Cotonsport de Garoua vies with Diallo Mouhamed Ali (left) of Moroccan team Raja de Casablanca in the 2003 CAF Cup final. Raja Casablanca won 2–0 in the two leg final.

FA Cup

It was in the offices of London newspaper *The Sportsman* in July 1871 that a small group of FA officials made the historic decision to introduce a cup competition. The key figure was FA Secretary Charles Alcock, an Old Harrovian, who formally proposed the idea for a challenge cup, basing it on the the inter-house competitions played at his old school. A trophy was ordered from Martin, Hall and Co. at a cost of £20 and in 1872 fifteen clubs vied to win it for the first time. Fittingly, Alcock's team, the Wanderers, beat the Royal Engineers in the final, which was played in front of 2000 people at Kennington Oval.

The first decade was dominated by home counties' clubs made up of gentlemen-amateurs. The Old Etonians' 1–0 victory over Blackburn Rovers in 1882 marked the end of an era. The following year the Cup went north for the first time, to Blackburn Olympic. Neighbours Blackburn Rovers then recorded a hat-trick of victories. This emulated the Wanderers' feat of the previous decade and under the rules should have earned the club in question the trophy outright. But the Wanderers had agreed to waive their right and hand the trophy back to the FA. This gave rise to the comical scene of Charles Alcock, the Wanderers' secretary, returning

Manchester United captain Charlie Roberts leads his team out for the 1909 final against Bristol City.

Police clear spectators off the pitch before the famous White Horse final of 1923.

**Frank Hudspeth is escorted from the pitch after
Newcastle United won the trophy in 1924.**

the trophy to the FA secretary – Charles Alcock! This altruistic act set a precedent and when Blackburn Rovers repeated the achievement the club received a commemorative shield to mark the occasion instead.

In 1884 Preston North End was disqualified from the Cup after openly admitting fielding professionals in a tie against Upton Park. A year later the FA realised that they were swimming against the tide and formally sanctioned professionalism. The trophy would remain in the hands of clubs from the Midlands and North until 1901, when Tottenham not only brought it back to the capital but in the process became the only non-League side to win it.

By then the competition had a new trophy. In 1895 the original was stolen from bootmakers William Shillock, where it had been on display. It was never seen again. Fortunately, the players who had won the Cup for Wolves in 1893 had been given miniature replicas by the club and it was thus possible to fashion a new trophy that was an exact copy of the original.

Between 1905 and 1911 Newcastle United reached the final five times. Crystal Palace, the Cup Final venue at the time, was not

mentioned in polite conversation on Tyneside during this period as Newcastle didn't win once there. The club's one victory in this era, over Barnsley in 1910, was gained at Goodison Park after the teams drew at Crystal Palace.

In 1914 King George V presented the trophy to Tommy Boyle, captain of the Burnley side which beat Liverpool 1–0. It was the first time that a reigning monarch had attended the Cup Final, beginning a tradition that would help to give the season's showpiece finale its special place in the sporting calendar.

In 1915 Sheffield United beat Chelsea in a match that was dubbed 'the Khaki Cup Final' as so many servicemen were in the crowd. Football had come in for some criticism for continuing while the conflict was raging; now the competition was suspended for four years.

Sheffield United had lifted a brand new trophy aloft. The design of the previous Cup had been copied for a competition in Manchester. The FA's response was to award the existing trophy to Lord Arthur Kinnaird, President of the FA and a man who had appeared in nine Cup finals in his playing days. Clubs would do battle for the third FA Cup until 1992, when the present trophy was presented for the first time.

After World War One Stamford Bridge staged three Cup finals, and in 1919–20 almost caused the FA a major headache as Chelsea reached the semi-final. Aston Villa's 3–1 win saved the administrators from having to face the problem of an FA Cup finalist playing at home, a breach of the competition's rules.

The new Empire Stadium, Wembley was ready in 1923 and the 127,000 capacity was thought to be more than enough to accommodate all fans who wanted to see the final. But the Bolton–West Ham match captured the imagination

**Stanley Matthews receives his cup winners' medal from the
Queen after the 1953 final.**

and supporters poured into the stadium, both through the turnstiles and by less legitimate means. More than 200,000 fans were said to be in the stadium by kick-off time and there was a 45-minute delay as thousands spilled onto the pitch. PC George Scorey and his white horse Billy became part of the game's folklore as they helped to restore order. Bolton won the match 2–0. The FA learnt their lesson and decreed that future finals would be all-ticket affairs.

In 1927 the Cup went out of England for the only time in its history. A hopeful long-range shot from Cardiff City centre-forward Hugh Ferguson was fumbled by Arsenal 'keeper Dan Lewis for the only goal of the game. It was one of the greatest shocks ever, Lewis blaming the slippery sheen on his new jersey. In future the Gunners made sure that all new kit was washed first.

1932 saw one of the most controversial incidents in the competition's history, and again it involved Arsenal. Leading Newcastle United 1–0, the Gunners' defence stopped when a ball looked to be well over the bye-line before Richardson crossed it. Jack Allen put the ball into the net and the goal was allowed to stand. Allen went on to hit the winner, leaving Arsenal fans staring ruefully at newspaper photographs of the game's turning point which suggested they had been hard done by. The following season Arsenal won the championship but fell victim to one of the great giantkilling acts in FA Cup history. Herbert Chapman's side was injury-hit but should still have been far too strong for Walsall, who were in the Third Division (North). The Midlands' side won 2–0.

Portsmouth held the Cup for seven years after their shock 4–1 win over Wolves in 1939, but only because of the outbreak of hostilities. When the competition resumed in 1945–46 the FA decided that ties would be played on a home-and-away basis. This increased the number of fixtures as the league programme wasn't restarted until the following season. The short-lived experiment gave rise to a curiosity: Charlton Athletic reached the final after losing a match. They had lost 2–1 to Fulham at Craven Cottage in the third round but went through on aggregate after a 3–1 win at home. In the Final Charlton went down to Derby County 4–1.

When Blackpool went to Wembley in 1953 they were desperate to avoid a hat-trick of defeats, having lost twice in the past five years. Sentiment was also on Blackpool's side as everyone wanted to see 38-year-old Stanley Matthews finally pick up a winners' medal. Opponents Bolton were 3–1 up with 20 minutes left but Matthews inspired one of the greatest Cup Final comebacks as Blackpool won 4–3.

The 1950s finals were blighted by a spate of serious injuries. It was dubbed the 'Wembley hoodoo' but many of the players put the misfortune down to the springiness of the

Spurs skipper Danny Blanchflower holds the Cup after beating Leicester in the 1961 final.

Wembley turf. Losing players in the pre-substitutes era was a major blow, but that didn't apply in 1956 when Manchester City 'keeper Bert Trautmann played on with a broken neck. City beat Birmingham City 3–1.

In the 1960s top-flight sides dominated the competition, Spurs winning the trophy three times. In the next 10 years three Division Two sides got their hands on the Cup. Sunderland's victory over Leeds in 1973 was one of the shocks of all time; Southampton turned over Manchester United in 1976; and a rare Trevor Brooking header gave West Ham victory over Arsenal in 1980. Fulham and Queen's Park Rangers were both Second Division outfits when they reached the final in 1975 and 1982 respectively, but they had to be content with runners-up medals. Perhaps the abiding memory in this era of the underdog was non-League Hereford United's victory over Newcastle in the third round in 1971–72. Having drawn at St James's Park against a team with one of the greatest Cup pedigrees, Hereford scored a famous 2–1 victory at Edgar Street. They went out to West Ham in the next round after a replay.

In 1982 Tottenham became only the third side of the century to retain the Cup. The great Spurs side of the early 60s had done so, in 1961 and 1962, and Newcastle United had also enjoyed back-to-back successes in 1951 and 1952. Iit would not be until the beginning of the next century before another name would be added to that list: Arsenal's victory over Southampton in the 2003 final was a rare victory for the holders.

The passion which the FA Cup arouses came to the fore in 1999–2000 when holders Manchester United were given dispensation to withdraw from the competition to enable the club to compete in a tournament in Brazil. Most fans were incensed, despite the fact that their own teams' chances might have been improved by United's absence.

Manchester United and Arsenal, the two most successful clubs in FA Cup history, contested the 2005 final. It was a 17th appearance in English football's showpiece for each, though United's 11 victories to the Gunners' nine gave the Mancunians the edge at the top of the all-time list. Arsenal closed the gap to one, though not without a slice or two of cup fortune along the way. There was a shoot-out victory over Sheffield United in the Fifth Round, after two titanic battles. And in the final Arsenal were second best to United but the game ended goalless. It was the first FA Cup final to be decided on penalties, and almost inevitably, United's failure to put away any of their chances came back to haunt them. Patrick Vieira, in his final game before

departing for Juventus, put away the decisive spot-kick. Arsenal's fourth final in five years yielded a third victory.

In 2006 Liverpool joined Aston Villa on seven wins, putting them fourth in the all-time list. Rafa Benitez's side accounted for both Manchester United and Chelsea, so it was no easy path to the Millennium Stadium. There they faced promoted West Ham, who had surprised everyone on their return to the Premiership. The Hammers led 2–0, and were 3–2 up with seconds to go, but Steven Gerrard's 35-yard screamer took the game into extra-time. It went to another shoot-out, and Pepe Reina made up for an indifferent 120 minutes with three excellent saves to give Liverpool victory.

In 2007, at the new Wembley, Chelsea scored the winning goal with four minutes of extra time remaining to prevent Manchester United pulling off their fourth Double.

Between 1872 and 2005 42 clubs have won the FA Cup. Manchester United is the most successful with eleven victories, followed by Arsenal and Spurs with ten and eight respectively. The romance of the competition begins each year in August as the non-League minnows battle hard simply to reach the third round, when the big guns of the Premiership and the First Division enter the fray. They harbour the dream of repeating Wimbledon's feet of 1988: from non-League status to FA Cup holders in barely a decade. Even the giants who have won the trophy many times regard FA Cup victory as something special. Such is the magic of the world's oldest cup competition.

2008 was the year of the underdog, a record 731-strong entry producing shocks a-plenty. Liverpool survived a Fourth Round scare against Conference South side Havant and Waterlooville, only to fall to Barnsley. Just half of the quarter-finalists were from the top flight, and that fraction was further reduced as Barnsley undid Chelsea and Cardiff won at Middlesbrough. It was a hundred years since the last four featured only one team from the top division. A Kanu goal gave Portsmouth victory over West Brom, while a volley from Cardiff-born Joe Ledley put his home city through to the final at Barnsley's expense. Kanu also scored the only goal at Wembley to give the south coast club their second Cup success, 69 years after their 1939 victory.

The cream rose to the top in 2008–09 as four of the Premiership's top five teams contested the semi-finals. Theo Walcott put Arsenal ahead against Chelsea, but Malouda levelled and Drogba hit the winner six minutes from time. It was the first time since 1947 that Chelsea had got the better of their London rivals in FA Cup encounters.

Manchester United went into their tie against Everton looking to add to a run of 13 successful FA Cup semi-final appearances. It ended at Wembley as Sir Alex Ferguson, with half an eye on the Premiership and Champions League

David Seaman and Patrick Vieira of Arsenal lift the FA Cup after defeating Southampton in the 2003 final.

campaigns, fielded an under-strength side. It was a game of few chances that looked destined to go to penalties long before the 120 minutes were up. Berbatov and Ferdinand had their spot-kicks saved by former United 'keeper Tim Howard, and although Tim Cahill blazed over, Everton's other takers found their mark and saw Everton through to their first final since 1995.

The showpiece got off to a dramatic start as Saha gave Everton the lead after 25 seconds, the fastest goal in the competition's history. Chelsea soon wrested the initiative, however, levelling through a Drogba header midway through the half. Frank Lampard's left-foot drive settled the issue on 72 minutes. Ashley Cole joined Saha in the record books, becoming the first player in over a century to pick up five winners' medals.

FA CUP FINALS

1872 Wanderers v Royal Engineers 1-0	1913 Aston Villa v Sunderland 1-0	1971 Arsenal v Liverpool 2-1 aet
1873 Wanderers v Oxford University 2-0	1914 Burnley v Liverpool 1-0	1972 Leeds United v Arsenal 1-0
1874 Oxford University v Royal Engineers 2-0	1915 Sheffield United v Chelsea 3-0	1973 Sunderland v Leeds United 1-0
1875 Royal Engineers v Old Etonians 1-1	1920 Aston Villa v Huddersfield Town 1-0 aet	1974 Liverpool v Newcastle United 3-0
replay Royal Engineers v Old Etonians 2-0	1921 Tottenham H v Wolverhampton W 1-0	1975 West Ham United v Fulham 2-0
1876 Wanderers v Old Etonians 0-0	1922 Huddersfield Town v Preston NE 1-0	1976 Southampton v Manchester United 1-0
replay Wanderers v Old Etonians 3-0	1923 Bolton Wanderers v West Ham United 2-0	1977 Manchester United v Liverpool 2-1
1877 Wanderers v Oxford University 2-1 aet	1924 Newcastle United v Aston Villa 2-0	1978 Ipswich Town v Arsenal 1-0
1878 Wanderers v Royal Engineers 3-1	1925 Sheffield United v Cardiff City 1-0	1979 Arsenal v Manchester United 3-2
1879 Old Etonians v Clapham Rovers 1-0	1926 Bolton Wanderers v Manchester City 1-0	1980 West Ham United v Arsenal 1-0
1880 Clapham Rovers v Oxford University 1-0	1927 Cardiff City v Arsenal 1-0	1981 Tottenham H v Manchester City 1-1 aet
1881 Old Carhusians v Old Etonians 3-0	1928 Blackburn Rovers v Huddersfield T 3-1	replay Tottenham H v Manchester City 3-2
1882 Old Etonians v Blackburn Rovers 1-0	1929 Bolton Wanderers v Portsmouth 2-0	1982 Tottenham H v QPR 1-1 aet
1883 Blackburn Olympic v Old Etonians 2-1 aet	1930 Arsenal v Hudersfield Town 2-0	replay Tottenham Hotspur v QPR 1-0
1884 Blackburn Rovers v Queens Park 2-1	1931 West Bromwich A v Birmingham City 2-1	1983 Manchester United v Brighton 2-2 aet
1885 Blackburn Rovers Queens Park 2-0	1932 Newcastle United v Arsenal 2-1	replay Manchester United v Brighton 4-0
1886 Blackburn Rovers West Bromwich A 0-0	1933 Everton v Manchester City 3-0	1984 Everton v Watford 2-0
replay Blackburn Rovers v West Bromwich A 2-0	1934 Manchester City v Portsmouth 2-1	1985 Manchester United v Everton 1-0 aet
1887 Aston Villa v West Bromwich A 2-0	1935 Sheffield W v West Bromwich A 4-2	1986 Liverpool v Everton 3-1
1888 West Bromwich A v Preston North End 2-1	1936 Arsenal v Sheffield United 1-0	1987 Coventry City v Tottenham Hotspur 3-2 aet
1889 Preston North End Wolverhampton W 3-0	1937 Sunderland v Preston NE 3-1	1988 Wimbledon v Liverpool 1-0
1890 Blackburn Rovers v Sheffield W 6-1	1938 Preston NE v Huddersfield Town 1-0 aet	1989 Liverpool v Everton 3-2 aet
1891 Blackburn Rovers v Notts County 3-1	1939 Portsmouth v Wolverhampton W 4-1	1990 Manchester United v Crystal Palace 3-3 aet
1892 West Bromwich A v Aston Villa 3-0	1946 Derby County v Charlton Athletic 4-1 aet	replay Manchester United v Crystal Palace 1-0
1893 Wolverhampton W v Everton 1-0	1947 Charlton Athletic v Burnley 1-0 aet	1991 Tottenham H v Nottingham F 2-1 aet
1894 Notts County v Bolton Wanderers 4-1	1948 Manchester United v Blackpool 4-2	1992 Liverpool v Sunderland 2-0
1895 Aston Villa v West Bromwich A 1-0	1949 Wolverhampton W v Leicester City 3-1	1993 Arsenal v Sheffield W 1-1 aet
1896 Sheffield W v Wolverhampton W 2-1	1950 Arsenal v Liverpool 2-0	replay Arsenal v Sheffield W 2-1 aet
1897 Aston Villa v Everton 3-2	1951 Newcastle United v Blackpool 2-0	1994 Manchester United v Chelsea 4-0
1898 Nottingham Forest v Derby County 3-1	1952 Newcastle United v Arsenal 1-0	1995 Everton v Manchester United 1-0
1899 Sheffield United v Derby County 4-1	1953 Blackpool v Bolton Wanderers 4-3	1996 Manchester United v Liverpool 1-0
1900 Bury v Southampton 4-0	1954 West Bromwich A v Preston NE 3-2	1997 Chelsea v Middlesbrough 2-0
1901 Tottenham Hotspur v Sheffield United 2-2	1955 Newcastle United v Manchester City 3-1	1998 Arsenal v Newcastle Utd 2-0
replay Tottenham Hotspur v Sheffield United 3-1	1956 Manchester City v Birmingham City 3-1	1999 Manchester United v Newcastle Utd 2-0
1902 Sheffield United v Southampton 1-1	1957 Aston Villa v Manchester United 2-1	2000 Chelsea v Aston Villa 1-0
replay Sheffield United v Southampton 2-1	1958 Bolton Wanderers v Manchester United 2-0	2001 Liverpool v Arsenal 2-1
1903 Bury v Derby County 6-0	1959 Nottingham Forest v Luton Town 2-1	2002 Arsenal v Chelsea 2-0
1904 Manchester City v Bolton Wanderers 1-0	1960 Wolverhampton W v Blackburn Rovers 3-0	2003 Arsenal v Southampton 1-0
1905 Aston Villa v Newcastle United 2-0	1961 Tottenham Hotspur v Leicester City 2-0	2004 Manchester United v Millwall 3-0
1906 Everton v Newcastle United 1-0	1962 Tottenham Hotspur v Burnley 3-1	2005 Arsenal v Manchester United 0-0 aet
1907 Sheffield W v Everton 2-1	1963 Manchester United v Leicester City 3-1	Arsenal 5-4 on penalties
1908 Wolverhampton W v Newcastle United 3-1	1964 West Ham United v Preston NE 3-2	2006 Liverpool v West Ham 3-3 aet
1909 Manchester United v Bristol City 1-0	1965 Liverpool v Leeds United 2-1 aet	Liverpool 3-1 on penalties
1910 Newcastle United v Barnsley 1-1	1966 Everton v Sheffield W 3-2	2007 Chelsea v Manchester United 1-0
replay Newcastle United v Barnsley 2-0	1967 Tottenham Hotspur v Chelsea 2-1	2008 Portsmouth v Cardiff City 1-0
1911 Bradford City v Newcastle United 0-0	1968 West Bromwich A v Everton 1-0 aet	2009 Chelsea v Everton 2-1
replay Bradford City v Newcastle United 1-0	1969 Manchester City v Leicester City 1-0	
1912 Barnsley v West Bromwich A 0-0	1970 Chelsea v Leeds United 2-2 aet	
replay Barnsley v West Bromwich A 1-0	replay Chelsea v Leeds United 2-1	

Acknowledgments

This book would not have been possible
without the help of
Rick Mayston and Natalie Jones at Getty Images.

Thanks also to
Karen Beaulah, Ian Brooke, Alison Kelt,
Richard Betts and Trevor Bunting.